P9-DBK-053

CREATIVE LEADERSHIP

PRENTICE-HALL INDUSTRIAL RELATIONS AND PERSONNEL SERIES

DALE YODER, editor

BELCHER · *Wage and Salary Administration*
BELLOWS · *Creative Leadership*
BELLOWS · *Psychology of Personnel in Business and Industry, 2nd ed.*
CARPENTER · *Case Studies in Collective Bargaining*
DANKERT · *Contemporary Unionism in the United States*
DANKERT · *Introduction to Labor*
DAVEY · *Contemporary Collective Bargaining*
DUBIN · *Human Relations in Administration*
GALENSON · *Comparative Labor Movements*
GOMBERG · *A Trade Union Analysis of Time Study, 2nd ed.*
HABER AND COHEN · *Readings in Social Security*
HARDMAN AND NEUFELD · *The House of Labor*
HENEMAN AND TURNBULL · *Personnel Administration and Labor Relations: A Book of Readings*
LINDBERG · *Cases in Personnel Administration*
MILLER · *American Labor and the Government*
OTIS AND LEUKART · *Job Evaluation, 2nd ed.*
PFIFFNER · *The Supervision of Personnel, 2nd ed.*
SHARTLE · *Occupational Information, 2nd ed.*
SMITH · *Collective Bargaining*
TAYLOR · *Government Regulation of Industrial Relations*
THOMPSON · *Personnel Management for Supervisors*
YODER · *Personnel Management and Industrial Relations, 4th ed.*
YODER · *Personnel Principles and Policies*

CREATIVE LEADERSHIP

ROGER BELLOWS

Professor, Rutgers University, and Director in Richardson, Bellows, Henry, & Co., Inc.

Englewood Cliffs, N.J.

PRENTICE-HALL, INC. **1959**

LIBRARY OF CONGRESS
CATALOG CARD NO.: 59-5062

PRINTED IN THE UNITED STATES OF AMERICA
19005

To

Carol

Foreword

This book on leadership deals with a timely, urgent problem that must receive rapidly increasing attention in the decade ahead. By 1970, we should know much more about leadership in a democratic society than we do today. This book provides a map of the road ahead leading to an understanding of leadership relationships.

The kinds of answers we shall find in our continuing search for clues to leadership are suggested by Dr. Bellows in this fascinating analysis of recent and current experience. The point of view of this book is one which should be most effective in opening doors and finding answers. Both the basic theory that underlies the entire analysis and the author's adherence to an empirical method provide essential foundations for continuing advances in this field.

The Bellows theory of leadership is eclectic. It discards such particularism as is evident in any simple "great man" theory, holding it evident that leadership is not simply a matter of inborn leader qualifications. The author notes the hazards of our inherited maze of superstition and folklore. He emphasizes the leadership syndrome—the whole complex of conditions that meld people into teams and that designate and "power" their leaders. He stresses the conception of leadership as a function of the group through the expression and participation of its members. He sees the conditions of leadership as dynamic and constantly evolving, so that present leaders must be different kinds of people from those who led in earlier societies, and future leaders must continue this evolution.

By his emphasis on the empirical, the author focuses attention on the only sure means of planned adaptation and growth in leadership. We must learn to develop more effective group action by the study of groups in action. We must work toward the discovery of consistent patterns in participation, status, leader acceptance, and leadership. We must garner our knowledge from the experiments of every relevant study and discipline.

This kind of a study of leadership is most appropriate at this particular stage in our social and political development. Our society must find the answers to new problems of "leading" in every major phase of our social activities. Nowhere is the problem of effective leadership more acute than in our employment relationships. The era of the empire builders and captains of industry has passed. Their demise has left us with traditional patterns of leadership and of status in our work teams that are quite inappropriate and not acceptable today. They will be much less appropriate tomorrow. This book points the way to real understanding of leadership and satisfying team-membership in tomorrow's society. The writing is nontechnical; it does not require previous training in statistics, psychology, economics, or sociology.

The author has benefited in this book from his wide experience as a teacher, laboratory research worker and director, and consultant. He approaches the subject with a thorough familiarity with what others have done and is generous in his crediting of insights and ideas to the many investigators who have helped to blaze a trail. The wide acceptance of his earlier *Psychology of Personnel in Business and Industry* has evidenced his ability to interest others and communicate effectively with faculty members and students. Our understanding in the whole field of employment relationships will benefit from this contribution. I welcome this addition to our Industrial Relations and Personnel Series.

DALE YODER

Preface

Creative leadership is needed if our present civilization is to survive. The thought has been voiced that physical science has made it possible for all men to die together; our growing knowledge of creative leadership must make it possible for men to live together.

Leadership is something more than management. It has a special meaning which includes *creativeness*. A manager—of a home, school, office, factory, labor union, state—may or may not be a creative leader. Creative leadership involves arranging the situation so that mutual goals and understanding meld people into harmonious teams.

I protest the notion that some men are born leaders. I would rather try to analyze and describe the situation in which the dynamic process of leadership takes place. By doing this, I hope to provide deeper understanding and vision for those who now manage situations of all kinds, for they are potential, creative leaders.

But the heritage of knowledge of creative leadership is as yet meager, and I approach the task with humility. The field of human relations is only a few decades old; the field of physical science, in contrast, is several centuries old. At last, however, the general area of behavioral science—an interdisciplinary approach—is well on the way to sound beginnings. There have been several research programs which have conducted important studies of human relations and leadership. These include programs of the Personnel Research Board at the Ohio State University and the Institute for Social Research at the University of Michigan. More than 1,000,000 professional man-hours have been spent on group research by these two agencies alone.

The concepts and methods discussed have been tried out by the writer and his colleagues in several kinds of leadership training situations during the past ten years. Acknowledgement is made to Drs. Charles Elmer Scholl, Jr. and Allen Ralph Solem who assisted in developing and trying out some of the materials included in chapters 14–16. Organizations in which the author has served as consultant and the executives of which have contributed to the practicality of the concepts and approaches to leadership have included the U.S. Air Force, Army, and Navy, U.S. Employment Service, Burroughs Corporation, Rockwell Spring and Axle Corporation, Great Lakes Mutual Life Insurance Company, Maccabees Life Insurance Society, J. L. Hudson Company, Nitrogen Division of Allied Chemical Corporation, National Bank of Detroit, E. R. Squibb & Sons Division of Olin-Mathieson Chemical Corporation, and the Western Electric Company. Leadership training seminars of the Society for Advancement of Management, the American Management Association, and Rutgers, the State University have tested some of the materials, and the author is indebted to the participants in these seminars for their contributions to the materials.

I have been lucky indeed to have had close association with a number of creative leaders in the field of behavioral science. Whatever value this book has may be traced to their influence. They include Drs. Robert Daniel Williams, Harold Ernest Burtt, Carroll Leonard Shartle, the late John Gamewell Jenkins, Marion Webster Richardson, Thomas Willard Harrell, and Frederick Kenneth Berrien. I am thankful to Dr. Stanley Emanuel Seashore for his constructive critique of parts of the manuscript. And I am, of course, indebted to the many behavioral scientists and their publishers who have given special permission to use their research results.

New Brunswick, New Jersey ROGER BELLOWS

Contents

One
VIEWPOINTS

Two
HUMAN MOTIVATION

Three
SOCIAL BEHAVIOR

Four
TENSION, CONFLICT, AND LEADERSHIP

Five
LEADERSHIP METHODS

Six

MEASURING AND IMPROVING TEAMWORK

Viewpoints

ONE

*

The force or strength of one man would hardly suffice
if men did not arrange mutual aid and exchange.

SPINOZA

I

Leadership for survival

Do you agree that a new kind of creative leadership is required if we are to survive and continue to progress? Methods of domination which have been used are more suitable for the jungle than for our present civilization. We are floundering for want of an adequate way of organizing our human resources: under present-day conditions, the "brutish force" that has been used in the past could result only in the "short life." We need now, perhaps more than ever before, a style of leadership which will emphasize moral principles and the freedom and dignity of man. Such leadership must have survival value for the man and for his family, community, world; it must have values for education, labor, and industry.

Survival requires progress

Survival means progress. If we do not progress we cannot survive. To stand still is to perish. Survival would seem, at first glance, to mean "to remain the same." Ordinarily, we would expect adequate results from merely holding what we now have. But today this will not work because of the dynamic way of the world around us. Survival requires keeping up with the times; preserving what we have is not enough. It is not enough because what we do is relative to what others are doing. And others are progressing. Four brief examples are:

1. In international relations, an aggressor nation, through progressive research, development, and organization of resources, can accumulate armaments sufficient to cripple all other nations and contain the resources that remain. The solutions are, in part, equal progress of all nations and leadership by the United Nations, to result eventually in common goals, common understanding, and mutual aid.

2. In business and industry, if one company does not progress in step with other companies, it cannot survive. It will fail, as scores of businesses fail each week, and its activities will be assimilated by other companies. Thus we see, in the industrial world, research and development, diversification and progress. The key is progress through leadership.

3. In labor organizations, which have done much for the general community welfare, there is need for harmonious management for integration within. There is also need for mutual goals and understanding with outside agencies, including private enterprise. Such organizations are relatively new. They are still growing. They have leadership problems. Present activity includes establishing union leadership academies for training union leaders, a step which should hasten progress. Numerical strength is insufficient; organizational harmony is necessary for continued progress. If policies and practices do not result in creative leadership, these organizations cannot survive over a long period of time.

4. The problems confronting education are tremendous, especially those resulting from population increases. If even the present level of adequacy is to continue, progress is urgent. Leadership—the marshalling of human resources to result from mutual goals and understanding—is the key to these problems.

In these four areas, and in many others, the *status quo* will result in disintegration and decay. The problems are dynamic because the scene is rapidly changing. The situation is similar to that which confronted the horse-drawn buggy industry in 1910. The advent of the automobile gradually but surely destroyed business enterprises concerned only with the manufacture of horse-drawn vehicles. Likewise the old fashioned whale- and coal-oil lamp, the gas light, the hand pump, the player piano, the electric automobile, the celluloid collar, the hoop skirt, quill pen, flint-lock gun, and wooden plow have left the scene.

Along with changes like these has come a complex industrial, economic, and political society. Our knowledge of creative leadership has not kept pace.

Changing times and leadership

Our changing times require a new style of leadership.

If the advances that were made during the past fifty years were to come upon us suddenly, as by waving a wand, they would be astounding. They have come upon us so gradually that we are not especially aware of them. Think of what has happened in transportation, with jet-powered air transports that cross the United States in a few hours; in communications, the advances in the telephone, the radio, and TV; in food processing and refrigeration, giving varieties in the diet unheard of before; and in medicine, surgery and pharmacology, the yield of antibiotic and other "miracle" drugs in prolonging life. These are technological advances.

At the close of World War II, one of our greatest scientists, Vannevar Bush,[1] pointed out that in the first half of the present century tremendous advances were made in physical science, invention, and technology. He prophesied that in the last half of the present century, advances of greater magnitude and importance would be made in human relations and leadership—in our ways of living and working and playing together. President Eisenhower, in a speech on future security, said [2]

> In this wonderful age we Americans have a special responsibility. . . . We must have people who can keep their heads and, in every field, leaders who can meet intricate human problems with wisdom and with courage. In short, we will need not only Einsteins and Steinmetzes, but Washingtons and Emersons. . . .

And the world's population, now 2.7 billion, is increasing at the fastest rate in history. Births are exceeding deaths by 123,000 a day. The world's people may reach 6 billion by the year 2000, and their economic

[1] Vannevar Bush, *Science, the Endless Frontier,* A Report to the President by the Director of the Office of Scientific Research and Development, July 1945.

[2] Dwight D. Eisenhower, speech to the nation, on future security, at Oklahoma City, November 13, 1957.

security is threatened. Technological advances have brought about vast changes in our way of life. They have made life more complex and have tended to minimize our feeling of closeness to our fellow-man. This is one reason why leadership is one of the most difficult problems of the era. Imagine for a moment life in a craft family 200 years ago. The workers or employees in this enterprise were usually members of a family group. Membership ties were strong in this small group. Communications were immediate. The group members lived together every day for seven days of the week; they lived and worked and played together. There was little remoteness, no isolation of any members of the group. A warm social climate was natural to their life. It was built in.

Today conditions are quite different. The warm "family" climate of the work place has given way to the cold efficiency of the modern factory with its impersonal time clock and automatic processes. Much of our crime, juvenile delinquency, labor unrest and dissatisfaction, our muddled decisions in management of business enterprises stem from lack of warm social climate. And the very fact of our great technological improvements have themselves brought grave problems in social organization and leadership. Children listen to the radio and TV rather than to their parents. Employees find social coldness in their work places. They form cliques and splinter groups. Through these informal social groupings they strive to provide for themselves at least a semblance of the warm human relationships that one time were enjoyed within the craft or farm-family circle.

Leadership problems have changed during recent times, and they are changing a great deal day-by-day. These problems are intensified now by automation—the advent of the automatic factory—and by our rapidly increasing populations. Each year brings more young families than the year before and more challenges to the human relations skills of everyone.

One of the essentials of effective leadership is that it must further the freedom and dignity of man. It is perhaps unnecessary to emphasize this, it seems so self-evident. And yet this principle is often neglected. Lincoln made this point in his Gettysburg address on November 19, 1863, and we may review part of it here.

Fourscore and seven years ago our fathers brought forth on this continent a new nation, conceived in liberty and dedicated to the proposition that all men are created equal. . . . It is for us the living rather to be dedicated to the unfinished work which they who fought here have thus far so nobly advanced . . . that this nation under God shall have a new birth of freedom, and that government of the people, by the people, for the people shall not perish from the earth.

While men are not equal psychologically, they are equal in their right to enjoy freedom and dignity. Lincoln would agree without question that any way of leadership must preserve these equal rights; social psychologists agree that equality in membership and approval in human groups are minimum essentials for mental health.

The wants, desires, strivings of man and groups of men center around the inherent motives for recognition of equality in this sense. Man as a slave who is owned, as a commodity that is purchased, ordered to work, imprisoned without a fair trial, oppressed by aggression—that man is not free or equal.

The leadership style of the past is for the jungle. Some of our bodily and psychological equipment is particularly adapted for primitive conditions of life where physical emergency effort was an everyday necessity. An example is a small gland, the suprarenal, located just above the kidneys. Its function is to inject small quantities of adrenalin, a powerful chemical agent, into the blood stream. When adrenalin is present in the blood stream, we experience certain changes in our bodies and in our behavior. These changes include: anger; increase in rate of breathing; increase in the blood clotting rate; increase in heart action. Such changes enabled man to survive in a jungle situation by making him stronger and less likely to die from his bloody condition after an encounter with wild jungle animals—or fellow men. In the jungle only the strong survive; the strongest become "leaders." They become dominant by virtue of brute strength. If people were to depend solely upon such jungle fighting to survive, life would be both brutish and short.

Brutish methods of domination persist somewhat in our society even today: unreasonable punishment of children by parents in the family group; crime and cruelty in the community; punishment without adequate trial in some foreign countries; rule of force over small nations by larger ones; ignorant, negligent and even cruel practices in education; violent tactics, even physical violence and assault in organizing and fighting by labor unions; inhuman and inhumane treatment of employees by company ownership and management.

"Climb the career ladder to success. Climb up on the backs of others; kick them down as you go. If they resist, cut their throats. Fight the organization!"

This is the brutish method. It is still practiced today. It brings the jungle right into the executive board, the club, the cocktail lounge, the drawing room.[3]

[3] See "Throat Cutting," (New York: *The Wall Street Journal*), November 30, 1957.

This corporate indoor sport has been known to work—for a time.

More than fifty executives in twelve cities who were interviewed by *The Wall Street Journal* reporters felt that, today, disaster is quite likely to befall the throat cutter. It may come immediately, as in the case of the salesman who was gunning for the vacant job of assistant sales manager. He spread rumors of his rival's propensities for high living. These rumors reached the ears of the boss. But the boss was something of a sport himself. He handed the job to the alleged sybarite and eventually fired the prude who started the rumors.

Delayed trouble may be the fate of the throat cutter. An executive of a Pacific Coast company was subtly but mercilessly attacked by his colleagues: they undermined his prestige and his competency until he was fired. Some time later, he turned up to haunt them as an executive of his original company's most important customer. With a fine sense of retribution he found placement of orders with competing firms more attractive.

A popular and subtle device for cutting down a fellow executive is to arrange for an "unbiased survey" of the company's top management needs. A vice-president in charge of supply and distribution for an oil company wished to expand his department to include some of the functions of the sales vice-president, thereby heightening his own chances for advancement. He arranged for an "unbiased study" which, to the surprise of no one, supported his proposal. In this particular case, his scheming was to no avail; it was evident to his superiors and no changes were made.

When throat cutting reaches epidemic proportions, as it has in several instances, the company may suffer severely in terms of its position in the trade. Internecine warfare so consumes the energies of the executives that production, sales, and personnel problems are swept aside. Obviously no one gains in the long run under these conditions.

The solution to this problem found most practicable by corporate executives is the cooperative, open communications approach. As expressed by an executive vice-president: "Everybody's criticized; sometimes feelings are hurt, but it's all in the open. By keeping an atmosphere of open criticism, we avoid most throat cutting." [4]

Times are changing: perhaps we are developing a social environment that lends itself to better leadership. Illustrations of evolution include historical facts from the changing scenes of industrial and labor relations conflict. Dead and gone are the redoubtable fighters for labor of the

[4] *Ibid.*, p. 8.

1930's: William Green, Sidney Hillman, and George H. Harrison; dead also are the top-billed warrior actors on the industrial side of the bloody drama: Henry Ford, Tom Gilder, William Knudson, Alfred Sloan. We are now ready, I believe, for an era of a new kind of leadership.

Common misconceptions

It is obvious to everyone that there is danger in short-cutting research and research results. A profession, art, or practice which aims to improve or remedy a situation is dependent on knowledge that has been gleaned from science. If one is aware of what is already known about a situation or a problem, then one has a head start on an approach to a solution to his particular, similar problem. This is the reason for recording scientific results so that others can profit by what has been found. A practitioner who is unaware of what has been found in the past is likely to make serious judgment errors. The medical practitioner, for example, who makes use of Berger rhythms in diagnosis need not necessarily have participated in research connected with electroencephalographic measurements of brain activity. He makes use of the results of the various steps which research has provided in understanding Berger rhythms; he has learned the significance of various patterns as indicators of states of health or disease within the brain.

The importance of research in aiding us to progress in the behavioral sciences in general, leadership study in particular, cannot be overemphasized. Misconceptions about the nature of man and his relationships with his fellow men are still rampant. There are misconceptions concerned with functions of the human body, the anatomy, physiology of the organism; there is even greater lack of knowledge of the psychological and sociological factors in human behavior.

Two surveys of common misconceptions are summarized in Table 1.1. Part 1 of the table shows erroneous ideas held by a sample of 1438 college students; Part 2 shows those of 169 foremen in an industrial plant. Note, in Part 1, item 8, "females are inferior to males in intelligence"—girls were less inclined to this misbelief than were men. Responses of college students to Part 1, item 3, may be compared to responses of foremen to a similar item, number 5 of Part 2 of the table, "fast workers usually make more mistakes than slow workers": 26 per cent of the students and 27 per cent of the foreman held this misconception.

Over half of the foremen believed that "any supervisor who really has the company's interest at heart can do his job well"; a fourth felt that "the best way to handle tough workers is to be tougher than they are," and one out of ten believed "most employees do better work when they get a good bawling out every so often." What kind of human relations should we expect to find in an atmosphere of such misconceptions?

TABLE 1.1

PART 1: Common misconceptions of 773 male and 665 female students in the beginning course in general psychology at Ohio State University.*

Misconception	Per cent incorrect responses Male	Female
1. Mathematics gives a logical mind	70	73
2. Shifty-eyed person is dishonest	23	36
3. Fast workers make more mistakes than slow workers	26	26
4. Can estimate intelligence by looking at face	23	29
5. Men are created equal in capacity	21	24
6. Receding chin indicates lack of will power	20	22
7. Palmistry can foretell the future	20	21
8. Females are inferior to males in intelligence	11	8

PART 2: Misconceptions held by 169 foremen, as indicated by the per cent of wrong responses to questions related to leadership and supervisory practices (Questions selected from How Supervise? test.)

Misconception	Per cent having misconception
1. Any supervisor who really has the company's interest at heart can do his job well	59
2. The average worker cares little of what others think of his job so long as the pay is good	38
3. Job evaluation is unnecessary if the supervisor knows his men well	34
4. Less intelligent workers tend to resent monotonous tasks more than the average individual	33
5. Fast workers usually make more mistakes than slow workers	27
6. The best way to handle tough workers is to be tougher than they are	24
7. Workers who are good on one job are usually below average on most others	15
8. A good supervisor can tell what a worker is worth the first time he talks with him	15
9. So-called "mental fatigue" is really nothing but laziness	14
10. Using production records alone to determine which worker to recommend for promotion (is satisfactory)	12
11. Most employees do better work if they get a good bawling out every so often	12

* Part 1 from W. L. Valentine, "Common Misconceptions of College Students," *Journal of Applied Psychology,* XX (1936), 633–58. Part 2 from a study by the author and colleagues, published in R. M. Bellows, *Psychology of Personnel in Business and Industry,* 2nd ed. (Englewood Cliffs, N. J.: Prentice-Hall, Inc., 1954), p. 141.

A number of misconceptions about people and leadership are engendered by the fallacy that some people have a very unusual faculty for sizing up men. (See items 2, 4, and 6 of Part 1 and items 3 and especially 8 of Part 2, Table 1.1.) What we now know from research that has been done on the selection interview suggests that, for the most part, interviewers do not agree very well even among themselves in sizing up people. Neither do we find very much validity in the interview. The best the interviewer can do, in general, is to attempt to make observations of the interviewee's bearing and manner, voice and language, and other obvious personal characteristics.

He would do well on other items pertaining to the person that he is interviewing to go to factual sources such as the application blank, and to quantitative measurements such as are derived from psychological tests. Research studies have shown these to be usually more valid than the interviewer's impressions. Judgments must be based on all of the data the interviewer has at hand, but several decades of research on these problems of assessment and appraisal—sizing up people—have not produced evidence that one person has any unique, mysterious, or unusual faculty or facility for sizing people up.

Studies have shown that some people tend to be more certain of their appraisals than others. Thus, personnel directors and interviewers stated that they were quite sure of their judgments when attempting to predict success by looking at photographs of Harvard graduates—photographs that had been taken before graduation some thirty years ago. Other subjects that were used in the experiment did not tend to be quite so sure as the personnel directors. It was commonly thought that personnel directors could do a better job of sizing up and predicting success through observation of photographs, since they had so much experience, but not so, according to the research results. However, it was concluded that the observers, whether personnel directors or not, had as much chance to predict success by looking at the back of the photographs as they had by looking at the pictures on the front.

Another study revealed that groups of judges agree significantly on leaders as judged from photographs—presumably they were using the same physiognomic cues as stereotypes—but their judgments were not related to the criterion of leadership. Their cues were of no value in predicting leadership.[5]

A tea leaf reader, a phrenologist, a graphologist, a physiognomist, or an astrologist will be able to tell you a very convincing story about your characteristics. This has been called the P. T. Barnum effect. The

[5] Donald J. Mason, "Judgments of Leadership Based Upon Physiognomic Cues," *Journal of Abnormal and Social Psychology*, American Psychological Association, Inc., LIII (1957), 273–74.

Barnum effect is simply the fact that we accept generalized descriptions of ourselves: you are honest, you are true, you are loyal, you are industrious, you are ever-loving, you are patriotic, you like people, you hesitate in making decisions, your decisions are firm when they are made. We like them. We are all more or less susceptible to the Barnum effect.

The variety of pseudo-psychologies that have been developed to attempt to satisfy man's desire to know more about himself and his fellow men is wondrous to behold. And these pseudo-psychologies still persist to a considerable extent even in our more enlightened world of today. Thus we see in our daily newspapers syndicated columns on astrology; publications pertaining to palmistry still appear in quantity, and they re-appear perennially. Phrenology, the pseudo-science alleged to teach the reading of character from the bumps on the head, has persisted to such an extent that businessmen still use it in isolated places as if it were a legitimate, valid tool.

In the upper part of the psychological underworld are: physiognomy, which has been shown to have little or no validity; body types, which has provided some systematic theory and has added somewhat to concepts forming the framework of careful investigations, but has as yet not yielded results of sufficient usefulness to enable it to provide a satisfactory tool for selection in any particular situation; and perhaps also graphology, the alleged science of reading character from handwriting. Virtually all of the research performed on graphology has proved that it is a fruitless technique—but not all. Some of the European studies of graphology seem to show that it has some substance. However, the validity may be said to be so negligible as to lack usefulness.

Why do these pseudo-psychologies remain in the mind of the public as valid and useful procedures?

"He is a born leader." This cliché becomes more and more absurd as we study the problem. Is leadership instinctive? Present-day psychology teaches that no complex organizations of behavior are inborn. An instinct is defined as an inborn pattern of behavior, unlearned, which is common to the race or species. Leadership could not be instinctive. The fact is that the word "instinct" when applied to integrated human behavior would be the lazy man's way of naming instead of describing behavior. Sometimes when we can conjure up a name for some complicated phenomenon we then feel we do not have to go to the trouble, take the time and energy, do the planning and work necessary to find how to describe behavior. Often, too, naming precludes description, having made us complacent and satisfied with the name by itself. So it is foolish to say leadership is instinctive. Leadership qualities are learned rather than inborn.

Looking ahead

If our present civilization is to progress—and it is evident that survival requires progress—then a creative, functional style of leadership is in order. It is the purpose of the succeeding chapters of this book to help provide a setting for such leadership by drawing upon social psychology and other behavioral sciences for help. We need to know the conditions under which such leadership may take place.

We have thus far had a brief look at human and inhuman relations and common misconceptions of them. Presently we shall examine the goals of leadership from the standpoint of the group and the team; we will look at the goals and motives of man, what individuals and groups of individuals want, the causes of action and behavior on the part of man and groups, and ways of analyzing man and groups. We propose to look at principles of team dynamics, since leadership depends upon the members of the team as much as upon the leader, and because we are working with dynamic, ever-changing processes. We then plan to have a look at ways of achieving both mutual goals and mutual understanding. Then we will consider the achievement of teamwork and the measurement of such achievement.

Improved leadership can result in improved health, both physical and mental. We have already touched upon the bodily and psychological equipment that man has been given through inheritance. It is suggested that some of this heritage is detrimental to his adjustment and chances for survival in our present life. Mental hygiene can be enhanced by functional, dynamic, creative leadership. Such leadership can reduce the tensions that most of us live under at the present time. For these reasons we shall be concerned with some facts relating to the conflicting goals that motivate us. We shall describe the aggressive man, the frustrated man, and the adjusted man, together with conditions which can tend to increase psychological well-being. Since one of the roles of the new, creative leader is counseling and guidance, we shall look into certain principles that pertain to these as they relate to leadership.

Leadership will later on be defined in terms of situations in which progress can be made toward goals—goals concerned with furthering the progress of man, families, workers, the community, the nation, education, labor organizations, businesses, and other management enterprises. The leader himself is one facet in this total "mix." He will have viewpoints and skills of such a kind that he will be able to arrange the situation for group work to be accomplished. It is necessary to put these new kinds of skills in proper focus so that such leaders can be developed.

Events are happening all around us to remind us that times are rapidly changing. Changing times require a new style of leadership. The brutish life which depended upon strength and ruthlessness is no longer functional, workable, human, or humane. The brutish life is a short life. Jungle leadership no longer has any place. Man has been attempting for a long time to find better ways of organizing a situation for leadership, but there have been few, if any, systematic plans and effective efforts. The new leadership will stress moral values: freedom and dignity of man.

Instead of the old, fallacious concept of power, as used in the Middle Ages, today we think of the leader as a man who has developed through learning certain skills. These skills are not in ways of manipulating groups, or in ways of forcing the members of the group to do his bidding, but in ways of establishing mutual goals and mutual understanding—ways of making use of warm social climates and communications and leadership techniques which cement relationships and bring about teamwork. It would seem that a fundamental grounding in behavioral science would be necessary and desirable if a leader is to use anything but rules-of-thumb, hit-or-miss chance procedures in his attempts to help people achieve their goals.

There are two ways to approach the facts, methods, and results concerned with leadership—defined as the process of arranging a situation so that various members of the group, including the leader, can achieve common goals with maximum economy and a minimum of time and work. One is to study better methods themselves; the other is to contrast common misconceptions with facts. The present section is concerned with common misconceptions. We all have these. Thus, we all have some unlearning to do. We can do this unlearning only if we are aware of our common misconceptions. They are pitfalls to leadership and team activity.

In the first place, it might be a good idea to consider how we have come by our common misconceptions concerning human relations and teamwork. Some of these misconceptions are grounded in ancient folklore, mysticism, and legend handed down to us. Our culture is immersed in misconceptions such as: criminals are born not made; criminals have marks upon them called "criminal stigmata"; the shape of our face and head gives us away as far as our abilities, propensities, instincts, emotions, tendencies, and aptitudes are concerned; when we have good fortune we must thank our lucky stars; compensation rather than correlation is the rule; a person behaving in an abnormal way must be possessed; familiarity breeds contempt. These misconceptions and a thousand others are habitual in our daily lives. They influence how we react to one another. It would seem self-evident that one of the first tasks for us is to guard against these pitfalls, if we are to understand human relations.

Man, ever since the dawn of civilization, has been in need of better understanding of his fellow man. He created what seemed to him, at first, logical descriptions and explanations of behavior. The psychology, or psychological philosophy, of the Greeks was the first recorded thinking of man on these problems. The early Greek was immersed in animistic ways of thinking. Animism seems to be the easiest way to try to describe how behavior becomes directed, organized, integrated, and adjusted to environment. Animism has "a little man within." The young child today is animistic. He thinks a toy is alive when he sees the toy move. By extension we can understand how primitive man "explained" many of the psychological phenomena which he saw all about him attributing them to mystical inner forces. Thus the cliché, "he is possessed," is a carry-over from this primitive way of thinking. The good spirit or force or power, or the bad spirit, the devil, the witch is the cause.

Man has always needed help in adjusting to his social environments. He needs help in explaining to himself his own behavior, the contents of his own mind. Often he goes for help to charlatans or to phrenology, astrology, and other pseudo-disciplines of the psychological underworld.

Several misconceptions are pertinent to our discussion: the leader is a power; leadership stems from the leader *per se;* people have inborn capacity for leadership; leadership skills are unlearned; people have power or faculties for managing men; some people have great intuition; great leaders have singular abilities and powers for sizing up people; people compensate for their weaknesses.

These common misconceptions and psychological underworld realms play an important, if insidious, role in our understanding of leadership. Members of working groups as well as leaders who arrange situations so that they can perform effectively need to know these pitfalls in leadership. Otherwise they cannot be aware of ways of overcoming these barriers to clear thinking and action in their attempts to achieve teamwork.

*

It has been the one song of those who thirst for absolute power that the interest of the state requires that its affairs be conducted in secret . . . But the more such arguments disguise themselves under the mask of public welfare, the more oppressive is the slavery to which they will lead. . . .

SPINOZA

2

The poverty of authority

Authority suggests power. It is a strong word. It has been associated in the popular mind with the police—"I am going to call the authorities." It is the purpose of this chapter to analyze the social function of authority, tell how it works and what its limitations are.

Is the leader a powerful man? If the answer is yes, then what kind of power does the leader have? Does he have great physical strength? Perhaps so, in certain leadership situations in the jungle or in primitive societies. In such situations he is able to beat his followers into submission and gain his authority status. In a military situation, the military force that has greatest might wins and, having subdued the enemy, rules for a time over the people. However, today we see all around us the signs of a more democratic, more participative, more permissive, more nondirective environment. We see that groups maintained by authority can swiftly bring sanctions into play. And in the history of the use of might and power, we have seen overthrow through rebellion and revolution. The reign of a power group is short-lived.

The word "authority" is itself somewhat abstract; it lacks concreteness. It is a word symbol that stands for something that itself is complex because it depends upon many factors that exist in our social culture and in our inter-relationships with people. We need a definition, and here it is: Authority is that which influences, or is a guide to, the behavior of a group of people or of a person under circumstances in which there is no participation in decision making. It is illustrated by factory rules of Amasa Whitney of 1830 in Figure 2.1. The people who are ruled by authority do not make up their minds, do not decide to act or behave in a certain way; rather, the person or the group takes orders from someone else who is "in authority." Authority is only one way of control; other ways will be discussed in later chapters. The earmark of the authoritative behavior pattern is the command. A command is a statement or directive concerning a behavior alternate of the receiver of the statement or directive. Authority is the attribute of the commander, or foreman, that enables him to expect that the command will be accepted by its receiver—it is the basis of choice of behavior.[1]

As an illustration, the foreman asks (commands, requests) Joe, a mechanic, to sweep up the work area. Joe demurs briefly, thinking to himself "that's the sweeper's job." But the sweeper is ill and absent that day. The foreman's request after compliance has taken place is authoritative—it has guided Joe's behavior choice; it has been the basis of his act.

Authority, then, implies and includes compliance. Authority flows in two directions: the command goes down to the receiver; acceptance or compliance goes up to the commander (if authority is "working"), as

[1] Herbert A. Simon, *Administrative Behavior* (New York: The Macmillan Company, 1947), pp. 125–34.

RULES & REGULATIONS
To Be Observed By All Persons Employed In The Factory Of
AMASA WHITNEY

FIRST: The Mill will be put into operation 10 minutes before sunrise at all seasons of the year. The gate will be shut 10 minutes past sunset from the 20th of March to the 20th of September, at 30 minutes past 8 from the 20th of September to the 20th of March. Saturdays at sunset.

SECOND: It will be required of every person employed, that they be in the room in which they are employed, at the time mentioned above for the mill to be in operation.

THIRD: Hands are not allowed to leave the factory in working hours without the consent of their Overseer. If they do, they will be liable to have their time set off.

FOURTH: Anyone who by negligence or misconduct causes damage to the machinery, or impedes the progress of the work, will be liable to make good the damage for the same.

FIFTH: Anyone employed for a certain length of time, will be expected to make up their lost time, if required, before they will be entitled to their pay.

SIXTH: Any person employed for no certain length of time, will be required to give at least 4 weeks notice of their intention to leave (sickness excepted) or forfeit 4 weeks pay, unless by particular agreement.

SEVENTH: Anyone wishing to be absent any length of time, must get permisison of the Overseer.

EIGHTH: All who have leave of absence for any length of time will be expected to return in that time; and, in case they do not return in that time and do not give satisfactory reason, they will be liable to forfeit one week's work or less, if they commence work again. If they do not, they will be considered as one who leaves without giving any notice.

NINTH: Anything tending to impede the progress of manufacturing in working hours, such as unnecessary conversation, reading, eating fruit, &c.&c., must be avoided.

TENTH: While I shall endeavor to employ a judicious Overseer, the help will follow his direction in all cases.

ELEVENTH: No smoking will be allowed in the factory, as it is considered very unsafe, and particularly specified in the Insurance.

TWELFTH: In order to forward the work, job hands will follow the above regulations as well as those otherwise employed.

THIRTEENTH: It is intended that the bell be rung 5 minutes before the gate is hoisted, so that all persons may be ready to start their machines precisely at the time mentioned.

FOURTEENTH: All persons who cause damage to the machinery, break glass out of the windows, &c., will immediately inform the Overseer of the same.

FIFTEENTH: The hands will take breakfast, from the 1st of November to the last of March, before going to work—they will take supper from the 1st of May to the last of August, 30 minutes past 5 o'clock P.M.—from the 20th of September to the 20th of March between sundown and dark—25 minutes will be allowed for breakfast, 30 minutes for dinner, and 25 minutes for supper, and no more from the time the gate is shut till started again.

SIXTEENTH: The hands will leave the Factory so that the doors may be fastened within 10 minutes from the time of leaving off work.

AMASA WHITNEY

Winchendon, Mass. July 5, 1830.

From Samuel Hopkins Adams, SUNRISE TO SUNSET *(New York: Random House, Inc., 1950). By special permission of Samuel Hopkins Adams and the publisher.*

Fig. 2.1 · Factory rules in 1830

shown in Figure 2.2. Compliance is manifested in that choice of behavior by the receiver that was called for by the command. What if the receiver does not accept the command—does not abide by authority?

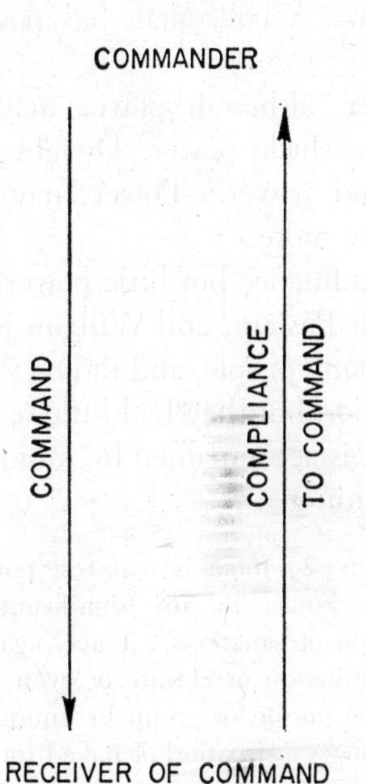

Fig. 2.2 · Authority flows in two directions

Power

There are two kinds of power with which we are concerned. The first is the power used by an authoritarian manager of an organization. The second is social force or power derived from interaction of group members. The latter power arises as a motivational condition to creative leadership. It implies consideration of alternate patterns of behavior and participation in decisions regarding behavior by the group as well as by the leader. Social power or force will be considered in detail in later chapters. Here we are concerned only with authoritative control.

Power is a significant aspect of regulation of behavior. Sociologists, social psychologists, political scientists, and philosophers have been concerned with its description for a long time.

Power need not be synonymous with prestige, fame, ability, or influence, although it may be related to any of these.[2] Power requires sub-

[2] See Robert Bierstedt, "An Analysis of Social Power," *American Sociological Review*, XV (1950), 730–36.

missiveness on the part of those who are influenced by it. Prestige, strength, or ability may not be accompanied by submission. Eddie Rickenbacker and Charles Lindbergh had prestige but little or no power. Adolf Hitler had both. A policeman has power but little prestige, a judge has both.

Ability is not power, although power may accompany it. Albert Einstein had ability but little power, Dwight Eisenhower has demonstrated both ability and power. Power may or may not stem from ability. It is something more.

One can have great influence but little power. Thus Rene Descartes, Sir Isaac Newton, Louis Pasteur, and William James had great influence upon the thinking of many people, and indirectly their works have modified thought and behavior, but they had little or no power.

Power, by definition, is accompanied by submission. Robert Bierstedt has proposed three definitions: [3]

> 1) Power is latent force; (2) force is manifest power; (3) authority is institutionalized power. . . . Force, in any significant sociological sense of the word, means the application of sanctions. Force, again in the sociological sense, means the reduction or limitation or closure or even total elimination of alternatives to social action of one person or group by another person or group. "Your money or your life" symbolizes a situation of naked force, the reduction of alternatives to two. The execution of a sentence to hang represents a total elimination of alternatives. . . . Dismissal or demotion of personnel in an association similarly, if much less drastically, represents a closure of alternatives. Now all of these are situations of force, or manifest power. Power itself is the predisposition or prior capacity which makes the application of force possible. . . . Power symbolizes the force which *may* be applied in any social situation and supports the authority which is applied. . . .
>
> The right to use force is then attached to certain statuses within the association, and this right is what we ordinarily mean by authority.

The creative leader, as contrasted to the authoritarian, does not depend upon status but rather upon human relations skills; he depends not upon latent force but upon mutual understanding; authority as defined may be completely lacking, since mutual agreement takes its place as a mode of control.

Authority and control

There are various kinds of situations in which controls on individual and group behavior are used. In most of them power and authority, as we have defined and discussed them, are present. But authority exists

[3] *Ibid.*

as a matter of degree. Surely in some, or perhaps most, situations power is intermingled with participation and mutual understanding. And in many others power is held back for use in an emergency, as it were, when communications and understanding break down.

We must say again—we said it a little while ago—that we are dealing with abstractions. The forces and conditions we are discussing lack the clarity that physical objects have. When a child learns the word for tree or dog or house, he has little difficulty—the percept of tree or dog or house is concrete—the name stands for a concrete object. Each time a tree is present, the parent says "tree," until the child says "tree" when he sees the object.

The concepts of power and authority are not present as tangible objects. They are none-the-less real. But how do we make them visible to the student of these phenomena? We have found no simpler or better way than to discuss them in connection with illustrative situations—this is analogous to associating "tree" with the object. In this way the student of these phenomena becomes familiar with them. He does not, of course, become as familiar with abstractions as a child is with objects in his environment. But we do "see" the concepts as working tools for analysis of the important social and psychological phenomena that exist in our environment.

Since power and authority exist in the various social situations around us, we can discuss a few of them. We might best start with extreme power situations and then gradually consider situations in which power is used to less degree or less frequently as a control. We may illustrate by situations involving coercion, political power, military power, wealth as a form of power, legal power, power in sanctions of approval-disapproval, and persuasion and manipulation.

Coercion is a form of power that lacks subtlety. In its nakedest form it takes the shape of blackmail: the blackmailer, with knowledge about a person which the person does not want divulged, may force the person to do what the blackmailer directs. Many forms of power are sometimes used in combination. Examples are the power of Hitler and Mussolini, both of whom used a number of power techniques, gaining their own ends through influencing the behavior of millions of people.

Political power, of course, is another form of control. A king during the Middle Ages made his own laws. Thus he could do anything with his subjects that he pleased. He was a monarch who had the power of life and death over his subjects; he maintained an owner-slave relationship.

The phenomenon of authority may be seen clearly in some military situations. In the army of Cæsar and in the authoritarian Prussian armed forces, authority was carried to a high degree of refinement through training, indoctrination, discipline, propaganda, and manipulation. And authority was used to a large extent in obtaining obedience in our own army during World War I. Military authority requires obedience. The orders were passed down through the line organization. Everything functioned like clockwork, like machinery; close order drill was said to be an "exact science." Men were drilled for hours each day. The purpose of this, according to military doctrine of the time, was to instill obedience, to cause men to act without thinking so that, in the face of the enemy, waves of foot soldiers would attack and, if destroyed, others behind them, following orders, would attack, also to be cut down. Authority in the Prussian army and in our own military establishments reigned supreme as the style of management. In World War II the picture was somewhat different.

In our present military organization, authority is still present, and the line of authoritarian organization is still paramount. However, authority to a considerable extent has given way to another form of motivation: mutual understanding and mutual goals. If one should review, for example, the organization in effect at a military outpost of the Air Force, it would be found that the line organization exists on the wall charts of the several squadrons and elements of the post. However, in the day-to-day activities one would rarely see the authoritarian organization in operation. Instead, the noncommissioned officers, warrant officers, the lower grade officers, and the higher level officers have a rather uniform fund of information and understanding. The goals are mutual goals; the understanding through communications, discussions, and closeness of groups in the organization, which is well knit perhaps because of the remoteness and smallness of the air base, is reasonably complete. There is a high degree of cohesiveness and social warmth.

Money or wealth in some form has been a source of power and authority ever since the dawn of civilization. There have been many examples of this. Before the turn of the century and shortly after, there were a number of "moguls." These were known by various terms: empire builders, tycoons, robber barons. Some of them were Cornelius Vanderbilt, John Jacob Astor, E. I. duPont, Daniel Drew, Jay Gould, Jim Fisk, John D. Rockefeller, Sr., J. P. Morgan, Sr., Philip D. Armour, Charles M. Schwab, Samuel Insull, Andrew Mellon, Daniel Guggenheim.[4] However, since shortly after the turn of the present century such tremendous wealth and power has gradually become more difficult to acquire.

Law has always been a source of power. Those who make laws can wield power in an influential way. Before the Magna Carta, when laws were made for specific purposes to further the advantage of a king or a certain individual, power was centered or focused, without diffusion. This is to be contrasted with our present lawmaking procedures which effect a diffusion of legal power in a more democratic mode of government. Not only the lawmakers, but also those who interpret the legal aspects of situations are vested with considerable power. Thus judges are authoritative.

An enterprise which conforms to a legalistic framework requires conforming behavior. Such behavior meets, in part, the requirements of the definition of authority. This is clearly seen in the authority of the policeman or police officer who enforces the law. In the next chapter, law will be viewed as one of the factors that limit the degree of freedom enjoyed by groups under a participative leadership style. In general, the law sets limits and determines the degrees of freedom within which individuals or small groups may function.

Social evolution gradually changes our mores so that what is acceptable to the group at one time may not be acceptable at another. Such change may take place in small groups without change in the larger group. Formal laws are not changed as readily as are customs; large organizations change more slowly than do small groups. Changes occur swiftly during revolution and quite slowly during evolutionary social processes. When mores change over a long period of time, these will gradually change the formal written laws.

Sanctions provide a way in which control may come into play. This is a way of saying that behavior is controlled by the authoritarian through punishment and reward. Animal trainers use punishment and reward; so do mothers and teachers, in child training. The same principle operates in the home, the school, and in the world of work. In the schools the teacher has the power of approving or disapproving through grade giving and honor systems. But the child in the home and the student in the school also have power. The child can indulge in negative behavior or repeatedly do wrong. A student in the school

[4] Stewart H. Holbrook, *The Age of the Moguls* (Garden City, N. Y.: Doubleday & Co., 1953), p. 373.

may disapprove of the instructor, may become delinquent or quit the school. Thus approval and disapproval work in both directions. One wonders, in these two kinds of situations, which is the leader—the mother or the child, the teacher or the student.

In business and industry the situation is very much the same. Whence comes the authority: from management of business or from management of the union? Does the president of the company or the president of the union local wield the most authority? Certainly, management operates in each of these kinds of organizations. The manager of the business brings certain sanctions into play if the workers do not work. He does not promote them if their work is poorly performed. He, in some instances, can fire them or lock his doors and close up shop. But the unions have counter measures at their disposal, so that if management does not come across in an appropriate manner in terms of working conditions, fringe benefits, wages, and other kinds of emoluments, then labor may exert its sanctions. Workers can quit *en masse* —a strike; they can slow down or sit down. Billions of dollars are lost to industry and the community as a result of invoking these kinds of sanctions.

Another form of control is persuasion. Advertising and motivation research are specific examples of its use as a device for begetting specific buying behavior. Peruasion is closely akin to manipulation, and it is also related to propaganda. Persuasion does not necessarily deal with the truth. It may deal in exaggerated claims or fabrications. Motivation research seeks to discover the tools for manipulation.

Whether such procedures for influencing the behavior of individuals are good and ethical is beyond the scope of our present interest. There is no doubt that these techniques have at least short-term effectiveness. Whether they are effective over a long period of time is doubtful.

Nonetheless, advertising which has been carefully developed through motivational market and advertising research does get results in terms of dollar expenditures. Not long ago a company which spends large sums on advertising had a meeting on Madison Avenue, the program for which was developed by its advertising agency. The title of the program was "the power of an idea." In the program, the studies and techniques which resulted in the highest sales were discussed. The advertising agency was selling the company and the company was selling the unsuspecting public. Manipulation that does not yield values to those who are manipulated may be shortlived. Manipulation may become weak and ineffective. Authority may end in poverty.

Control in social groups

In a family, an attempt is made by some parents to use authority almost exclusively as a control device. In others, authority is almost never used. In some families, authority is used as a last resort—a procedure brought into play when all else fails. But in most families there is a gradual lessening of authoritarian control as children become able to think for themselves. The father of a patriarchal family is said to have the power of an authoritarian and, indeed, the word patriarch suggests ruler.

Authority comes into play sometimes when children "get out of line." It is similar to the kind of authority we have in a policing activity. Authority is, in most family organizations, highly diffuse. It is nominally vested in the father, who is thought by some to be the stronger. In any case, the mother tends to make the father believe that he is the authoritative one, and when it comes to the final decision he is the one to make it. However, the father is not present most of the time and the mother is in charge, or in authority, in the home. Authority becomes diffuse. Management is not closely held by the mother. Authority is handed away to the father and to the children. When extreme situations occur, when understanding and mutual goal approaches seem to fail, the mother falls back upon the old authoritative manner. It would seem that her task is to establish mutual goals and understanding, to hand away authority whenever she can.

The control that is found in a church organization, in contrast, is somewhat more subtle and complex. The church leader is influential only through belief, trust, confidence, prestige. He, of course, would prefer not to be authoritative but would like to engender mutual feelings, mutual religious affectivity, mutual understanding and, of course, mutual goals. It is his purpose to be nonauthoritative and to enlighten rather than to direct. Thus he engenders understanding and insight into life's problems.

The relationship of physician to patient is, in some respects, similar to the relationship of a minister, rabbi, or priest to his congregation. In the case of the doctor-patient relationship, often it is to the interest of the patient for the doctor not to tell the patient what is wrong, so that whereas a mutual goal—a healthy patient—is common to both the doctor and the patient, mutual understanding may not be. In another situation, the physician is too busy to explain the intricacies of the malady to the patient, so he adopts an air of superiority, chilling the climate of their relationship; or he may just choose to be esoteric, believing that this will result in higher prestige, and that the patient will submit with docility to his instructions.

Some conditions of authority

Why do people accept authority? What are its basic conditions? Among those conditions that appear to be significant for our purposes are: (1) belief in the goals of a group or organization, (2) economic security, (3) confidence in the ability of those in power to achieve these goals, (4) fear of punishment, (5) social customs and institutions and the need for group approval, (6) lack of knowledge of the problems about which decisions are made, (7) ability of those who accept orders to carry them out.[5]

1. Some social groups, collectivities, or systems function because there is strong belief by group members that the cause is right, moral, or just. Segregationist groups may thus accept an authoritarian and follow him in the segregationist pattern because of their belief in the system, not necessarily in the authoritarian. In national or international relations we behave in terms of belief in "the cause." Employees behave in certain ways because they believe in the company's way of doing things. Religious groups believe in the cause, including the teachings of their particular religious organization, and their behavior pattern is regulated by this belief. If such faith is lacking, authoritative power diminishes.

2. Authoritarian systems may work because the groups and group members have more security when their behavior conforms to the wishes of the autocratic manager. Employees may lose their jobs if they do not follow orders or if they are insubordinate. In both industrial and military organizations, promotion—and hence greater economic security—results from conformance. In labor organizations, members conform—join and pay dues, for example—in large part for economic security. If such economic security is not forthcoming, the hold the authoritarian has on the group becomes loose and the members escape.

3. The third contributing condition to acceptance has to do with confidence in the authoritarian. Such phrases as—"I don't understand it, but the boss must be right"; "He is a wise man—I'll do it, but I don't see just what might happen"; "He's always been right and I'll do it"; "There must be a reason for it"—these suggest confidence in an autocrat. Such confidence may stem from irrational, emotionally toned acceptance engendered by manipulation or propaganda. If confidence stems from

[5] Herbert A. Simon, *Administrative Behavior* (New York: The Macmillan Company, 1949), pp. 125–34.

rational analysis, then the conforming behavior would not be brought about by authority but rather by mutual understanding. In this case, the leader would be obtaining conforming behavior through participation, not by authority.

4. Fear of punishment is an obvious condition that is quite frequently present when authority is observed. This is related to economic security and also to group membership security and approbation. The people who have been conquered by military force conform to the edicts of the occupying commander through fear of reprisal. People conform to laws for the same reason. Prisons conform to prison rules through fear of increased punishment. Children fear punishment for wrong behavior.

When the authoritarian utilizes this fear as a basic condition for achieving his wishes, his power is suspended by a slender thread. The nature of the thread is clearly psychological.

5. Social customs and institutions and our need for group approval tend to keep us in line with authoritarian desires. This condition is related both to economic security and fear of punishment. Through economic security we maintain certain accustomed group memberships. Such memberships, and the group approval and approbation that accompanies them, satisfy some of our social needs. This motivational condition is discussed in some detail in later chapters.

Fear of punishment likely involves fear of social disapproval by some group or groups in which the individual holds informal membership. Ridicule and loss of face, prestige, acceptance, approval or membership in the group is a powerful force.

Such losses take place as a result of lack of compliance with authority when its power lies in established customs and institutions. These customs and institutions establish modal behavior—behavior patterns that are expected. We expect a child to obey its mother; obedience is the modal behavior. We expect subordination, for it is part of our culture. Family and community behavior conforms to the established, customary pattern. For an employee to "blow his top" is unusual; it can be as embarrassing as going to a formal social event in improper attire.

6. A condition of authority is ignorance of the receiver of autocratic orders. During World War II, German, Italian, and Japanese authority was based in large part on fear and ignorance of the masses. Secrecy is an authoritarian technique. Groups cannot participate in decisions, think through problems and their solutions, or contribute suggestions if they do not have requisite knowledge and skill.

Children cannot participate in family planning, employees cannot help in management decisions, the community members cannot help solve problems unless they have the necessary knowledge of the difficulties involved and the approaches to their analysis for considering and weighing alternative behavior. They take orders from those in authority; there is nothing better to do. But, in general, people are becoming better educated, more knowledgeable, less prejudiced and more enlightened. Groups are beginning more-and-more to ask "Why?"

7. On the other hand, ability to carry out orders on the part of the order receiver is a prime requisite for authority. It cannot exist on the basis of willingness alone; the receiver must have the necessary equipment, both psychological and physical, to do the task as ordered by the autocrat. This condition does not contradict the one discussed immediately above. The receiver must be able to obey. If the mother tries to make the child read, but the child is not yet ready to learn, authority is not present. Military authority fails if troops are untrained. Management of a factory likewise fails, and authority is lacking, if workers are untrained or are not provided with tools and equipment to accomplish the goals of management.

This is a rather serious limitation of the authoritarian style of management, for two reasons. (1) When subordinates are trained, they begin to become knowledgeable about decisions made by superiors, to assess them and become critical of them. Authority does not flourish in such an atmosphere. (2) Training goes forward faster when the trainee knows what he is being trained for. He is poorly motivated for learning if he does not see the larger picture. He can obtain understanding if he gets the "big picture" in a participative climate rather than under an authoritarian one.

The poverty of authority

For one reason or another, the person or group of people who may be in power at one time find themselves in a state where their authority becomes weak. They find that no longer is power available to support authority. Power is transient, temporary, loosely held, almost ephemeral. This state of affairs has been called "the poverty of authority." This is a multiple factor phenomenon, brought about by many forces and conditions.

In the ontogenetic development of the child, the mother or one of the parents takes an authoritative role. That is, the parent, by a kind of force, takes care of the infant, since it cannot do many things for itself. Later on, language is developed and communications between the child and the mother become functional. During the early period of communication, the mother directs or orders the child; sometimes the child obeys. By school age, the child may be found to develop a negative pattern of behavior toward orders. This is the period which might be called the dawn of simple insights and understandings in the child. The stage is being set for a new and different style of leadership by the mother—the style of leadership that depends upon understanding and mutual goals rather than force and power. When the negative patterns of behavior in the child bring about sanctions, the mother may, at first, be startled. After a brief period of uncertainty and, in some cases, even panic, the mother may cast about for a new method. She hits upon understanding as a key mode of managing the child. She begins to perceive the child's role, and the child begins to perceive her role, always in terms of their own backgrounds and psychological equipment. A social climate rather than authority is operating. Acceptance on the part of the child is present, but it is an acceptance by mutual understanding rather than an acceptance of the power of authority.

Another illustration is concerned with the relationship of the slave owner to his slaves. At one period in this relationship, the slave owner, as in the barony in Europe in the fifteenth century, ruled his serfs with an iron hand. They accepted and followed his edicts without question. They did not analyze the situation. They did not think for themselves. They perceived his role as all-powerful. They looked upon him as a giver of orders and these orders were to be obeyed.

Then came the dawn of enlightenment. This may have come from contacts with the outside, from knowledge of better treatment of serfs in a neighboring barony. Slaves began to see their role in its truer light: they were being imposed upon by the one in power. They began to form cliques or social groups that discussed ways and means of reducing the power of the baron. These ways sometimes eventually took the form of outright physical revolt. More usually, subtle forms of sanctions were adopted, such as taking orders literally to the extreme, as was done by the IWW, an anarchist labor movement of several decades ago, to obfuscate the formal organization.

Slaves slowed down their work or invented physical or mental illness. Gradually the baron, the once all-powerful one, came to realize that he must cast about for a different way of managing his serfs. After a period of trial and error he may have hit upon ways other than physical coercion to deal with them. The baron, finding, as many a chagrined mother has found, that the authoritarian power no longer worked, may have tried propaganda and manipulative techniques or persuasion. Or he may have tried sincere efforts to reach mutual goals and mutual understanding. He found that his serfs, through the kinds of sanctions that they could exert when they began to gain enlightenment and insights into the situation, were as powerful as he. He then realized the poverty of his authority.

Many other examples demonstrate the poverty of authority and the shift from power to consideration as a human relations and leadership technique. The foregoing illustration of the relation of serf to master has a parallel in the history of the relationship between king and subjects; military authorities and rank-and-file privates; employer and employees; heads of unions and members; management and labor; a politician in high office who wields power ruthlessly through a spoils system and the people under his regime; aggressive nations and nations that are dominated for a time by the aggressor.

We have emphasized in the best way we know, by the use of illustrations, that authority flows in two directions: if orders are not accepted and obeyed, authority does not exist. Power as the basis of authority can be possessed by both sides. Destructive sanctions can be used by both sides, reducing the situation to the question "Who has the most power?" and resulting in chaos. We need a better, more constructive way of control.

Fortunately a more constructive way of control exists. It depends not upon imposing the commander's will upon group members, but rather upon establishing mutual understanding and mutual goals. It may be called "creative leadership." The next chapter, "Leadership and Social Climate," contrasts the authoritarian with the creative leadership style.

*

No normal person is happy in a situation which he cannot control to some extent.

WILLIAM FOOTE WHYTE

3

Leadership and social climate

In ancient times when a chieftain ruled the clan—through authority vested in him by blood relationship to a former chieftain, or mystical powers breathed into him by a god, or by his skill as a high priest or medicine man, or by sheer physical prowess—he was able to control behavior and obtain obedience. Sometimes power of this kind was accompanied by mutual understanding and mutual goals; as often as not, however, it had force or authority without understanding as its principle feature. Some of the kings of the Middle Ages wielded this absolute power.

What style of leadership has been developed to take the place of this? Virtually nothing. At the present time, man, in his various organizations, is groping for better leadership, but he is having difficulty in achieving it. His difficulty stems from two facts: first is the extreme complexity of the problem that he has encountered; second, and important, is the inadequate thought given to human relations. There has been precious little systematic effort—quite unlike the conditions that exist in technological advances. A bona fide way of leadership—a kind of leadership that is sincere, functional, workable, and reasonable—is urgently needed.

Today many organizations are mismanaged through autocratic and authoritative power. However, by virtue of increases in formal education and effectiveness of communication, there is a growing unrest and intolerance of the autocratic and authoritarian way of control. The per cent of high-school-age youth in high school has increased 28-fold and per cent of college age in college has increased 18-fold since 1870.[1] Perhaps, as a result of changing times, increased education, and a feeling of need and readiness, many people want to study and improve leadership. This chapter will consider leadership style, requirements for participative leadership, degrees of freedom permitted, and two cases of participative leadership.

Leadership style

Three styles of leadership, which are accompanied by three different social climates, are recognized. These are most often called "democratic," "autocratic," and "laissez-faire." These terms are perhaps unfortunate because of their political connotations. We would prefer to coin new terms or use a symbol to designate them, to avoid their contaminating associations, which tend to distort their precise intended meaning as they apply to phenomena of small social groups and organizations. We may, however, avoid these harmful associations by being aware of them.

We have examined in the previous chapter the mode of management and supervision which utilizes authority: the autocratic style. It endeavors to control behavior through power. We have seen in the section on the paucity of power that this power does not endure and that it sometimes fails as a basis for control. In its extreme form the autocratic style

[1] Source: U.S. Office of Education, *Biennial Survey of Education in the United States, 1950–52* (Washington: Government Printing Office, 1955), Chapter 1, tables 11, 34.

of control attempts to hold unlimited and independent authority over a group. The democratic style also endeavors to control group behavior. However, this mode of control relies upon the group itself. The control is not independent of the group but rather makes use of motivational forces within the group. The laissez-faire style relies on the autonomous characteristics of the group to the extent that the leader does not intervene. He may be present to give information when the group asks for it. He does not, however, plan policies or set goals or arrange the group situation so that goals can be achieved.

It should first of all be emphasized that none of these three styles of control exist in absolute form. Rather, we may think of them as a matter of degree. All of them are blended in each situation. Thus we think of a situation as being relatively more autocratic than democratic; somewhat autocratic but predominately democratic; almost entirely laissez-faire; alternating between democratic and autocratic. Figure 3.1 is provided to illustrate this relativity concept.

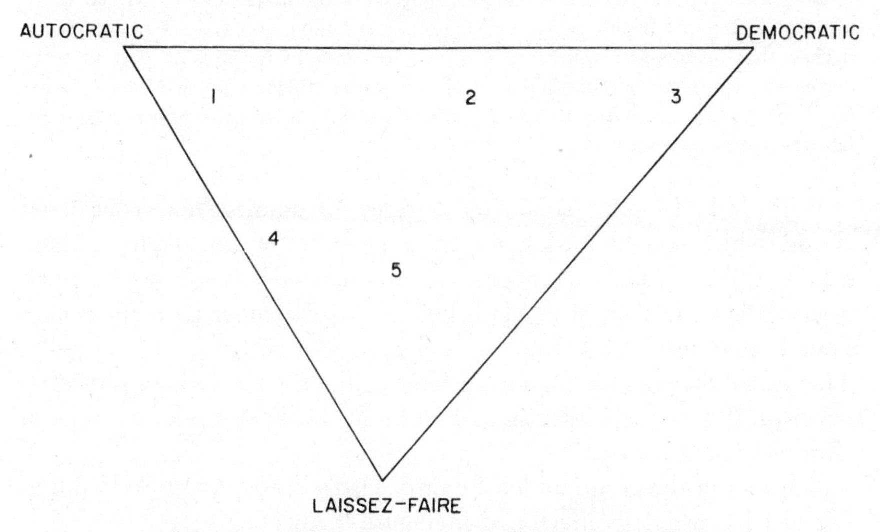

Fig. 3.1 · Degrees of three leadership styles

We can, then, designate the leadership style of a particular situation at any given time by reference to a position within the triangle in Figure 3.1. Thus, an autocratic supervisor would be located at the number *1* in the figure; a democratic leader would be at *2;* a strongly democratic one would be at location 3. A laissez-faire leader would be located at 5, whereas one with some tendency toward the authoritarian, autocratic style would be in position *4*.

The roles assumed by supervisor or leader in a study of the three social climates—authoritarian, democratic, and laissez-faire—are discussed by White and Lippitt [2] as follows

Authoritarian: All determinations of policies by the supervisor; techniques and activity steps dictated by the authority, one at a time, so that future steps were always uncertain to a large degree; the leader usually dictated the particular work task and work companion of each member; the dominator tended to be "personal" in his praise and criticism of the work of each member, remained aloof from active group participation except when demonstrating.

Democratic: All policies a matter of group discussion and decision, encouraged and assisted by the leader; activity perspective gained during discussion period—general steps to group goal sketched, and when technical advice was needed, the leader suggested two or more alternative procedures from which choice could be made; the members were free to work with whomever they chose, and the division of tasks was left up to the group; the leader was "objective" or "fact-minded" in his praise or criticism, and tried to be a regular group member in spirit without doing too much of the work.

Laissez-faire: Complete freedom for group or individual decision, with a minimum of leader participation; various materials supplied by the leader, who made it clear that he would supply information when asked—he took no part in work discussion; complete non-participation of the leader; infrequent spontaneous comments on member activities unless questioned, and no attempt to appraise or regulate the course of events.

White and Lippitt [3] conducted a series of studies, now considered classic, which sought to describe certain aspects of leadership. These studies utilized four experimental groups of ten-year-old boys. Each group of five members worked on hobby projects under an adult leader. Four leaders were shifted among the groups at intervals of six weeks. The leader changed his leadership style with each new group, providing opportunity for observation and recording of behavior under each social climate or leader style.

Behavior of the group under the three leader styles, resulting in different social climates, is illustrated in Figure 3.2.

The experimenters were able, from the observations and data collected during these studies, to describe: (1) supervision or leader behavior

[2] Ralph White and Ronald Lippitt, *Leader Behavior and Member Reaction in Three "Social Climates" in Group Dynamics*, eds. D. Cartwright and Alvin Zander (Evanston, Ill.: Row, Peterson & Company, 1953), p. 586.

[3] *Ibid.* See also R. Lippitt, *An Experimental Study of the Effect of Democratic and Authoritarian Group Atmospheres*. University of Iowa Studies in Child Welfare, XVI (1940), 43–195; and R. Lippitt and R. White, "The Social Climate of Children's Groups," *Child Behavior and Development*, eds. R. G. Barker, J. Kounin, and R. White, (New York: McGraw-Hill Book Company, Inc., 1943), pp. 485–508.

Autocratic atmosphere with leader playing role of strict supervisor.

Laissez-faire atmosphere with leader standing aside and responding only when questioned.

Democratic atmosphere with leader playing the role of a "regular member."

By permission from D. B. Klein, MENTAL HYGIENE *(Holt, 1956) and Professor Ronald Lippitt.*

Fig. 3.2 · Group behavior under the three social climates

under each of the three social climates; (2) differences in group members' behavior for the climate that resulted from the leader style.

1. Leader behavior differed for the three social climates with reference to giving orders, giving disruptive commands, and giving criticism.

The autocratic supervisor's verbal behavior consisted much more of order-giving than was the case in the other two kinds of leaders; for example, "Get your aprons on" and "All right, put your brush away." Also, the autocratic leader gave more disruptive commands and more nonobjective, personal criticism and praise than the other two kinds of leaders. The table below, Table 3.1, shows the present or total behavior for the three kinds of leaders.

TABLE 3.1 · Differences in Leader Behavior

Verbal behavior	Per cent of total verbal behavior for:		
	Autocratic	*Democratic*	*Laissez-faire*
Ordering	45	3	4
Giving disruptive commands	11	1	1
Nonobjective criticism and praise			
Criticism	5	1	1
Praise	11	7	5

TABLE 3.2 · Suggestions and Information-giving by Leader

	Per cent of verbal behavior		
	Autocratic	*Democratic*	*Laissez-faire*
Guiding suggestions	6	24	14
Giving information	15	27	47

Leader behavior differed also in other ways, including differences in total verbal behavior of leaders in giving guiding suggestions; for example, "Did you ever try going the other way—against the grain?" and giving information. The democratic leader gave many more guiding suggestions and information than the autocratic leader, as shown in Table 3.2. Criticism and praise were more objective, evaluative, and analytical and less personal in the democratic style; for example, "That's good, because if you leave as big a piece [of soap during the carving period] as that, you can try again [if the first try fails]."

Democratic leaders tended to avoid the "I" in their conversation, and they were more equalitarian. Thus, a democratic leader would tend not to say "I'm going to pick out the best one when you get done" or "I don't like it yet."

2. Differences found by experimenters Lippitt and White in group behavior under the three social climates are interesting indeed.

Under the laissez-faire leader style less work was done, the group was not as well organized, it was less efficient and "definitely less satisfying." The group was absorbed in work activity some 33 per cent of the time under laissez-faire, as contrasted to 55 per cent under democratic leader style. "Play-minded conversation with other boys was more than 2.5 times as frequent in laissez-faire."

The democratic groups were efficient. While autocracy achieved work goals and laissez-faire play goals, democracy achieved both. The autocratic groups were absorbed in work 74 per cent of the total time. "On the other hand, the amount of genuine interest in work was unquestionably higher in democracy."

One group reacted aggressively to the autocratic set-up. In this one, work time decreased from 52 per cent to 16 per cent when the supervisor left the room. In the three groups which reacted submissively to the autocratic leader, the decrease in work-involved behavior was from 74 per cent to 29 per cent. But in the democratic atmosphere, the group members kept on working when the leader left the room.

Other conclusions drawn from the study by the investigators had to do with hostility and aggression, discontent, dependence and individuality, group mindedness and friendliness.

In one of the four groups, aggression under the autocratic rule was evident. The other three groups were submissive. Friendly ascendance occurred 24 times under the autocratic style and 230 times under the democratic. Definite hostility occurred 186 times in the autocratic group and only 6 times in the democratic; "destruction of own property was conspicuous at the end of the meeting of the autocratic group, and did not occur at all in the democratic group."

The investigators further conclude that discontent, not apparent on the surface, can be fostered in autocratic groups; that there tended to be more dependence and less individuality in autocracy; there was more cohesiveness or group mindedness, and more friendliness in democracy. Friendly remarks, praise, and willingness to share group property were more frequent in the democratic social climate.

Leadership by democratic procedure involves decision making by the group. The decision making process includes three steps: becoming aware of alternatives of behavior which are relevant to the decision being made; definition of these alternatives, together with study of probable outcomes of each line of behavior; and making a choice between the alternatives.

In the complete democratic procedure, how many of these three steps are accomplished by the group and by the leader? The answer is all three of them. The third one, making the decision, is done by consensus or vote of the group. Participation in the first two steps would provide only a portion of the democratic procedure.

Participation of group members is the basic characteristic of the democratic leadership style. Members contribute their ideas, feelings, and preferences. They help decide on goals to be achieved. They help plan activities and decide between alternate approachs to accomplishing goals. There are certain minimum group requirements for such participation.

Requirements for participation

Requirements for group participation include:

1. Provision for education for participation
2. Appropriate communications media
3. Adequate time for participation
4. Economy
5. Adequate and ready interrelationships within the group and among related groups, and stability of these relationships

1. Not always are group members prepared to participate in decision making. If members are accustomed to autocratic leadership, they are not in the habit of stating problems, analyzing situations, considering alternatives and discussing probable outcomes of decisions. Such work may be something new to them. Participation requires both a change in set and an increase in knowledge. These can be learned by group members through training and education and practice in use of democratic procedures such as conference, counseling, and role-playing, to be discussed in detail in later chapters.

2. In addition to education and training in the participative procedures, wide-open channels of communication to keep participants continously informed on all relevant matters are required. These may include information conferences and meetings, information bulletins, and interviews.

3. The first two items above require time. In addition, the meetings for participation and study of decision alternatives take time. Is such time available? Not in emergency situations. Since most decision situations are not of an emergency nature, it would seem feasible in most

instances to provide sufficient time; however, the fourth item—economy—is tied in with the time element.

4. Economy is important in those leader situations in which profit, services, productivity, or money is involved. In highly competitive enterprises, profit is the main goal. Will the advantages that may accrue from democratic leadership warrant the expense involved in education, communications, and participation conferences? Since, at present, sufficiently accurate measurements of outcomes of different leadership styles are difficult to obtain, it is not as yet feasible to convert outcomes to money values. Outcome values can be estimated, and such estimates can be made in terms of short- and long-term effects. On the expense side, however, costs can be accurately computed. Such computations can be compared to estimated outcome values to obtain approximate information concerning relative economy.

Possible values of democratic leadership are: (*a*) ease of management—less close supervision needed, authority is diffused through the group, acceptance is also diffused, resistance is lessened; (*b*) management decisions are improved in quality—many heads are better than one; (*c*) economy in time and money in reaching the goal, for example, of production—greater interest and motivation of team members; (*d*) less absenteeism and turnover—group is more cohesive; (*e*) smoother relationships among group members; (*f*) greater satisfaction.

5. Above all requirements, the group members, and those of related groups in an organization, must be psychologically ready for participation. One cannot decide to use the democratic method one day and install it the next. Readiness implies interest and felt need on the part of members of the participating group. It implies a social climate and cohesiveness among group members. It assumes sufficient knowledge of group goals, that each group member will want to solve the problems confronting the group rather than his own problems. "We-ness" or group feeling must be present.

Furthermore, those who have been in power or authority in the past must be willing to share information in such a way that the former power, held by virtue of ignorance of members of the group, will be lessened. Readiness for group participation by those in related groups is needed. In one company, leaders in middle management stated that they believed the participative style was potentially valuable, but they could not use it because managers at higher levels would not understand it, and their adverse criticism destroy its value.

These requirements for participation are related to limitations upon freedom, discussed below.

Freedom and democratic process

Certain limitations are imposed upon the democratic process. There are *degrees* of freedom. Some of these restrictions come from outside; others from inside the group. The same dilemma exists for any individual anywhere. The leader and his group are free and at the same time, not free. One is free to behave within certain fairly well-defined limits. Murder is an act, for example, which he is not free to commit. Similarly, we can consider degrees of freedom of democratic groups.

Such degrees of freedom are limited by certain outside restraining forces: (1) laws; (2) economics; (3) contracts; (4) acceptance of arbitrators, umpires, or moderators; (5) ethics; and, (6) accepted policy, customs, and moral codes.

1. *Law* sets the outside limits of decisions of all kinds of democratic groups. A leader may want to allow complete freedom, but he cannot. A family acting as a democratic group might decide that a school-age child should be taken out of school to work and contribute his earnings to the family budget. It cannot do this—he has not reached the legal age for leaving school. A business establishment may want to monopolize its industry. It cannot. A state university may want to decide to conduct a profitable business: the law prevents this. Thus democratic process may go so far as the law allows—the public good, not the good of the group or isolated organization, is the concern of the law of the land.

2. The *economics* of a situation, like laws, often determine the limits of group behavior. It would be unrealistic for a large, poor family to decide to send all their children to expensive colleges. It would be foolhardy for a business to expend all of its assets on community goodwill—it could not survive an economic crisis. Military decisions are made in terms of economics. Small group decisions are contained by economic barriers.

3. *Contracts,* as legal agreements, sometimes set limits for group freedom. Thus if a family, borough, or industrial firm is obligated by contract to pay a debt it cannot reasonably decide to spend the money in another way. A decision cannot reasonably be made to increase wages if all assets of the company are obligated by contract. Management development or product research cannot reasonably be performed if contractual obligations preclude this. Diversification may be decided upon but agreement with other companies precludes this.

4. If a small group has agreed that a decision by an *arbitrator, umpire* or *moderator* will be final, then it cannot itself, through democratic

process, make its own decisions. It is limited to decisions not included in the agreement to abide by outside arbitration.

5. *Ethics,* as a higher order of social pressure than that brought about by laws, exerts control on decisions of small groups. This control pertains especially to professional groups. A group of physicians or dentists may not decide to advertise or split fees—such practices, while not illegal, are unethical and are frowned upon by the profession. Should a small group persist in either practice it risks loss of professional society membership. Thus ethical codes impose limits to degrees of freedom of small groups.

6. It is obvious that *policy, customs* and *moral codes*—codes imposed by the general social order—also establish limits to freedom of small groups. Such mores act as informal laws, to restrain groups. It is not customary for a family to spend and live very far below or above its income. A miserly or spendthrift family has sanctions placed upon it, such as loss of group membership, by the community. Custom results in social pressure, maintaining, within broad limits, a modal pattern of small group behavior.

A case of changed social climate

Instances of changed social climate may be available from the experiences of the reader. Perhaps it is not usual for most of us to observe closely such changes. One of the purposes of this and following chapters is to prepare the student of human relations to observe, analyze, and assess —not only the fact of such changes but also their impact on group behavior.

Changes in social climate may have beneficial or harmful results. The direction taken by group behavior, beneficial or harmful, depends upon many variables contained in the total dynamic situation over a period of time. One cannot in any way generalize and say that a participative, consultative leadership style will always foster higher productivity, morale, and achievement by groups. Group behavior is exceedingly complex. It depends upon the myriad conditions existing before the change, the nature of the change, the impact of successive conditions on social forces that themselves change from one episode to the next. It must be remembered also that changes in one small social group are influenced by the organization, system, community, or collectivity of which the small group is a part.

The reader may best come to grips with the complexity of actual situations by considering case problems from time to time. The following case, from Berrien and Bash, is presented for this purpose.[4]

Mr. Schwartz, Production Manager of Lyson Cotton Mills, was agreeably surprised as he inspected the production figures from the winding room. At the same time he was somewhat mystified. Production per employee hour had increased according to the figures in front of him from approximately 29 lbs. to 36 lbs. in the interval between May and December. Total daily production had mounted in the same period from 25,000 to 33,000 pounds. What brought this 32 per cent increase in productivity?

Schwartz scratched his head and began to review in his own mind what had happened. So far as he could remember there had been no changes in methods of work. Up to May, the winding room had been under the general supervision of Hans Heinkle, who had come to Lyson from another cotton mill in order to straighten out difficulties in the winding room. Heinkle was a trained engineer with many characteristics of the Prussian militaristic class, believing that once an order was given it was to be followed without question. Generally, he operated in an authoritative fashion, paying attention to the employee's grievances only when they reached critical or loud proportions. He tended to remain in his office adjacent to the winding room, circulating about the department only when a special problem demanded his presence among the machines. In the course of his 5 years with Lyson he instituted many technical changes designed to speed production and reduce labor costs. In many instances the improvements were reflected in increased production. Schwartz further recalled that Heinkle was an enthusiastic planner, but often failed to carry through his plans if they met minor obstacles.

In May of the next year Heinkle was lured from the Lyson Mills by another company to assist them with certain production problems. It was with some reluctance that Schwartz accepted Heinkle's resignation.

The winding room in the Lyson Mills operated on a two-shift basis with a total payroll of 120 women. Each operator was in charge of 6 winding machines set in a row about 25 feet long, moving back and forth placing empty spools on the spikes when a spool was filled and replenishing the bobbins of yarn when they were exhausted. From time to time it was necessary to tie broken threads. Two shift foremen had reported to Heinkle and were the immediate supervisors of the women. In addition, approximately 20 other workers were under these foremen and were assigned inspection and packing duties. That is to say, the spools of thread were trucked to an adjacent room where these latter employees inspected the spools for poor workmanship and subsequently wrapped and packed the spools for shipment.

In June the CIO Textile Workers Union negotiated increases generally throughout the industry and, at Lyson, finally reached an agreement on a 6c per hour raise on the base pay. This meant that the first shift women operating

[4] F. Kenneth Berrien and Wendell H. Bash, *Human Relations: Comments and Cases* (New York: Harper & Brothers, 1957), pp. 463–71. By permission of the authors and publisher.

between 6:30 A.M. and 3:00 P.M. received 76c per hour base. In addition, an incentive system was in use providing additional earnings according to output. The majority of the women were skilled in their assignments.

Shortly after Heinkle left Lyson Mills, Tony Nassi, a former secretary of the local union, came to Schwartz and told him that he had been promised by Heinkle a promotion to a supervisory job. Nassi was not particularly popular with Schwartz or with the general manager, because of his incessant talking and theorizing about labor relations and wages in terms of the "party lines" of the labor unions. At the time Hinkle left, Nassi was a spinner mechanic. In conference with the general manager, Schwartz presented the problem which Nassi posed. How could the management accept such an individual and yet in view of the promise made by Heinkle, it seemed unlikely that they could easily sidestep some kind of official recognition, especially because of the vacancy created by Heinkle's resignation. Schwartz finally reached what he thought was an adequate solution by cutting off the inspection and packing section of the winding room into a separate department and putting Nassi in charge. However, Nassi was first given four weeks training in the winding department so that he would understand the operations and problems involved.

For a period of two weeks after Heinkle left, Schwartz puzzled about the means of filling Heinkle's position. At the end of that time he finally told each shift foreman that each would run his own shift by himself without other supervision. Within these first two weeks after Heinkle left Schwartz was also confronted by a grievance from the employees which had apparently been ignored by Heinkle.

The difficulty revolved around the disposition of damaged bobbins of yarn. After the bobbins came from the spinning room they occasionally were cut or tangled so that the winding operation was made difficult. Whenever an operator received such a damaged bobbin she placed it to one side. These damaged bobbins were eventually collected. Heinkle had adopted the policy of giving them to one operator on a particular day and rotating the assignment to these damaged bobbins among the various operators. Quite obviously the production of the operator assigned to these damaged bobbins was thereby lowered. The women operators wanted a guaranteed hourly wage for these days equal to their average wage when they were on regular work. Schwartz objected to this on the ground that it was in effect a raise in the base rate. In a meeting with the women he suggested a procedure whereby each operator used all the bobbins distributed to her regardless of whether or not they were damaged. In this way, it was felt the damaged bobbins would be distributed evenly and would not on any one day seriously interfere with anyone's production. The operators seemed satisfied with this solution but they raised the question of pay they had lost by reason of the former procedure. Since their average earnings were down when they worked on damaged bobbins, it was felt that they were unduly penalized and should receive at least their average daily wage. After considerable discussion with the union committee, Schwartz agreed to pay the difference to those who had not made their normal "take home." In total it amounted to $100. Schwartz stipulated that hereafter such requests or grievances should be dealt with immediately if possible by the foremen rather than delaying the issue for two or three months.

About the same time Schwartz learned through the foremen that the women wanted their restroom painted. Because it was exposed to the sun they asked further for shades and an electric fan. Without hesitation Schwartz told the maintenance crew to go to work on the job. In addition he told the foremen to feel free to handle such minor grievances and requests on their own authority hereafter.

Within the next month (July), the third issue was presented. Production had not increased up to this time and was approximately 150,000 lbs. per week (25,000 lbs. per day). This time the women complained that when working a six-day week and changing from one shift to another they were compelled on alternate weeks to work until 11:30 on Saturday night and then report for work again at 6:30 Monday morning. Schwartz listened to their complaint and expressed his sympathy with the short week end but said that production was still lagging and he could see no solution to the problem unless they could meet their production quotas by some other means. In looking over attendance reports he called their attention to the poor absentee records and intimated that if workers were more regular in attendance, production could be increased and the necessity for working six full days would be minimized. At this time he indicated that if production reached 30,000 pounds per day, he could then institute two short shifts on Saturday running from 6:30 A.M. to 12 and 12 to 5:30 P.M. which would then meet the request of the employees. Within a very short time (3 weeks) production reached the level indicated. Unfortunately Schwartz was again in a difficult position because the New York office demanded even more production to meet their orders. Schwartz then had to go back to the women and ask them to continue on the six-day schedule for another few weeks until the orders were filled. Although there was some grumbling, most of the women continued to operate with greater vim and the foremen felt there was no noticeable drop in morale. Late in September the press for more production was reduced somewhat so that it was possible to institute the short day on Saturday beginning about October 1.

Morale during this time had definitely increased and Schwartz was pleased with the cooperation which the employees had given him. He had the feeling (although he could not recall any specific evidence to support it) that a certain suspicious attitude formerly directed toward Heinkle had been dissipated by placing the major supervision in the hands of the foremen. Earnings of the employees had moved from 90c per hour to $1 and sometimes to $1.05 per hour. The general manager in November began to wonder whether the rates in the winding room were, therefore, out of line and he accordingly called Schwartz' attention to the possibility. The union contract specified that no changes in rates would be made unless elements of work were added or subtracted. The general manager was insistent upon this point and wondered therefore whether some elements had been subtracted without the foremen realizing it and reporting the changes. Schwartz began to check on the winding room and discovered a number of minor variations which might be contributing factors to the high wages being earned. Recent changes in the weight of the thread being manufactured had reduced the weight of the spool. The operator's bonus was originally figured in terms of weight and then converted into spools and the number of spools produced was used as a short-cut means of determining wages. It was felt that the change in the weight of the thread had, therefore, made the work easier without any downward revision in wages. About the middle of October Schwartz called the union committee for a conference and proposed that the basis on which the bonus was computed be changed in such a way that 110 spools would be required for the same bonus which formerly 100 spools had earned.

Moreover, another factor entering into the determination of the bonus was the number of knots tied per spool. This latter factor was somewhat complicated. Bonuses above the hourly base rate were dependent upon 2 factors, (1) the number of spools wound per hour and (2) the number of knots tied per spool. The first of these could be counted easily and a careful record was kept of each operator's production. The second could not easily be counted for each operator. Therefore, an agreement had been reached with the union that spot checks would be made once a week and bonuses would be figured on the average count for the whole department. Furthermore, some leeway was permitted in the knot count so that if the average count fell between 4 and 5.9 the operators would be paid for 5; if it fell between 6 and 7.9 they would be paid for 7; etc. A shift from one knot count bracket to a lower one meant a drop of about 70c per day.

In this manner the operators were not penalized in their earnings if the thread delivered to them was of inferior quality. The spool count would go down and the knot count would go up. If the thread was running well, the knot count would drop, but the spool count would rise and earnings should theoretically remain the same if effort were constant.

The operators were not entirely satisfied with this arrangement. Schwartz was reasonably sure that the women preferred to tie knots rather than set up new spools. The effort required to walk to a spool bin, bend over to pick up a spool, place it on the machine and start it winding seemed to be greater proportionally to the time, than tying knots. Moreover, as long as the count remained on the low side of the average (that is between 4 and 4.9) they were making an excessive bonus but if it dropped to 3.9 the bonus was less than the effort expended.

The foreman's clerk posted each day the earnings of each operator for the previous day and also the number of spools required to make 100% of standard production (this would vary depending upon the knot count) and the number that represented 167% of standards.

Actual counts made at the time of this agreement showed the number of knots generally fell between 4 and 5.9. A new count revealed in October that the number of knots per bobbin approximated 3.4 and accordingly some downward revision in rates seemed to be indicated. The union committee protested that the drop was too great in take-home wages. Schwartz, however, pointed out that the women "had been making more than they should" for some time and it was management's turn to have the advantage of the low knot count. However, considering the lighter weight of the thread, the union and Schwartz agreed to an increase from 100 to 106 spools for the same bonus, but the knot count average used for figuring the bonus was left at the old figure of 5 for the time being.

As Schwartz thought more about the situation he recalled that someone had suggested shifting some of the machinery around to make a wider aisle on one side of the room for the trucks to deliver the thread and take out the filled spools. The foreman had gotten the credit for this idea but Schwartz thought that some of the women might have talked about it first—he was not sure.

Then there was Tony Nassi. Since he had been given the job as foreman he had ceased to talk so much about labor problems. Schwartz found him a more agreeable person. Instead of always complaining and theorizing, he was genuinely interested in getting inspection and packing done quickly. With his original crew he was keeping up with the winding room in spite of the increased rate of work.

The whistle was another funny thing. It had been the habit of the foreman to blow a whistle in the winding room at the beginning and end of the shift as well as at six-minute rest periods and at lunch. One of the women had suggested that they use the public address system, having the foreman say, "All right girls, time to begin" or "It's 10:15 and you have a six-minute rest." Some of the women smiled about it at first and seemed to ridicule it with remarks like, "Gee, what's this place coming to?" but in a few days they took the announcement as a matter of course. Once the foreman was busy when the lunch period ended and failed to make the announcement but the women went back to work just the same. Later even the announcements were dropped yet the women started and stopped work at the specified times just the same. Between October 1 and December the daily output of the winding room had grown steadily from 30,000 to about 33,000 lbs. except for one incident in November and early December.

In the latter part of November the New York office complained that the thread was coming through with unbleached spots and urgent orders were dispatched to the plant to cease shipment of such inferior thread. Schwartz walked down to the winding room and stopped all machines in which the thread was in any way defective. This, of course, cut production immediately to approximately the level in the early summer (23,000 pounds per day). Within an hour the union committee descended upon Schwartz demanding in excited tones that he explain the reduced production schedule. Many of the women had no work and were drawing only straight time without a chance for a bonus. Schwartz explained the situation as best he could, pointing out that the outmoded bleaching equipment was partly responsible but inferior workmanship on the part of the men in the bleaching room was also a factor. On the afternoon of the day in which production was curtailed the union committee, on its own initiative, took the bleach men from their department and showed them the inferior thread which was being delivered to the winding room. The union committee became insistent that the bleach operators do their job so as to avoid jeopardizing the jobs of the women in the winding room. Within three weeks, by making certain technical changes and in part through the effort of the employees themselves, the bleaching department was turning out a good quality of thread and output in the winding room was raised to its former level.

But Schwartz was puzzled. He could not understand why production was up 32 percent.

This is a case of changed social climate. Its outcomes are provocative and one is tempted to generalize: to say that, since Hans Heinkle's autocratic style seemed to hold down production, this style is not effective in any situation. Such a generalization would be hazardous, even foolhardy. All we can say is that changed social climate seemed to contribute markedly, during the episode considered in the case, to production. Perhaps later on other less desirable outcomes would appear, as they did in the situation discussed below.

Participative leadership that failed

A dramatic result, exemplifying the potential influence of social climate on both morale and productivity, is reported by William Foote Whyte.[5]

The observations were made in a plant that manufactured wooden toys, such as wooden animals and pull toys. One set of tasks consisted of spray painting the toys as they hung on hooks carried by a conveyor belt to drying ovens. A group of eight girls sprayed the partly finished toys as they passed through the spray booths on the hooks. There was at first much absenteeism, turnover, overt evidences of dissatisfaction, and low morale.

Management decided upon a learning bonus for the learning period of six months and on a group bonus plan. Engineers determined the speed of the conveyor which traveled the endless chains of hooks on which the toys to be painted were suspended. The speed "standard" was determined by time study.

The girls, as is usual, complained that the speed was too fast; they also complained bitterly that the ventilation was poor.

The painting operation became a trouble spot in the plant. A consultant was brought in. He suggested that the foreman have meetings with the girls. The foreman—albeit reluctantly—consented to the meetings, an unusual occurrence in the plant. This was the advent of a democratic, participative leader style, for good or ill a forerunner of a warmer social climate—at least for a time. At the first two meetings they asked for ventilating fans. Finally their request was granted; both production and morale improved. "Whatever the actual efficiency of these fans, one thing was clear: the girls were completely satisfied with the results, and relations between them and the foreman improved visibly." Little did the foreman realize the ultimate outcome of the subsequent meetings.

The girls were eager to meet with the foreman. They brought up the problem of the speed of the conveyor. Their leader said, "Let us

[5] This investigation, its results and implications are reported as Chapter 10 in William Foote Whyte's *Men, Money, and Motivation* (New York: Harper & Brothers, 1955), pp. 90–96. The chapter was written by George Strauss; the unnamed consultant referred to in it was Alex Bavelas.

adjust the speed of the belt faster or slower, depending on how we feel." This was a bombshell. But to make a long story short, the boss of the boss and the engineers consented: they installed a control lever and a dial at the booth of the group leader.

The girls were enthusiastic: during lunch periods they avidly planned; they decided to set the dial at slow, medium fast (considerably above the constant rate standard the engineers had decided upon, based on time study) and fast, at various times during the work day.

The results may be discussed as (1) immediate effect inside the group and (2) outside impact and implications.

1. In the small group the production increased markedly—30 to 50 per cent higher performance than had been originally determined by the engineers as standard in terms of units produced. Quality as well as quantity was high; there was no increase in rejects. High morale was evident—for a little while.

The girls' earnings were much higher than had been planned. They still had two months of the learning bonus to go, they were earning a high group bonus under the plan that had been agreed upon, and they had their base pay in addition.

2. Trouble began. Skilled workers elsewhere in the plant were making less. Complaints to management poured in. "The situation came to a head when the superintendent, without consultation, arbitrarily revoked the learning bonus and returned the painting operation to its original status: the hooks moved again at their constant, time-studied designated speed, production dropped again, and within a month all but two of the eight girls had quit. The foreman himself stayed on for several months, but feeling aggrieved, he left for another job." One of these factors concerns related elements of the system, other parts of the organization. These must be integrated into the leadership style. Change within one small social subgroup of an organization is not enough. The creative leadership style must pervade the entire organization; the organization must be immersed in it. Mutual goals and understanding must be present up and down and across the system.

Thus the change in social climate just reported was both highly successful and a dismal failure.

Leadership is not solely a function of a leader, acting by himself, as is commonly thought. Leadership depends upon the relationship of all the members of the group. The leader may be thought of as standing for the group, a "front man," a prestige symbol. Group behavior may be thought of in terms of the leader. Leadership stems from the interaction of the group members out of which group goal-seeking behavior emerges. Group behavior does not stem solely from the acts of the leader that are themselves goal-seeking. He works with and through others. The leader may do a large share of the group planning; he is active in arranging the situation; he is acting indirectly toward the goal, whereas actually the rank-and-file accomplish the goal by direct action. Thus we see in the leader's activity not a man who is necessarily at the head of the column of the rank-and-file group members, but rather one who is in a role of arranging the situation for the group.

We turn, in the next chapters, to motivation: human needs, analysis of needs of situations, attitudes, and principles of motivation.

Human Motivation

TWO

*

He cannot live in complaisance with others. . . .
Complaisance is the characteristic of a slave.

ARISTOTLE

4

Human needs

Satisfaction of human needs may be considered from two viewpoints: external and internal. The discussion that considers the external viewpoint spotlights the features of the social environment in which the person interacts. Such factors as friends, cooperative supervisors, helpful teachers, loving members of the family are considered as outside need satisfiers. In contrast, the internal viewpoint focuses upon inner needs, drives, urges, desires, strivings, wants. These are exemplified by primary drives such as hunger, thirst, sex; by social needs such as interaction, participation, belonging, friendship, love—these are within the organism. They are sometimes called "organismic" or "ego needs."

From this point of view, motivation is seen as a condition of unsatisfied need. And personal and emotional well-being, contentment, and morale are seen as the dynamic process of resolving tension, accomplishing goals of group membership and approval, and achieving need satisfaction.

The purpose of the detailed consideration of human needs in this chapter is to set the stage for understanding motivation and leadership. The treatment of these topics throughout succeeding chapters is consistent with the brief definitions of motivation given above. Basic to sound leadership is an understanding of human social needs. They are:

Activity and variety
Basic achievement needs:
  security of status
  sense of personal worth
  sense of participation
  group membership
Secondary achievement needs:
  personal development
  release from emotional tension

A discussion of these needs, which have been called "basic" by S. J. Haden, will, I think, be of interest and value in connection with leadership defined as "arrangement of the situation so that group results may be achieved." These needs, if observed in connection with group activity and interaction, have important implications for motivating people.

To be sure, everyone has need for food as well as for other physical needs. But these needs, in our present economy, are not felt *per se*. Rather, they are intermingled with the social needs. Such needs are rarely if ever observed in pure form. We may, therefore, go directly to a more detailed account of the social needs.

Activity and variety

The need for activity, variety, and novelty is considered by some behavioral scientists as a basic need. In the case of an animal or infant, we see mass behavior and exploratory movements which appear to be a part of the life process. These, however, become quickly differentiated into organized behavior that has meaning in terms of a social relationship, for example, the relationship of child with mother. Gradually, such mass behavior becomes organized toward the satisfaction of low-level social needs. It is virtually impossible to conceive of a person who indulges in activity that is isolated from some small group or collection of people.

That the human need for activity and variety is a motivating force is seen in a treatment of the nature of motivation by Hadley Cantril.[1]

For all human beings whom we could call normal, living is thus a constant flow from established form. There is in all "normal" human beings an apparent craving for novelty, a desire to escape boredom and ennui. The human being wants to test his assumptions in new instances. He wants to experience new qualities of satisfaction. . . . Each of us can see in our own lives we are motivated by the desire to experience qualities of value which we feel will somehow be more satisfying than those which constitute our living so far.

Haden mentioned, in an unpublished list, certain factors that influence the desire for activity, variety, and novelty. These factors include the determination of proper limits of the job or task; opportunity for physical movement; relief from monotony; rest periods; recognition of individual differences; change from job to job within limits; change of job within group; and opportunity for initiative. Some of these items have to do with situations in the community, in the home or off the job, whereas others pertain to work or job situations. If management has set limits to the job in such a way that there is little opportunity for physical movement, or if the job is exceptionally monotonous, then we would look upon the job as not satisfying the desire for activity, variety, and novelty. We would say that the job is not a very challenging one and does not provide what is needed to prevent monotony.

Again, if the leader, who establishes the conditions under which the work will go forward, does not recognize the fact of individual differences, we would expect that the worker might be either overplaced or underplaced. If underplaced, he does not have sufficient motivation; he would say "my job is too monotonous, too routine."

Another factor that is cited is the change that might be made from one job to another. A number of companies have practiced job rotation to provide variety and novelty in the activities of various members of the group. This suggests that a job incumbent can satisfy some of his needs if departmental lines of the company can be so arranged that the worker can move from one element of the company to another.

Opportunity for initative in thought also can be arranged by the leader. Again, this bears on the satisfaction of the need for activity. Physical activity is not the only kind of activity that is indicated in this need: mental activity, including problem solving, learning, development of new

[1] Hadley Cantril, "The Qualities of Being Human," *American Quarterly,* VI, No. 1 (1954), 6.

skills, and related activities challenging to the individual would help satisfy this need.

Having proper recreational facilities and making provision for social activities off the job can break up monotony and add variety and novelty. The fact of the social need aspect for activity, variety, and novelty is evident. The satisfaction of the need for social activity presupposes group membership, recognized achievement by the individual, and acceptance and approval, at least to some degree in the group.

Basic achievement needs status

We have listed six kinds of achievement needs. These are social needs. The first one has to do with security of status. All status is of the social kind. We not only need status; we need to preserve it, make it secure. Often status is nothing more than membership and approbation; sometimes an individual may require a high degree of status, which suggests social hierarchy and level. This may mean being chosen, in the sociometric sense, by a number of people: people want to be with him; want to eat lunch with him; want to work next to him; want to be on his bowling team. It does not necessarily mean stratification, that different prestige levels are present. It may mean the less formal, less tangible friendship kind of status that all human beings seek—acceptance by their fellow man.

The status of a person is relative to that of other people around him. In a formal organization or system, such as a school, factory, or office, there are several earmarks of status. These include grades or earnings, equipment, assignments or job duties, responsibility. One who earns more, has a more artistically appointed office, has better equipment, or cleaner working conditions is rated higher in performance of duty or learning achievement. He has relatively higher status.

In smaller, informal groups these status symbols may play a part in sociometric choices, determine whether one person is popular with others and sought after as a companion or rejected as an isolate. But the status symbols that are effective in being chosen frequently by many other group members vary with the group values. For example, a child dressed neatly and in style may be rejected by one group and popular in another, depending upon the situation and the value placed on dress as a status symbol by members of the group.

It is evident that need for status is a motivational factor. The term "status anxiety" suggests that people are sometimes emotionally disturbed about status and its security. In later chapters it will be shown that need for status, which is closely tied to group approbation and approval, is in reference to a particular group and that this fact is of importance to leadership. For example, does a worker identify himself with—have a felt need for status in—the group that is *for* production or *against* it? If he is in the group that is for production, he is said to be company or management oriented; if against production, he may be labor-union oriented or merely "in" with a clique of slow workers. Knowledge of the factors contributing to status security and insecurity is thus a part of the leader's equipment.

Status of membership in an occupational group has been studied by several investigators. One study reported by Carroll Shartle [2] summarizes the results of almost 3000 interviews concerning the status of 90 occupations. It was found that U.S. Supreme Court Justice ranked highest; electrician was ranked in the middle; carpenter was somewhat below the middle; janitor was nearer the bottom of the list; garbage collector was among the lowest.

Assignment of duties within a job is of considerable importance in determining status. William Foote Whyte [3] discovered that restaurant workers' status is affected by job duty assignment. Among cooks, those who prepare chicken have higher status than those who prepare meat. Even among the chicken chefs, those who work with the white meat are higher in status than those who work with the dark meat!

Provision of job security and a stable economic system can be accomplished in part by the individual employer. To some degree it calls for harmonious policies on the part of industry, labor, government, and other groups in our economic system. It is taken for granted that many companies today meet the elementary standards of job security. Such items as protection from arbitrary discharge, seniority provisions, and in-plant promotion hardly need to be urged. The question arises whether more can be done.

In some instances, employers now are being asked for pension and welfare plans or guaranteed annual wages. Since these minister so clearly to the need for security, they are obviously desirable from the psychological and ethical points of view. They also serve a major economic interest of the employer, since a stable and satisfied working force is more efficient. At the same time, they raise other vital economic questions. Instability has so characterized our economic life, for example, that many companies with excellent human relations have hesitated to make such commitments.

[2] Carroll L. Shartle, *Occupational Information,* 2nd. ed. (Englewood Cliffs, N. J.: Prentice-Hall, Inc., 1952), pp. 114–17.

[3] William F. Whyte, *Human Relations in the Restaurant Industry* (New York: McGraw-Hill Book Company, Inc., 1948), pp. 33–46; see also Keith Davis, *Human Relations in Business* (New York: McGraw-Hill Book Co., Inc., 1957), pp. 106 ff.

On the other hand, labor's legitimate desire for security is a force that is bringing pressure to bear upon many firms to reconsider possibilities for increasing job stability. Where the reason for previous instability has been the seasonal nature of an industry, some companies have found that planning, storage, and diversification have made stable production possible. Indeed, one of the first firms to offer guarantees was operating in a highly seasonal industry.[4]

Fourteen factors which affect security of social status are:

( ) Security of employment and income
( ) Pension systems
( ) Seniority
( ) All types of insurance
( ) Definite and understood promotion policy
( ) Company stability
( ) Company reputation
( ) Good company discipline
( ) Impartial treatment of employees
( ) Freedom from coercion
( ) Stability of purchasing power
( ) Confidence in management
( ) Opportunities to maintain personal habits
( ) Confidence in the social order

The first twelve items pertain mostly to work situation; two relate to general conditions.

How many of these fourteen features of your situation have been arranged favorably for you? It would be a simple matter for you to check off or enter a plus mark for each of those that have been so arranged and a minus mark for those that have not been arranged favorably. One could do this for other individuals and for other groups which can be observed or about which one knows in detail the situation as it exists. Such an analysis would approach a systematic method of assessing a situation and roughly appraising the quality of the leadership that has been operating over a period of time. This, too, would be an analytical way to arrive at corrective action for a situation.

Attitude surveys illuminate status conditions in an environment, often revealing feelings of insecurity about employment and income. Less frequently, employees are dissatisfied with the pension systems. Seniority is, to a large extent, satisfactorily controlled for the rank-and-file employees by union negotiations and union-management agreements. More and more companies are emphasizing various kinds of insurance, to

[4] American Business Leaders, *Human Relations in Modern Business* (Englewood Cliffs, N. J.: Prentice-Hall, Inc., 1949), pp. 38–39.

give the feeling of security; the so-called major medical insurance provides virtually complete security in case of serious disability from common illnesses.

Employees may say that there is no definite and well understood promotion policy in a company. They say that promotion policy is not effective because the company pays very little attention to excellence of performance. They say that the leaders in the company have not set up adequate means of assessing performance and do not have adequate records by which they are able to take into account superior performance and to reward it with promotion. The groups that have been surveyed by the use of attitude scales tend to say that cumulative, meaningful records based on impartial judgments of performance would greatly help in promoting a feeling of security of status and progression within the company.

Other items have to do with company stability and company reputation. Good, impartial company discipline is considered by many to be important—if discipline is sporadic, if it lacks uniformity, it germinates a feeling of insecurity of status. Uniformity of disciplinary procedures is, we believe, an exceedingly important item not only in business and industry but also in the family and in community, state, and national affairs.

Children, for example, sometimes feel that they will not be disciplined and punished unless the parents are in a peculiar mood. Thus the child is heard to say, "I hope my dad is in a good humor when he comes home from work tonight, otherwise I'll get a licking." A violator of a traffic regulation who is caught in the act may say, "I hope the judge got out the right side of the bed this morning."

Related to uniformity of discipline is impartial judgment, a difficult achievement, particularly in assessing performance. Human judgment, when other human beings are concerned, is fallible. Judges of human behavior are under the influence of contagious bias and stereotyping, and must guard against halo and favoritism. Knowing this, we feel insecure, because our efforts may be misunderstood or not impartially observed and judged.

A feeling of futility often stems from the lack of stability of purchasing power. The dollar that we earn and put away to satisfy our need for security of status later on may decrease in value during an inflationary period. If we buy government bonds or insurance as a form of saving for the maintenance of our future social status, such investments do not increase proportionately in times of inflation.

A fundamental need is freedom from coercion by unions or by managements. We do not want to have our behavior unduly controlled. We speak of freedom as "the American way." But, indeed, this is jeopardized by coercion from any source—blackmail is the extreme form of coercion. Similarly, our security of status is influenced by our own and others' confidence in our family, community, company, and nation.

We need an opportunity to maintain our personal habits. We need confidence in the social order. For some time, our society has been beset by fears of unwelcome outside influences, the aggressive isms of the twentieth century. These insecurities give rise to unreasonable degrees of tension and frustration that affect the need for security of status.

Personal worth

Every man has need for personal worth or dignity. One of the appeals used by labor union organizers is employee dignity. Unions claim the ability to maintain and preserve the dignity of man. And they contend that managements have worked, in the past, in an opposite direction, that managements have depreciated and dissipated the dignity of the worker.

We observe in isolated, unusual cases, perhaps occurring today in a frequency of one out of a thousand men, the severe personal maladjustments that sometimes result from loss of the feeling of dignity. Loss of dignity is the felt lack of acceptance by any group; the dreadful feeling that no one cares; the withdrawing; the egocentric, disorganized behavior of the psychotic. The schizophrenic is an example. The functional hypothesis of the etiology, origin, or cause of schizophrenia claims that a person has lost the feeling of belonging.

One factor which affects the sense of personal worth is an autocratic disciplinary system. We feel that discipline belongs farther over toward the autocratic and the authoritarian part of the autocratic-democratic scale. However, in the best possible form of democracy, discipline must be resorted to from time to time. The democratic form of discipline is fair, impartial, impersonal, and uniformly administered in the democratic setting; the autocratic is more personal, biased, and lacking in uniformity, as discussed in the previous chapter.

Man is an individual but at the same time he is a social being. He wishes to develop his own personality and self-respect; he desires opportunity to achieve and to create, and he delights in the self-assurance that derives from possessing real ability and the chance to use it. But few persons would be content to be hermits, even though they could demonstrate to themselves a thorough mastery of their environment. Indeed, self-esteem is founded only in part upon an inner conviction of worth. To a large extent it is a by-product of recognition given by others.

So interrelated are these feelings that it is often impossible in practice to say whether a given program is aimed at man's need for self-respect or at his desire for recognition from others.

Policies directed at affirming the basic human dignity of employees at the same time imply the employer's esteem for them. Nevertheless, there is a broad distinction between programs giving the employee a chance to develop himself, and those that recognize his achievements.[5]

Sense of participation

Suggestions made by members of a group constitute recognition of the members only if the suggestions are recognized, approved, and acted upon. Recognition and use of suggestions of members of a group are part and parcel of the democratic, participative style of leadership. We may perceive, broadly speaking, two kinds of situations in which suggestions are made use of by the participative leader: (1) informal provision for recognition by use of suggestions, and (2) highly developed, systematic plans. Informal suggestions are made use of in informal groups; formal plans are generally set up by highly organized systems and larger group organizations.

The degree of formality of the group does not necessarily refer to the degree of cohesiveness of a group. We may have a highly cohesive and tightly knit group—for example, the family group—in which suggestions are used as a natural part of the participative process. In such a group there is no need for a formal system for suggestions. A somewhat more formal setting is exemplified when formal rules of procedure for conducting a group meeting are used. A chairman of a school board, a board of directors of a company, or a board of trustees of a university asks for suggestions when he calls for discussion of a motion before the board.

Formal employee suggestion systems have been in existence in business and industry for a long time. More than 75 years ago a suggestion system of a formal kind was used in Scotland at the William Denny Shipbuilding Company near Glasgow. At the same time, the Yale and Towne Manufacturing Company in Stamford, Connecticut developed a suggestion system, and just before the turn of the present century the National Cash Register Company set up a formal plan for the study, appraisal, and execution of suggestions made by employees. The East-

[5] *Ibid.*, p. 21.

man Kodak Company and the Bausch and Lomb Company started plans at about the same time; and some ten years later both Westinghouse and Western Electric had plans, as did the United Shoe Machinery Corporation and the Public Service Company of Northern Illinois. A number of other companies had suggestion systems of a highly organized kind before World War I: the Public Service Corporation of New Jersey and Philadelphia Electric Company, Stromberg-Carlson Company and the Firestone Tire and Rubber Company were included in this list. During the early part of World War II the War Production Board encouraged use of suggestion plans in industry, and at that time the National Association of Suggestion Systems was formed. A survey conducted at mid-century indicated that 39 per cent of all companies were using formal suggestion plans. At one time the chairman of the War Production Board stated that "production suggestions are saving the nation at a conservative estimate . . . the equivalent of the full-time labor for an entire year of an army of about 80,000 workers." The General Motors Corporation announced that one million dollars was paid for employee suggestions in a five-year period. It is clear that in industries, suggestions are big business.

It is noteworthy that some suggestion systems work quite well without money awards to the employees who make the suggestions. One of the prerequisites of a suggestion system is a sincere desire on the part of the leadership to make use of the suggestions. The social climate must be right before a suggestion plan can work effectively. Several reasons have been given for the failure of suggestion plans:

1. Supervisory resistance and indifference on the part of management
2. Lack of know-how—proceeding on a hit-or-miss basis rather than by establishing a sound policy before installing the program
3. Inadequate rewards for adopted ideas and carelessness and undue delay in handling suggestions
4. Lack of an educational program to teach employees how to submit workable suggestions [6]

The results of a suggestion system are the same as the results of any consultative, participating, or "we" procedure. They are tangible and intangible. In some situations, productivity or effectiveness of the group is clearly increased. Intangible results, harder to observe and measure, accrue at least in some, perhaps in many, situations in terms of morale,

[6] From F. A. Denz, "Why a Suggestion Plan?" *Getting and Using Employees' Ideas*, Production series #165 (New York: American Management Association, 1946), pp. 3–6.

feeling of acceptance, feeling of worth, approval, and, indeed, "favorable notice." They may act as a tool for the elimination of barriers to understanding. They can act as a communications device arranged by the leadership of any kind of group, informal or formal, small or large.

A suggestion system is related to a counseling plan. Appraisal and discussion of a suggestion affords an opportunity to counsel with the suggester. It is a nondisciplinary setting for nondirective communication. Its main value in leadership is its nondirective aspect. A suggestion system properly handled by leadership can establish a social atmosphere which lends itself to working with, advising, discussing, and communicating in a situation of social interaction which has *rapport* as its basis. And suggestion plans are related to action research, the process of the development, evaluation, and application of new and better ways of doing, with the participation of the user. In the suggestion plan, the user initiates the actual research process by raising the question, "Can we do this more effectively?" By using his experience and ingenuity, perhaps with tryout and simple experimentation to test his ideas, he then submits them for assessment and recognition of others.

Group membership

A child, as soon as he is able to walk and talk and have a feeling of belonging to a group, says, "Wait for me. I want to go too. Where are we going? What are we going to do?" When he might be inadvertently left out of a conversation he says, "What is going on?" Or simply, "What goes?" He wants to be communicated with, to know about activities of the group, in terms of his own interaction with it. Further, he wants to be chosen and felt to be a part of the whole.

Later on he asks why things are done in a certain manner. Many of these *why's* have to do with social customs, social norms, and mores. These are more intangible than actions of the group toward its physical environment. The individual's need for communication includes the need for knowing the use of the end products of the activity of his group. Furthermore, he has a need to help determine the conditions within which he works, produces, acts, or behaves. He wants to know what the relationship of his behavior is to the finished product or to the final action. He wants to know something of the relations that he has with his fellow workers. With whom am I working? What are my personal relationships? Where do I stand? Then, as he sees his group is related to other groups, he wants to know how this relationship works and what his part is in the relationship. Much of our day-to-day conversation is concerned with the discussion on a casual level of these relationships. When we consider the enormity and complexity of the relationships of individuals to groups and of groups to other groups, we sometimes wonder how individual and group behavior can be organized as adequately as it is. And the size and complexity of group memberships are becoming greater as organizations become more intricate. It is in this area that leadership may play a significant role in the preservation and continuity of our civilized life as we live it today.

The individual also wants to help in the administration, policies, planning, and execution of plans. He wants to know his relationship to that of the nominal leaders or supervisors of the job; how far he can go in yielding suggestions, discussing problems, and advising on solutions. He is anxious for a knowledge of the future plans of the company, of the committee, of the classroom curriculum. He wants to "think ahead of his teacher." Pilots often say, "We have to fly ahead of the airplane."

The individual needs to satisfy his yearning for a sense of citizenship in the community. What else prompts men and women to assemble at parent-teacher meetings, to work in their off-hours at service clubs or community welfare, to form community improvement associations, to participate in welfare funds, to vote at the polls? And the individual has need for a sense of participation in group recreational activities. For many people, participation in group recreation supplements participation in more gainful efforts and enterprises. For others, whose participation in gainfully occupied groups is thwarted, group recreational activity yields a sufficient outlet and they become clock watchers in school or at work. What proportion of the population of working people and those in school would fall into this classification? The percentages are, of course, unknown; a good guess perhaps would be half. But there are some signs that suggest that leadership, in general, is becoming more enlightened, learning to direct this energy along a productive course; that the pendulum is swinging in the direction of participative leadership, toward satisfaction of social needs.

What can be said for satisfaction of the need for group membership, itself? Some groups provide badges or lapel buttons signifying membership. Why do people wear them? It must be concluded that they derive pleasure or satisfaction from being recognized as a group member. It is often a symbol of a rather high degree of morale, equivalent to saying that this group is a good group or that this company is a good company. The person who wears a gold emblem in his buttonhole which is a symbol of 25 years of service with his company is saying, "I continue to be happy in this company. It is a good company." For some men, the company has a halo. It is globally good. A certificate of membership in a professional or social organization is likewise valued. Some individuals carry a dozen or more membership cards; others are content with one or two. Often the cards are not shown to anyone from year to year as they are renewed, but they provide some sort of satisfaction—otherwise they would not be carried.

Most of the groups to which we belong are not so formal. Many of them are not named. Some of them lack cohesiveness and are not closely knit. Others have a high degree of cohesiveness, depending upon whether goals are clear-cut and the activity and interaction of the membership fosters participation in the group goal activity. If group membership is attractive in a sense that it satisfies a number of the basic needs which we are discussing, it tends to be more cohesive. Amounts and degrees of cohesiveness are hard to measure, although social scientists are working toward the development of such measurements.

An example of one index is ERI, an index of employee relations.[7] The employee relations index has been developed by social scientists working on experimental situations in the General Electric Company. The ingredients which have gone into the employee relations index include amount of turnover of groups, the amount of absenteeism, the number of suggestions contributed to the suggestion system plan, the number of initial visits to the medical room or dispensary, and the amount of participation in voluntary employee benefit plans. It will be mentioned again in Chapter 17 in connection with methods of measuring syntality. The measurement of cohesiveness is also discussed in that chapter.

Some behavioral scientists feel that the quantification of the variables that are involved in the satisfaction of needs is both feasible and desirable and that after they learn through experimentation to develop, evaluate, and use better methods for objective analysis, the mysteries of leadership will unfold, revealing improved methods that may be generalized from one situation to another. Other social scientists, particularly those who follow the Harvard tradition for methods in the study of groups and group interaction, believe that, for the most part, quantification destroys the essential elements of the problems involved and that more adequate descriptive, nonquantitative efforts will constitute the answers for the future.

[7] Willard Merrihue and Raymond Katzell, "ERI—Yardstick of Employee Relations," *The Harvard Business Review* (1955), 91–99.

Internal social needs

Most investigators study satisfaction of needs—morale—by observing how people look upon their external environment. The needs that have been discussed above were perceived for the most part in terms of the environmental viewpoint. Investigators have usually used such questions as "Do you like work?" "Do you enjoy family life?" "How do you like your teacher?" If respondents make high scores—answer such questions favorably—it is inferred that satisfaction or morale is high, that internal needs are being satisfied.

Another method, used for example by Gordon,[8] emphasizes the internal needs that are being satisfied.

Gordon, in his comprehensive study of internal human needs, revealed a general factor which he interpreted as general satisfaction of all needs. He defines morale, in terms of this factor, as over-all satisfaction of needs. He found that the smaller the group the higher the degree of need satisfaction. In addition to the general global or over-all satisfaction factor, Gordon isolated two others which he named "need for recognition of status" and "need for self-respect." One of the productivity scores of the groups, obtained by Gordon before the need satisfaction questionnaire was administered, was found to be related to both the need for self-respect and the need for social recognition of status as measured. Among Gordon's conclusions was the following:

> These findings can lead to suggestions for programs of action. By noting which needs are not being met in various groups . . . steps can be taken to better satisfy these needs. The ability to satisfy needs has often been described as a chief attribute of leadership. . . . Further, in view of the noted relationships, management may expect certain need-fulfilling programs to affect morale and others to affect production.[9]

Secondary achievement needs

Whether need for personal development *per se* is basic is argumentative. It is probable that this category of needs is encompassed by the other needs that we have discussed; that it is secondary rather than primary. A primary need is social recognition.

Again, can we say that the need for the release from emotional tension is a basic one? Perhaps not. We believe that some degree of emotional

[8] Oakley J. Gordon, "A Factor Analysis of Human Needs and Industrial Morale," *Personnel Psychology*, VIII (1955), 1–19.

[9] *Ibid.*, pp. 17–18.

tension is necessary. Some tension is desirable as a requirement for psychological activity such as thinking, problem solving, learning, progress toward goals. If emotional tension is severe, then we do have a need for alleviating such tension. A little tension is a stirring thing: it engenders growth, development, progress, and morale. Too much tension thwarts and distorts. A good balance supplies the raw materials for progress, sets the stage for need satisfaction.

We need not emphasize further that to be human is to have social needs; that to have social needs is motivation; that their satisfaction is morale. In the next chapter we shift to larger groups and explore ways of analyzing situational needs.

*

Every concrete activity is the solution of a situation. . . . When a situation is solved, the result of the activity becomes an element in a new situation.

THOMAS AND ZNANIECKI

5

Analysis of human needs

Success in leadership may be said to depend on ability to analyze situations and identify problems, to conceive solutions to problems, and to remedy situations. The goal of a leader is to contribute to the value of a group enterprise through leadership as we have defined it.

So complex and dynamic are human social needs that their observation is not yet an exact science. Situation analysis, the first step in leadership research, locates and describes leadership problems. Behavioral scientists seek ways of measuring various aspects or dimensions of social groups. Some progress has been made in this direction—much more is required before the dynamics of groups can be adequately described.

More progress has been made, and research has been done more frequently in industrial and work settings than in other situations. This chapter will therefore discuss approaches to situation analysis and cases in which whole situations have been analyzed to illustrate methods, dynamic problems, and possible solutions. The next chapter will present a whole case analysis, together with analysis of attitudes. Later chapters will include summaries of some results of research studies of small groups within organizations.

Analysis of whole situations [1]

Leadership is not yet an exact science, although it does, to some extent, depend upon research. Leadership research is the development, evaluation, and application of a body of knowledge and techniques with which the creative leader works. If a leader does not know the products of research, he can do no more than make rule-of-thumb applications. Over-and-over again he may make the same mistakes that were made in the past without the benefit of the results of research. To practice the art of leadership effectively, he needs to have knowledge of the techniques and products that have been derived from research; he needs to know the results of research in human resources and social science; above all, he needs experience in analyzing group situations in which problems exist.

Case problem solutions deal with employee relations and human dynamics. An example of a human relations solution is increased employee participation in management decisions. A primary goal is harmonious relations, not production—although this solution could result in higher production.

If we view in perspective the historical changes in personnel management, we see three eras that have evolved. First, at the turn of the century, was Taylorism, seeking to find ways to get employees to do more work through engineering the work situation by speed-up and motion-and-time study. Second, beginning in 1915 approximately, interest was turned to techniques for selection, classification, and placement. Third, beginning in the 1920's, attention was directed to social and other felt human relations needs of the employee.

[1] Adapted from Roger Bellows, *Case Problems in Personnel Management* (Dubuque, Iowa: The William C. Brown Co., 1955), by courtesy of the publisher.

In the first and second eras, management was primarily production oriented; in the third, and current, era it is employee oriented. Industrial psychology began in the second era; it started to contribute tools for personnel selection, in response to managements' demands for higher production. Such aspects as social or human relations needs of the worker were not emphasized. No effective employee oriented advances were made in so-called employee motivation until the late 1920's. It was not until the major labor-management clashes of the 1930's and the concurrent strengthening of labor organizations that managements were forced to become employee oriented.

Managers now seek the causes of industrial strife and peace. They need harmony. Their goal is no longer a short-term production record. Their newly acquired employee orientation makes them conscious of two goals: high production coupled with employee satisfaction. They are finding these two goals to be compatible. In seeking ways of achieving industrial harmony, managers are emphasizing peaceful relations by working together with employees. Seemingly inconsequential meetings, in which managers and workers join in solving problems, have been found to have subtle but powerfully constructive influences. Harmonious relations often depend on such slender threads.

The two kinds of solutions—those aimed at increased production, and those aimed at increased harmony—overlap in two ways. First they overlap because, in the long-range economic view, increased production may result in increased job security and better living standards. Second, and more important, the development and use of improved procedures can be accomplished by participation of employees. This is sometimes called "action research." If developed and used in this way, improved procedures serve as employee communications tools and, as such, can result in increased worker satisfaction and worker-management harmony.

The first approach to solution of a case problem is its analysis. A Case Problem Analysis Check List is illustrated in Figure 5.1. It is designed as a systematic aid to analysis of cases and with modifications can be used for cases other than those in industrial settings.

The check list form is designed so that the analyst can record, for each of twenty or more items or aspects of the personnel situation, the degree of need of the situation. Four columns are provided for the analysis: *irrelevant or no information, adequate, improvement needed,* or *critical.* Each of the twenty items is to be checked in one of these first

a. In view of the problems in this case, check the items below in column I, II, III, or IV by placing (X) in the appropriate column opposite each item. b. Then, in column V, place a number 1 opposite that item you believe should have highest priority for remedial work; use number 2 for second priority and 3 for third priority, if work on more than one item is indicated. c. Then, in the space provided on the reverse of this form, write a brief statement telling what you would do to improve the situation.		Irrelevant or no information I	Adequate II	Improvement needed III	Critical IV	Priority V
1 Personnel policies and practices survey	1					
2 Organization chart	2					
3 Selection of executives for efficiency	3					
4 Selection of supervisors for efficiency	4					
5 Selection of personnel to control turnover	5					
6 Training employees in human relations	6					
7 Training supervisors in human relations	7					
8 Training top management in human relations	8					
9 Attitude-morale surveys	9					
10 Exit interview	10					
11 Employee benefits	11					
12 Employee services	12					
13 Employee counseling	13					
14 Employee communications	14					
15 Employee participation in decisions	15					
16 Supervisor participation in decisions	16					
17 Suggestion systems	17					
18 Upward communications	18					
19 Employee evaluation procedure, criteria	19					
20 Use of employee evaluation procedure	20					
21 ____________________	21					
22 ____________________	22					
23 ____________________	23					

Adapted from Bellows, CASE PROBLEMS IN PERSONNEL MANAGEMENT

Fig. 5.1 · Case problem analysis check list

four columns. The fifth column is to be numbered for priority—what should be worked on first, second, etc., in solving the problem for the company. Usually not more than three or four items are numbered; sometimes only one or two numbers will be entered in the priority column. For example, if a personnel policies and practices survey is indicated as number one in priority, then the designation of other items that are in need of improvement might await the results of the personnel policies and practices survey. It should be noted that more than one remedial step could, in some cases, be taken concurrently. Thus it is possible to have two, or even more, items checked as highest, or number one, priority.

Space is available at the bottom of the check list for writing in other items that are inadequately handled by the company. Use of this space for write-ins is encouraged.

The following functional descriptions of the twenty check list items are presented to aid in uniformity of definition.

1. *Personnel policy and practices survey.* A general assessment of over-all personnel policy and practices of an enterprise is sometimes needed. Such a survey is itself a detailed analysis of the company situation; it may be much more detailed than would be possible with the use of the present check list. The check list items for the survey would be specifically designed for the particular company.

The survey is usually performed by having knowledgeable managers and supervisors complete the prepared forms. Sometimes representatives of rank-and-file employees participate, an activity to be encouraged for the communications value that this approach yields.

2. *Organization chart.* Adequate organization planning is important in all enterprises for: flow of communications, delegation of authority, fixing responsibility, establishing career ladders, supervisory orientation and training, and developing replacement schedules. The need for it is most evident in case problems in which supervisors do not know to whom they report and when employees have more than one boss. The story is told of a Pentagon office worker who, on his way out to lunch, called back over his shoulder, "If the boss phones, get his name."

3. *Selection of executives for efficiency.* The term "executive" is here used to include all of management above direct-line supervision. Although executive selection is, in some cases, of prime importance, other factors—organization, communications and training—are sometimes basic.

Selection and promotion from within is generally to be preferred to selection from outside the firm as it enhances security and cohesiveness.

4. *Selection of supervisors for efficiency.* Too often a serious problem emerges when a good rank-and-file worker is promoted to foreman or supervisor on the basis of his superior performance. Other psychological characteristics are needed for supervision; the solution frequently is to take these into account in selection for promotion.

5. *Selection of personnel to control turnover.* An excessive number of employee quits is expensive and wasteful. The problem is caused by two general classes of factors: (1) selection that has not provided for weeding out the turnover prone applicant, and (2) conditions at work, especially those involving employee dynamics, that foster dissatisfaction. We are concerned in this item only with the first of these causes.

An applicant may be turnover prone for two reasons: he may not have the aptitude or skill to perform efficiently on the job, or he may be unstable. Selection for efficiency is taken care of by adequate interviewing, aptitude and trade testing. We are here concerned with job stability from the point of view of factors in the individual's make-up, other than his efficiency, which are associated with short tenure and which can be identified at the hiring point. Sometimes application blank items, such as marital status and number of dependents, are found to be valid predictors of job tenure.

6. *Training employees in human relations.* Human relations training—how to get along with others—is generally considered not as important for rank-and-file employees as for supervisors and executives. However, in many case problems in which communications are inadequate, such training can provide a medium for transmission of information and mutual understanding. Some of this can be accomplished as part of induction training.

7. *Training supervisors in human relations.* Human relations training sometimes goes by various names, such as employee good will, management-worker relations, living and working together, how to motivate employees, direct line supervision, and many others. A heritage of knowledge has come from research in the areas of group dynamics and leadership, and this furnishes the basis for superior human relations training. For such programs, conferences or seminars are arranged—from ten to twenty meetings of from one to eight hours each, in which from eight to twenty supervisors and a conference leader participate. A typical outline for a course of ten sessions is:

Session	*Topic*
1.	Orientation to human relations methods; concrete problems of group members
2.	Leadership; conference leader techniques
3.	How to view human problems objectively
4.	Attitudes
5.	Frustration
6.	Motivation; levels of aspiration
7.	Counseling and the counseling interview
8.	Nondirective methods in human relations
9.	Role-playing and role-playing analysis
10.	Group discussion procedure; summary and evaluation

8. *Training top management in human relations.* Managing heads of companies—president, executive vice-president, treasurer, secretary, controller and vice-presidents—are harder to reach with human relations training programs than are supervisors. Yet the need is very often greater at that level, as revealed, at least somewhat dramatically, in several of the case problems that follow.

Ideally, the course content and sessions would be arranged the same as for foremen and supervisors. Few companies have achieved this ideal, although some actually have round-table conferences on these topics without regard to the level of status of the participants; the communications values that stem from this arrangement are obvious.

Quite often the approach to training top managers must be handled in a more subtle way. An example is ostensibly accomplishing a position analysis or job shredout to conserve time of the top executive, which allows exposure time for discussion and counseling on communications and human relations problems. This approach will provide a suggested solution for both of the case problems to follow.

9. *Attitude-morale surveys.* An employee or supervisor attitude is a predisposition to behave toward a situation in a certain way. An attitude may be measured fairly accurately by scaling attitude techniques applied to questions, or it may be estimated roughly by questionnaire or interview approaches. Questions are usually broken down to reflect attitudes of the worker, or supervisor, toward aspects such as working conditions, his job and job relationships, supervision, management policy, hours, pay rates, benefits and services, promotion. Respondents are usually anonymous, and confidences should be respected.

The terms "attitude survey" and "morale survey" are generally synonymous. Morale pertains to over-all feelings of the worker toward the work situation and may, for present purposes, be considered as the total or synthesis of his attitudes. A detailed summary of results and recommendations from an illustrative attitude survey is included in Chapter 6, pages 94–98.

10. *Exit interview.* Some companies regularly ask questions of a terminating employee, seeking to reveal reasons for employee turnover, to enable remedial action—perhaps training supervision—or to save the employee by transfer or ironing out difficulties. Unless a depth interview of long duration conducted by a highly skilled interviewer is utilized, there is usually little chance that the information obtained will be useful.

11. *Employee benefits.* This area includes the many arrangements to help employees, which may be required of management by union organizations through collective bargaining. Examples of benefits are: paid vacation, sick leave, company credit union, guaranteed annual wages, retirement benefits.

12. *Employee services.* Employee services are usually not specified in labor contracts but are provided thoughtfully by management. Employee services may include items such as adjustment counseling, legal counsel, medical and nursing care, restaurant and parking facilities.

13. *Employee counseling.* This advisory service facility provided by management is designed to help adjust employees socially or emotionally —sometimes by professional nondirective therapy: to iron out petty grievances between employees; to give information, especially during induction and orientation to a new job or department; to help the employee by job counseling or by use of criteria of degrees of attained success.

Counseling often acts as a two-way communications channel, helping the employee understand management's problems and vice versa. It can aid in establishing mutual goals.

14. *Employee communications.* In many of the case problems encountered the cause of lack of employee-management harmony is found to be inadequate transmission of information up-and-down-and-across the organization. The "grapevine" is a most unsystematic, unsatisfactory communicating medium. Other devices, such as bulletin boards, letters from the president, house organs, and conferences are helpful.

It should be stressed that indirect communications through counseling and by research programs, with emphasis on action research, are often most helpful in fostering teamwork based on mutual goals.

15. *Employee participation in decisions.* During the last few decades much emphasis has been placed on democratic, as opposed to autocratic leadership. This emphasis is grounded in research findings in the area

of employee-management social dynamics. Participation by employees—taking an active part—in arriving at decisions is an essential characteristic of democratic organization. This has been found to be an effective solution to a number of case problems.

16. *Supervisor participation in decisions.* A predominating trouble factor in some case problems that will be analyzed will be found to be inadequate supervision. This not infrequently stems from faulty communications between planning engineers and foremen, or between top management and foremen. The direct line supervisor is sometimes the forgotton man.

If foremen are brought into management policy and decision meetings, mutual understanding of problems will tend to be increased.

17. *Suggestion systems.* Most companies would profit by use of well-planned and maintained suggestion systems. The most important value of an adequate suggestion system is thought generally to be communications. The suggestion system committee itself acts as a catalyzer in bringing about employee participation in improvements.

18. *Upward communications.* While organizational planning gives attention to downward flow of information, seldom is emphasis placed on the need for upward flow. Employee gripes often stop at foreman level. The door of the department head is not always open, or, if it is, he is likely to be out. Some company managements make personnel policy with no knowledge of the worker's felt or actual needs.

Counseling, attitude surveys, suggestion systems, employee participation, and open-door policy all contribute to planned upward communications.

19. *Employee evaluation procedure, criteria.* This is considered as the most important single item for improved personnel methods. Employee evaluation is a kind of worker analysis in which assessment is made of the worker's job performance. Evaluation is done by merit rating or by objective scores such as production per unit of time or errors made. These procedures yield job scores or criteria of effectiveness of employee performance.

Adequate criteria are, among other things, realistic, statistically reliable, and reasonably related to other possible measures of job success.

Criteria form the basis of objective evaluation of various personnel tools and procedures such as employee selection and training programs.

20. *Use of employee evaluation procedure.* Cases are included in which the results of adequate employee evaluation are *not* used. For example, one of the more important uses of criteria is job counseling.

In this procedure the counselor tells the employee, in a nondisciplinary way, his weaknesses and strengths. This enables him to correct his faults, gives him confidence in his ability to do the job. Another example is the failure to use available criteria for validating data used in employee selection.

Solution of case problems

There are five steps in the analysis and solution of case problems.

1. Become familiar with the several aspects of the situation as described in the case problem.
2. Work out a tentative analysis of the case problem by use of the Case Problem Analysis Check List (Figure 5.1).
3. Refer to textbook sources and other references for information related to the problem. *Psychological Abstracts* will locate additional sources of information.
4. Revise the check list analysis as needed in light of what you have found from textbook and related source materials.
5. Prepare a write-up of your solution. The write-up of report and recommendation for solution conforms to the check list for each case.

An illustrative case [2]

In this case problem we are interested in methods of payment which will yield the greatest incentive for higher production among power sewing machine operators. The plant is located in Atlanta. It fabricates simple articles of clothing including overalls, aprons, dresses, and pajamas. The plant is a modern one and the most efficient machinery has been installed in it. The firm, Artistic Textile Corporation, is a subsidiary of a larger textile manufacturing company which is located in Stamford, Connecticut. The Atlanta installation is solely a production plant.

The plant superintendent is John Pritchard. The head of the fabricating department, which employs 628 people, is Ivan McKesson. Fifteen foremen and 65 group leaders supervise the work of 435 female power sewing machine operators, the largest group in the plant. The sewing machine operators have relatively little education, averaging 7 years of schooling. The 15 foremen, all men, average 13 years of school, and the 65 group leaders, who are women, average 7 years of grade school. There are 3 sections in the fabricating department: sewing, inspection, and folding and packing. There are 28 employees in inspection, and 85 in folding and packing. These also are female employees.

A personnel director, Peter Clancy, has recently been employed. Personnel was formerly handled by another unit in the Atlanta organization headed by an office manager. The office manager's office was responsible for payroll, but the payroll unit has recently been shifted to the personnel department. A centralized

[2] *Ibid.*

personnel department was established to work out an incentive procedure to increase production. Peter Clancy was selected for this position because of his experience in pay incentive work in the textile industry. John Pritchard had for some time been contemplating a change-over from the hourly rate now being paid the power sewing machine operators to a piece-rate pay basis.

Both the personnel director and head of the fabricating department believe that there are certain theoretical advantages in the piece-rate method. These include equal pay for equal work. It was thought that each employee would work harder and be happier in the thought that she was actually being paid for the amount of production she, herself, achieved. If production could be increased, with overhead remaining approximately the same, the company would make a higher amount of profit on the work of the sewing machine operators, and at the same time could afford to pay them more for their work: part of this added profit could be split with the employees. Thus, the employees would, on the average, make a higher amount of take-home pay. This fact in itself was believed by these gentlemen to be sufficient for increasing worker satisfaction. They felt that the main thing the worker desired was the amount of actual pay that she took home in the pay envelope weekly.

It was also realized that there were some advantages to the hourly rate of pay. First, it was certainly easier to administer; and second, it was easier for the worker to understand. It was simpler all around. Then, too, the workers would at all times know how much they are making. Employees generally, especially in the South, are skeptical of complicated pay plans. Withal, however, the advantages of the piece-rate as an incentive device seemed to Pritchard, McKesson, and Clancy to outweigh the disadvantages in this procedure. The various aspects of production in the workrooms of the fabricating department seemed to them to lend themselves to piece-rate payment practice. Piece rates had been used successfully by other competing companies, both in the New England area and in the South.

Peter Clancy had worked out a criterion of performance for the female employees based on a daily errorless production figure. Errors were caught in the inspection department; the power sewing machine operator who made the error was identified in each case and a slip was forwarded to payroll indicating the number of production units that were to be subtracted from the total daily output of each employee. Clancy worked out a learning time adjustment for trainees. It has been known from job analysis and motion and time study that it required two and one-half weeks of training for the average sewing machine operator to reach normal production. For the first three weeks, a new employee was to be placed on a straight time pay basis as a trainee, and after the three weeks of training, each employee was to be placed on the daily average errorless production incentive plan.

It seemed natural to Pritchard, McKesson, and Clancy to keep the new plan a secret until the details had been worked out by them, with only 3 of the 15 foremen involved in the development of the plan—"for security reasons." The plan was to be announced and put into effect on the first of the month without knowledge or participation of the rest of the foremen, the group leaders, or the power machine operators themselves. The plan was duly installed on the first of the month. After the first 30 days it was found that it was not at all well received by the employees or the group leaders. The results were something less than favorable—they were nearly disastrous to the company. The turnover among employees had jumped from the usual 7 per cent a month to 18 per cent a month. There were other evidences of dissatisfaction. The production activities of the Atlanta plant were beginning to fall apart.

To sum up, here are three hard-boiled and practical management people, Pritchard, McKesson, and Clancy, who have worked out a plan for piece-rate incentives. The plan was carefully conceived in all aspects except one. Remedial procedures, though not simple, are fairly straightforward.

What would you do to remedy the situation?

Mr. Pritchard and his managing co-workers have overlooked important aspects of the situation: human relations, communication, participation. In Figure 5.2 a check list analysis of the situation is shown. It would perhaps be best for them to start over again and go back to the hourly pay basis for some months while gradually indoctrinating, through meetings and discussion groups, all of the foremen, group leaders, and employees in the advantages and disadvantages of the piece-rate incentive system.

Complete participation of all employees in decisions regarding the piece-rate pay plan is recommended. The group of operators could be divided into committees of from ten to twenty each. It would take perhaps as much as twenty hours of exposure time with each committee, with well worked-out presentations and provision for adequate participation and discussion, to get across the purposes and design of the piece-rate plan and how this plan would favorably influence the earnings, well-being, and security of the employees, and to achieve the needed participation in a decision to use it.

No attempt should be made at any time to superimpose the piece-rate plan against the will of the employees. The goal of employee participation in decisions would be a unanimous agreement.

The key is "let the employees decide." This is not, of course, a *laissez-faire* procedure. It illustrates the principles of democratic *vs.* autocratic forms of management. A second illustrative case [3]

Approximately ten years ago, this company moved its operations from Brooklyn to Texas. The move was occasioned by the fact that legislative controls on this kind of business were less rigid in Texas than in New York State. Whereas the company has enjoyed increasing profits from year to year since its move to Texas, it may be said that its personnel practices leave something to be desired.

[3] *Ibid.*

a. In view of the problems in this case, check the items below in column I, II, III, or IV by placing (X) in the appropriate column opposite each item.
b. Then, in column V, place a number 1 opposite that item you believe should have highest priority for remedial work; use number 2 for second priority and 3 for third priority, if work on more than one item is indicated.
c. Then, in the space provided on the reverse of this form, write a brief statement telling what you would do to improve the situation.

	Item		Irrelevant or no information I	Adequate II	Improvement needed III	Critical IV	Priority V
1	Personnel policies and practices survey	1			X		
2	Organization chart	2	X				
3	Selection of executives for efficiency	3	X				
4	Selection of supervisors for efficiency	4	X				
5	Selection of personnel to control turnover	5	X				
6	Training employees in human relations	6	X				
7	Training supervisors in human relations	7				X	4
8	Training top management in human relations	8				X	3
9	Attitude-morale surveys	9	X				
10	Exit interview	10	X				
11	Employee benefits	11	X				
12	Employee services	12	X				
13	Employee counseling	13	X				
14	Employee communications	14			X		
15	Employee participation in decisions	15				X	1
16	Supervisor participation in decisions	16				X	2
17	Suggestion systems	17	X				
18	Upward communications	18			X		
19	Employee evaluation procedure, criteria	19	X				
20	Use of employee evaluation procedure	20	X				
21	____________________	21					
22	____________________	22					
23	____________________	23					

From Bellows, CASE PROBLEMS IN PERSONNEL MANAGEMENT

Fig. 5.2 · Case problem analysis check list for Artistic Textile Corp.

Several indices of employee unrest—employee turnover, slowdowns in work among clerical workers, absenteeism, and grievances—all tend to indicate that the corporation is in an unhealthy condition personnel-wise. At first, this would seem to be a mysterious malady, inasmuch as the company has put a good bit of effort into personnel policies and practices, but the personnel techniques that have been developed have not been put to proper use.

The company is directed by Saul Brenner, president, and Robert Gregg, vice-president and general manager. These two gentlemen accomplish all policy formulation and management of the organization. The organization is divided into seven elements: the legal department, which employs 14 people; the controller and main office unit, 55 personnel; claims adjustment and possession department, 7 employees; advertising and public relations, 5 employees; two closely controlled subsidiary companies (that operate two secondhand merchandising establishments for repossessed goods on which chattels have been held by the company), 52 employees; personnel and payroll department in the main office, comprising 18 employees; a branch office unit including 8 field supervisors who establish liaison, communications, and control links between the main office and the branch offices.

The Personal Loans Acceptance Corporation operates, in all, 43 branch offices. Each of these offices has a branch director and from one to three assistant branch managers. One of the assistant branch managers is the credit man for the branch. The branch offices on the average employ four teller-cashiers and two billing clerks. The total number of personnel employed by the corporation as a whole, including its two small subsidiary companies, is over 500 people.

Philip Mudd is personnel director for the corporation. He has had experience and training in personnel methods and procedures which would seem to be sufficient to accomplish the execution of the personnel policies and practices of the company which are, in part, firm and sound. The main exception to the soundness of the personnel developments is the fact that they have been created in a vacuum—without collaboration of supervisory and rank-and-file employees other than those in the personnel department.

For example, a job evaluation study was conducted during the past several years, including the development of job descriptions for all jobs in the company. The jobs were grouped into pay-rate ranges on the basis of: job specifications (formal and informal training and experience and other psychological characteristics required for successful accomplishment of the job duties); responsibilities (for employee relations and supervision, for money, for confidential information, for public relations, and for property of the company). The only people who have worked on the job descriptions and pay-rate ranges by job evaluation procedure have been personnel department technicians. There has been no communication and no participation in planning with employees in the company to which the job evaluation system has been applied. Philip Mudd has thought it unncessary to bring in other people in the company for participation. He erroneously contends that this slows down the development of the needed tools and results in an unnecessary waste of valuable working time on the part of employees and supervisors, both inside and outside the personnel department. Brenner and Gregg realize that the tools, though technically excellent, are not working and have brought in a qualified personnel consultant, James Evans, with a view to remedial effort.

In brief, this company, in spite of the fact that it has increasing profits from year to year, and in spite also of the fact that it has a considerable number of what would appear on the surface to be excellent personnel developments, can be given something less than a good bill of health as far as employee satisfaction and morale are concerned. There are many signs of employee unrest. It seems clear that there is a blind spot in the thinking and planning of Mr. Mudd in the development, verification, and application of personnel policies and practices in the Personal Loans Acceptance Corporation.

If you were James Evans, who is being brought in as personnel consultant, what would you recommend as a remedial procedure?

The blind spot in Mr. Mudd's planning and execution of studies, it would be agreed, is lack of provision for participation and communication. The solution seems fairly simple. Figure 5.3 shows a check list analysis for this company. To increase employee communications, James Evans would recommend that two steps be taken: (1) Publish a bimonthly employees newsletter of 1500 to 3000 words reporting plans of the company and activities of supervisors and employees. (2) Institute a formal counseling program and an open-door policy to enable free communications between supervisors and employees for the dissemination of information up, down, and across the organization.

It would be desirable for Mr. Evans, as consultant, to recommend that the job evaluation program be redone, emphasizing its use as an employee communications device. It would be conducted as a project in action research. Committees comprising representatives of rank-and-file and supervisory employees, to whom the job evaluation system is applied, would be set up to achieve their participation. A letter from the president, Saul Brenner, would announce that a revision is being made in the job evaluation plan and that committees are being established to plan and execute the program. A suggestion system might be considered for aiding in accomplishing the same purposes—more adequate communications with employees. In addition, a morale survey would probably help management spot weaknesses in their policies and practices.

Two cases have been analyzed as whole situations. Both of these case analyses have revealed dynamic conditions concerning interrelations of people within small groups and of small groups within the organization and system. Use of the analysis check list is seen to focus the analyst's observation on specific needs of the total situation.

a. In view of the problems in this case, check the items below in column I, II, III, or IV by placing (X) in the appropriate column opposite each item.
b. Then, in column V, place a number 1 opposite that item you believe should have highest priority for remedial work; use number 2 for second priority and 3 for third priority, if work on more than one item is indicated.
c. Then, in the space provided on the reverse of this form, write a brief statement telling what you would do to improve the situation.

	Item		Irrelevant or no information I	Adequate II	Improvement needed III	Critical IV	Priority V
1	Personnel policies and practices survey	1			X		
2	Organization chart	2	X				
3	Selection of executives for efficiency	3	X				
4	Selection of supervisors for efficiency	4	X				
5	Selection of personnel to control turnover	5	X				
6	Training employees in human relations	6	X				
7	Training supervisors in human relations	7			X		
8	Training top management in human relations	8				X	
9	Attitude-morale surveys	9				X	2
10	Exit interview	10	X				
11	Employee benefits	11	X				
12	Employee services	12	X				
13	Employee counseling	13				X	
14	Employee communications	14			X		1
15	Employee participation in decisions	15				X	
16	Supervisor participation in decisions	16	X				
17	Suggestion systems	17	X				
18	Upward communications	18			X		
19	Employee evaluation procedure, criteria	19			X		
20	Use of employee evaluation procedure	20			X		
21	____________________	21					
22	____________________	22					
23	____________________	23					

Fig. 5.3 · Case problem analysis check list for Personal Loans Acceptance Corp.

We believe also that his view may be more objective and impartial with this analytical approach.

We should continue to emphasize first that analyses as made in these two cases do not get at elemental essentials for describing, in minute detail, group dynamics. Second, findings from such cursory analysis cannot be generalized to other complex whole situations.

The analytical procedures that have been used as an aid in describing human needs in whole situations are, we consider, a first step in approaching descriptions of leadership situations.

Subsequent steps might include, depending upon the cursory whole situational analysis, one of three areas for further study: choices of members of groups for other members; interpersonal perception of roles of members; attitudes of members toward external environment, with special reference to fellow workers, supervisors, and leaders. The next chapter will discuss human needs and their analyses in a whole situation and the attitudes of members of an organization.

*

And no one shall work for money, and
no one shall work for fame;
But each for the joy of working. . . .

—RUDYARD KIPLING

When Earth's Last Picture Is Painted

6

Needs, motivation, and leadership

People have various kinds of urges, desires, strivings, wants, or needs, and these control our behavior, in part. The psychologist calls this area of problems *motivation*. By analyzing these wants or needs we are better able to understand and describe behavior. If we can describe man and groups of men in action, we will then be better able to understand leadership.

We have both direct and indirect wants, as suggested in Chapter 4. Our direct wants, in our civilization, are not so very important. The indirect wants—those dictated by our social environment—are the wants of the utmost importance to our analysis.

The bare essentials of life

Our direct needs include food, water, some adequate shelter, and all of those things that enable the individual to keep on living in the biological sense. Biologists also include sex as a requirement for the continuation of the race. These are direct or primary needs.

Now it so happens that in our civilization it is rare, indeed, that we strive to satisfy these needs and only these needs. They are usually satisfied automatically. It might be argued that satisfaction was not automatic during the depression, when many people were hungry to the extent of ill health. But they were not hungry for a very long time, because government, state and local aid programs stepped in to supply the bare necessities of life. The need to get food, a direct biological need, is rare in the United States. However, man does sometimes find himself in need of food and striving to obtain it. We may say that the food goal or the food need has set up a tension, arising from a condition of unsatisfied need.

Tension

To carry this description of man in a state of tension one step farther: when a man is in a condition of unsatisfied need, we may say that motivation is present. This tension exists between the man and his environment.

As soon as a tension or unsatisfied need occurs the man may be said to become a psychological being. Before the tension existed and while his needs were satisfied by routine, automatic, or habitual behavior—with no barrier in the way of the satisfaction of a simple need—the person was living more like a vegetable than a psychological man. He did not have to take advantage of his psychological equipment, that is, his intelligence. If he has no problem, he has no reason to use intelligence. So we may conceive of the person as being in a nonpsychological condition, or as leading a nonpsychological, unmotivated existence. Man's psychological existence emerges when there is a barrier or problem in the pathway of the routine satisfaction of a need.

This idea of the emergence of psychological behavior is quite different from most concepts to which we are accustomed. Because of their unusualness, such ideas are elusive when we try to grasp them. We do not in our everyday work and life think in these terms. Figure 6.1 presents,

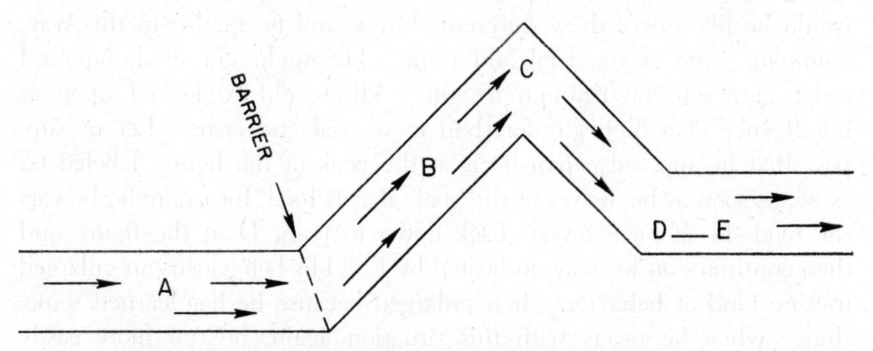

Fig. 6.1 · The emergence of psychological behavior

in a schematic way, the emergence of psychological behavior. The left segment, labeled *A*, represents routine behavior, the kind of behavior that we indulge in most of the time. The arrows in that part of the figure designate our behavior as it flows along in a smooth way. It appears as if we are quite well adjusted through habit to our environment. We eat when food is placed before us, satisfying the primary or direct biological need for food. Most of our other needs of the direct biological nature are satisfied in this way, by routine habitual behavior.

However, when a man comes to a barrier in the pathway of the satisfaction of a need, it could be said that he is alerted, that there is a tension, however minor or however strong. This stress is occasioned by the barrier placed in the way of routine behavior. He then has to solve the problem, surmount the obstacle, get out of the difficulty. If he is not able to do this, he may substitute a different goal that would satisfy the need, or he may become maladjusted and frustrated, or he may not survive in the situation for lack of achievement of the goal—he may die.

If the barrier to achievement of the goal is not too rigid and insurmountable, if the problem is not too difficult for him, he may be able to solve it. Part *B* of the diagram represents problem-solving behavior. He is analyzing the situation. He may set up an hypothesis: he says to himself, "If I do this, I shall be able to achieve the goal."

After our problem-solving person states the problem, sees it clearly, and formulates a hypothesis concerning how he might solve it, he then perhaps indulges in some trial-and-error behavior. He tries out his hypothesis to see if he can achieve the goal in terms of the solution that he has developed for himself. Instead of indulging in sheer trial-and-error behavior, however, he might sit back and imagine what it would be like to try these different things, and he might, in this way, eliminate some of the trial and error. He might cut it all out and arrive at a solution through insight. This could be looked upon as intelligence of a higher order than mere trial and error. Let us suppose that he succeeds, then he is at the peak of the figure, labeled *C*. Now, as soon as he arrives at the goal—if it is food, for example, he eats the food—he at once reverts back down to point *D* in the figure and then continues on his way, indicated by *E*. His behavior is an enlarged routine kind of behavior. It is enlarged because he has learned something: when he meets with this situation again, he can more easily surmount the difficulty. He then falls back into a kind of patterned behavior which is habitual and routine, which again could be called "nonpsychological." From this viewpoint we see that we are psychological beings only part of the time. Perhaps for some people almost all patterned behavior is of a routine, habitual, automatic kind. For others, perhaps as much as 50 per cent of the behavior is problem solving and the other half of a routine kind.

Later on we will develop the thought that an administrator is one who handles routine problems, whereas a creative leader is one who indulges in this kind of psychological behavior. In leadership there are added complexities, some of which will be discussed in the paragraphs immediately following.

Social needs

Direct needs have been discussed in a simplified way. We have also suggested that they are rarely, if ever, isolated from the indirect, social needs. The satisfaction of the needs for food or earnings are often mixed in with the satisfaction of the more significantly important social needs.

For example, a friend who likes to call himself a gourmet claims that his tastes, likes, and dislikes in food are highly developed. He has a particularly strong yen for eating in an attractively decorated restaurant that provides Cantonese cuisine. He claims that Cantonese style cooking satisfies his well-being and his appetite.

How do we acquire needs for specialties such as pressed duck Cantonese? Why is it that the term "exotic drinks" may appeal to our sense of romance or our need for gaiety? Our likes and dislikes are almost totally learned. We tend to like the same kinds of things that we have been taught to like, at first in the family circle, later on in school, later still in the work place, and in the community. What we like depends largely upon the social groups in which we move and live and which control our behavior in the sense that they set up the indirect or social goals to which we aspire. They provide the environment in which we behave as social beings. They set the stage for the very satisfactions which enable us to return to a routine, unmotivated kind of existence—until new and additional aspirations of a social kind appear on our horizons.

The gourmet has acquired his tastes as a form of social learning; his highly directed and integrated behavior patterns are aimed at the satisfaction of certain social needs which impinge upon him. His needs may be strong. His behavior may be as highly motivated, goal driven, as strong in terms of social forces that activate him as the needs of the starving man striving to satisfy direct biological needs.

It is interesting to note what surveys have shown that employees feel they need. Status security appears to be a predominate need. In one study, 1400 department store employees were surveyed by Kolstad.[1] Intrepreting the results of the survey, he ranked their answers in the following order of importance: promotion of best qualified person; help to get results expected; encouragement to offer new ideas; fair hearing on grievances; and pay increases when deserved. Another survey of 325 factory workers was made by Wyatt, Langdon, and Stock.[2] Again in their interpretation of the replies, the authors ranked the factors. The results were as follows: ranked first was steady work; next was comfortable working conditions; next good working companions; then good boss; next was opportunity for advancement; last was high pay and opportunity to use ideas.

Another study by the National Industrial Conference Board [3] which surveyed some 6000 workers found that they tended to list most frequently job security, chances to get ahead, and wages, in that order. In still another study, Clifford Jurgensen [4] found that woman employees —there were 1189 men and 150 women in the survey—were somewhat less interested in security, advancement, and benefits than were men.

Donald Baier who has conducted timely studies on how to reduce shortages of engineers and scientists concludes that provision of oppor-

[1] A. Kolstad, "Employee Attitudes in a Department Store," *Journal of Applied Psychology*, XXII (1938), 470–79.

[2] S. Wyatt, J. F. Langdon, and F. G. L. Stock, "Fatigue and Boredom in Competitive Work," *Industrial Health Research Board Report No.* 77 (1937).

[3] National Industrial Conference Board, Inc., "Factors Affecting Employee Morale," *Studies in Personnel Policy, No.* 85 (1947).

[4] Clifford E. Jurgensen, "Selected Factors Which Influence Job Preferences," *Journal of Applied Psychology*, XXXI (1947), 559–61.

tunities for professional development and satisfaction are exceedingly necessary. He cites a National Industrial Conference Board report[5] which showed the percentages of engineers who believed the following statements to be true:

	Per cent
Engineers are given too much routine work	77
Pay not high enough	76
Engineers not kept properly informed of company policy	61
Too little chance to use creative abilities	45
Company does not help to further his education	44
The engineer needs some sort of union to represent him	17

Needs and attitudes in a large organization

As we discussed in the previous chapter, the social needs felt by members of an organization can be analyzed in a rough way for the whole situation, as observed in two situation cases. Attitude surveys tend to pinpoint these needs somewhat more closely in terms of what people say they want from a complex social environment. Such studies get at external environmental conditions, as pointed out in a previous place.

We may now analyze a whole situation and then narrow down our analysis to specific group attitudes about what is needed. Let us use an organization[6] called Glowacki, White, and Stern as an illustrative case. This is a certified public accountant firm that serves clients throughout the country. Its home offices are in Buffalo, and most of its 14 offices are located in the Midwest. Robert Glowacki is managing partner of the firm, and Walter Leske is personnel director. The firm has 805 professional personnel consisting of some 16 partners, 24 managers, 103 seniors, 282 semi-seniors, and 380 juniors. In addition there are 125 clerical personnel, bookkeepers, typists and messengers.

The firm is one of the most prestigious of the ten prominent national public accounting firms. It ranks seventh in size, gauged by the total assets of the clients of the firm. Unlike many public accounting firms, this one serves a large variety of clients, having no single sizeable client.

Responsibility for personnel management, including recruiting and selection, is decentralized to the resident partners who manage the firm's activities in each of the fourteen cities. There is a central personnel policy committee which consists of Glowacki, Leske, and the resident

[5] National Industrial Conference Board Inc., "Unionization Among Engineers," *Studies in Personnel Policy #155* (1956).

[6] Adapted from a case discussed in Bellows, *Case Problems in Personnel Management* (Dubuque, Iowa: The William C. Brown Co., 1955), pp. 1–17, by courtesy of the publisher.

partners. It meets not less frequently than every six months. Recruiting is achieved by visits to college campuses, made either by Leske or resident partners. It has recently been found that it is possible to utilize, on an internship basis, students who are to graduate in June. They can be used on inventory work during the Christmas vacation period, giving them an opportunity to get acquainted with the firm, and giving the local office managers an opportunity to get acquainted with them. Selection in the last few years has been based on observations of these so-called interns. The beginning rates for juniors are the same throughout the various areas in which the firm operates, regardless of cost of living differences between the different areas.

All the men who are selected as junior accountants are college graduates with a major in accounting. The central personnel policy committee has been concerned with selection of juniors, realizing that its load during the next few years will be quite high, and there is a considerable need for feeding juniors up into the senior classifications. There is need for selecting juniors so that they will have the characteristics necessary for manager status. There has been some hiring of seniors and managers from the outside because of heavy turnover among juniors during the last five years. Actually, the firm as a whole has lost 310 juniors in five years through turnover of two kinds: inefficiency or quitting to get jobs in controllers' offices of industrial and business firms which the company serves. The central personnel policy committee has faced up to the problem of turnover and the evident job dissatisfaction of juniors.

Today the committee is meeting to decide what to do. Leske emphasizes that personnel matters are too often left to chance. This public accounting firm is not particularly different from others. In the nature of the work, the task of supervision is difficult. Junior and other public accountants work with exceedingly remote supervision; they are out in the clients' offices. The supervisor makes a general assignment but, in normal course, does not accompany the employee to the location of the work. Sometimes the employee is out in the field for as much as three or four weeks at a time without even seeing his supervisor.

Glowacki insists that the problem is one of selection, not of supervision. Leske attempts to persuade him that turnover causes are of two general kinds: selection and conditions at work. Most important is the relationship of the junior to his supervisor. All of the members were in agreement that something must be done to improve the personnel situation. The main question in their minds was what to do.

To sum up, here is a firm of professional personnel that is having difficulty with employee turnover and dissatisfaction, particularly among its junior professional employees. The nature of the work and the working situation precludes close supervision and close communications between supervisor and employee. What should the personnel policy committee of the firm do to correct the situation?

The organization has begun to realize the need for more adequate personnel practices and relationships with junior employees. It appears that a number of remedial procedures are needed (see Figure 6.2). Among the needed procedures seem to be an attitude survey, employee counseling, and communications; those should probably be worked on early in the remedial program.

The firm clearly needs to make supervisors conscious of their responsibility for accomplishing communications and employee goodwill. If the supervisors cannot be close enough to the junior accountants to enable a fair amount of counseling and communications, the problem cannot be solved. An attitude survey, by use of questionnaire, preferably conducted and analyzed by a consultant from outside of the organization, would be one of the several possible starting points.

Remedial work should be done as a project in action research—management or a consultant should not do the work alone. All managers and employees involved should participate. The attitude survey setup enables close participation by the employees and acts, itself, as a communications tool. Management should be cautioned that it may do more harm than good if it is not willing to follow through by making the results of the survey common knowledge and taking action in terms of the findings resulting from the survey.

These findings would be a guide to the thoughts and work of the personnel policy committee and would form the basis for long-range personnel planning.

The situation that requires remedial work in one of the specific offices of this CPA firm, made on the basis of attitude survey results, follows.[7]

The staff attitude survey was conducted at the request of a partner as one approach to gaining some insights into problems related to turnover and its control, as well as for guidance in the development of sound personnel policies. First, several meetings were held in considering the areas to be included in the survey. A printed questionnaire with 90 items was developed during these meetings.

[7] From an unpublished study by Roger Bellows and Associates, 1952.

a. In view of the problems in this case, check the items below in column I, II, III, or IV by placing (X) in the appropriate column opposite each item. b. Then, in column V, place a number 1 opposite that item you believe should have highest priority for remedial work; use number 2 for second priority and 3 for third priority, if work on more than one item is indicated. c. Then, in the space provided on the reverse of this form, write a brief statement telling what you would do to improve the situation.		Irrelevant or no information I	Adequate II	Improvement needed III	Critical IV	Priority V
1 Personnel policies and practices survey	1				X	
2 Organization chart	2	X				
3 Selection of executives for efficiency	3	X				
4 Selection of supervisors for efficiency	4			X		
5 Selection of personnel to control turnover	5			X		
6 Training employees in human relations	6	X				
7 Training supervisors in human relations	7			X		
8 Training top management in human relations	8			X		
9 Attitude-morale surveys	9				X	1
10 Exit interview	10			X		
11 Employee benefits	11	X				
12 Employee services	12	X				
13 Employee counseling	13			X		
14 Employee communications	14			X		
15 Employee participation in decisions	15			X		
16 Supervisor participation in decisions	16	X				
17 Suggestion systems	17			X		
18 Upward communications	18	X				
19 Employee evaluation procedure, criteria	19			X		
20 Use of employee evaluation procedure	20			X		
21 ____________________	21					
22 ____________________	22					
23 ____________________	23					

Fig. 6.2 · Case problem analysis check list for Glowacki, White, and Stern

Technicians trained in survey work gave the survey to 48 staff members. Among the group were 12 seniors, 15 semi-seniors, and 21 juniors. Most of the group had been with the firm from 1 to 5 years, although 10 had been there less than a year, and 4 had been there 6 years or longer. Sixteen of the group had CPA certificates. Two were female.

The conditions under which the survey was administered were kept uniform in each of the sessions. A prepared speech was given, furnishing information about why the survey was being given and the kinds of information it would likely yield. The surveys were filled out anonymously, although information was requested about the job title, length of tenure, and CPA status of each individual.

The questionnaire was divided into 3 parts. The first part contained 71 questions, with several alternate answers from which to choose. These questions related to management-employee relations, job conditions and employee benefits, advancements and promotions, supervisory-employee relations, training and development, the job itself, the firm, fellow employees, and social relations. The second part of the questionnaire was a unit containing 18 questions about aspects of job satisfaction. The third part provided space for the staff members to write any suggestions, comments, or criticisms. The survey blanks were tabulated in several ways, in an effort to identify any particular groups who were dissatisfied about specific areas.

TABLE 6.1 · Level of Job Satisfaction

Group	Number in group	Range	Average
All staff members	48	54–90	71
Job title			
Junior	21	55–80	69
Semi-senior	15	54–90	71
Senior	12	60–80	73
Tenure			
Less than 1 year	10	55–90	71
1–5 years	34	54–83	71
6 years or more	4	65–73	68
CPA status			
Had CPA	16	59–90	72
Did not have CPA	32	54–83	70

The level of job satisfaction was determined by scoring the 18 questions of Part II of the questionnaire. Very favorable attitudes were indicated by high scores (90 was highest possible) and unfavorable attitudes by low scores (18 was lowest possible). A score of 54 indicated a neutral level of job satisfaction.

In the survey the unit of 18 statements was included to provide an independent estimate of the level of over-all job satisfaction.[8] The statements, 9 of which were favorable things to say about one's job and 9 of which were unfavorable, were of the sort, "I feel that I am happier in my work than most people." The employee was asked to express his opinion about the statement by checking the extent to which he agreed with it. A score was derived for the unit of 18 items. Favorable opinions or attitudes received more weight than unfavorable or negative attitudes. Scores could range from 18 (unfavorable attitudes) to 90 (favorable attitudes), with a neutral point of 54. The scores for each of the groups surveyed are shown in Table 6.1.

The range of scores for the total group was 54 to 90, with an average score of 71. This suggests that none of the staff was dissatisfied. On the contrary, over-all morale and job satisfaction were quite high. Seniors showed a slight tendency, on the average, to have higher morale than juniors. Persons who had been with the company less than 5 years showed a wider range of level of job satisfaction (54 to 90) than those who had been with the company longer than 6 years (65 to 73). People who had their CPA's tended to have slightly higher job satisfaction than those without. The most satisfied was the senior who had been with the company 5 years or less and who probably had his CPA certificate. The most dissatisfied was the junior who did not have the CPA.

It should be noted, however, that morale of the entire staff seemed to be high, as compared with other firms. There were no expressions of over-all dissatisfaction in the firm, even though other parts of the survey results suggest specific areas about which the employees were concerned.

Seventy-one questions were asked about management-employee relations, superior-employee relations, public accounting as a career, pay and hours of work, the supervisors, training and development, and advancements and promotions. The first two of these major topics will be discussed separately below. Comments bearing upon the areas will be drawn into the discussion when appropriate. It is interesting to note that 29 of the 48 individuals surveyed (60 per cent) offered comments and suggestions at the end of the survey in addition to comments on specific questions. The results follow.

[8] The scale was developed by Brayfield and Roth and is described in A. H. Brayfield and H. F. Roth, "An Index of Job Satisfaction," *Journal of Applied Psychology,* XXXV (1951), 307–11.

Management-employee relations

This area is concerned with the closeness of communication of ideas, policies, and general information between management and employees. It includes how much information they were given when they started with the firm, whether or not they feel a part of the firm, adequacy of work reviews and counseling, favoritism, and the policy of referrals of staff members to outside jobs.

1. *Policy of job referrals.* Over half of the group (52 per cent) felt that the firm was not fair in its handling of referral of staff members to outside position vacancies. Thirty-one per cent felt they were, and 17 per cent did not answer the question. There were more comments written in about this problem than any other in the survey. In general, the complaints were that the firm seemed reluctant to refer its good men to attractive positions, so that if a person was referred, it was because the firm was dissatisfied with his work. They felt that if a person indicated he would like to leave the firm, all employment opportunities known to the firm should be made available to him. Several people indicated that the firm's policy on this subject was not clear, that they depended upon the grapevine for their information.

The results bearing on this problem, and others to follow, indicate the need for clarification of the firm's policies, whether this is done by manual, by meetings, or by personal counseling situations. Improvement of communications with employees seems indicated.

2. *Work reviews and counseling.* Most people feel free to go to the partners of the firm with their problems—personal or otherwise—although 36 per cent rarely or never feel free. One person commented that he favored personal interviews twice a year, as this seemed to be the only time personal problems could be freely discussed. Sixty-six per cent said they had had no occasion to find out if the counseling and advice given by the firm was sufficient; 19 per cent felt that it was fairly helpful or very helpful; and 15 per cent said it was not very helpful. Concerning work reviews, a large majority (80 per cent) felt that they were adequate and helpful, but nearly half of the group felt that they were not told promptly and regularly whether their work was satisfactory. Two people commented about this item: "Management usually tells us once a year how we have performed the preceding 12 months . . . it is possible to go a considerable length of time without knowing how one stands." If an employee is doing unsatisfactory work, the group felt on the whole that he would be warned and given a chance to improve before being released. Six people mentioned that they did not know the policy on warnings, and three others indicated that supervisors were a "little weak in this! Have noticed some buck passing and failure to tell to one's face."

The area of work reviews (to be discussed again on the next page) needs general revision. Many of the comments offered in several parts of the survey indicate that people are not told often enough how they are getting along. Work reviews are not systematically conducted by the supervisors, and although the reviews conducted by management are adequate and generally helpful, they are not offered often enough.

3. *Favoritism.* Thirty-five per cent of the staff felt that some or much favoritism was shown in the firm. Eight per cent said none was shown, and 55

per cent said very little. Only two comments were made: "Not aware of any favoritism if it is shown" and "ability and personality are recognized."

It is doubtful that "favoritism" as such is shown, inasmuch as nowhere in the survey results were there any indications of dissatisfaction because of it. No mention of it was made in connection with pay, nor with supervisors, nor with promotions. On the contrary, the group felt that the firm knew who was best qualified for promotions. It appears that "favoritism" is another label for not knowing why the firm makes the decisions it does.

4. *Information about the firm.* When the employees first started at the firm, 27 per cent felt they did not receive adequate information about the firm's rules and personnel policies, although 83 per cent said that the job itself was described fairly and honestly. Twenty-seven per cent felt that the firm did not keep them well enough informed about its activities. Thirty-three per cent felt that they were made to feel part of the organization not at all or to a small degree. In commenting on these related items, two people mentioned that not enough was known about the job titles and wage levels in the firm—as one expressed it, "most of information obtained from cashier who is poorly informed. Rest of information through grapevine." Three people used the phrase "very little" in describing how much information was given. "We were expected to know what public accounting was like."

Supervisor-employee relations

More questions were included about this topic than any other in the survey. Several aspects of supervision were investigated: closeness and adequacy of supervision, regularity and manner of work reviews, and the example supervisors set in their own work habits.

1. *Work reviews.* Only twenty-three per cent of the group felt that their supervisors told them regularly and promptly if their work was satisfactory; indeed, 44 per cent indicated that they were "rarely" or "never" told. Newer staff members seemed to feel that there was a greater need for constructive criticism of their work. One of them stated, "One thing I have found out is that they don't seem to let you know just where you stand. I don't know if I have made any progress in the firm or not; I don't know if my work has improved or become worse. If mention is ever made as to how you are doing, it is very general and to no use as far as I'm concerned. I want to know where I am weak and what I can do about it. Also you really cannot learn as you should on the job because everyone is working so darn fast to cut the budget that they can't take the time, or if they can they don't, to explain things to you. As an example: why am I doing this particular share of the job and how does it tie in with the job in its entirety? You really don't know these answers, but you go ahead and do the work because somebody did it last year and you refer to last year's working papers to do it this year." Another said, "It is believed that supervisors should in all cases advise assistants as to the type of work done on the job, and any criticisms should be related to the assistants as a help for other assignments. This is usually done, but in some cases supervisors are lax in this respect." One person pointed to this situation as "another reason why I would favor twice yearly personal interviews."

Opinions on this question are reflected in several other parts of the survey and in the comments offered by the group. It is probably the most critical area of any surveyed, largely because not enough reviews are held.

When unusually good work is done, 50 per cent said they were usually or always recognized by their supervisors for it. Thirty-one per cent said they were sometimes recognized for it, and 17 per cent said they were rarely recognized.

2. *Criticism of work.* The staff members almost unanimously said that they were rarely or never criticized in front of others by their superiors. When their work is criticized, they agreed (94 per cent) that it was done in a friendly and helpful way.

3. *Suggestions for better ways of doing.* About a fourth of the group said they were not given much encouragement to offer ideas and suggestions for new or better ways of doing things. However, when asked if they would get credit for a suggestion if they made it, 81 per cent said they felt they would. Four people made the same general comment that whether or not they received credit for a suggestion depended upon the person to whom it was made, and whether or not it would be withheld at some level on its way to the top.

We have seen from this situation analysis coupled with an attitude survey that high global, or over-all, morale is insufficient. Serious shortcomings, both in management-employee relations and supervisor-employee relations, were revealed. They were pinpointed by the attitude survey. This enabled remedial work which consisted in large part in closer working relationships developed through communications and counseling. Feelings of mutual understanding were fostered by the attitude survey. Employee oriented counseling, in which assistants were told how they were doing on their assignments, did much to develop the needed rapport. This counseling technique will be discussed in detail in Chapter 16.

Tension in an organization can be either destructive or constructive. Destructive tension arises from insecurity and lack of mutual understanding, and is common in autocratic, authoritarian atmospheres. Constructive tension leads to problem solving, mutual understanding, mutual goal effort, and teamwork.

Analysis of organizational needs and attitude surveys can assist, as has been shown in this chapter, in deciding on what remedial steps to take. Such analytical tools are used by leaders to help accomplish group goals.

We turn in the next chapter to problems of goals, aspirations, motives, and ideals as related to learning and improvement of teams. The case problems of Glowacki, White, and Stern will be used again in the next chapter to illustrate creative learning.

*

One quickly gets readiness in an art
where strong desire comes in play.

—THOMAS MANN

7

Motivation and learning

We are surrounded, when studying leadership, by the intriguing problems of the dynamics of social groups. We are also involved in problems of the dynamics of the individual. The leader, while primarily interested in achievement of a team, works with individuals as basic units of a team. To understand, describe, and endeavor to appraise, predict, or control teamwork, it is necessary to work with the individual team member.

In this chapter we concern ourselves with aspirations, drives, motives, and ideals—static and dynamic conditions. We emphasize that leadership and learning are much the same and that each requires the dynamic situation. We illustrate a few principles of motivation and learning (only a few are known) by reference to two of the case situations discussed in previous chapters; we then attempt to identify some earmarks of easy and difficult leadership situations.

Our social aspirations are satisfied by membership in, and approval of, groups. It may be a formal group or an informal group. We are concerned about how the groups to which we belong look upon us. Do they approve or disapprove of what we do?

Aspirations

An elemental kind of behavior indulged in by children and some adults is boasting about accomplishments. Such behavior stems from unrealized aspirations. A person who brags or boasts, who tells of his own alleged achievements with a swagger and flourish, with a bluster and bravado, who indulges in exaggeration and tall talk—this pretentious, bombastic, pompous person is playing to the grandstand for attention, recognition, approval, and applause. His listeners will say about him "he's putting on a big show" or "he is making a grandstand play."

The boastful man aspires to approval. He has an unsatisfied social aspiration. Many examples more subtle than the braggart are readily visible all around us. The wage earner who gets a raise comes home eager to tell the story. It may be a factual story or it may have some degree of exaggeration. The approving remarks of wife and other members of the immediate family circle actually motivate this man, day-after-day. They motivate him to do, in the eyes of his boss, a better job, so that he can achieve this kind of distinction at home. But it certainly goes farther than the home. He is recognized in the community as a progressive, successful man. If the raise is large enough, you may see presently several signs of increased wealth. You may see that the old model automobile, which still ran quite well and economically, too, has been traded in, and in the driveway there is a new model, larger car. This is keeping up with the Joneses. It is looked upon in the community as a sign of success; wages and salaries are ways of keeping the success score. The wage earner does not necessarily need additional money to survive. He does, however, need this to maintain and augment his sense of dignity.

Man is, then, not only a psychological individual, as discussed in the first part of the previous chapter, but more than that—a socio-psychological being. He becomes a socio-psychological being when he is solving problems which enable him to satisfy indirect social needs, such as those illustrated by the man aspiring to an increase in his pay envelope. We may refer back to Figure 6.1 in the previous chapter. The left end of the figure represents behavior of a man who is in a phase of routine behavior, having for the moment no particular social aspirations. He does not need especially to influence his fellow men. This is being done through automatic, routine, habitual behavior. Then a problem appears. His friends have bought new cars. He feels the need for a new car, but, alas, he does not have the old car paid for. How can he get out of this difficulty? So, we enter the second part of the diagram. An impediment has been presented. He begins to analyze the problem. He begins to worry. He goes to his boss. He asks his boss what he needs to do to get a raise. The boss tells him—or maybe fires him. In any case, he casts about for a solution to the problem, forming various hypotheses. His problem is one of great complexity.

The man in social need usually does not analyze his situation in this systematic manner. He sometimes has a vague feeling of worry, anxiety, and unrest. Often social goals are not as concrete and specific as in this illustration. However, our particular individual strives until he achieves a greater salary. If he fails in this, his behavior may become disorganized. He may be able to cast about to shift his goals. For example, he may move from a community in which he lived to a simpler community where the social pressures will not be as great. Nevertheless, if he does achieve the goal of higher earnings, he then purchases a new model automobile. He settles back into routine behavior and goes along in this way until another problem—usually again of the nature of keeping up with the Joneses—appears upon his horizon. His aspirations are again elevated. Perhaps he achieves the goal. And the cycle repeats itself over and over again.

This is life in our modern civilization. It would appear as if we have been caught in an inexorable environment that puts pressures on us from all sides—from as many directions as we have formal and informal group memberships. Advertisers have studied these phenomena. We are bombarded intermittently by advertising reinforcements of these indirect social needs through radio, television, newspapers, magazines, and billboards. There is no place to hide from the ad men. They want to shorten the time interval between cycles.

Drives, motives, and ideals

A certain drive or urge has been designated by a minority school of psychologists, the Freudians, as *libido*. This is the sex drive or urge.

Generally speaking, when we use the word *urge,* the goal is not as well identified as it is in the case of *drive.* We define a drive as unsatisfied need with special reference to the primary or biological needs. Satisfaction of these needs results in survival of the individual and the race. Included among them are the need for food, the hunger drive; the need for water, the thirst drive; the need for sexual outlet, the libido or sex drive.

We have seen that a man becomes a psychological being when his drives are thwarted, when there is a barrier to the satisfaction of needs. Drives are satisfied somewhat more immediately and more simply, in terms of the patterned behavior involved, than is the case with motives. Motives involve social goals; needs arise from memberships in formal or informal social groups. These have been illustrated to some extent in the above discussion. The satisfaction of these secondary needs calls upon the individual for much more intricate, complex behavior patterns. There the satisfaction, too, is somewhat more remote in time. Thus the wage earner may be confronted with the need for increasing his pay envelope in order to do certain things that will enable him to be accepted in the community group to which he aspires, to keep up with the Joneses. However, his plan of attack upon the problem and the solution to it may take one or two or several years for achievement.

Still another condition, which may be designated as *ideals,* exists in our physical and social environments and our relation to these environments. An ideal is quite different from a drive and somewhat different from a motive. In the condition which we call "an ideal," the satisfaction of the condition—which is again a social need—is remote. In fact, an ideal may never be achieved, although the striving for it may be intermittent or continuous over a long period of time. Thus, an ideal can guide our behavior for many years.

The tensions and stresses that are set up by an ideal are not usually intense, although they may be, as in the case of a religious or health fanatic. We may conceive of such stresses and tensions as being quite intense and lasting—modifying and largely determining patterned behavior of a very complex kind. Ideals of people may include such things as health, wealth, sociability, knowledge, beauty, and righteousness. It is not unusual for a person to spend a great deal of time quietly contemplating his ideals. This reverie may bring about a considerable degree of personal serenity and tranquility, providing, of course, that the tensions and stresses are not acute or extremely intense, and assuming that achievement is thought of as something in the remote future rather than the immediate or near future.

Consider the case of a man who plays duplicate bridge in tournaments and seldom finishes near the top. He does fairly well at the game, but one of his ideals is to become a good bridge player. The need for this kind of social approbation—his need to excel—is not intense, however. He does not particularly care whether he becomes a good bridge player within the next few years or next ten years. He plays bridge, he says, for social purposes and to become a better player. It could be said that one of his ideals is to become a good bridge player. Since he is not progressing rapidly, his goal is indeed a remote one. He is not aggressive in the situation and is quite content with his lot.

The Freudians have the framework of their system built upon the fact of conflicting needs. Often, in our day-to-day life, drives conflict with motives; drives conflict with ideals; motives conflict with ideals; one drive may conflict with another; a motive may conflict with another motive; and an ideal may conflict with another ideal. The stresses and tensions that arise from these conflicts may be severe. They stem from our membership in different groups from which we obtain our unsatisfied social needs. The person who is adjusted to his socio-psychological environment, the well-integrated person, the person whom we might look upon as having an over-all "good personality" is one whose psychological equipment is functionally adequate to modify and adjust his conflicts in a realistic way. We say that the psychologically adjusted person "maintains his affairs with ordinary prudence." We say that the person suffering from schizophrenia or other psychotic condition has not integrated his conflicting drives, motives, and ideals; we say he is not adjusted to his social environment. He is a person who does not handle his affairs with ordinary prudence. Indeed, he may be so maladjusted that he is completely dissociated from social reality.

Static and dynamic conditions

We have seen that people strive in various ways to satisfy their needs and that most of these needs are of a social kind. A condition is said to be a static one when the behavior is of the routine kind. When behavior is on a level plane, when there is no particular need involved in behavior, we say that the person in this condition is more like a vegetable than a man. He is not a psychological being. He is, rather in a merely satisfied state, a state of no tension, no stress. There are no dynamics involved in the situation. He may be utilizing energy and skills which he has learned in the past, as in driving a car. However, there is nothing new in the situation. There is no barrier to the smooth flow of already learned behavior.

A dynamic condition is much different. This is a condition of unsatisfied need—whether the need is of a direct biological character or an indirect social kind.

This distinction between static and dynamic conditions is an important one, for it bears significantly upon leadership. In the system of leadership that is being discussed, leadership does not exist under static conditions. Rather, administration is in order—administration of the *status quo*. It is only when there is a dynamic condition that leadership comes into being. It is because of this that leadership is to be considered in social and psychological terms. Other conditions require other kinds of management of the situation. A program that is generally routine, conducted in a quiet atmosphere after the planning and problem solving has been accomplished, is managed or administered; no creative leadership is involved.

Learning requires the dynamic condition [1]

Most psychologists believe that if we could tie down, analyze, and describe all the conditions that are involved in the learning process, we would have answers to all of our questions in psychology, including complex questions concerning leadership. What the psychologist wants to do is to describe in a complete way how it comes about that man's behavior is directed, adjusted, orderly; how it comes about that he can solve problems and reach solutions; how he differs from vegetative beings, an imbecile, or a paranoid. How is it that he can handle his own affairs with ordinary prudence? It is through "learning." However, learning is an exceedingly complex phenomenon. Just to call it learning—to name it—is not to describe it or explain what happens.

Learning, then, could be called the most important area in all of psychology as well as in leadership. The leader helps the group achieve its goal. He is concerned with improving the behavior of the group. When learning is defined as improvement of behavior, leadership may be defined as arranging the situation so that learning—improved goal-achieving behavior—will take place.

There are hundreds of viewpoints, theories and systems, rules, principles, and so-called laws of learning. These have been expounded during the past 2000 years. They fall into two classes: those which pertain to the physiology and neurology of learning; those which concern themselves with psychology.

[1] The theory of equilibrium in this section is adapted from the author's "Learning as Perceptual Evolution," *Psychological Review*, XL (1933), 138–59. By special permission of the American Psychological Association, Inc.

Attempts to explain learning by describing what happens inside the body—the physiology and neurology of learning—have failed. According to Lashley ". . . it is doubtful that we know anything more about the mechanism of learning than did Descartes when he described the opening of the pores in the nerves by the passage of animal spirits. His statement sounds remarkably like the reduction of synaptic resistance by the passage of the nerve impulse." [2] And events during the past several decades have not thrown sufficient light on the physiology of learning. However, the psychological approaches to learning have been, I believe, more helpful.

Of the various approaches and viewpoints to learning, the configurational viewpoint seems to us the most fruitful. It is based on the dynamics of the learning situation. It emphasizes goal activity. It defines learning as evolution of perception—as changing ways of seeing things, especially our relations with people in our environment. Learning is a transformation of the relation of a person with others and with objects in the environment.

There are a number of conditions for human learning. These are prerequisites, the events or states that must be present before learning can take place. In attempting to get at these conditions, we are confronted by a problem of logical classification. If we were to choose a single condition of learning, that condition would probably be physiological differentiation or maturation, or the acquisition of basic skills or understandings, the other various conditions falling as subentries under that one. We may arbitrarily fix the prerequisites for the learning process as three.

1. There must be a person who has developed to a particular stage or degree of physiological specialization. This differentiation is not of the sensory, central, or motor parts alone, but differentiation and integration of the person as a whole. The amount of differentiation or growth must be adjusted to the scale of acquisition or to the difficulty of the problem which is to be learned. The lower or less differentiated person is necessarily limited in acquiring skill or dexterity of performance, owing to his lack of specialization and integration.

The memory phenomenon has been one of the enigmas of psychology. Many names have been given to it, and sundry neurological explanations have been offered. Semon called it "mneme." Spearman referred to it as a group factor, almost as universal as his "G" in determining

[2] K. S. Lashley, "Learning: I. Nervous Mechanisms in Learning," *The Foundations of Experimental Psychology*, ed. Carl Murchinson (Worcester, Mass.: Clark University Press, 1929), pp. 369–76.

intelligence test results. G. E. Müller insists upon his perseverative tendency. D. Q. Adams called retentivity a "universal property of protoplasm."

The power of retentivity is included under the first condition of learning. Although no specific neurological correlate can be postulated, a relatively permanent reorganization no doubt takes place in the organism as a whole. In regard to this, Herrick states, "The change in the 'set' or organization of the reacting substance probably involves a slight chemical readjustment of autocatalytic type such as to make a repetition of the discharge easier. It may be transitory or long enduring. This is organic memory." [3] Thus memory might be called that inferred physiological change of the person as a unit which enables him to attain more intricate performances on successive trials and to duplicate these performances after long, latent periods.

Memory is, in reality, a psychological affair because the physiological trace, whatever its locus or nature, is initiated by relation of the person to his environment. A living, moving person is necessary before learning can take place. The power of retentivity is inherent in such a system. Functional changes which are rudimentary forms of learning take place at very early stages in the life cycle. Examples of such early learning are the activities of sucking, grasping, and winking. These activities are learned before birth in many cases. The problem of learning is thus a matter of degree of behavior change rather than one of kind. The person must be considered as evolving structurally and functionally, as a unit.

2. The second condition for learning is concerned with the needs or requirements that we have discussed. R. M. Ogden considered learning to be nothing but an improved method of behavior. His concept of improvement "includes both the satisfaction of the creature's needs and solution of its problems." [4] These are interwoven with the matrix of biological requirements. The different types of needs thus interact with one another.

3. The third condition for the learning process is an obstruction to the smooth activity which might result in the resolution of tensions or the satisfaction of needs. If the behavior resulting in the satisfaction of needs were never blocked by an environmental obstacle, the person would always be in perfect balance with field forces.

[3] C. J. Herrick, *Neurological Foundation of Animal Behavior* (New York: Henry Holt & Co., 1924), p. 57.

[4] R. M. Ogden, "Learning as Improvement," *American Journal of Psychology*, XXXIX (1927), 235–58.

Learning was referred to earlier as the evolution of perception. *Perception* is here used to designate the fact that a dynamic relation exists between the person and the many potential constellations of the environment, and that one of these is *figure,* the rest *ground.* One dynamic relation is effective upon the individual at a particular cross-section in time.

Dynamic relation means any situation in which the person is in a state of unsatisfied need. It may be a combination of needs. When needs are not immediately satisfied, an obstruction to the routine passive form of activity is present. This obstruction increases the tension, or condition of imbalance between the person and the environmental forces, which was brought about by the need. Such an organismic situation is a dynamic relation, as opposed to the vegetative type of relation which usually persists in the lower, less differentiated forms of life.

Learning is a process of psychological transformation which is not dissimilar to evolution in the biological realm. In the learning process, which eventuates from the three conditions given above, is evidenced the emergence of new patterns or forms. In the Darwinian notion of organic evolution, new and higher types come about in the animal world as a result of the operation of natural selection. A particular species survives because it is suitable to the environment to which it is subjected. There is at each step a resultant adjustive pattern, and the result is survival and adaptation. The end is attained by the interaction of natural forces.

The growth or evolution of perception and goal behavior of a group or team is more difficult to observe than is the evolution of morphological types. Nevertheless, such psychological evolution takes place. It is the learning process. This evolution of perception may be observed to follow a particular sequence.

In the learning process, the perceptual field may be seen to evolve and differentiate through four stages in the following chronological order: (1) a homogeneous perceptual field to which the person or group responds passively by the routine life processes, in which there is no imbalanced relation between the person or group forces and those of the environment; (2) definite figure-ground relations in which the passive state of the person or group is imposed upon by social need which terminates this passive condition of the perceptual field; (3) distortion of perception resulting from obstructed goal activity, causing reversed figure-ground relations which result in poorly defined goals and dynamic relations; (4) dissipation of this distortion of the perceptual field, eventuating from reorganization of the field with personal or group goals clearly redefined, a condition in which the person or group is sufficiently adjusted to the acquisitional level so that consummatory or goal activity results.

Motivation and learning illustrated

The dynamic principles of motivation and learning discussed above may be illustrated by reference to two case situations discussed in previous chapters. Stages in solution of these cases through leadership—goal behavior shared by the group, arranged by the leader of the group—passed through the four stages of evolution discussed immediately above.

In one of the illustrative cases—Glowacki, White, and Stern (see Chapter 6)—a leader perceived a problem in group dynamics. Although the firm was productive and making money, the routine phase, he felt that some of the professional employees were dissatisfied. He perceived some trouble with morale and a rather high rate of turnover.

This is the second stage in the evolution of improvement of behavior through leadership and group improvement. Social needs had made themselves felt, and a leader perceived them. Thus "definite figure-ground relations" were perceived by the leader.

But the picture as seen by the leader was distorted. This is the third stage in motivated, problem-solving behavior. The organization, at the suggestion of the leader, decided to do two things. First the situation was analyzed by use of a systematic procedure. This revealed the need for an employee attitude survey. After this survey was conducted, the problems in morale, and what to do about it, were revealed more clearly in the perceptual field. Solutions were made visible by the attitude survey.

When these solutions were achieved—the solutions took the form in large part of counseling employees in terms of their performance and future outlook for advancement in the company—the tension that existed in the situation was dissipated. This is the "back-to-normal" phase—a condition of reorganized behavior.

Another illustration may be drawn from "the case that failed" (see Chapter 3). In this case a problem had arisen, breaking up what might have been a routine activity. The girls in the paint shop had complained of inadequate working conditions, especially with reference to poor ventilation.

The consultant perceived this and offered a proposal which involved participative or democratic handling. The perceptual field of the girls and foreman changed: the foreman saw meetings in a new light; the girls saw participation in meetings as desirable. The ventilation problem was, as far as the girls were concerned, solved. They became satisfied on that score: tensions had been resolved; the perceptual field, once cloudy and distorted, had cleared—but only temporarily.

A second cycle ensued. The girls, having had a taste of participation in decisions, wanted to regulate their own output standards. The old familiar sequence took place: distortion and stress; goal behavior, again in the form of a participative meeting; goal achievement. Higher production and profit for the company and higher earnings and morale for the girls resulted within the small group.

But these conditions did not last very long. What was happening inside this group affected other nearby groups in the organization or system. The girls were earning more than workers in other groups, so routine in the girls' group was broken up. Distortion and stress again made itself felt.

Thus cycles of activity—problems and distortion and goal achievement —occur without end in a dynamic society. Perhaps the presence of these continuing cycles makes possible improvement, evolution, and progress.

Difficult vs. easy problems

Some leadership tasks are easy; others are difficult or impossible. Although it is rare to obtain, in our field of leadership, principles that are general enough to work in all situations, in the case of identifying the earmarks of easy leadership situations, we can state such principles.

In general, three features of a situation, taken together, determine whether goal activity, learning, or leadership will be successful. The task problem to be achieved must be in proper relation to the facilities of the group that aspires to achieve it. And the group must be motivated. To put this another way and somewhat more analytically, the following variables or factors operate to determine the difficulty of the leader situation: the level of aptness of the group; the severity of need or amount of motivation; the complexity of the problem or rigidity of the obstruction to its solution.

The first factor is the level or aptness of the group. This includes more than problem-oriented knowledge or skill. It includes skill in working together as a team. Leadership and appropriate group interaction enter here. With adequate leadership, problem-solving tends to be easy, other things being equal.

The second factor is the degree of motivation. It is in part dependent on the situation as a whole and in part dependent upon the leader who, to some extent, arranges the situation. If motivation is too weak—needs not clearly felt by group members—no progress is made. If motivation is too strong—tensions too severe—disorganized behavior results.

The third factor involves the difficulty of the task at hand or the rigidity of the obstruction. How hard is the problem itself? It is clear that these three factors are interrelated. If the group does not have requisite skills or is poorly integrated by the leader, even easy problems cannot be solved. Furthermore if motivation is too low or too high, either nothing will happen or group behavior will be disorganized.

Thus it is seen that these three general factors are not absolute, but relative: one depends upon another. The entire situation, seen as a dynamic whole, must be taken into account if group goal behavior is to be described, explained, appraised, predicted, controlled, or regulated by the leader.

When tensions are strong, either group learning or disorganization takes place. We have discussed and illustrated several principles of group improvement by use of a theory of equilibrium and group dynamics. The next chapters will make use of this theory in discussing how we view ourselves and others and what these perceptions have to do with social behavior.

Social Behavior

THREE

*

And I see but shadows around me,
Illusion is everything.—SIR ALFRED COMYN LYALL

8

Behavior: person-to-person

Leadership depends upon interpersonal activity. Behavior is person-to-person, person-to-group, group-to-person. Social psychology, as we define it today, is a study of this behavior. Man has, since time began, wanted to fathom the mysteries of such interpersonal activity. At the very dawn of civilization, he thought of the mind or spirit as being all-powerful in determining it. The most common view of early man was that the mind influences matter, and the mind or spirit directs behavior. This view was not very helpful to him. Today we still define the mind as that which expresses itself in behavior. But in behavioral or social science we do not pay very much attention to the mind *per se*.

Imagine a primitive man sitting on a stone, if you will, pondering the mysteries of human nature. Perhaps he is thinking about the behavior of a neighboring tribe. Members of this tribe had attacked his cave and carried off several of the adolescent girls. Our primitive man sitting on the stone is most likely asking himself not why they did it, not how he can recover the loss, but how he can retaliate. It is possible that if immediate activity of the "get even" kind is not open to him, he may feel some degree of frustration. He may be tense or angered. He may feel an unrest. He has a problem-solving situation. Since there is lack of immediate behavior, he may possibly be pondering the causes of the behavior of the wrongdoers. He is, however, likely not to be analytical. He tends rather to think in terms of an evil spirit, a devil within the wrongdoers. He invests the spirit of the wrongdoers with the spirit of the devil or the devil god. Primitive man and we, today, tend toward what might be called "universal animism." We invest a living human being with a kind of spirit. This spirit activates the mind of the actor or doer.

Animism is modern

We may only speculate as to how primitive man, as well as some modern men, attempted to explain mysteries of behavior in terms of animism —the good or evil spirit within. "He is possessed." "What possesses him?" These expressions, in use today, give away the basis of our day-to-day interpretation of the behavior of our fellow men. We are not far removed from the witch hunts of the inquisition.

The earliest psychology is recorded in the literature of Greek writers several centuries before Christ. Virgil in the *Aeneid* revealed the basic elements of the Grecian approaches to psychology, and his discussion of spirits is the root of our present-day psychology. A strong, lingering influence of primitive and early man as well as of the Greek philosophers shows through in our own language, thought, and culture as it pertains to our understanding interpersonal behavior. Early man, it is believed, came to view interpersonal behavior as guided by a spirit or *psyche*. Probably the basis was his dreams. During periods of dreaming and imagery he could see in his mind, by introspection, the vague, ephemeral, cloud-like image of a person who is not present before him. Indeed, he could see the spirit of a person long since dead. What was more natural than for him to believe that spirits departed the body and re-entered it? Primitive man could see visions of friends, acquaintances, or members of his family who were actually away at far distant places or deceased a long time ago. This caused him to believe that the soul left the body at times during life, certainly at the time of death, and that the soul or spirit was all around him, invading one's mental content, and viewable in imagery and reverie. The contents of his psyche or mind were believed to be spiritual.

But divorcing ourselves from the past is somewhat difficult for us to do, a difficulty which partly explains the common misconceptions which we discussed and listed in Chapter 1 (see Table 1.1). When a person is doing something harmful to us, something we do not like, some act that is distasteful or repugnant, we tend to blame the man rather than to look into the background of the episode and objectively attempt to discover what are the factors in his behavior and our response to it.

It is a fact that the phenomena we are studying are of great complexity: there is nothing more complex in existence than living protoplasm. It is the most intricate substance known. Behavior is one of the properties of protoplasm. When we come to person-to-person interaction, this even further increases our difficulties of description. It is no wonder that ancient man attempted to satisfy his curiosity concerning the problems of nature by investing psyche with the spirit of gods or devils, benign or evil spirits—universal animism. Even physical objects were animated and deified: when the ocean was turbulent, Neptune was angry; when it was calm and smooth, Neptune, the God of the Sea, was in a beneficent, placid mood. Illustrations and experimental evidence that proves the prevalence of animism in modern thinking will be presented a few pages farther on.

Subjective and objective approaches

The paragraph above focuses our attention on the difference between the subjective and objective outlook. When we are being subjective in reacting to another person, we tend to blame him; this is the usual way. If a person steps on our toe in a crowded subway or bus, we are momentarily angered. This is a blame response. We may tend, if we do not hold ourselves in, to respond to this behavior with a snarling word. But sometimes our code of courtesy saves us. A man may say, "I beg your pardon. It was an accident." Then we realize more of the factors involved and look upon the incident as an unmeditated act.

Inappropriate behavior on the part of another may be seen as influenced by his past background and training. It may be understood on this basis. We would do well to look to the background factors that are involved in behavior. This is the objective approach, as contrasted to the subjective, emotionally-toned, personal response that we are so wont to make. One who has an objective outlook on his interpersonal relationships is not likely to blame the other person. He is not so likely to retaliate or to want to punish another. He directs, supervises, and tries to guard against a repetition of unacceptable behavior. Modern criminology teaches the objective, analytical approach to the treatment of criminals.

The objective view will tend toward leader behavior less contaminated by erroneous cultural stereotypes. For example, punishment of "witches" by burning and the inquisitions of the Middle Ages were behavior based on such cultural stereotypes. An objective view would tend to eliminate unjust sanctions based on ignorance; it would tend to substitute understanding for ignorance.

The creative leader, in contrast to the authoritarian supervisor, is concerned with understanding behavior rather than punishment or retaliation. He uses, as his fundamental tool, techniques for understanding rather than power of sanction and punishment.

We may safely say that all behavior is brought about by influences in the background of the people involved in the episode and by the immediate conditions of the physical and social environment. When we speak of our psychological background we refer to the fact that we have learned many patterns of behavior. We discussed, in Chapter 7, some of the forces involved in learning. If we look into these behavioral factors, it is easier for us to understand the people, individuals, and groups with whom we interact hour-by-hour and day-by-day. If we endeavor to understand behavior in this way, we can hope to improve our behavior toward others; we can enable others to improve their behavior toward us and toward the group goal. This is creative leadership—it is the arrangement of the situation so that the activity can proceed in a most economical way toward the common goal.

Social stimuli constellations

Some behavior patterns are simple stimulus-response activity. This, in its simplest form, is exemplified by stimulating a person with an electric shock and watching him jump. You turn your head and orient your body toward a sudden loud sound; if lightning illuminates the sky, you look toward it. It is noted that in these simple forms of stimulus-response behavior, as well as in more complex forms, the immediate cause of the behavior is the stimulus and that it comes before the behavior itself. We may abbreviate these three factors by the symbols *S* for stimulus, *P* for person, and *A* for activity or behavior—*SPA*. We are not so much interested in the stimulus or in the person or in the activity for its own sake, but we are interested in the outcome of the activity, that is, what it achieves. This we may call the "results" and use the symbol *R* to stand for it. We may then try to describe interpersonal behavior in terms of *SPAR*.

It is of interest and value to emphasize two things about the objective view of *SPAR*. In the first place, we are dealing with conditions and events that are not concrete, as contrasted to the study of *things* in the physical sciences, which deal with concrete entities. We are dealing with highly abstract forces, conditions, and phenomena. In the second place, these exist along a time line. In behavioral science we observe the conditions and events that exist in one cross-section of time and study them along the time line as a succession of caused episodes.

For example, when we are considering the *P* part of *SPAR*, we think of the person as he now exists; but in so doing, we must think of his complex background: what he has *learned* up to this particular time. Another phase of the same problem is concerned with *R*, the results of his activity *A*. We are actually observing a *dynamic series of events*. The acting person or group brings about the response of another person or group, so that a whole cycle of events is continued. In this sense, we are dealing with serial responses, not cross-sectional ones. Words are symbols for *dynamic events*, not static things. They stand for on-going, flowing process. Our words do not stand for something that you can reach out and feel or see, as in the case of physical things. Verification and reverification, checking and rechecking the information that flows through our experience when observing a series of activity is necessary if we are to achieve an objective, impartial, and analytical observation of interpersonal behavior.

We tend to lose sight of the trite fact that a person is what he is because he has become what he is. As we observe him he is becoming something else. He is in a dynamic state of change. We are interested in the flow of behavioral events, and we must think about what has happened to him in the past as well as what is happening to him now. In the past he has learned various behavior patterns. If the psychologist could describe adequately all there is to be described about learning, our problems of predicting and control of behavior would be solved, as was suggested in Chapter 7.

If a subject in an experimental laboratory under instruction is told to respond by touching a telegraph type key when he hears a sound, as from a sound hammer, this stimulus might be called "a simple stimulus." We could observe and measure his reaction time by hooking up a time measuring device. An electrical circuit would be so arranged that when the sound hammer was activated a clock would start; and when the subject touched the key, the clock would stop. The elapsed time would be his reaction time to the stimulus. This is an example of a relatively simple environment.

Let us take another example of a more complicated physical environmental stimulus, or we should perhaps say "a constellation of stimuli." Suppose we are testing the reaction time of a group of automobile drivers. We show a movie to people who are sitting in simulated automobiles—driver-training simulators. Each subject is under instructions to make specific responses to a certain combination of events. If the automobile in the movies is approaching an intersection and a red traffic light appears, he is to put his foot on the brake pedal and to give an appropriate stop signal at the same time. He is also under directions to maneuver his car into the right-hand lane. This is a somewhat more complicated situation. We cannot say that there is unit stimulus. The stimulus is not simple, as in the reaction time example above. Thus, we should revise the *S* part of *SPAR*, so that we can designate the degree of complexity of the stimulus. We could let *Ss* designate a simple unit stimulus and *Sc* designate complicated stimuli, or a constellation of stimuli, which may be impinging on many different sense organs at the same time from different sources.

It would be well for us to differentiate between not only *Ss* and *Sc*, as simple and complex physical stimuli, but to differentiate also among *Sc*, indicating physical stimuli; *Sp*, which stands for a stimulating person; and *Spgr*, which stands for configurations of social stimuli—groups of people. Thus we have, on the *S* side, as major factors in understanding leadership:

S	Stimulus
Sc	Constellations or configurations of physical stimuli: a situation without person-to-person or person-to-group involvement
Sp	Constellations or configurations of stimuli including a person as a component: a social situation
Spgr	Constellations or configurations of stimuli consisting of people in groups: a social group situation

We would all, I am sure, agree at once that the subject matter that interests us in leadership is concerned with *Spgr*. The first example that comes to mind is social activity in a school. Certainly, there are many stresses and tensions in the psychological make-up of the pupil that are occasioned by friendship or hostility with other pupils or groups of pupils and the teacher. The teacher herself responds, for the most part, with activity that is concerned with configurations of *Spgr*. The activity *A* that a given constellation of stimuli *S* elicits from a person *P* depends in very large part on whether the *S* is present with or without social or group components. All that this involved sentence means is that the presence of people makes a difference. But the way the small group of people is structured, set up, or organized is significant. "Groups put pressures on group members." How does this work?

P sometimes submits to, sometimes resists, group pressure. Group pressure is part of the controlling constellations of environmental stimuli. The so-called influence of suggestion and prestige are examples of such pressures.[1]

Asch [2] collected data on eight group members who were instructed to judge length of lines. They were asked to match the length of a particular line with one of three lines of unequal length. The conditions of the experiment were arranged so that: (1) each member of the group announced his judgment so that all the others could hear; (2) each member except one was instructed to announce an erroneous, prearranged judgment. The one member, the critical one, was not "in the know." All except the critical person had been instructed to respond with a wrong judgment. These wrong judgments were unanimous except for the one critical person. Imagine his surprise when confronted with this condition of pressure—either he was the only one who was wrong, or all the others were wrong! An interesting *Spgr* situation was set up in such a way that conditions could be controlled and activity attributed to these controlled conditions. The experiment was repeated with eight member groups a number of times, so that Asch was able to report results on a total of fifty critical subjects.

The majority, that is, the other seven subjects, knowingly reported erroneous judgments; the errors were large, ranging from 1½ inches to 1¾ inches. Thus the majority group, in relation to each critical subject:

[1] See, for example, Irving Lorge, "Prestige, Suggestion and Attitudes," *Journal of Social Psychology*, VII (1936), 386–402.

[2] Solomon E. Asch, "Effects of Group Pressure upon the Modification and Distortion of Judgments," *Group Dynamics—Research and Theory*, eds. Dorwin Cartwright and Alvin Zander (Evanston, Illinois: Row, Peterson and Company, 1956), pp. 151–62. Also H. Geutzkow, ed., *Groups, Leadership and Men* (Pittsburgh: Carnegie Press, 1951).

contradicted the evidence of his senses. *a*) The critical subject was submitted to two contradictory and irreconcilable forces: the evidence of his own experience of an utterly clear perceptual fact, and the unanimous evidence of a group of equals. *b*) Both forces were part of the immediate situation; the majority was concretely present, surrounding the subject physically. *c*) The critical subject, who was requested along with the others to state his judgments publicly, was obliged to declare himself and take a definite stand *vis-à-vis* the group. *d*) The situation possessed a self-contained character. The critical subject could not avoid or evade the dilemma by reference to conditions external to the experimental situation.[3]

The results of the experiment revealed that the fifty critical subjects tended to report errors that conformed to those reported by the majority. A third of them reported errors identical to those of the majority, but control groups in which there was no prearrangement for distortion made virtually no errors. However, 68 per cent of the critical subjects resisted the pressure of the majority and reported judgments "as they saw them." These differences among critical subjects are attributable to the *P* rather than to the *S* aspects of *SPAR*, since the *S* aspects were controlled by the experimental design.

It is quite evident that the social setting determines in part the outcome of the response. If we were to take into account only the physically given constellations of stimuli, *Sc*, we would be omitting from consideration the very factors that we wish to examine. The crucial factors are social—the *Spgr* factors.

It looks as if we have here at least one generalizable set of facts: responses are, in part, determined by the constellations of social stimuli that impinge upon the individual. Behaviorial scientists seek general principles.[4] Here is one that is applicable to all situations. The principles concerning the *P*, *A*, and *R* aspects to be discussed immediately are equally generalizable.

The person is a social being

Attention is now invited to a no less interesting, albeit complex, part of the *SPAR* set of concepts: *P*. This symbol is intended to encompass

[3] Asch, *ibid.*, 152–53.

[4] See, for example, George C. Homans, *The Human Group* (New York: Harcourt, Brace and Company, Inc., 1950). In the introduction to this book Robert K. Merton says, "Mr. Homans' major purpose is to work toward a sociological theory which will state, in convenient and compact form, the interconnected uniformities detected in the behavior of men in groups." p. xvii. George Homans' is a *conceptual scheme* which consists of persons and three elements of their behavior; *activity*, *interaction*, and *sentiment*. Out of these elements of behavior he endeavors to develop a set of hypotheses and principles which will apply to the study of all groups, no matter where they find them. He is interested in generalization. See p. 44.

all of the factors that go together to make up the acting person. Whether or not a child trembles with fear when he hears thunder depends upon his past experience: what he has learned, how he has learned to react to thunder. The scope of this book does not include a detailed statement of the facts, methods, and results from research studies pertaining to the field of learning. Several conditions of learning have been discussed in the previous chapter. Gradual progress is being made toward adequate knowledge of the personal factor. We may say here that the person involved in the situation is of paramount importance. His background and what he has learned in the past help the leader to understand him, adjust him to the situation, and to meld each individual into a team in such a way that the individuals on the team will interact freely, having mutual understanding and goals.

We may discuss some of the *P* factors of *SPAR* with a view to fostering a more objective approach to *P*, the person; to *A*, his activity; and to *R*, the results of his activity. We may look upon a person as a bundle or mass of integrated protoplasm, in a physical sense, as *P*; or we may look at him as a person interacting with another person, as *Pp*, a social being; or we may see him as a social being related to a social group, *Pgr*:

P
Pp
Pgr

Further, we may look at his activity, *A*, as simple stimulus-response behavior patterns, or as response to another person, or as interpersonal activity in which the social group plays a part:

A
Ap
A, gr

Similarly, we may be content to view the outcome, achievement, or results, *R*, of his activity as simply responses which have an impact on him, the person, alone; or we may view his activity in its impact on each of several individuals in his social environment; or we may view the results of his activity as changing the group as a whole:

R
Rp
R, gr

It is easy for us to prove the human tendency of *P* to seek cause of behavior where there is no cause—to look for the cause in the wrong place. Some suggestions of this tendency come from observation of childlike behavior; real proof comes from experimental evidence.

The behavior of a ship at sea or on a lake is difficult to understand. So one tends to personify the ship: "*She* is pounding . . . *she* wants to tack . . . *she* is broaching to." We personify the auto: "*She* is ready to go." The child animates moving toys, referring to them as *she* or *he*, explaining movement by imputing "a little man within" as the cause and director of the movement.

And *P* likes to see striving or goal behavior when, in reality, goal-seeking behavior is not present. *P* observes from a distance two men talking in an animated way: he reports that they are fighting or arguing rather than merely talking. He tends to observe emotion—anger or fear—when there is no evidence that the men are angry or afraid. Such casual observations suggest that tendency to impute cause and effect of behavior in animistic terms is universal and a part of our cultural behavior pattern. Experimental evidence provides more rigid proof of the same thing.

That primitive animism as a basis of interpretation influences our perception is shown clearly by the experiment of Heider and Simmel.[5] These investigators presented a two-minute movie film to groups of adult observers. The film showed them only three geometrical figures in motion. These were a large triangle, a small triangle, and a circle. These figures moved near and around a rectangle, one corner of which could be opened and closed as a gate or door (see Figure 8.1).

Heider and Simmel used two different groups of subjects or observers. The members of the first group were merely instructed to report what they observed; the members of the second group were requested to consider the figures to be human and to report what they saw.

Now there was, as far as the geometrical figures or instructions were concerned, no reason for the first group of observers to see people. But they did see people in the movements of the figures. Not only did they see humans acting, but they also tended to invest them with personalities. Almost all subjects animated the figures. They personified them. They reported a series of causal, meaningful, orderly, motivated events.

The second group, instructed to see the figures as human, all personified the figures. One observer reported that

[5] F. Heider and E. Simmel, "A Study of Apparent Behavior," *American Journal of Psychology*, LVII (1944), 243–59; see also Solomon E. Asch, *Social Psychology* (Englewood Cliffs, N. J.: Prentice-Hall, Inc., 1952), pp. 152–69.

From Heider and Simmel, OP. CIT.

Fig. 8.1 · Three figures shown in various positions and relations on a movie film

A man has planned to meet a girl and the girl comes along with another man. The first man tells the second to go; the second tells the first, and he shakes his head. Then the two men have a fight, and the girl starts to go into the room to get out of the way and hesitates and finally goes in. She apparently does not want to be with the first man. The first man follows her into the room after having left the second in a rather weakened condition leaning on the wall outside the room. The girl gets worried and races from one corner to the other in the far part of the room. Man number one, after being silent for a while, makes several approaches to her; but she gets to the corner across from the door, just as man number two is trying to open it. He evidently got banged around and is still weak from his efforts to open the door. The girl gets out of the room in a sudden dash just as man number one gets the door open. The two chase around outside of the room together, followed by man number one. But they finally elude him and get away. The first man goes back and tries to open his door, but he is so blinded by rage and frustration that he cannot open it. So he butts it open and in a really mad dash around the room he breaks in first one wall and then another.[6]

[6] Heider and Simmel, *ibid.*, pp. 246–47; also Solomon Asch., *ibid.*, pp. 154–55.

Apparently, some people have unusual facility for personification. There are, no doubt, differences in people in this facility. The figures seemed to the subjects to be capable of independent movement. The above illustration serves to show how far one's tendency toward animism can go under conditions that conduce its free use. Other studies verify the results of Heider and Simmel. One of the more clear-cut and striking illustrative studies of this kind has been made by Michotte.

Michotte also presented figures, in the form of colored rectangles, to his observers. He could control the speed of movement and the direction and distance moved by the rectangles. In Figure 8.2 the rectangles are represented by *A* and *B*. Michotte's observers did not see *A* and *B* as separate moving rectangles. Rather, they saw cause and effect in their movements; their responses indicated that they saw *A* moving near *B*, causing it to move out of the way. The subjects injected functional connections and causation into the situation, when in actuality there was no functional connection or interdependent causation. When *A* moved

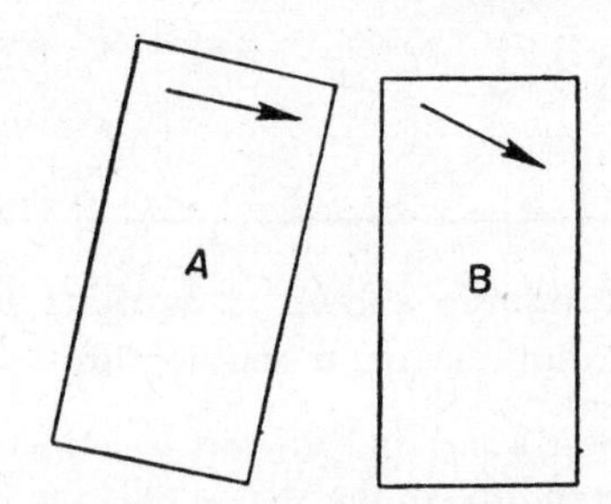

Fig. 8.2 · *A* and *B* represent rectangles in motion seen as cause and effect

and bumped *B*, *A*, for the observers, had set *B* in motion. If *A* moved close to *B* and hovered there, and they both then moved off in the same direction, the observers stated that *A* came by and enticed or attracted *B* away.[7]

We appear to like to see causal effects in the events around us and tend to use simplified explanations to explain the unknown. It seems more comforting or pleasant to us to interpret events in terms of a simple and apparent, if incorrect, cause. Michotte pointed out that the

[7] A. Michotte, "The Emotions Regarded as Functional Connections." By permission from *Feelings and Emotions*, edited by M. L. Reymert. Copyright, 1950. McGraw-Hill Book Company, Inc. Also A. Michotte, *La Perception de la Causalité* (Louvain: L'institute supérieur de Philosophie, 1946).

observers used the language of human emotions to describe the motions of the figures.

It seems natural for people to do this. It was not unusual for observers to say that *B* joined *A*, that *B* and *A* then disagree, have a quarrel, and separate, but come together again when they cease to be angry; or that *A* was afraid of *B* and ran away. It is more than likely that when we perceive social behavior we are likely to type or stereotype it in terms of arbitrary, fallacious categories of cause and effect. In this way we tend to "close" an episode. It is closed when we have an explanation, insight, or understanding of it. And it matters little whether the explanation is in reality correct or true in fact. Its main characteristic to the observer is closure.

The *P* factors in *SPAR*, then, are to be viewed in terms of these tendencies that we have to interpret events in a subjective and emotional—as contrasted to a cautious, objective, analytical, unemotional—way. *P* tends to see cause-and-effect where there is no cause-and-effect. *P* tends to have fallacious insights, followed by closure. These facts have important implications for nondirective counseling that is discussed in Chapter 16 as one of the creative leader's techniques.

We may now return to Asch's studies of group pressure to discuss the differences among his critical subjects. It will be recalled that of the fifty critical people in his experiments, about a third conformed to pressure—"got on the band wagon"—and 68 per cent were more independent. There were differences among those who yielded to pressure; differences were also noted among those who remained independent and "called them as they saw them."

An interview was held with each critical subject after his series of judgments were made to find out from them whether they were suspicious of collusion among the majority and reasons given for yielding to the majority judgments. It was found that instances of suspicion were rare. The results of the interviews revealed some interesting differences between the independent and the yielding subjects. One illustration for each is given below:

Independent. After a few trials he appeared puzzled, hesitant. He announced all disagreeing answers in the form of, "Three, sir. Two, sir." Not so with the unanimous answers. At trial 4 he answered immediately after the first member of the group, shook his head, blinked, and whispered to his neighbor, "Can't help it, that's one." His later answers came in a whispered voice, accompanied by a deprecating smile. At one point he grinned embarrassedly, and whispered explosively to his neighbor: "I always disagree—darn it!" During the questioning, this subject's constant refrain was: "I called them as I saw them, sir." He insisted that his estimates were right without, however, committing himself as to whether the others were wrong, remarking that, "That's the way I see them, and that's the way they see them." If he had to make a practical decision under similar circumstances, he declared, "I would follow my own view, though part of my reason would tell me that I might be wrong." Immediately following the experiment, the majority engaged this subject in a brief discussion. When they pressed him to say whether the entire group was wrong and he alone right, he turned upon them defiantly, exlaiming: "You're *probably* right, but you may be wrong!" To the disclosure of this experiment, this subject reacted with the statement that he felt "exultant and relieved," adding, "I do not deny that at times I had the feeling: 'To heck with it, I'll go along with the rest.' "

Yielding. This subject went with the majority in 11 out of 12 trials. He appeared nervous and somewhat confused, but he did not attempt to evade discussion; on the contrary, he was helpful and tried to answer to the best of his ability. He opened the discussion with the statement, "If I'd been the first I probably would have responded differently." This was his way of stating that he had adopted the majority estimates. The primary factor in his case was a loss of confidence. He perceived the majority as a decided group, acting without hesitation: "If they had been doubtful I probably would have changed, but they answered with such confidence." Certain of his errors, he explained, were due to the doubtful nature of the comparisons; in such instances he went with the majority. When the object of the experiment was explained, the subject volunteered, "I suspected about the middle—but tried to push it out of my mind." It is of interest that his suspicion was not able to restore his confidence and diminish the power of the majority. Equally striking is his report that he assumed the experiment to involve an "illusion" to which the others, but not he, were subject. This assumption, too, did not help to free him. On the contrary, he acted as if his divergence from the majority was a sign of defect. The principal impression this subject produced was of one so caught up by immediate difficulties that he lost clear reasons for his actions, and could make no reasonable decisions.[8]

The interviews also yielded information as to reasons for independence and yielding to group pressures. The independent subjects differed in that they had more confidence in their perceptive judgments. They did experience some conflict but were vigorous in their self-dependence. Some of the independent ones tended to be withdrawn from the group, and others seemed to be task- rather than group-oriented.

Some of the subjects who yielded to group pressures, on the other hand, reacted to the stress of the situation as if their perception were distorted. In more cases of yielding subjects, judgment was distorted; they judged that their perception of the lines must be inaccurate; they lacked confidence in their perception in the face of group pressures. Some of the yielding subjects submitted to group pressures as a matter

[8] Asch, "Effects of Group Pressure upon the Modification and Distortion of Judgments," pp. 154–55.

of distortion of action. These, according to Asch, "suppress their observations, and voice a majority position with awareness of what they are doing." These categories provide examples of differences of people in the face of group pressures.

Social activity and its results

We have seen from the experiments of Heider and Simmel, Michotte, and Asch that people differ in the way they interpret simple constellations of physical stimuli. They do not respond to, or describe, such environmental stimuli as physical stimuli at all. Rather, they respond to them in terms of the social configuration that exists in the environmental situation.

Ever since Wilhelm Wündt (1832–1920) established the first formal psychological laboratory at Leipzig in 1879, classical experimental psychology has been almost solely interested in physical environmental stimuli. The behavioral sciences have gone far beyond consideration of physical stimulus or constellations of such stimuli. Wündt has been called the founder of modern psychology. However, "a science which hesitates to forget its founders is lost." [9] Whitehead felt that we should not have a reverential attitude toward the founders of a science. And psychology, at least social psychology, has moved far away from the stimulus-response psychology, recognizing that the meat and substance of the discipline is not to be found by studying simple physical stimuli and response.

We need to emphasize social configurations in which the person finds himself. The presence of forces of the social person *Pgr* responding to the forces of social stimuli *Sgr* is abundantly clear. The concrete experimental results of the few well-controlled studies we have selected emphasize to us our need for seeing social activity in terms of dynamic concepts.

Social activity can only be described in terms of social group configurations of *SPAR*. This set of concepts helps us to view social activity objectively and impartially. We are not so apt to blame a person for his actions; rather, we look at his actions in terms of the whole configuration of forces which influence the situation. Such a viewpoint is perhaps unnecessary when power, as it manifests itself in authority, is utilized as a way of managing people. But such power fails, as discussed in

[9] Alfred North Whitehead, *The Aims of Education* (New York: The New American Library, 1929), p. 112, which reprints as "The Organization of Thought" his presidential address to Section A at the New Castle Meeting of the American Association for the Advancement of Science, 1916.

Chapter 2. Creative leadership is the utilization of socio-psychological forces; the leader's function is to understand and use these forces for achieving results which are the goal of the group. These results constitute the *R* of *SPAR*.

Results of action, *R*, have serial influences on subsequent social activity. Results achieved by a person or group influence the dynamic interrelations for the next action. For example, group decisions are made to solve a problem; as a result, other problems arise on which decisions are to be made. The action, a decision, has an impact on the social situation, so that the social environment is changed.

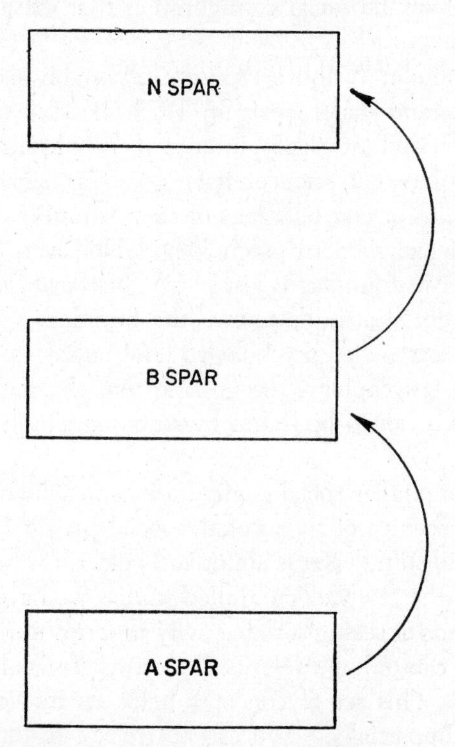

Fig. 8.3 · Each episode is related in a dynamic way to its predecessor

This fact of serial process may be illustrated as in Figure 8.3, in which *A SPAR*, an episode with a result of activity, has an impact on another episode *B SPAR*, *etc.* so that there is a series of episodes, *N SPAR*, each related in a dynamic way to its predecessor. We have viewed the various episodes in the cases that were analyzed in chapters 5 and 6. The analysis of needs and attitudes—and remedial human relations procedures that were instituted as a result of such analysis—were discussed. These, as well as other similar cases, can be seen as the serial impact of results *R* of group activity *A*.

In this chapter we have emphasized again, as we began in Chapter 1, that all of us tend to have common misconceptions regarding the actions of people. Modern man is not free from primitive animism.

The concept of SPAR, an analytical view of the Situation, Person, Activity, and Results of activity in the social setting, has been illustrated by the findings of research studies designed to control and isolate some of the factor areas involved. It is shown, for example, that the presence of a small group of people acting in a certain way can be so powerful a determinant of activity that a person simply cannot believe what he sees! The results of social activity are seen to have impact on other episodes, so that we cannot consider one episode as isolated from previous or subsequent events.

In the next chapter, we are concerned with further aspects of interpersonal perceiving—how we perceive ourselves and others and how they perceive us—with emphasis on roles and on problems of empathy.

All the world is queer save thee and me,
and even thou art a little queer.

—ROBERT OWEN
On severing business relations with his partner

9

Perceiving and predicting social action

The leadership situation depends in part upon how people perceive one another. Robert Burns was striving for clarity in self-perception when he made the plea, "Oh wad some power the giftee gie us to see oursels as others see us!" The ways we see ourselves and others around us is a highly personal, contagiously biased procedure. It is the aim of this chapter to discuss the psychology of how we perceive the people around us in their various roles, how contagious bias operates to distort our perceptions of others, and how our background and set disturb the clarity of our perceptions. *Empathy* will be defined, and some experimental studies will show the relation of empathy and its cousin, predictive abstracting, to leadership. Empathy will be contrasted with projection, and the significance of these two mechanisms for creative leadership will be considered.

Psychologists have been studying perception for a long time. Most of the earlier studies dealt with philosophical or logical theories and systems of perception. The mentalists held that perception is the state of the mind in which such mental contents as sensations, images, and feelings were combined to create awareness of an environmental object. The object may be an apple, a tree, a building or a person, or a group of these. Later on, and shortly after the turn of the present century, psychologists began to view perception as a response to an object out in the environment. That is, instead of saying one has a mental state in which "house" is represented in the mind, the psychologist would say the person responds to "house." Thus, these later psychologists attempted to simplify what they were observing and describing by referring to observable activity rather than to personal introspective mental content of a person.

Distorted perceptions

Any school of psychology, whether mentalistic or behaviorist or configurational, will agree that we do have illusions of perception. All will agree also that it is not possible for the sense organs of the body to be activated by everything in the environment but that we fill in what we are not directly aware of.

A quaint notion, held by some philosopher-psychologists shortly after the Middle Ages, was that each object in the environment gives off miniatures of itself. These miniatures fly around in the environment, and some of them get through our sense organs and into the mind. Thus, when we perceive a tree: little trees are given off from the real tree, and the mind (in some mysterious way) becomes aware of the tree. These miniatures that were given off from the various objects in the environment were called *idola.* The authors of this primitive view of perception would describe imperfect perceptions as imperfect miniatures that have been thrown off by the tree.

Today, psychologists describe illusions as distorted sensory perceptions. The distortion comes about in the "perceptual filling." All of our perceptions contain some filling. When we see an apple, we do not see the back of the apple, but we have learned to respond to the sensory cues available as if we saw the whole apple. We respond, in reading, to an

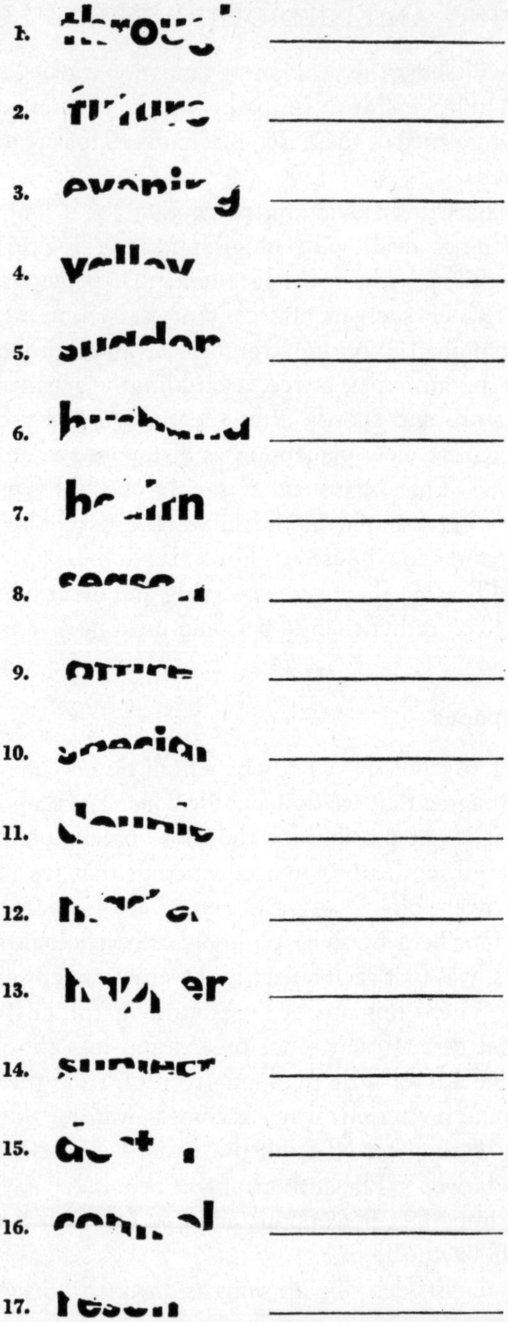

1. ______________________

2. ______________________

3. ______________________

4. ______________________

5. ______________________

6. ______________________

7. ______________________

8. ______________________

9. ______________________

10. ______________________

11. ______________________

12. ______________________

13. ______________________

14. ______________________

15. ______________________

16. ______________________

17. ______________________

From Edward E. Cureton and Louise Witmer Cureton, THE MULTI-APTITUDE TEST *(New York: The Psychological Corporation, 1955).*

Fig. 9.1 · The Gestalt or closure test illustrated by word recognition

abbreviated word as if it were the entire word. Our past experience and background learning enable us to fill in and close up the word. This is illustrated in the *Gestalt* or word closure test, officially called "Word Recognition," which appears in Figure 9.1. The reader will experience closure of the words that he can complete from minimal cues given on the page. The score is the number of words properly completed in a short time limit.

The phenomenon of illusions, agreed to exist by all schools of psychology, proves that even in the case of the perception of simple objects, our senses deceive us. There are some interesting and dramatic examples of illusions. The first is the Müller-Lyer illusion, shown in Figure 9.2. Two lines, *A* and *B,* actually of equal length, appear different in length.

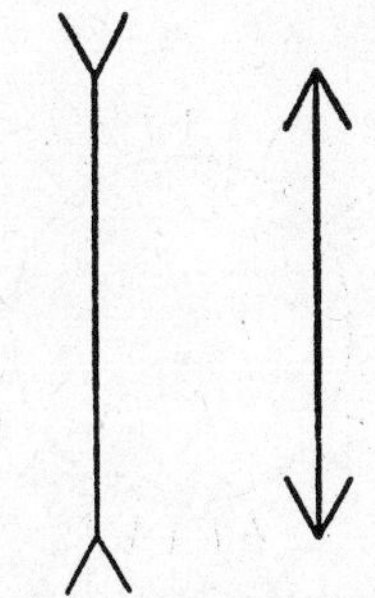

Fig. 9.2 · The Müller-Lyer illusion

Another example is the flying staircase illusion, sometimes called the tumbling or reversible staircase. After looking at Figure 9.3 for a little while, the observer will see first the staircase apparently from above and then, alternately, from below.

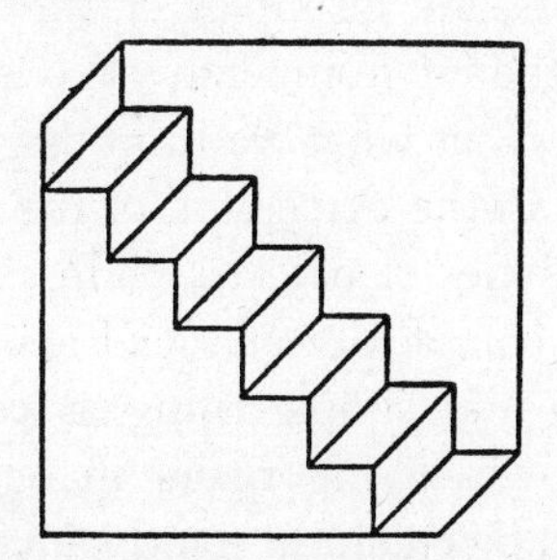

Fig. 9.3 · Flying staircase illusion

A fourth example of distortion in our perceptions will suffice to show that we are prone, even in the perception of objects, to false experience.

We see something that is not immediately given in the environment. This final illusion from the area of sensory perception has to do with the "phi" illusion, so-called by its inventor, Max Wertheimer.[1] This illusion has some practical uses and can be observed on the highway at some railroad crossings. It is apparent movement of a light, as if a lantern were swinging, where there really is no movement at all in the environment. Two stationary lights, *A* and *B* as in Figure 9.4, are so arranged that the first one is turned on and off, then the second is turned on and off, and so on. Under certain conditions of optimal distance between the lamps, optimal duration and succession of on and off, and optimal intensity of the lights, the observer reports that he sees a single light swinging back and forth.

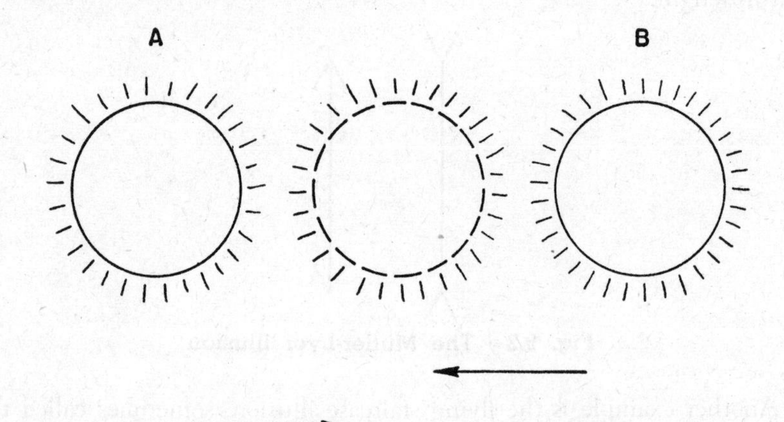

Fig. 9.4 · The "phi phenomenon": apparent movement of two lights

These several illusions are examples of the fact that we do not see what is "out there" in the environment. We are quite liberal in filling in what we think is there, or what we think is going on. We are likely to be even less accurate in the perception of the activities of other people than we are in the activities of objects. This is readily understandable when we think of the complexity of social activity. A physical object is a relatively concrete and simple thing as compared with the most complex substance known—living tissue in action. But living tissue from a physiological and biochemical standpoint is less complicated when an individual is viewed behaving by himself; group behavior is infinitely

[1] Max Wertheimer, "Experimentelle Studen über das Sehen von Bewegüngen," *Zeitschrift für Psychologie*, LXI (1912), 161–265.

more complex than individual. That human behavior consists largely of responses which are actually interactions with other people was emphasized in Chapter 8 which described experiments dealing with the impact of the presence of other people—social pressure—on perception.

Contagious prejudice and halo

The many factors that dictate what we will see in other people and what they see in us may be likened to a triangle: (1) on one corner of the triangle are factors contained in the observer or the person observing us; (2) on another part of the triangle are factors or forces that are contained in us that make us behave or move or appear in a certain way to the observer; (3) on the third corner of the triangle are clusters of factors relating to the total environmental situation, mostly social; and these, for want of a better term, may be referred to as the social climate—cold or warm.

We may first have a look at factors that relate to the background of the observer—this is the *P* portion of *SPAR* discussed in Chapter 8—which may determine what he perceives in other people.

A sociologist [2] had the task of employing and training a number of people to interview indigent, homeless men of New York's Bowery, in connection with a study of social failure. Several interviewers were involved, and each of them was responsible for quite a large sample of these men. It so happened that one of the interviewers was an ardent prohibitionist. He reported that many of the homeless men in his sample were in this plight because of liquor and had so described the situation themselves. He said that 34 per cent ascribed their destitution to alcohol and 43 per cent to industrial conditions.

In contrast, another interviewer in this study was a socialist. His personal conviction was that the woes and ailments of society had to do with the inequitable distribution of wealth. He found that 60 per cent of the homeless men owed their difficulties to economic conditions and only 11 per cent to liquor. He reported their downfall as resulting from lack of economic opportunity to satisfy needs. Thus, these two interviewers were reacting in terms of their own background and personal biases. We all have these predispositions, preconceptions and stereotypes about people, in greater or less degree.

The problem here is one of accurate observation and intercommunication. If we would get the facts, we first must recognize our prejudices

[2] Stuart A. Rice, "Contagious Bias in the Interview: A Methodological Note," *American Journal of Sociology*, XXXV (1929), 420–23.

and biases and not allow them to influence contagiously our observation and interpretation of another's responses. This is not a usual precaution. In our day-to-day interrelationships with other people we frequently allow these predispositions to determine what we see in them. We have, all of us, a large number of prejudices which depend not only upon our background and training but also upon the particular social pressures of the groups in which we have membership.

How the bias of a group in which we have membership may affect our social perception is most interesting. Haire asked two groups to describe the personality of a man. They saw a picture of him and were also given a brief description of him. One of the groups was composed of union representatives, the other consisted of management men. Each group was split into half: one half of each was told the man was a union leader, the other half that he was a member of management. Here is what the groups saw in the man: [3]

> Managers, when told he was a management man, saw him as
> "honest, conscientious and adaptable."
> Managers, when told he was a union man, saw him as
> "alert, determined and aggressive."
> Labor leaders, when told he was a union man, saw him as
> "active, alert and capable."
> Labor leaders, when told he was a management man, saw him as
> "active, aggressive and alert."

An investigator [4] wanted to know how two groups of students would react to a visiting lecturer if he were introduced to the two groups in slightly different ways. In the one group, called the "warm" group, the lecturer was introduced in terms such as *industrious, critical, practical, highly determined, a very warm person.* In the other group, called the "cold" group, the same lecturer was introduced as a person who was *industrious, critical, practical, highly determined, with a rather cold personality.*

The same lecture was presented in the same manner to the two groups. Two measures were taken from each of these groups at the end of the lecture session. One examined what the students thought of the visiting lecturer as a person, from their own observations of him. In the "warm"

[3] Mason Haire, "Interpersonal Relations in Collective Bargaining," *Research in Industrial Human Relations* (New York: Harper & Brothers, 1957), pp. 187–88.

[4] H. H. Kelley, "The Warm-Cold Variable in First Impressions of Personality," *Journal of Abnormal and Social Psychology*, XVIII (1950), 431–39.

group, such comments were made of him: *considerate, informal, sociable, good-natured.* The "cold" group made comments such as: *self-centered, formal, unsociable, irritable.* Another measure was taken. This revealed the amount of participation in the discussion after the lecture. The "warm" group had significantly more participation and discussion (56 per cent participated) than the "cold" group (32 per cent). Thus, we see that a significant amount of predetermining can take place by establishing a set in the subjects with only one or a very few words, for example, "warm" versus "cold personality," as was the case in this investigation.

There tends to be a constant and all-pervading error in our observations of other people. This error was called the "halo effect" by E. L. Thorndike, who wrote about it back in 1920. This is our tendency, in rating a person formally or judging him informally, to let a strong impression on one or two characteristics color our judgment of other, unrelated characteristics. For example, a high-pitched voice may be quite irritating to a particular employment manager. Through the operation of the halo effect, an applicant with this trait may be rated as "poor" in honesty, neatness of work, and sociability. The manager himself is not aware that this particular kind of bias is operating in his evaluation of the applicant. Similarly, a very attractive single characteristic of a person may produce a "halo" for other characteristics. The war hero whose advice is sought in matters such as community planning and child-rearing is, through the "halo effect," imbued with wisdom that there is no rational reason for attributing to him.

The "halo effect" has as its end result a simplification of the process of making judgments about others. That we often err through oversimplification is clear. By stereotyping, we may carry one step further this attempt to make the difficult easy. Here we paint broad pictures of groups of people: the soulless, ruthless businessman, the absent-minded, impractical college professor, the scatterbrained, lovesick adolescent; and willy-nilly, without any thought at all, we try to fit individuals into our stereotyped cubbyholes. They automatically are imbued with the traits that go with the stereotype.

The effective leader will tend to perceive accurately other persons, arriving at judgments relatively uncolored by the halo effect or stereotyping. *Empathy* is another type of understanding which a leader may utilize to reach below surface superficialities and further a warm social climate in which mutual goals are achieved.

Empathy

Although there has been a great deal of research reported on empathy during the past two decades, mostly from experimental studies on interpersonal perception, it has not yet been sufficiently applied to leader behavior. We will try in this section to define and illustrate this phenomenon in terms of leader behavior.

A counseling situation that arose as the result of the behavior of one of the selectmen in a town hall meeting illustrates empathy:

Mr. James North was acting as chairman of a meeting of selectmen. The purpose of the meeting was to plan a financing program for a new playground for the community. Seven selectmen were present. George Zober violently opposed a proposal to increase real estate tax assessments. He wanted a bond issue. Other members were in favor of the real estate tax plan. When it became apparent that his arguments failed to impress the others, he stomped out of the meeting room in a rage. Next day Mr. North called on him to discuss the matter in a quieter, less emotional setting. Mr. North believed he could see Zober's viewpoint. Since Zober had real estate holdings in the community, part of his opposition to the new tax assessment was based on personal economic considerations, but not all. Zober had no children.

North's task was a kind of nondirective counseling. In preparing for this counseling, North put himself in the place of Zober. He asked himself what he would have done if he had been in George Zober's shoes. He, in a sense, imagined that he had Zober's mind and appreciated his logic, felt his feelings and emotions, and knew his motives. His approach was to use group pressure to bring Zober around, to make a unanimous group decision for the good of the community. North believed that the net outcome of empathizing (not sympathizing) and counseling might achieve the desired result. In any case, it would do no harm. Logic or power approaches, he thought, would surely fail.

This case illustrates empathy, defined as *the state of perceiving the feelings, attitudes, and state of mind of another*. The term was first used to designate "feeling with" or "into" the thoughts of others. It is an aspect of social perception.

Empathy, or the German equivalent of it, *einfuhlung*, was first used as a major portion of a system of psychology by Theodor Lipps (1851–1914). Lipps was interested in esthetics and developed a theory of esthetics based on empathy. When we appreciate a work of art we "feel" ourselves into the mind, or behavior, of the artist. To appreciate a symphony, or a play, is to play with the players. Not with overt but rather with covert, implicit movements. Appreciation is awareness of such movements.

As a part of our psychological equipment, each of us has this special ability or skill of seeing into another's mind or behavior. This special social feeling for others is an important component of over-all skill in dealing with people. Successful salesmen are believed to have this attribute to a rather high degree. The good salesman knows what the prospect is thinking about. The good interviewer has an awareness of what the interviewee is thinking and feeling. We may experience empathy when we are spectators at a sports event or when we see a movie or a TV show. This is perhaps a reason we feel tired after seeing a movie: we have played the role of the leading player or character in the story. We empathize with him.

The counselor, for example, in vocational and educational counseling or psychotherapy, helping the patient gain better insights into his own life adjustment, uses empathy to a large degree. He "feels into" the mind and behavior patterns of the patient. In this way he is able to understand better the problems that confront the patient. Through empathy the bond that is established is made more firm—between interviewer and interviewee, counselor and counselee, mother and child, supervisor and employee, or teacher and pupil. Empathy is related to mutual *rapport,* the bond of mutual understanding.

It would be supposed that a good facility in empathy would be necessary for a high degree of success in jobs such as salesman, supervisor, executive and manager, counselor and therapist. Empathy is assumed to be a characteristic that is needed by the leader who works in a democratic as opposed to an authoritarian, disciplinarian, or autocratic atmosphere.

Most of us as individuals have in our make-up a need for empathy. We like to feel that other people understand us. This is one of the satisfactions that an actor gets from his work. It constitutes a motivating force to make him improve himself to the extent that he can be empathized by large audiences. This need is, of course, tied up with the social need of approbation and acceptance by various social groups. Empathy does not always, of course, require that we approve of the acts of other people.

Empathy and leadership

Do group leaders and other members feel the feelings of the others in the group? Does the leader make use of empathy in engendering mutual understanding and in developing mutual goals? Does he make more use of it than members of the group who are not leaders? Do differences between people exist in empathic ability? Is empathy measurable? Answers to some of these questions will be treated here. Approaches [5] to answers to these questions have been made.

Attempts to measure empathy have been of two kinds. The first, a direct method, consisted of a list of questions that would presumably measure how effective a person is in making judgments of the feelings, knowledge, set, attitude, and future behavior of others. The test allegedly measured "understanding and anticipating reactions of other people."

Rosalind Dymond in an article considered a pioneering effort in the definition and study of empathy indicated that there is not one but many definitions of empathy. She uses the word to denote the ability to see things "from the other person's point of view." [6] She attempted to develop a test, using the direct method, to measure empathy. This investigator reported evidence that tends to confirm the possibility of its measurement. Future research may yield more precise and useful techniques for its measurement. Chapter 18, which is concerned with the earmarks of the successful leader, will discuss the status of further attempts to measure ability in social perception in the selection of leaders.

The direct approach was used by Kerr [7] who reported very high correlations between scores on his Empathy Test and performance ratings and sales records of automobile salesmen. Furthermore, Kerr found very high relationships between the Empathy Test scores and six criteria of performance of labor union business agents. These performance criteria were: (1) performance record in settling disputes; (2) recruitment of new members; (3) proportion of votes received in union elections; (4) enforcement of rules and regulations; (5) leadership rank; (6) knowledge of supervisory principles.

The degree of association of Empathy Test scores with performance in such jobs as salesman and labor union agent was high enough to suggest

[5] R. M. W. Travers, "A Study in Judging the Opinion of Groups," *Archives of Psychology* (Washington, D. C.: American Psychological Association Inc.), 260 (1941), 348–57. Also Rosalind F. Dymond, "A Scale for the Measurement of Empathetic Ability," *Journal of Consulting Psychology*, XXXIII (1949), 127–33 and "Personality and Empathy," *Ibid.*, XXXIV (1950), 343–50; W. A. Kerr, "The Empathy Test," (Chicago: Psychometric Affiliates, 1947) and W. A. Kerr and B. J. Speroff, "Manual for the Empathy Test (Chicago: Psychometric Affiliates, 1951); W. M. Patton, Jr., "Studies in Industrial Empathy: III, A Study of Supervisory Empathy in the Textile Industry," *Journal of Applied Psychology*, XXXIV (1954) 285–89; C. G. Browne and R. P. Shore, "Leadership and Predictive Abstracting," *Journal of Applied Psychology*, XL, 2 (1956), 112–16.

[6] Dymond, *ibid.*

[7] Kerr, *op. cit.;* also Kerr and Speroff, *op. cit.*

that it might be an effective device for identifying some pertinent characteristic of leaders. If so, it would have two valuable purposes: it would enable more adequate description of leader behavior than we now have; it would, furthermore, be of immediate use in selecting leaders (treated in Chapter 18).

Unfortunately, other studies of the validity of the Empathy Test—degree of association of test scores with performance in jobs which seem to require it—have not proven out. In one study [8] the Empathy Test was administered to a sample of automobile salesmen to determine whether its scores would identify outstanding salesmen. No correlation at all was found between supervisor's merit ratings of the salesmen and test scores.

Likewise, McCarty,[9] in a study of the difference in Empathy Test scores of executive secretaries contrasted with scores of nonexecutive secretaries, found no validity. Since executive secretaries would be expected to have greater facility in dealing with people, we would assume they would have greater degree of empathy as measured by the Empathy Test. The findings of the study show that they did not. A somewhat more crucial study of the Empathy Test was conducted by Siegel.[10] He started with the assumption that clinical psychologists possess empathy in greater degree than experimental psychologists who do not deal with people in their day-to-day activities. If the Empathy Test measures empathy, then clinical psychologists should make higher scores than experimental psychologists. He found no difference in the scores made by the two groups. Again, no validity.

The indirect approach [11] has been more fruitful. It consists of predictive abstracting. Browne [12] believes that the meaning of the term *empathy* is too broad for our purposes in studying leadership. It refers generally to "knowledge of others," whereas leadership is concerned with a narrower, more specific aspect of empathy. He maintains that

> The essence of the leadership variable . . . does not include either (a) the taking on of the experience and the emotion of another individual, or (b) the

[8] Roger Bellows and associates, *Validity of the Empathy Test,* 1952. An unpublished study.

[9] John J. McCarty, "Validity Information Exchange," *Personnel Psychology,* X (1957), 202–3.

[10] Arthur I. Siegel, "An Experimental Evaluation of the Sensitivity of the Empathy Test," *Journal of Applied Psychology,* XXXVIII (1954), 222–23.

[11] H. H. Remmers, "A Quantitative Index of Social Psychological Empathy," *American Journal of Orthopsychiatry,* XX (1950), 161–65.

[12] C. G. Browne and R. P. Shore, "Leadership and Predictive Abstracting," *Journal of Applied Psychology,* XL (1956), 112–16.

necessity of learning specific knowledge regarding another person's experiences through any specific channels. Rather the leadership variable relates to an individual's ability to take from all of his knowledge of individuals or groups those particulars which will prove to be determiners of the behavior or attitude, etc. of an individual or a group on any given question at any given time. Fundamentally the process involved in the process of abstracting, which is the process of selecting certain details from an event and eliminating other details which are included in the same event . . . the extent to which any individual is able to predict the attitudes, etc. of any other individual will be dependent largely on the extent to which he is able to select details from an event which are pertinent to and have an influence on the areas to be predicted.

Browne and Shore look upon the term *predictive abstracting* as a better operational designation. They make two hypotheses at the beginning of their study: (1) predictive abstracting, as defined above, is a function of leadership, and (2) a relationship or association exists between a person's ability in predictive abstracting and the level he has achieved in an organization. They did not define *echelon level* in terms of height achieved—top, middle, or bottom of the organization—but rather in terms of the focal level of communication.[13] They used 83 subjects at 4 echelon levels in a factory: 5 department managers, 9 general foremen, 17 assistant foremen, and 52 nonsupervisory personnel.

Predictive abstracting was measured by use of a questionnaire. It consisted of 27 statements concerned with attitudes toward job satisfaction, economic issues, and social issues. The indirect measurements were obtained as follows. Each of the subjects first completed the attitude questionnaire in terms of his own attitudes. Then each department manager filled in the questionnaire in terms of the way he predicted the nonsupervisory employees would do it. Then each general foreman and each assistant foreman filled in two questionnaires: in one they predicted or estimated how the nonsupervisory personnel would respond to it; in the other they predicted how the general managers would do it. These data gave a basis for comparison of actual responses with predictions: comparisons of actual responses of employees with the predictions by each of the three levels of supervision; and comparison of actual responses of each supervisory level with predictions made by employees and members of other supervisory levels.

Browne and Shore found that the higher the echelon of the predictor the more accurate the prediction. The second hypothesis, that a relationship or association exists between a person's ability in predictive abstract-

[13] C. G. Browne, "The Concentric Organization Chart," *Journal of Applied Psychology*, XXXIV (1950), 375–77.

ing and the level he has achieved in an organization, is affirmed by the results of the study.

The results bear less precisely upon the first hypothesis, that predictive abstracting, as defined above, is a function of leadership. If leadership were defined simply as level in the organization, then the hypothesis would be affirmed by these results. But this definition is, of course, untenable by us. Such "leadership" could depend solely on a position of power as it manifests itself in institutionalized authority (see Chapter 2), and our definition does not include use of such power.

Insofar as the higher echelons in the Browne-Shore study could be assumed to be leaders the first hypothesis can be said to be affirmed. The results of Browne and Shore suggest strongly that predictive abstracting is an aspect of leadership

> with the following specific observations: (a) the supervisory personnel predicted more accurately than the nonsupervisory, and (b) the more focal supervisory echelons predicted more accurately than the less focal. A study is needed which will test the extent to which predictive abstracting is a function of the individual and/or a function of the position which the individual occupies.[14]

Other available studies confirm the reality of empathy, that it can be measured, and they shed additional light on interpersonal perception.

One of these is a study by Remmers and Remmers.[15] Their investigation of empathy used the indirect method to measure the way union leaders perceive management people. *How Supervise?* a questionnaire test of knowledge of supervisory relations, was used as the method of observation and measurement. The study was divided into several parts: (1) union representatives were asked to fill in the questionnaire in terms of how they thought members of management would be able to answer it. That is, they put themselves in the place of management and filled out the forms for them. (2) Then the management people were asked to fill out the questionnaire forms for themselves. This enabled a comparison of what the union people thought of management with what management thought of themselves.

The results of the study clearly indicated that the union leaders, when they responded as they thought management would respond, thought managers did not know very much about supervision. The scores given

[14] *Ibid.*, p. 116.

[15] L. J. Remmers and H. H. Remmers, "Studies in Industrial Empathy: I. Labor Leader's Attitudes Toward Industrial Supervision and their Estimate of Management's Attitudes," *Personnel Psychology*, XII (1949) 427–36.

the managers by the union leaders were significantly below the scores made by the managers when they filled out the questionnaire themselves. This study revealed that there was a considerable amount of prejudice or lack of accurate social perception on the part of the union leaders in their estimation of how good the managers were as supervisors.

Another study in the same series [16] was conducted by Wendell M. Patton, Jr. He wished to uncover the relationship of empathic ability to level in the organization, since this ability has been shown by other studies [17] to be significant for the direction of others. He also sought to determine the relation of empathy, as measured, to other psychological characteristics such as intelligence. He employed the indirect method used by Remmers and Remmers, gathering data from the *How Supervise?* attitude measure from 54 front-line supervisors, 18 members of top management, and 243 employees.

His findings may be divided into three parts. First he revealed that top managers made highest scores, supervisors made next highest, and employees earned lowest scores on the *How Supervise?* test when they filled it out for themselves.

Second, he found that none of the groups could predict accurately the attitudes and knowledge, as measured, of other groups. The supervisors tended to impose (or project) their own attitudes upon, or into, the employees, rather than to empathize with them. Patton feels that one of the greatest difficulties in constructive leadership is the lack of ability of managers to empathize with employees and, conversely, the lack of accurate empathy on the part of employees toward supervisors. He concludes that "The principal reason for the failure of supervisors to understand management and labor is the projection of their own feelings, attitudes and knowledge upon these groups." [18]

Projection has been defined in clinical psychology as the process of ascribing to others ideas, thinking, feelings, attitudes, motives, and tendencies emanating from one's own experience without noting or recognizing the personal source of the ascription. It is seen in its extreme form in delusions of persecution of the schizophrenic individual. It appears that it exists in most or all people in greater or less degree.

[16] Wendell M. Patton, Jr., "Studies in Industrial Empathy: III. A Study of Supervisory Empathy in the Textile Industry," *Journal of Applied Psychology*, XXXVIII (1954) 285–89.

[17] L. M. Libo, *Attitude Prediction in Labor Relations.* Studies in Industrial Relations No. 10 (Stanford: Stanford University Press, 1948).

[18] *Ibid.*, p. 288.

Imposition (projection) is the opposite of empathy (social perception) as defined. We could thus consider a scale with these two variables in a continuum, as in Figure 9.5.

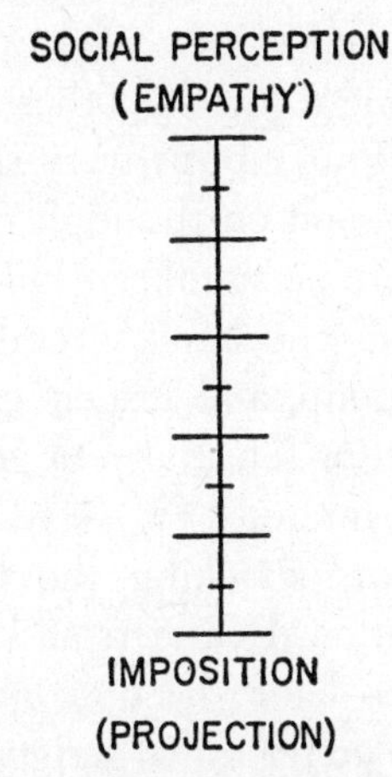

Fig. 9.5 · The empathy-projection continuum

Another promising approach to social perception is the work of Chowdhry and Newcomb.[19] They utilized existing small groups "to test the hypothesis that chosen leaders of a group are superior to non-leaders in estimating group opinion on issues of high relevance to that group, but not superior to them on issues of little relevance."[20] The groups used for study were a religious group, a political group, a medical fraternity, and a medical sorority. Leadership status was determined sociometrically, that is, by choices expressed by the group members themselves in response to questions such as, "Who are the three persons who most influence the opinions of the group?" "Who are the three persons most capable of acting as president of your group?" Those with a large proportion of choices were designated "leaders." Those with no choices were called "isolates," and the rest, "nonleaders." Each group responded to an appropriate attitude questionnaire which dealt with subjects of common interest to the group at three levels of relevance. For example, the content for the religious group in the first part dealt with Christian doctrines and practices; the second part was concerned with the church as a social institution and Christian attitudes toward

[19] K. Chowdhry and T. M. Newcomb, "The Relative Abilities of Leaders and Non-Leaders to Estimate Opinion of Their Own Groups," *Journal of Abnormal and Social Psychology*, XLVII (1952), 51–57.

[20] *Ibid.*, p. 51.

war; the third (least relevant) part covered broad economic and political issues.

In presenting results, the authors computed a mean error score for each individual by subtracting his estimate from the actual group estimate for each item. Plus and minus signs were ignored, since direction of error was not germane to the hypothesis. It was found that, in general, the leaders of the four groups were superior to the isolates in ability to evaluate group opinion on the high relevancy items. On the least relevant items there were no significant differences between leaders, nonleaders, and isolates. A check of several variables—chronological age, length of time in the group, and academic level—showed that none of these was related to superior sensitivity to group attitudes on matters relevant to particular group interests.

A number of investigators attacking the broad problem of social perception—among them Patton, Remmers and Remmers, Dymond, and Chowdhry and Newcomb—have been concerned essentially with empathy. The reader may prefer other designations for this social skill which has been shown to be of importance to the leadership function—for example, "predictive abstracting" (Browne), "ability to estimate group opinion" (Chowdhry and Newcomb)—however, it is felt that no violence is done to the theoretical positions taken by the various researchers if it is said that they have all been dealing with aspects of empathy or social insight in group situations.

The authoritarian manager orders the people in the group to comply with his wishes. He projects or imposes his desires and needs upon the group without insight into their feelings and needs. He uses power of sanctions as a way of control. The creative leader, in contrast, works in terms of the desires and needs of the group members. To do this it is necessary for him to know the feelings and needs of the group members. The creative leader thus tends to utilize empathy; the authoritarian manager does not. Acceptance by the group may be said to depend in large part on ability in social perception which results in mutual understanding and group effort shared toward mutual goals.

We have endeavored in this chapter to describe additional aspects of interpersonal behavior with particular reference to interpersonal perception. Our perceptions even of simple physical constellations of stimuli are frequently distorted. Our views of ourselves and others—social perception—are even more erroneous. Contagious prejudice and halo distort our view of the actions of others.

We have examined a facility or talent called "empathy," and a narrower, more specific, related phenomenon, "predictive abstracting." We have seen by reviewing controlled research studies that aspects of empathy can be operationally defined and measured, that people differ in their empathic skill or in their use of it, and that it is related to level in an organization. It is likely that empathy is a leader talent or skill. It is the opposite of projection of one's own feelings into others; it is, rather, the accurate understanding and prediction of another's attitudes and behavior patterns. As such, it is part of the social climate that is conducive to teamwork; it is believed to be a significant attribute of creative leadership.

In the next part of the book, Part 4, we concern ourselves with theories, facts, methods, and results bearing upon problems of tension, conflict, and leadership. In the next two chapters we are concerned with leadership and tension, conflict, aggression, and frustration.

Tension, Conflict, and Leadership

FOUR

As with all gregarious animals, 'two souls,' as Faust says, 'dwell within his breast,' the one of sociability and helpfulness, the other of jealousy and antagonism . . . WILLIAM JAMES

10

Tension and conflict

The new style leader is, in part, a mental hygienist. One facet of the new leadership is the art of keeping people, such as those in a small group or team, mentally healthy. In this chapter we take a look at some viewpoints on mental health and some facts and theories concerning tension, conflict, frustration, and aggression. We are all victims of conflicting ethics. What can the leader do to meliorate these conflicts and thereby increase team efficiency?

Viewpoints

Not many centuries ago, those afflicted with mental ailments of various kinds were thought of as witches or demons and were burned at stake. In the Middle Ages they were treated with the utmost horror. John Calvin, a relentless religious reformer, thought the devil was inborn in every child and must be extirpated by rigorous means. Even at the turn of the present century, G. Stanley Hall believed that everyone tends to sow wild oats and that abnormal tendencies were inherent in human nature. And following John Calvin, he believed that strenuous measures must be taken to prevent the child from sowing his wild oats. The Children's Bureau, U.S. Department of Labor, beginning in 1914, brought out pamphlets entitled *Infant Care,* which claimed that the only way a mother could handle the recalcitrant child was by stamping out uncivilized and asocial tendencies by ridicule and punishment. These methods have changed radically, so that now love and affection, the warm climate, is recognized as significant.[1]

The present-day enlightened view is typified by the following passage: [2]

> Unpossessive, unconditional love provides a child with the sense of security necessary to mental health.
>
> Each child should be accepted for what he is. "Children need a human relationship far more than they need a perfect relationship."
>
> We must remind ourselves how frustrating childhood is. . . .

Since the child is "father to the man," we would expect that childhood frustrations—many of them "normal" in the sense that they are experienced by *all* children, as well as those arising out of adult interaction with various groups—would sometimes result in tension and conflict. The leader, then, will be concerned with doing something about keeping people mentally healthy. Conflict and hostility detract from effectiveness of behavior patterns of a group. A leader is in the position to set the stage for mental health.

One of the most fundamental causes of mental ill health stems from loss of the feeling of worth, dignity, and group acceptance. When a person is thwarted on every hand, when he is barred from group member-

[1] M. Wolfstein, "The Emergence of Fun Mortality," *Journal of Social Issues* (1951), pp. 15–25.

[2] June Bingham, "Do Cows Have Neuroses?" (Raleigh, N. C.: Health Publications Institute, Inc., 1948, 1950), p. 15. Originally published by The Mental Hygiene Association of Westchester County.

ship, acceptance, and approval, his orientation can turn in no direction other than inward. He simply does not have *rapport* with anybody. When this happens to an inordinate degree, his mental state is said to be *unhealthy*. He is said to be in *poor adjustment* with his social environment. His feeling of worth and his self-respect fail him. The various mechanisms that everyone has for self-defense begin to function. We say that he has become dissociated from his social environment. In its extreme forms this state of being is labelled *psychosis*. He is a psychologically maladjusted person.

Each of us is in delicate balance with his social environment. When we think of the intricate combinations of organizations of men, morale and motivation, money and machines that constitute our social, economic, physical, and psychological environments, one cannot help but wonder how it comes about that we are adjusted as well as we are. There are no concrete statistics that would demonstrate to us that mental ill health is on the increase, in spite of the fact that the proportion of hospital beds occupied because of psychological ailment is now one-half of all of the beds occupied for any reason. However, specialists on the statistics of psychological maladjustment agree that every person is mentally disturbed from time-to-time, and that this disturbance cuts down efficiency—at work, at play, in community activity, and in every phase of our behavior.

We are more likely to see this kind of maladjustment in other people than we are to see it in ourselves, since we possess, through learning, common mechanisms of a defensive kind to guard ourselves against knowledge of our psychological deficiencies. We see such deficiencies more clearly in others.

If we were to make a guess as to how much the lack of social adjustment of people to their environments detracts from the total of their efficiency, we could not help but conclude that the loss is very considerable. Could we be 10 per cent more efficient than we are? Could we be 50 per cent more efficient than we are? The amount of loss is not known because of the lack of appropriate procedures for its measurement. Precision must await the research development of more adequate techniques for observation and measurement of such losses. (Methods that are now available are discussed in Chapter 17.) And for one reason or another, perhaps because of the very defensive mechanisms that we use to guard ourselves against psychological harm, we are loathe to discuss these problems.

In an advanced orientation seminar for business executives who were studying human relations and organizational techniques at the American

Management Association, the topic of mental health of supervisors, executives, and other managers in business and industry was proposed as an appropriate topic for leader trainees. The seminar was devoted to the general subject of men, management, and machines. Some forty-five executives were asked to check their preference for ten possible topics to be used for lecture and discussion.[3] The topics included the following items: communications, human relations, organizational techniques, management and supervisory development, techniques for motivation, group dynamics, overcoming resistance to change, the use of money incentives, the relation of morale to productivity, and mental hygiene for executives. The data obtained from the preference check marks of the forty-five participants in the seminar were summarized in such a way that the different items could be ranked from most preferred to least preferred. It happened that the topic mental hygiene for executives earned the lowest rank on the list—the executives at the conference reported that they were not interested in this topic.

At this point it was thought that these executives might possibly be reluctant to indicate any possible need for instruction and discussion on the topic. The results of this little survey were made known to the respondents. It was explained that the original idea was to impart to them information about mental hygiene so that they, as leaders, could set the stage for a more meliorative environment—an environment that would be conducive to mental health—for their underlings. The instruction would be given so that they could help others, not themselves. When this became clear to the seminar members, they were again asked if they would like to have discussion on this topic. Their replies in the second survey were quite different from the first one. Mental hygiene was given a high preferred rank.

It seems that the mental hygiene topic has, in general, the aura of a taboo. People would prefer to receive information about the topic by mail, in a plain unlabelled wrapper, like sex. There is still reluctance to talk openly about mental hygiene. This situation is unfortunate. It stems perhaps from the history of beliefs of witchcraft and false starts in attempts at therapy.

Tension

The motivated person or motivated group is under a degree of tension. The field forces are such that he is not at complete equilibrium with

[3] These data were collected in collaboration with F. Kenneth Berrien and Louis Allen.

his social environment. Tension or a set of stresses between the person and his social environment may be either constructive or destructive.

Tension can be constructive, as pointed out by Anthony H. Richmond.[4] "Only in a completely static society," he says, "can conflict be completely eliminated." He points out that primitive tribes, undisturbed by outside influences and isolated from nonindigenous social contacts, remain unchanged over long periods.

If tensions and stresses upon the individual are too severe, the individual will be in a state of frustration. He cannot achieve the goal. He is unhappy. He does not have syntality. A decrease of stress might make it possible for him to achieve the goal toward which he aspires and strives, and then he would be satisfied and happy. Syntality or happiness comes only from the results of activity which is productive in the sense that needs are satisfied. A constructive tension results in syntality. A destructive tension is one which is overly strong; it results in frustrated goal-seeking behavior.

Tension may provide a conflict situation in which the person is motivated to achieve two or more goals, for example, by having membership in two or more groups which conflict with one another. Thus a public enemy, a criminal, has membership in a number of different groups, one of which might be a Sunday school group, and the other might be his gang, as in the actual case of John Dillinger. Membership in the gang may require him to rob and kill with the other members of the gang. But membership in the Sunday school group would require an opposite pattern of behavior, if he is to be an accepted and approved member. Thus this individual would have strong tensions in opposite directions. Goals are conflicting. If he achieves syntality from one group, he would be ousted from the other group; at least he would not be approved by it. Such conditions bring about conflict.

In the workplace, similar conditions sometimes exist. We may illustrate with the extreme case of an agricultural industry that was developed by new outside influences on a remote island in the South Pacific. Some of the natives are brought in to work on the plantations. Their productivity is so low that their work is unsatisfactory. They have not learned as a tribe to value money. It has no prestige value for them, and they can satisfy their physical needs by waiting for food to fall from the trees and by catching fish on the beaches. Why should they work ten hours a day on a plantation? Such work will help to satisfy

[4] Anthony H. Richmond, "Conflict and Authority in Industry," *Occupational Psychology,* XXVIII (1954), 24–33. London: National Institute of Industrial Psychology.

neither primary biological needs nor social needs. The management of the plantation would likely say that these natives are lazy savages, uncivilized, and without culture. But this is from the point-of-view of the manager of the plantation, not from the point-of-view of the natives. The manager either does not have or does not use empathy.

The plant manager may, as a destructive leader, enslave the natives, forcing them to work through a dictatorial, authoritarian approach; on the other hand, he may attempt over a long period of time to re-educate them. He may attempt to develop social needs and cultural changes in much the same way that such changes have evolved on the mainland. And this is exactly what has happened on the islands of Hawaii, for example. But more than a century was required in this "civilizing" process. Whether this process has been good or bad is a question which is beyond our scope.

Conflict

Although it is usual to view conflict as a destructive psychological force, Mary Parker Follett [5] argues for constructive conflict. Her position is that, for dynamic motivation, some degree of conflict is necessary. Some conflicts are synonymous with tension or stress as we have defined it. Conflict is the opposite of equilibrium. When some conflict does not exist in some degree there are no dynamics in the situation; then there can be no creative activity. Conflicts, then, can be either constructive or destructive.

Destructive conflict differs from constructive in two ways: severity and kind. If the conflict, like the tension or stress, is too strong, disruption, disorganization and lack of teamwork ensues. Aside from strength or amount of conflict, what kinds of conflicts are destructive and what kinds are constructive?

In a lucid technical analysis of conflict, Anthony H. Richmond [6] points out that conflicts may be either reintegrating (constructive) or disintegrating (destructive). He contrasts *manifest objectives* of the organization with *latent objectives* of the members.

Production is an example of a manifest objective of many organizations such as an industrial enterprise. Career goals of a member—to get ahead personally, regardless of the goal of the organization—is an example of a latent objective. When these two objectives are brought together

[5] Mary Parker Follett, "Constructive Conflict, An Essay in Dynamic Administration," eds. Metcalf and Urwick (Bath: Management Publications Trust, 1949).

[6] Richmond, *loc. cit.*

through reintegrative conflict with outside forces, that is, with the larger social systems and institutions, then conflict is constructive within the small organization. When manifest and latent objectives do not jibe within the smaller organization, disintegrative, destructive conflict results.

Stated simply, destructive conflict is present when the individual's goal is different from that of the organization. The "rugged individualist" is interested in the size of his share of the pie rather than in joining the organization to make a bigger pie.

Frustration and aggression

The fact remains that many conflicts and frustrations have arisen through a clash of individual and group goals. *Frustration* is defined as a psychological state resulting from interference that bars attainment of the objective of goal-directed striving. It is the opposite of syntality. In the case of the natives of Hawaii, frustrations arose from the superimposition of new motives upon old. New tension structures arose in the group which were in conflict with the old. Re-learning and re-education—a mass change of attitude—were necessary before the natives could achieve syntality, or a reasonable resolution of tensions.

Hypertension leads to frustration. Hypertension is a condition or set of forces in the social field of a person or group in which there are exceedingly strong pressures of the social kind—pressures for approval are examples. Several outcomes may stem from frustration: aggression, self-abnegation, solution.

Aggression is a name given to the condition that we so often find in the maladjusted person when he is striving for something that is impossible for him to achieve. It is an unproductive kind of behavior and does not lead to syntality on the part of its victim or the group around him; it is not favorable to mental health. Mental hygiene is concerned with aggression for this reason.

Examples of aggression are available within the experience of everyone. A youth who does not have ability to achieve college courses in engineering, perhaps because of a lack of number facility and other aspects of scholastic aptitude required in engineering courses, becomes frustrated. These handicaps are of such a nature that they are barriers to his success in engineering courses, yet this young person has a strong felt need for membership in the professional group of engineers. Vocational guidance, defined as the process of aiding him to choose, train for, enter upon and progress in an occupation, might have prevented his difficulty. It might have oriented him toward goals that he could reach.

If the young person does not have the advantages of vocational guidance counsel, if he is strongly motivated toward the goal but cannot achieve it, he runs, time and time again, headlong into the barrier, and, in the usual course of events, flunks out of college. He may become aggressive, tend to be angry with people and the world in general. He becomes morose and tends to display envy or jealousy of those people who are progressing toward this profession.

Frustration arising from conflicting goals stems in large part from the fact that everyone is a member of more than one group, each of which is attractive. Each group exerts a "pull" or, in terms of the group dynamicists, has cohesiveness.

Two goals may be equally desirable, or nearly so, but may not be mutually compatible. They may be conflicting. This is sometimes what is meant by the saying "you cannot have your cake and eat it too." This popular cliche refers to the fact of conflict. Such condition arises from membership in two groups; the two groups were incompatible in the sense that they have approved opposite kinds of patterned behavior. The two goals may have equal valence to the individual, but one of them will have a negative valence, the other a positive one to the members of the two groups. Thus arises conflict.

An anecdote is sometimes told of vacillation: a mule stands in the center of a circle; all around its circumference is a ring of fragrant hay. The mule is hungry. There is no wind blowing, no breeze to waft the fragrance more strongly from one direction than another. The goals, equally attractive, surround the mule. He remains in the center and starves to death.

A common example of this condition is a college student confronted by two classes, equally desirable, both required, both scheduled at the same time. Which shall he choose? The student has two desirable goals of equal valence. He vacillates between the two.

We might consider a case of a John Dillinger-like youth who bears strong membership ties in a Sunday school and church group and at the same time has equally strong membership bonds with a group of young hoodlums who constitute a juvenile criminal gang. This young church-going hoodlum is torn by an incompatible dual allegiance. Both groups have need for him, and he has need for them. He is interacting simultaneously with two diverse, conflicting groups. It is obvious that the activity patterns that will be elicited from him by the hoodlum gang will be diametrically opposed by the kind of behavior acceptable and approved in his church associations. After a while, a part of his energies are devoted to (a) keeping the gang from knowing about his membership in the church group and (b) trying to reconcile conflicts by aggression or rationalization. Lack of syntality, feelings of remorse and futility resulting from these conflicting valences are the outcomes.

Another type of conflict is conflicting avoidance. When a person has a choice between two alternative directions of action, each of which has approximately equal negative valence, in which direction will he go? This is sometimes called an *avoidance conflict.*

Yet another type of conflict, that of approach-avoidance, has been illustrated by reference to a child approaching a growling dog. The child reaches out to pet the dog. He seems to seek satisfaction or group syntality that comes from interaction in this peculiar group relationship. However, the dog is growling, which appears to suggest to the child that there may be danger in his approach; he vacillates. His behavior is said to be ambivalent—one of the valences in the situation is positive, the other is negative. Here resides another source of conflict in many organizations.

We may consider the example of a factory situation in which "binging" is practiced and observe the case of an employee who exceeded the informal production standards. These production standards were set by a small informal group of people who were attempting to keep down production so that they would "get ahead of" and "outsmart" the management of the formal organization. Their goal was to keep down production, and the goal of management was to keep it up. A young man, John Cadwallader, exceeded production. He forgot about this upper limit that had been informally agreed upon between the members of the small group, the group that obtained syntality by restricting production.

When John Cadwallader came in and took his position at his workbench the day after he had exceeded the informal rate standard, several of his fellow workers greeted him. The first said "Gee, you sure busted our rate yesterday." Then he "binged" him. This consisted of a half-friendly, half-warning blow on the biceps. Each man in the department greeted him the same way—first with a wisecrack and then—bing! on the muscle. John's muscle was sore, and he did not feel very much like working rapidly that day.

These men, John and his fellow workers, like the workplace. Their morale is high. They have a good time together. They enjoy playing this game on management. So when you ask them how they like their work they say, "Fine. It's a good place to work. We get by with a lot of things." They might include the last sentence in an informal, confidential, or "depth" interview. So each of these individuals would show low productivity and high satisfaction. But the satisfaction that they get is with reference to their little informal group. They are against the organization. Herein is the conflict, at first mysterious. It is hard to understand why morale and productivity, as management views it, do not go together. Many studies have shown that there is no correlation between morale and productivity when global, over-all morale is considered, operationally defined as it is measured through morale surveys.[7]

A task of the constructive leader is to rearrange the dynamics of the social situation so that goals are realigned—so that the goals of the "binging" group will be the same as the goals of the organization. All members of the collectivity could then derive syntality from the situation. Thus, in a sense, the leader's job is to create common syntality.

We may therefore see the leader as a mental hygienist who regulates situations so the activities of individuals and groups will be adjusted to one another. Conflict will be minimized; group members will act in a way that is constructive and adjusted, as contrasted to maladjusted, destructive, nonsatisfying, and stultifying behavior. The relationship between the constructive leader and the mental hygienist seems clear. Leadership is, when viewed in this way, meliorative mental hygiene.

Aggressive behavior, as we have seen, is elicited when hypermotivation is present, when the barriers that bar the individual or the group from the goal are so high that the person is unable to surmount them. This may be shown, as is done in Lewin's field theory, by a simplified diagram, as in Figure 10.1. When achievement of the goal, or syntality, which

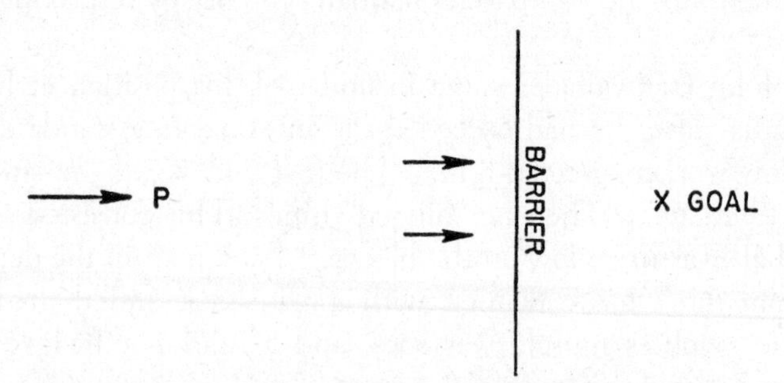

Fig. 10.1 · Goal behavior thwarted by a barrier

[7] Arthur H. Brayfield and Walter H. Crockett, "Employee Attitudes and Employee Performance," *Psychological Bulletin,* LII (1955), 396–424.

is the satisfaction of needs, cannot be achieved, conflict tensions continue. The arrow in the diagram to the left of *P* shows a strong motivational force or problem or unsatisfied need symbolizing the stress or tension of the person. The arrows to the right of *P* suggest fruitless activity: bumping into the insurmountable wall. Goal and syntality are not achieved.

This is something like giving a person a problem so difficult that he can never solve it and then giving him a strong electric shock at intervals, telling him he will receive the shock until he does solve it. If, in some mysterious circumstance, you were put into this situation and the shock that you were given was excruciatingly painful, what kind of behavior would you show? It would perhaps not be a warm or friendly kind of behavior. You would probably blame the person who got you into such a predicament. An observer might express the behavior as frustrated and hostile, but there is another aspect of this behavior which can be noticed.

The behavior that would be elicited by this predicament would probably be of a random nature. You might rant or declaim or cry out. These responses would have no apparent relation to reaching the goal; they are behavior patterns which have no rational basis. This is one of the main characteristics of frustrated behavior. It is wasteful and destructive, since it is not reaching the goal. Destructive behavior of this kind which is not goal-directed is labelled *aggressive activity.* A child, a pupil, an employee, a member of a service or church group or town meeting sometimes reverts to aggressive behavior. We refer to such acts as "angry," "disorganized," "maladjusted." The person becomes angry at his fellow group members. He might want to fight them. Hostile acts of this kind are acts of aggression. The behavior is an end in itself, not a means to an end. Maladjusted behavior is of this kind: it does not provide syntality. It is destructive behavior. It is characteristic of neurotic and psychotic people in its more extreme form.

Frustration and aggression are destructive for both the individual and the group because aggression does not further either the syntality of the person or the group. We find other examples of overmotivation and extreme tension, frustration, and aggression everywhere. A mother attempts to teach her preschool child to read before the child is ready to read. A teacher attempts to motivate a child—turn the screws down—to learn more rapidly than his ability permits. She tells him that he will surely fail if he doesn't get busy and get to work. This is hypermotivation, resulting in hypertension. Failure is embarrassing and frustrating to him because his fellow pupils will look upon him as dull; he will tend to be an outcast, a social isolate. This brings about envy and jealousy of the other pupils and often-times hatred for the teacher and for the school. It is aggressive behavior. Aggressive attitudes become generalized. When the pupil becomes a social isolate, he is maladjusted. He strives, as his attempt at solution, to join others who are like him and to whom he is acceptable. And often these are anti-social gangs who work in directions opposite from the goal of the majority groups. Juvenile delinquency is brought about often in this way.

Scapegoating is one form of aggression: this is termed "displaced aggression" by Hilgard.[8] He refers to displaced aggressive behavior of the poor whites of the South. When cotton prices decrease, aggression begins; and the Negro, who is entirely innocent in the situation, bears the brunt of the wrath of the poor whites. They blame him. And as Hilgard points out, Germany, following World War I, suffered low living standards and poor economic and social conditions. The Nazi party in both its early and late phases picked the innocent Jewish minority as a scapegoat. They blamed it, during the twenties, for their condition. Such aggressive activity was harmful and destructive.

Conflicting ethics

Conflicts arise from the facts of living. To virtually everyone, "Complete isolation is unbearable and incompatible with sanity."[9] We are social beings. There is interdependence between one person and another person, between one person and a group, between groups. Conflict arises out of this interdependence. This fact, at times, has been called the conflict between the *individualist ethic* and the *social ethic*. We are individuals and sometimes like to feel that we are self-sufficient. We should—as Horatio Alger had his fictional characters do—win our own way by our efficient intelligence and brute strength. His characters fought their way up the ladder of success to the top of our organizations. The very culture in which we learn our patterns of social behavior is brimful of conflicting teachings. A child is taught humility, righteousness, and fair play; only the meek shall inherit the earth. And at the same time he is taught to exceed, excel, to compete, to fight. The fighting spirit is what counts. Win the game. A loser is a failure.

[8] Ernest R. Hilgard, *Introduction to Psychology* (New York: Harcourt, Brace and Company, Inc., 1953), p. 185.

[9] Erich Fromm, *Man for Himself* (New York: Rinehart & Company, Incorporated, 1947), p. 58.

Similarly, our theories on human nature—particularly as they relate to child-rearing—are ambivalent. We know the immature human being as, on the one hand, a nasty monster that must be rigidly curbed for his own and society's good ("spare the rod and spoil the child") and, on the other hand, as an innocent *tabula rasa,* inherently good and reasonable, and highly amenable to control through love and explanation. Although during recorded time, one or the other of these theories has been upheld as the correct one, it seems they have existed side-by-side, providing a source of conflict for the individual at an early age. The history of philosophical thought yields two theories of social control which closely parallel these theories on human nature. Jesus emphasized the dignity of the individual and the salvation of society through care of the weak and downtrodden, the essential goodness of man who was created in God's image. Christianity points to democracy in the political sphere; Nietzsche's philosophy points to dictatorship, aristocracy, or the rule of the weak by the strong. His advice to a would-be manager:

> Beware of good natured people! Dealings with them make one torpid. All environment is good which makes one exercise those defensive and aggressive powers which are instinctive in man. All one's inventiveness should apply itself to putting one's power of will to the test. Here the determining factor must be recognized as something which is not knowledge, astuteness, or wit. One must learn to command the times,—likewise to obey.

And again, Nietzsche speaks out against John Stuart Mill,

> I abhor the man's vulgarity when he says "what is right for one man is right for another" and "do not to others that which you would not that they should do unto you." Such principles would fain establish the whole of human traffic *upon mutual services,* so that every action would appear to have a cash payment for something done to us. The hypothesis here is ignoble to the last degree . . . "reciprocity" is a piece of egregious vulgarity.[10]

Nietzsche spoke out against the Christian ethic as the code of slavish masses; he preached the brutish life, might, the morality of the strong which, for him, is above good or evil. His influence on German thought reached its zenith in Naziism, a code of the superman which did not fulfill its promise for world leadership.

Man's nature we know to be neither evil nor good. He is, rather, a psychological creature to be described by the *SPAR* factors discussed in

[10] Oscar Levy, ed., "The Complete Works of Friedrich Nietzsche," *The Will to Power* (London: The Macmillan Company, 1925), Vol. 15, Books 3–4, Part 2.

previous chapters. A constructive view of him emerges only if we view his behavior as it unfolds in his particular social climate.

That conflict as an integral part of human society is both an historical fact and a present reality no one would argue. The nature of conflict and the function of the leader relative to it are matters of time and place as well as point of view. Plato's solution was the development of inner strengths and resources and the denial of outer, crass reality: "There is no world but the world of ideas." Every man here is king. Nietzsche, on the other hand, despised the individual *per se,* seeking solutions to conflict by the application of power, the authority figure managing the masses by sheer force.

Currently, we have a picture of conflict between what William H. Whyte, Jr. has chosen to call the Protestant Ethic *versus* the Social Ethic. The Protestant Ethic, religious peruasion notwithstanding, is synonymous with the Horatio Alger American Dream emphasizing and glorifying the "sacredness of property, the enervating effect of security, the virtues of thrift, of hard work and independence."[11] The Social Ethic, according to Whyte, embodies a belief in the group as the fountainhead of productivity and the success of the individual as ultimately measured in terms of his success in achieving "belongingness" to the group. This leads only to mediocrity and the conforming "gray flannel suit" figure of big business—the organization man. The conflict arises, Whyte believes, in our giving lip service to the Protestant Ethic while becoming progressively more stultified by the Social Ethic.

We have seen that one aspect of leadership is mental hygiene. Frustration decreases team efficiency. Mental hygiene is the art of arranging the situation so that frustrations are lessened and teamwork is increased. We continue discussion of this role of the leader in the next chapter.

[11] William H. Whyte, Jr., *The Organization Man* (New York: Simon and Shuster, 1956), p. 5. This author is not to be confused with William Foote Whyte whose viewpoints and research approaches are quite different.

*

We are not only gregarious animals, liking to be in sight of our fellows, but we have an innate propensity to get ourselves noticed, and noticed favorably, by our kind. WILLIAM JAMES

11

Conflict and leadership

The effective leader will try to understand individuals not only in terms of the conflicts present in the social environment, but also in terms of psychological defenses or mechanisms commonly resorted to as safety valves to relieve severe tensions. We will now consider defense mechanisms used to resolve conflict and to maintain psychological and social adjustment.

Defense against conflict

One set of psychological facts of importance in leadership is concerned with the psychological phenomena which we call "mechanisms for defense." These are part of the psychological equipment—the make-up—of each of us. These are simply ways which we have learned to preserve our own dignity. The Japanese say "saving face." These phenomena are bound up with our needs for group membership, approval by others, approbation and social rewards: the system of social needs that we have discussed in a previous section. The fact that we are usually unaware of the operation of these mechanisms presents a difficulty in assessing their importance for an individual at any particular time. They are emotionally toned and not immediately accessible to intellectual observation by the individual.

These mechanisms consist of self-deception in either the form of denial or disguise. We may deny certain facts in order to preserve our dignity or disguise them in a way that makes them more palatable. Defense mechanisms may be either positive or negative, beneficial or harmful. For the most part, these forms of psychological activity are beneficial. They are harmful only when carried to such an extreme or abnormal degree that they interfere with handling affairs, our own and those of a group, with ordinary prudence. The first, and perhaps the one most often observed in ourselves and others, is *rationalization*. Its common form is called "sour grapes." The child wants the grapes, reaches for them, finds that they are out of reach, and deceives himself by prematurely saying the grapes are sour and he didn't want them anyhow. A mother sees her school child defeated in a spelling match. Concluding that there are many other things in life more important than expertness in spelling, she says that she is really glad her child is not a bookworm. She may go farther and say that the child makes up for his lack of spelling ability by being very good in arithmetic. Here is a combination of rationalization and another defense mechanism known as *compensation*. The child allegedly compensates for the lack of one ability with great proficiency in another area.

A somewhat less common form of defense mechanism is called *projection*. The term is used in several contexts. Its present context is different from that in which the term was used in Chapter 9. There, its meaning was the opposite of empathy; here it refers to a mechanism of defense. In projection, the individual thinks of himself as similar to a person whom he respects and admires. Thus a boy projects himself into the behavior of his father or his teacher. The employee projects himself into the role of the foreman; the executive projects himself into the role of president of the company.

Regression, as a defense mechanism, involves resorting to behavior appropriate to an earlier (simpler?) stage in our development. "You're acting just like a baby" is a lay description of regressive phenomena.

When employees complain in inordinate and unreasonable ways about working conditions, such complaining may be a mild form of regressive behavior. Either crying, slandering, or unreasonable complaining helps the person to relieve frustration. But such activities tend to cause others to dislike the person. This leads to a state of social isolation, so that such behavior results in an even more frustrated condition than before. We see here a spiral of episodes which may end in maladjustment.

Resignation is a state of "giving up." The person resigns himself to his fate. He stops trying to do anything at all. In one of its extreme or ultimate forms, it is known by specialists of abnormal behavior as catatonic schizophrenia. It is a final stage in frustration in which the person simply stops interacting; he even loses the ability to take care of his most simple needs. He leads a vegetative existence.

Repression is the mechanism for the convenient and expeditious forgetting of things that are unpleasant or frustrating to us. This tendency may be so strong in some people that it is impossible for them to remember any details of a recent unpleasant event. A boy may be embarrassed in a group of people when he suddenly bursts into the room with incorrect or incongruous clothing. He backs awkwardly out of the room and the next week is unable to recall any details of his recent predicament. Memory of the event has been repressed.

Another and perhaps most significant form of defense mechanism is *sublimation* or *substitution.* Here the defensive person substitutes an achievable goal for one that cannot be achieved. This is avoidance of prolonged frustration in the grand manner. It can be a healthful form of defense. It brings about adjustment often in the most effective manner. Freud and his followers have based the theory and practice of psychoanalysis largely on sublimation, the substitution of one goal for another. All behavior according to Freud and some of his followers is in the beginning grounded in the sex drive which he terms "libido." But in our society, behavior cannot obtain an outlet directly in the sex act because of mores, customs, taboos, and the resulting social pressures, so the individual learns to sublimate. He substitutes socially appropriate goal behavior. Barnyard behavior, not acceptable in the drawing room, is changed through the shifting goals to acceptable forms of behavior such as ballroom dancing, card playing, conversation, and other important forms of life activity such as study, work, community activities, church affiliations, and current events. Thus, Freud would interpret adapted, organized behavior as a sublimated form of a primitive drive—a rather extreme view indeed.

In any case, whether or not we adhere closely to the somewhat bizarre views of Freud, we see substitution in our own behavior and in behavior of the people around us. To be sure, we do not observe it as sublimation in the Freudian sense, but we may see it if we observe it closely, as shifting goals in terms of circumstances. We have seen in other sections of this book that striving for achievement of social goals can bring about frustration; that if barriers are high and goals are strong, the only courses of action left for the individual are appropriate substitution or maladjustment.

Our defense may take the form of flights from reality. The crux of the matter is how readily we make the return trip to our everyday problems. All of us indulge to some extent in phantasy and daydreaming. This defense mechanism is operating when we imagine that in a meeting with a friend we said those right things we actually didn't say at all; when we think of ourselves ten years hence as a head of the company or a revered leader in the community, as the President of the United States; or when we have, in a dream, achieved our fondest career goals; or when we indulge in reverie, looking back over some period in life, changing the outcomes, making ourselves the hero, the one approved above all others.

In extreme cases, these flights take the form of dissociation in which a person ceases to interact successfully with other persons and with his environment: he lives in his own private world. "Nobody likes me" leads to "people are no good" which may, in turn, lead to withdrawal from society. Delusions of grandeur as well as the delusions of persecution of the paranoid schizophrenic are examples of dissociation in which the individual has parted company with reality and in which this separation remains in effect over a long period of time. Paranoid schizophrenics are said to result from complete loss of self-respect, loss of dignity, the feeling of despair and panic, of not belonging to any group —the feeling of utter and complete failure.[1]

Our account of dissociation or extreme maladjustment may not be amiss for two reasons. First, in leadership situations such cases are encountered, although quite infrequently. Second, this consideration is worthwhile for a reason suggested by specialists in the fields concerned with understanding behavior: we can get insights into the more normal

[1] Of the 150,000 people who enter state or private mental hospitals for the first time each year, 20 per cent, or nearly 30,000, are diagnosed as schizophrenic, and a share of these are of the paranoid type.

behavior patterns by considering the abnormal. This cursory account is in no sense designed to cover the various aspects and complexities of abnormal psychological phenomena.

A relationship has been known to exist between maladjustment and lack of effectiveness of social interaction among the psychologically abnormal, such as the psychotic. Does this relationship exist with more normal people? This question has been answered for us in a study by Fine, Fulkerson, and Phillips.[2] For their first measure [3] they used a score derived from three aspects of social attainment: educational and occupational achievement, maturity and responsibility in the area of sex and marriage, and participation and adequacy in social relations.

For their second psychological maladjustment measure, the investigators used a Rorschach index developed by Fisher.[4] They obtained these two measures—social efficiency and psychological maladjustment—for a sample of 74 normal community members. The sample consisted of male factory workers, white-collar workers and foremen: people who would be considered as fairly well adjusted. The measuring instruments used were sufficiently sensitive to differentiate these people in terms of amount or degree on both variables.

The results of their study indicated "a highly significant relationship" between degree of maladjustment and social attainment, including interpersonal relations, as measured.

This conclusion suggests only that adequacy in participation and group membership by normal people is tied to freedom from maladjustment. It does not tell us directly that there is necessarily a causal relation between the two. The likelihood is implied, however, since the two variables go together, that a change in one variable would result in a change in the other, that is, if psychological adjustment is increased, then higher social attainment, participation in group activities, and more appropriate personal interaction would result.

Hypermotivation

An individual attempting to come to terms with his social environment often is not aware of his own limitations. The social pressures may be so strong upon him that he finds himself striving toward a goal that, for him, is impossible. Under these conditions defense mechanisms are

[2] Harold J. Fine, Samuel C. Fulkerson, and Leslie Phillips, "Maladjustment and Social Attainment," *Journal of Abnormal and Social Psychology,* L (1955), 33–35.

[3] This measure had been developed by L. Phillips and B. Cowitz, "Social Attainment and Reactions to Stress," *Journal of Personnel,* XXII (1953), 270–83.

[4] S. Fisher, "Patterns of Personality Rigidity and Some of Their Determinents," *Psychological Monographs,* LXIV (1950) No. 1. (Whole No. 307).

sometimes brought into play, sometimes substitute goals are set up either by accident or design. The leader can serve, through his understanding, by redesigning the situation to adjust tension. Several life illustrations follow.

Martha, a member of a church congregation, aspires to become a singer in the choir. Her parents are eager for Martha to sing in the choir and have encouraged her; they have used a number of different approaches to motivate her. She had a trial audition, and it was judged that her voice was inadequate for choir singing. It would have been discovered, had she been tested by a musical talent test, that her tonal memory and rhythm scores were so low that she could not possibly make a singer.

When she was turned down as a choir member, she had a strong feeling of rejection and frustration. It appeared that Martha was neither able to rationalize this failure nor to readjust to the situation and set up new aspirations. It happened that she had had training on the piano and was considered a fair pianist. Some additional training at the organ would have enabled her to become a passable organist. She claimed that she was not interested in playing the organ—only in the choir.

A man, John C., had for some years been a member of a service club, the Kiwanis, of a small city. He was well received by some of the members. There were several cliques in the club. He was not recognized as a very efficient person by the board of directors or by the president. He aspired to be a member of the board of directors, but each time he approached one of the directors on the matter he was put off. He had been trying hard for several years. His eagerness placed him in an awkward relationship with the directors. Mr. C.'s failure to achieve his aspiration caused frustration, so that he began to lose even the relationship that he had enjoyed with one of the cliques. He began to feel outcast. Instead of working diligently on the committees of the organization, he began to get the reputation of "trying to play politics all the time to get to be a director, and doing nothing constructive." The thought that he had been a failure in the club began to haunt him. And not having mechanisms for justifying to himself his apparent failure, he was morose, dissatisfied, and unhappy. Tensions were too strong, motivation was too much, aspirations were too high; he couldn't adjust himself. He became frustrated and aggressive.

A girl, Ruth G., was applying for a position as card punch operator in the comptroller's office of a large production organization. She was highly motivated to get this position and to perform successfully in it.

Her older sisters had been working while she completed her course, a commercial curriculum, in high school. She did not have much clerical ability but felt that she did have good finger dexterity. The company trained card punch operators for three weeks before they put them on productive work. The policy of the organization was to use aptitude tests for the selection of the trainees. These tests did not include achievement measurement, and no experience was necessary for the position. However, a certain level of performance on the aptitude test battery, which consisted, in part, of the Minnesota Vocational Test for Clerical Workers, number-checking and name-checking, was required. This test had been found by the company personnel research people to be relatively highly valid to predict the success of trainees—those who made high scores on the test also tended to finish the training course and to become high producing workers on the job.

It happened that Miss G. had obtained a copy of the test form from a friend of hers whose brother worked in the employment office, and she practiced for some hours on the test before she went to the employment office to be examined. This practice gave her a significant advantage over the other examinees, so that her test scores placed her in the upper 10 per cent of employees now working there. The employment office said that she had about 9 chances out of 10 of becoming a highly proficient worker; her test scores indicated that she would most likely be in the upper third in terms of errorless productivity on the job after six months of training and experience.

Ruth made borderline progress as a card punch operator trainee. She learned the card punch operations from the standpoint of the manual and finger dexterity involved fairly readily; however, she failed in the tests which measured achievement of coding speed and accuracy. The training supervisor was mystified at Ruth's poor performance on the clerical part of the training. Learning coding skills should have been easy for her, judging by her test scores. Little did he know that she had the doubtful advantage of having had practice on the test before she took it at the employment office. The placement officer finally recommended, with some misgivings, that she be tried out in the job.

She was placed on the job and became a member of a clique of girls in the card punch operating group. She was, at first, quite well received and became friends with several of the girls. However, her work did not progress. She seemed to reach a plateau after the second week and could not get above this, no matter how hard she tried. At the end of the fourth week she was producing approximately one half as many errorless cards per hour as the average of the girls who had graduated from the training course at about the same time she had graduated. At a conference between the key punch operator pool supervisor, placement officer, the testing examiner in the employment office, and the personnel research technician who served the company, it was decided that she simply did not have the ability to go forward in the job. They decided to relieve Miss G. of her duties and to pay her two weeks termination pay. This committee decided that she was one of the rare cases of failure for no apparent reason. They had never seen a girl who made such high aptitude test scores fall so far below the group.

Needless to say, Ruth felt sorry for herself. She was in a highly frustrated condition. At the time of the exit interview she broke down and cried before the exit interviewer, telling him that she felt that she had a fair trial, but that she just couldn't do the work. She did not, however, reveal to him that she had practiced on the aptitude tests before the aptitude examination was given her at the employment office. The net result was: Miss G. had wasted several months of her time and left with frustrated, maladjusted attitudes and reactions toward society, attitudes which developed into aggressive behavior. For the company, there was tangible loss of several hundred dollars in terms of employment, training, and related turnover costs and possibly intangible loss in morale and satisfaction of employees and supervisors.

Leadership applications

If we define the leader role as one which arranges the situation so that the activities of a group may go forward in a shared direction, we might look at a new case, and the examples just given, which are concerned with hypermotivation, to see whether a constructive leader might have arranged the situation somewhat differently. What would be involved in the home situation in which the mother is forcing the child of preschool age to learn to read before the child is ready? The mother in a creative leadership role could have recognized her error of motivating the child too strongly. Seeing the hypertension and resulting frustration, she might have directed the energies of her child and herself into more appropriate channels, for example, finger painting, simple clay modeling, or picture recognition games. In modern school systems, a school psychologist is generally available to advise parents—not only those who are members of the Parent-Teacher Association, but others in the community —concerning management of learning. This mother could have discovered the facts concerning reading readiness and, by playing the role of an understanding leader, could have saved her child from these early frustrating experiences. Perhaps the fault was with the community. If adequate leadership were present, facilities for advising mothers might have been made available to her; instead, through ignorance, she created tensions in her child.

Similarly, in the case of Martha, who aspired to sing in the choir at her church, conditions could have been arranged to provide a situation which would not have resulted in the extreme frustration that the girl experienced in failure. But the parents were not constructive leaders in this case—they motivated the girl in a way that did not take into account her potentiality. Thus the parents and the girl as well as the community were losers in the situation. No satisfaction was achieved anywhere because nothing useful was produced. Had the direction of goal-seeking been slightly shifted toward practice and achievement as a choir organist, the girl might have provided some degree of syntality and satisfaction for herself and the various persons that were involved in this interaction.

In the case of John C., the service club member, similar principles apply. Here is a case in which the directors, or one of them, could have counseled Mr. C., who aspired to a directorship in the club. It is probable that a real contribution to the syntality of John C. and others in the organization could have been made had a leader played the role of counselor and arranged the situation so that John could have shifted his goal from immediate member of the board of directors to a functioning, contributing, and valuable member of one of the committees. The man was trying too hard; no one advised him through nondirective, permissive discussion, and counseling.

In the case of Miss G., the card punch operator aspirant, it is evident that the machinery for constructive leadership had been set up but that it did not work in this particular case. The program for aptitude testing, selection of trainees, training and placement of trainees on the job was somewhat more mechanical than human. Little personal contact between the individual and manager of this work situation was provided. Rather, decisions were made only on the basis of quantitative test scores.

If it had been possible to provide and plan for orientation counseling, the end result might have been different. The use and purposes of aptitude tests and the fact that the aptitude test system had been set up as much for the applicant as for management might have been explained to applicants and employees. It is doubtful whether Miss G. would have prepared for the selection tests in an illicit, undercover manner if there had been mutual understanding of their purposes. It is clear that she did not understand the purposes of aptitude tests. She probably looked upon them simply as a hurdle to surmount before she could be on her way to her chosen career as a card punch operator.

However, what of the many companies that have not progressed in their human relations program to a point where they have screening tests? And roughly half of the companies do not provide such aptitude test screening services. In most companies, there is no available method to prevent frustration from overplacement. Usually, hit-or-miss, rule-of-thumb methods are used. Employee selection and job placement without the aid of predictive techniques, which normally worked well in this company, engender frustration and dissatisfaction as well as lack of efficiency. Creative leadership requires use of all available human relations methods.

In each of these cases—Martha, the aspiring singer; Mr. C., aspirant to the board of directors; and Miss G., who wanted to be a card punch operator—more creative leadership was needed.

The method of the leader would seem to be, first, situational analysis. This was discussed and illustrated in chapters 5 and 6. Through observation, discussion, counseling, and study of the situation, the leader ascertains what the forces are which cause members of the group to behave as they do; he is objectively dealing with a situation. He is formulating insights and plans for coping with it. It is hoped he can do this with the participation of the group.

Again pointing to the classic studies at the Hawthorne Plant of the Western Electric Company, frustrated behavior of a junior executive was found, upon analysis of the situation, to be brought about by the simple fact that the junior executive had been assigned a single pedestal desk when others of the group, his peers, had double pedestal desks. The solution to this problem was a simple one; it involved only a change in furniture. However, the background factors behind most cases are more subtle and complex. Some of these may involve changes in the person; others, changes in group members; still others may entail changes in group member relationships.

An anecdote [5] may be recalled of a little boy whose teacher considered him a problem child and trouble maker. He had fights with other children and created disturbances in the class. The teacher was understanding. She decided that the child was probably frustrated, as she knew

[5] Told to the writer by Allen R. Solem.

his home life was unhappy and that his parents quarrelled in his presence.

This is what she did about it: She had the child go down to a room in the school basement where there was a large pile of old tin cans. She gave him a little mallet and encouraged him to flatten the tin cans so that they could more easily be hauled away to the junk yard. The boy pounded and flattened tin cans furiously for about an hour. After that he felt better and came back to the classroom smiling and quite happy. Thereafter, whenever the child was hostile in the classroom the teacher would ask him if he would like to flatten some more tin cans. She let him express his hostility in a harmless way.

Perhaps one of the best ways to relieve frustration is to permit harmless aggression by the listening technique: encouraging a person or group to talk out their feelings. As in the counseling interview, this is a technique used by nondirective leaders. Frustrated behavior is stubborn and hostile, and it has as part of its background stubborn and hostile attitudes. The leader in counseling in the nondirective style does two things: he establishes a bond of communication and understanding with the person, and he also enables the person to feel that an understanding person is listening. This is the same as saying that there is interaction and syntality. Through this understanding the leader is able to get insights into the problem which enable him to rearrange the frustrated person's interaction patterns and to articulate him with others in the group. The constructive leader who uses the counseling interview learns about the factors which are causing the frustration. These are usually found to be concerned with the relationships of the person to members of the group to which he belongs. Such counseling interviews sometimes take a long time; they may require a number of sessions to get depth of understanding. This technique is considered in detail later on in Chapter 16.

In our set of *SPAR* concepts in Chapter 8 we referred to the person *P*, immersed in a total social environmental situation: we referred to the activity *A*, which this set of conditions elicited, and the results of this activity, the *R* of the set of concepts. Frustrated behavior is an activity that can best be described in terms of the *SPAR* set of concepts. We need to approach the complex phenomena of maladjusted behavior from an analytical, objective viewpoint.

The implication for leadership seems clear: the leader may give attention to conditions which reduce hypertension, frustration, and aggression with benefit to the group. Although he cannot control the past environments of the group with which he is concerned, he can contribute to improved present and future adjustment by establishing meliorative conditions in the present social environment. And, broadly considered, if each leader during the life history of present team members had given attention to mental hygiene factors, we could hope for more effective social interaction and teamwork.

This chapter has dealt with conflict and psychological defense viewed from a mental hygiene point of view. In developing insights about groups and the individuals who compose them, a leader may utilize this information to further personal and social adjustment. Chapter 12 discusses attitudes, their learned aspects and durability, prejudice, and attitude change.

*

Every day and every hour we are engaged in accommodating our changed and unchanged selves to changed and unchanged surroundings . . . when we give up the attempt we die. . . . SAMUEL BUTLER

12

Attitude change

What is it that determines a response? This is what concerns the leader—he wants to arrange the situation so that he can predict and control the activity of a group to achieve group goals. A naïve view is that the determiner of activity is inside the person. The word *attitude* is a term used by laymen and psychologists alike in referring to this determination. We use the term attitude to stand for regulating forces. Here it is necessary for us to guard against the nonproductive principle of "naming versus describing." In seeking those forces which lead to the activity on the part of the person or group and determine its course, it is all too easy for us to fall into the fallacy of naming the phenomenon and then not describing it.

Actually scores of different terms have been used to designate this regulator; there has been a long history of attempts to describe it.[1] Names such as *Aufgabe,* "psychological set," "anticipation," and "posture" have been used. Philosophers have sometimes suggested that man has a vital spark within him, an *élan vitale.* The nature of this impalpable mental content or force has been mysterious to philosophers, associationists, and personal psychologists, as well as behaviorists, throughout the centuries. An attitude differs from a set and from a motive. A set is considered as a highly specific temporary regulator of behavior; it regulates activity in a particular current situation. Attitudes, on the other hand, are somewhat more durable regulators. An attitude is a predisposition to patterned activity which has been learned and is thus tied to the history of the individual.

Attitudes deserve the degree of attention and emphasis in our consideration of leadership that *P,* the person, deserves. But this is only one aspect of the conditions which engender adjusted, efficient team behavior. We must bear in mind that the situational dynamic tensions or valances of a group are also regulators. An attitude predisposes an individual to certain kinds of activity within the tolerance of these forces.

This chapter is concerned with attitude formation, attitude change and resistance to change. It includes discussion of opinion and prejudice as aspects of attitude. Attitudes, being learned, can be changed. Some leadership procedures for changing attitudes are considered briefly here and in greater detail in the next several chapters.

Durability of attitudes

How permanent are attitudes? Can they be changed quickly by changing the social atmosphere that pervades a home, office, factory, a school situation, or a town meeting?

We may turn again to the classical Hawthorne Plant, Western Electric Company studies. Behavioral scientists were brought into the situation by the engineers who were confronted by mysterious increases in productivity. The behavioral scientists decided that the explanation of the increase was to be found in attitude changes of the employees.

[1] For example, G. W. Allport, "Attitudes," *Handbook of Social Psychology,* ed. Carl Murchinson (Worcester, Mass.: Clark University Press, 1935), Chapter 17; see also J. F. Dashiell, "A Neglected Fourth Dimension to Psychological Research," *The Psychological Review,* XLVII (1940), 289–305; W. Edgar Vinacke, *The Psychology of Thinking* (New York: McGraw-Hill Book Company, Inc., 1952), p. 18.

The engineers were concerned with the way productivity was affected by aspects such as illumination, rest pauses, and length of workday. A group of skilled girl employees who had been working in the large assembly room at coil-winding benches were put on the same kind of jobs in a special experimental room. They worked with the same materials and tools and produced the same products as those in the larger room. The job was set up in such a way that they took many small parts and assembled them into an electrical relay and then dropped the finished relay into a box. The amount of production was measured in terms of number of finished relays per day. A continuous record of production was maintained.

Working conditions in the special experimental room were somewhat different from those in the large assembly room. In the test room the length of the workday was varied, as was the number and duration of rest pauses. Another difference in the experimental room was that instead of many girls working in a large room under the direction of a foreman, five girls worked under the direction of an observer. The observer was not a foreman, nor did he try to act like one. Instead of giving orders, he saw his job as that of keeping supplies on hand and getting the cooperation of the girls. He encouraged the girls to talk about any problems they had in connection with the job.

A number of experimental phases were set up by the engineers. Each phase lasted from two to about thirty-two weeks. At intervals the conditions under which the girls worked were systematically changed, so that for one month they were given one fifteen-minute rest pause during morning and afternoon; then for another three weeks they were given the same amount of rest, but it was broken into three five-minute periods. Also other conditions were varied, such as length of workday, giving the girls morning and afternoon refreshments, such as coffee and a sandwich. The production of the girls increased. At the end of the seventh experimental period, the original working conditions were restored.

One would expect that if changes in lighting, rest pauses, and refreshments were responsible for increased production, then reinstatement of original conditions would tend to cause production to return to its original level. However, when the original conditions were reinstated, production was considerably higher than it had been at the outset, even though there was no reason to believe that the girls had any greater skill than they had at the beginning. This result was surprising to the engineers, so they continued varying the conditions and found that there was little relationship between the engineering changes made and the amount that the girls produced. No matter what observable factors were varied, production continued to increase. And at the last experimental period, the productivity of the five girls had increased from an average of about 48 units an hour to more than 66 units an hour, where it leveled off. This was a very large increase in production, which could not be accounted for by variations in the workroom factors being studied.

Enter, behavioral scientists. The experimenters concluded that some as yet unknown factor or forces were responsible for increased productivity. They asked behavioral scientists to study the problem. Emphasis was now placed on attitude changes and the nature of the social rather than the physical environment of the experimental room. It was found that changes in the attitudes of the girls were taking place; they reported a pleasant, relaxed feeling in the experimental room; they had more freedom as to what they did and how fast they worked. They said that by working with the observer instead of the previous foreman they felt that they were being helped and that there was more "consideration" and approbation.

They of course did not use such terms as change in the social climate; they did not report that their needs were being satisfied; but they did say that a friendly feeling had been developed, both toward one another and toward the supervisor. One girl, when she wasn't feeling very well, said that the others were exceptionally cooperative and would do more work to make up for her slower production. When a girl wanted to do some shopping or run an errand by taking a longer lunch period, the other girls would do extra work, so that the production of the unit held up.

There was group feeling. This was not present in the large assembly room. The change in attitude was reflected in syntality of this small interacting, cohesive group. The girls sensed that they were participating in an important activity, that the company had a special interest in them, as they were being shown attention which they had not previously experienced. They reacted favorably. The behavioral scientists concluded that the changes in attitude were responsible for the increase in syntality of thc group.

What we say about the treatment that we receive or about conditions that surround us is to a large extent determined by our attitude, which in turn is a part of our psychological make-up—the *P* aspect of *SPAR* as discussed in the previous chapters.

Several examples from situations at home, school, work, and community further illustrate the role of attitude change in leadership. In the home, the mother has the job of creative leader. She hopes to engender a spirit of teamwork on the part of other members of the family group. She hopes that they will be satisfied with her efforts in the kitchen and in managing the household. The husband's responses toward the wife's efforts will tend to show approval or disapproval in terms of his attitude. But we think of the wife and mother as a leader who arranges the situation so that there is high syntality, shared satisfaction in living together; and that leadership is not a thing of force, power or influence that is created by one person alone.

The husband is also to be considered as a leader. He, too, arranges the situation so that high syntality—group productivity and satisfaction—is the result of team activity. He shares the leadership of the family group. When attitudes are right, acceptance and approval come from interaction. The mother indulges in activities that are concerned with the development of the children. If she has a wholly disciplinary, inconsiderate approach, hostility, aggression, and other forms of uncooperative behavior may appear. Lack of communicative interactions, of *rapport* and "we" feeling characterize the family group that is deficient in creative leadership.

The teacher maintains a number of relationships which include the principal, other teachers, pupils, and parents. Her greatest amount of time is spent in contact with the pupils. Her task as a creative leader is to arrange the situation so that academic progress on the part of her pupils will result. Her objective is the achievement of each child's highest potential. She can approach this objective in one of two ways. If she approaches it in a disciplinary, authoritarian manner she develops an attitude of either passive acceptance or active resistance. There is little mutual understanding. The goals of the teacher are not the goals of the pupils. The pupils are in one "we" group, and the teacher is an isolate. The teacher may be "in" with the principal, top management, or the administration, in which case she would be comparable to the production- or management-oriented supervisor. She would not be comparable to the creative leader in business and industry, shop, office, and factory. The attitudes and behavior tendencies of the pupils designate the way they will accept the efforts of the teacher. Her leadership style helps determine their attitudes.

In the office and shop, employees have various attitudes toward such things as pay, working conditions, food in the cafeteria, the closeness of inspection, their supervisor, overtime, merit rating or performance review program, safety program, and the training program. An illustrative attitude survey and its results were outlined in detail in Chapter 6 in connection with the discussion of social needs of such groups. Employees have an unfavorable attitude toward the pay they receive if they have a generally unfavorable attitude toward supervision. If the worker group in a union shop has a high degree of cohesiveness, and the union takes the stand that the pay is too low, then the worker reaction toward pay would tend to be unfavorable.

On the other hand, if the union and management have agreed amicably at the bargaining table on a job evaluation method and the contract, and the union tells its members that the rates are fair, equitable and agreed upon, then the attitude of the employees toward their pay would tend to be favorable. In a situation without a labor union, if management has worked out the detailed decisions by participation with the employees in job evaluation and pay rate policies and procedures, then the employees would tend to have a favorable attitude toward pay; but if management has neglected participation of the employees in setting pay rates, attitudes would tend to be unfavorable.

If multiple management, that is, participative leadership, is entirely foreign to the enterprise, and pay rates are set without the employees knowing how or why they were set, then we would expect an unfavorable attitude. Attitudes of employees are favorable in proportion to the amount of mutual understanding coupled with feeling of mutual goals. Mutual understanding and mutual goals may be engendered by participative, permissive, considerate, democratic approaches; unfavorable attitudes toward conditions in the workplace are likely to be engendered under the authoritarian or autocratic style of direction and organization in which there is no permissiveness, no toleration of suggestions, no sharing of management, no mutual arrangements.

A town meeting tends to be a cohesive group not only if it is based upon the philosophy of democracy, but if the participative style is used as a basis for leadership. However, such meetings are not as likely to lend themselves to creative activities for the common good if one man or a small clique becomes powerful, perhaps as a result of democratic processes, and switches over to the autocratic, authoritative style.

It sometimes happens that a person duly elected through democratic procedures becomes an autocrat. This is true in the case of the spoils system, where a successful politician has power to pass out jobs and rewards for loyalty. He then can wield influence, as the traditional autocrat does, through sanctions—punishment and rewards—*if* the individuals and groups within the organization respond in the way that he wants them to respond. As shown in Chapter 2, "The Poverty of Authority," his power and its institutionalized authority depend upon their acceptance. Authority, by definition, cannot exist if it is not accepted. An order is not an order in the complete sense unless it is received and carried out. If obeyed, an authoritarian order becomes completed when it *per se* becomes a guide to the behavior of the receiver. Theirs is not to reason, but to follow orders. The authoritarian establishes control over behavior by limiting understanding of those led and offering no choice of goals. The authoritarian goal is not the goal of the group but rather the goal of a particular individual. This is the kind of control characteristic of a dictator, a dishonest politician, a fascist, or a communist.

Attitudes are learned. Attitudes are behavior tendencies which are learned. They are learned "through experience." The experiences which teach us most are those that are important or vivid to us. They determine our future attitudes. A child experiences fright in a dark place; he develops an attitude of fear, a predisposition to a behavior pattern. This attitude manifests itself in certain kinds of patterned behavior such as trembling, screaming, running to hide, or simply wanting sympathy from his mother. A child is not innately afraid of the dark. Rather, *"A great source of terror in infancy is solitude."* [2] If the child in the school has an unpleasant experience with his teacher, if an employee has an unfavorable experience with the company, it is quite likely that an unfavorable attitude will be developed toward the teacher or toward the supervisor and the company. A negative behavior tendency is thereby established. Such experiences are unpleasant because they do not contribute to, but rather hinder, the satisfaction of social needs.

We may consider pleasant experiences to have, in general, the opposite effect. If a teacher is kind to a child, the child may develop a favorable attitude toward teachers and school in general. Similarly, a supervisor who provides pleasant experiences on the job will tend to create favorable attitudes toward the company as a whole. These illustrations suggest the simple effect of experience on the formation of attitudes. Our social environment, the *S* of *SPAR*, is an important factor in shaping our attitudes.

Persons are not usually aware of the genesis of their attitudes. When we have a national election, roughly half of the people usually vote one way as Democrats, and about half vote the other way as Republicans.

[2] William James, *Psychology*, 1892.

Why should this be the case? Persons in a particular age group have a greater tendency to vote for one party. The facts of income, geographical region of residence, whether residence is in a large city, a village, or the country, occupation, and other factors are related to political attitude which, in turn, is reflected in activity at the polls. The voter himself is often unaware of the ingredients of his particular political attitude. He may say he "studied it out" and just voted for "the right man and the right party." In his case, "right" may be the party his father supported or that of his neighbor, a much-admired bank president. Although our attitudes emerge from our background, experiences, and learning, we are not commonly aware of their origins. Our tendency is to intellectualize them, deny, in essence, their existence as determiners of behavior in favor of "considered judgment" or "the normal way."

Opinion and prejudice

The *opinion* of a person is only slightly different from his attitude. An opinion might be said to be made up partly of our attitudes and partly of the facts that reside in the situation. Some opinions are formed largely from facts; others may be formed largely of attitudes, as illustrated in Figure 12.1. Opinion *A* in the figure is based somewhat on fact but largely on attitude. Opinion *B* is half and half, whereas opinion *C* is more factual. It is based largely on fact and somewhat on attitude.

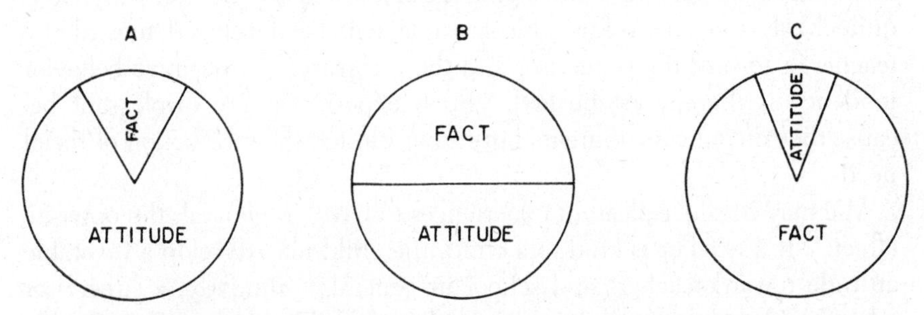

Fig. 12.1 · Opinions consist of attitudes and facts in varying amounts

Prejudices are opinions that are made up largely of attitudes and very little fact. A prejudice is to be contrasted with an opinion based largely on facts, as shown in circle *C*, Figure 12.1. Prejudice is illustrated by a glance at Figure 12.2.

Prejudice contains only a negligible ingredient of fact. The word *prejudice* stems from "prejudgment," and most students of this phenomenon have defined it in this way: prejudice is a predisposition to action which involves judgment of a person, thing, or situation before the facts are in.

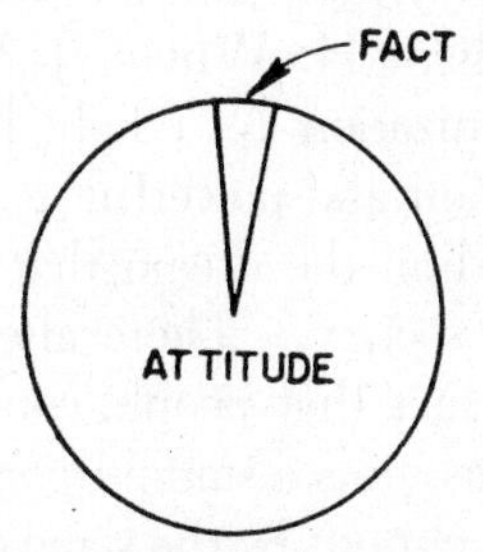

Fig. 12.2 · Prejudice contains a small amount of fact

Prejudices are emotionally toned and often fallacious. In addition to those we pick up unintentionally from our immediate environment—prejudices about racial, religious, and economic groups for example—we lug around some foisted upon us intentionally. They are invoked by social labels, propaganda, and advertising—manipulative techniques which appeal to emotions to change attitudes and responses. Hitler wanted to build up prejudice. He maintained in *Mein Kampf* that a public speech could more readily develop prejudices if it were given at night when the "will" of the audience was less strong than in the daytime.[3] His aim was to weaken the will, the force of his listeners. He wanted to do this when they were lulled, when they did not have "full command of their energies and their willpower." The philosophy of the destructive executive or dictator is to view followers as weaklings, without will or intellect strong enough to participate in decision-making or to combat his influences. The felt need for development of prejudice through manipulation underlines the "poverty of authority." It is a technique used by those who would bend the activities of groups throughout their organization to the benefit of themselves.

It is easy for the dictator or the destructive executive, administrator, or supervisor to rationalize such techniques as being in the interest of the people. "Any excuse will serve a tyrant."[4] The philosophy of Friedrich W. Nietzsche in his "Will to Power" illustrates this plainly. Most men, he believed, are weaklings who realize their weaknesses and their need for strong direction. They want to be slaves under the domination of a powerful dictator; therefore, all good stems from power. This is not the kind of leadership that assists a group or organization to serve the

[3] Adolf Hitler, *Mein Kampf* (New York: Renyal and Hitchcock, Inc., 1939), p. 710.

[4] Aesop, "The Wolf and the Lamb," 550 B.C.

community. There is in our culture today, as pointed out in Chapter 11, conflict between the individual and an outside power—the organization, as depicted by William H. Whyte, Jr.[5] The organization man ". . . must *fight* the organization . . . fight he must, for the demands for his surrender are constant and powerful . . . it is wretched, dispiriting advice to hold before him the dream that ideally there need be no conflict between him and society. There always is; there always must be." Whyte decries the fact that people conform to the organization. The organization, he claims, puts a stamp upon its members so that they appear as if each had been cut out by the same cookie cutter. Their uniform is the gray flannel suit; they work for the team. They are organization men. They are a group of mediocre Milquetoasts who have no actual power at all, says Whyte. The organization deals out a neat set of attitudes and values that they must make their own.

The destructive manager of the organization relies on emotionally loaded, manipulative techniques for his power and influence, just as the hypnotist arranges the situation so that his subject is in the state in which he does not ask questions, but can only obey. The hypnotic state is an extreme example of submission to authority. The destructive procedures which foster prejudice as an emotionally toned attitude to result in submission to a powerful director are of the same order.

Changing attitudes

Meanings change when attitudes change. Consider this series of seven words: table, glass, bottle, alcohol, noise, woman, white coat. As you look at this list of words see if they, when viewed together, give you a picture of some kind. The picture is one that you yourself created. Nothing has been furnished to give you a particular picture. All we have done is provide some words, and you have made whatever you wanted out of them. What if you add the word "dog" to the list? Were changes necessary? Now add the word "microscope." Does the picture stay the same? If you add this word to those you already have and still make sense out of it, then you may have changed the picture that was aroused with the first seven words. Suppose now that you add to the list "Bunsen burner." Can these words be put in the picture and have the picture make sense?

Now you might describe the picture that you have with this complete list of words. What was the formation of your mental pictures? What

[5] William H. Whyte, Jr., *The Organization Man* (New York: Simon and Schuster, 1956), p. 404.

kind of a table did you see at first? Was it in the home, in a restaurant, or in a bar? Did it have a tablecloth? What happened to the picture of the table when you saw the word "glass"? Was there a sheet of glass on the table, or was there a drinking glass on it? With the word "bottle" added, did your glass become a small glass on a bar with a bottle of whiskey nearby? Is this the kind of alcohol suggested by the next word on the list? The word "noise" could fit into the picture of a barroom scene, and so could "woman," but what happened when the "men in white coats" were added? Were they waiters, or did you find yourself starting all over again and viewing the words in the context of a hospital? Perhaps adding the word "dog" made it a veterinary hospital. But then the word "microscope" made the hospital into a laboratory, perhaps. If you now have a concept of laboratory, the table is probably white-topped or stainless steel. Changing your frame of reference from that of a bar to that of a laboratory is similar to what happens when you undergo a change of attitude.

Now we might take different items and see what picture develops. Consider the items: high production, no smoking, close inspection, low tardiness, high quality, must attend company functions. As you look over these words what kind of picture do you get? Is it the kind of place where you would like to work? If you think you would not particularly care to work in a place like this, why would it not be a good place? Notice that we have not said anything about what kind of a company this is; who the supervisor is; what work you have to do. We merely said some things, and you have placed a particular frame around those things and filled in the picture so that they mean something to you. You have built up your own picture. The picture you get may not be a highly favorable one. Suppose the items shown below were added to the words that we listed above: supervisor has you participate in setting goals of production; you feel free to discuss problems with your supervisor; your supervisor is always ready to give your personal problems a hearing. Does this or does it not change the picture? Does it change for better or worse?

We note that the picture changes for most people with the supervisory style that is suggested by the added three phases that modify the picture. By adding several things to the picture, we have changed the frame of reference by which you viewed the picture. Notice also that we changed the picture, not by changing the things that were already in it, but by adding some new things about your supervisor. The information about the supervisor brought about a change of attitude, did it not?

How did the new backdrop—the addition of these three items—change your attitude toward the picture? Your first mental picture, which was an attitude formed by the original list of words, may have suggested a factory situation—especially if you have had experience in a speed-up, a production-centered supervisory scheme. The frame of the picture changed by the addition of several items, so that you might now say that high productivity means to you that the group was "on the ball." The "no smoking" item in the first scene might have meant that management didn't let you smoke because they felt that you wasted too much time that way. In the new scene, however, "no smoking" may come to mean that there is a fire hazard. "Close inspection" in the first scene might mean that the inspectors and management had you do a lot of things over-and-over again. However, in the new scene, "close inspection" might mean that you would like to turn out things of high quality. Similarly, in the first scene, "low tardiness rate" might mean that you had better not be tardy or else you might be penalized, might be fired for it. In the second scene, "low tardiness" might mean that you would not want to let your fellow workers down. "High quality" in the first scene might mean that the company was extremely strict and forced you to work slowly and carefully. In the second scene, "high quality" might mean that you felt like doing the work better. Likewise "attending company functions" in the first scene might mean that management watched closely to see whether or not you attended company functions. In the new scene, it might mean to you that you really enjoyed the company parties and didn't want to miss them.

If we say that there are five ways by which the leader can create more favorable attitudes, this would be an oversimplification; a cook-book approach. These five principles really may not generalize to every situation. However they may clarify approaches. Here they are: (1) a general change in *S*, the situation; (2) leadership training; (3) free discussion; (4) learning about attitudes; and (5) listening.

1. *Attitudes can be changed by changing the situation, S,* as discussed in previous chapters in connection with the *SPAR* concepts. A very significant part of the variance that is responsible for changes in activities *A*, and in results of activities, *R*, lies in the situation *S* rather than in the person, *P*. It would seem most economical to try to alter *S* rather than *P* to achieve desirable changes in *A* and *R*. Attitudes defined as behavioral tendencies may be altered by changes in the situation. We have noted that unfavorable attitudes exist in the authoritarian situation; by improving the conditions in the situation, attitudes can be

made favorable. This is the same as saying that behavior tendencies, activity, and resultant components of activity of individuals and groups can be improved. And in the art of leadership we are interested in improvement. Executives, administrators, managers, and supervisors who desire to seek ways of creative leadership will give consideration to the improvement of attitudes of the members of small groups that comprise units of the organization.

2. *Attention may be invited to leadership training as a device for engendering attitudes which are favorable to the goals of management.* We have noted that management takes place in all of the personal interaction in which we are concerned. These include, for example, family, school, labor union, business and industrial enterprise, and town hall situations. Such training may rightly be said to be one of the primary influences upon leadership effectiveness. Yet training may be based on various philosophies of needs of the trainees. Education alleges to fit one for life work. Specific leadership training alleges to fit one for leading men. Diplomatic requirements and training fit one, it is said, for work in international relations. Experiences lead to attitudes and opinions: opinions may be either factually based or emotionally toned.

Leadership training is designed to provide a hurry up way of changing attitudes and opinions; it endeavors to supply facts which will hopefully result in more effective teamwork. Our discussion of an analytical approach to changing attitudes suggests a way for planning such training. It would seem that supervisory or management training might include, or indeed emphasize, leadership training. Such training, if accomplished in accordance with the concepts that have been outlined, might prove to be highly effective.

Leadership training combines two features. First, it is planned to provide experiences which lead the group member to change attitudes toward the situation. This means understanding of goals in terms of satisfying needs that are the same for leader and group members. And secondly, such training would alter the situation in which the employee or group member finds himself. This latter change could be effected by the leader as one of the important elements of his role. Thus leadership training—whether it is concerned with family, school, work place, community, or national activities—would emphasize leadership style as we have defined it in various places throughout this book. Such an approach to leadership training takes into account the needs of trainees. It is concerned with changes in attitudes, both of the leader himself and of the other members of the group who are themselves potential leaders.

3. *Freedom of discussion is one of the primary approaches for improving attitudes.* It depends upon absence of superimposed authoritative coercion or threat. It is a way for permitting groups to express feelings in a permissive setting. Such discussion may involve informal conversation, or it may be planned in a somewhat more formal way with a discussion leader. It does not exercise censorship or discipline over the feeling expressed but instead it encourages further expression of feelings and problems. These may be of a personal nature. Such discussion, whether guided by a skillful discussion leader or not, develops communications from group members to the leader and from one group member to the other. It encourages expression of feelings directed either toward other members of the group or toward the leader.

Suppose that we have a situation in which feelings are heavily loaded with hostility, discontent or pronounced prejudice. If these feelings are brought into full cognizance by the various group members, would it not be likely that greater mutual understanding would result?

But the supervisor who believes in authority, who believes essentially in the incompetence, weakness and subversive nature of group members, would not perceive the value of such an approach. He would say that the people being led are not able to understand or to participate in decisions; that they rely upon authority, the autocratic style. Such a person might be called administrator, executive, manager, or supervisor; he would not be called a leader in terms of our definition. He would not be a person who would be able to change attitudes which would be for the benefit of the greatest number. He would feel that the people under him are his charges and that their very existence depends upon their compliance to his orders; orders which, in fact, he is merely conveying downward from above. He would not be concerned with the changes in attitude because he is not concerned with mutual understanding and mutual goals; rather he is concerned with productivity, as any production or management oriented executive is. He would not use free discussion because free discussion is foreign to the authoritarian approach.

But just as free discussion is used with proven beneficial effects in therapy,[6] it can be used in creative management. In another place we are concerned with free discussion and nondirective counseling. These are tools of the constructive leader. Free discussion is permissive and enables the person to express hostility. By so doing, hostility may be dissipated.

4. *Learning more about attitudes and their formation* is one way

[6] George A. Meunch, "An Evaluation of Non-Directive Therapy," *Applied Psychology Monographs* No. 13 (1947) 160.

that the leader may change attitudes for the mutual benefit of the group. In the same way it is possible for the leader, as part of his technique for arranging the situation, to increase the knowledge of the members of the group concerning facts, methods, and results of attitude formation.

Members of the group may increase their tolerance toward other people who respond to situations differently from themselves if they have an objective, impartial, unbiased, and unprejudiced view of attitudes and behavior of fellow team members. The considerate way is the understanding way. It means openly viewing behavior—not blaming others of the group who behave in a way that is, or appears to be, maladjusted. Without such knowledge of attitudes members of the group think of others as stubborn, incompetent, guilty, blameful. When the leader and, through him, the members become analytical of behavior, there ceases to be a tendency towards blame based upon prejudice and retaliation.

5. *Listening is a permissive way of altering attitudes.* It is not used by the authoritarian; it would only be observed as a technique of the constructive leader. It is implied as part of the role played by the discussion leader in the free discussion method as a technique—not a manipulative procedure—used as a way for changing individual attitudes. Suppose a child is obstinate and negative; an employee is hostile, bitter, and says he is ready to quit; an organization of employees threatens to strike. These are themselves overt manifestations of power. The first impulse of a manager, confronted by a hostile employee, would be to assert his authority. The man might be told to "quit talking or get out." He might be told that if he did not quit talking he would see himself "walking out there in front of the plant on Route 25." The authoritative way would be expected to lead to unfavorable action tendency on the part of the individual. At the least we would expect argument.

Listening by the leader might result in a quite different activity. The troubled person would, as in the case of a nondirective counseling interview, have an opportunity to blow off steam and would probably emerge from the discussion with a better adjustment to the situation. Listening is said by the proponents of the nondirective approach to provide a setting which tends to increase the factual content of opinion and to reduce the amount of emotional loading that an opinion may have. In other words, it tends to reduce the percentage of emotional blocking and, hence, the degree of prejudice. And by listening, the leader learns the approaches that he may make in altering either the situation or the person in such a way that the activity will result in adjustment.

Attempts to change attitudes do not constitute manipulative devices in the same sense that propaganda does. Propaganda is a short cut which does not depend upon the creation, on the part of the group, of mutual goals and mutual understanding. Ways of creating attitudes which include changing the situation, providing leadership training, permitting free discussion, learning about attitudes, and listening—all engender mutual understanding and mutual goals. And for that reason these five procedures are used by the creative leader.

Attitudes are behavior tendencies. They are emotionally toned and not based entirely on fact. An analytical, objective approach is helpful in interpreting them. Opinions consist largely of attitudes; prejudices consist mostly of emotional attitudes with very little factual component. Attitudes are learned; they can be changed. One aspect of the leader role is to change attitudes through mutual understanding.

Training methods as considered in detail in the next section are devices for attitude change for the mutual benefit of group members.

Leadership Methods

FIVE

As soon as everyone can be brought to the place where his best energies may be unfolded . . . mental dissatisfaction in the work, mental depression and discouragement may be replaced by overflowing joy and perfect inner harmony.[1] HUGO MÜNSTERBERG

13

Leader training

Leaders are made, not born. Our changing times require more and better leaders. How can we get them? The answer: train them.

You, the reader, may not entirely agree with this answer. You may feel that selection, rather than training, should be the key to the problem. You may believe that there are many people who are highly potential leaders if we could readily identify and appoint them for the leader role

[1] Quoted by Rinehard Bendix, *Research in Industrial Human Relations.* New York: Harper & Brothers, 1957, p. 6.

in each situation. And you are, in part, right. Selection, picking the right man for each situation, is important. Its values and limitations will be treated in detail in Chapter 18. In the present chapter and in chapters 14, 15, and 16 we are concerned with several aspects of training and development: general training problems and procedures; the conference and role-playing; nondirective counseling.

At present, then, we are interested in "best" ways for training and development of leaders. And we wish to keep these three old and familiar ideas before us—leaders are made, not born; leadership is diffuse, that is, several people, not just one, participate in group leadership; leadership depends upon mutual goals and mutual understanding. We shall endeavor in the following pages in this chapter to discuss use of situation analysis and what we may call "leader trainee needs analysis." Then we want to go to the problem of communications, attitude surveys and related personnel procedures, and action research, in their relation to leadership. Decision making and the preliminary conference sessions as leadership training will then be examined.

Training leaders is a double-barrelled process: it pertains to both leader and participants. Since each follower is to some extent a leader, participating in leader activity—that is precisely what makes a team—the followers, too, need human relations training. To achieve mutual understanding, followers must know what the leader is doing and his purposes in doing it. The discussion of human relations training in this and in the next three chapters is, therefore, oriented toward both the team leader and the team members.

Situation and training needs analysis

Situations differ so much in terms of kind of leadership required that there are no cook-book recipes that apply to all of them. If one should say, "We need leadership in our club; what should we do?" there would be no pat answer except "It depends upon the situation," which does not seem to be an answer at all. And yet this phrase starts us off in the right direction.

A situation may be analyzed in the way discussed in Chapter 5. The illustrations used there dealt with industrial and business settings. However, the same general approach and the check list aids may be modified to fit other settings, including labor unions, government, military, and community groups and organizations in which leadership takes place. In that chapter we said of the leader, "Above all, he needs experience in analyzing group situations in which problems exist."

In Chapter 5 we noted, in the case of the Artistic Tiles Corporation, the need of highest priority was training leaders and followers in employee participation in decisions. Other high priority needs were revealed by situation analysis: training supervisors to participate in decisions; training top managers in human relations; training supervisors in human relations. And in the case of the Personal Loans Acceptance Corporation, discussed in the same chapter, we found that employee communications had highest priority and that attitude-morale surveys were second in terms of needs of the situation.

Chapter 6 discussed a case in which situation needs were analyzed. The analysis went a step further. It included survey of attitude-morale of the group involved. The situation analysis revealed that an attitude-morale survey was needed as a matter of highest priority. The survey itself, a further analysis, revealed where the emphasis should fall in remedial work. It revealed that although general morale was high (see Table 6.1), certain factors in the situation were causing trouble.

For example, in that situation more than a third of the staff men involved rarely or never felt free to go to the partners of the firm with their problems; one comment concerning work reviews, that is, telling the staff man how he is doing, was that supervisors were "a little weak on this. Have noticed some buck passing and failure to tell to one's face." Another said "One thing I've found out is that they don't seem to let you know where you stand." It was found that the area of work reviews needed general revision. More counseling was needed.

If the potential leader conducts or participates in situation analysis of the kind illustrated, he is training himself in leadership. He is beginning to view the situation in terms of its deficiencies. The point is that such participation is itself leadership training: how else can a potential leader be more effectively informed concerning the needs of the situation in order to help arrange it so that mutual goals and mutual understanding can be achieved?

Training needs of "followers"

It appears that emphasis is being placed on the leader as a person who is sensitive to the needs of followers. The leader, then, would be thought of as a personnel man? Yes, by all means. While his title may not contain the word "personnel" in it at all, every leader is a personnel man in the fullest sense of the phrase—he is personnel oriented; his interest is in the group of people who comprise the team; his role is to assist them to go forward toward mutual goals. Thus his interest encompasses the attitudes, knowledge, and skills of the group with specific reference to needs. What does the group or organization need to do its job?

An example of a problem of training needs of an organization in World War II illustrates the point.[2] It is in the area of needed mechanical skills. In an Army training situation during World War II, some 100,000 men entered Ordnance Automotive Maintenance Schools each month. Of these trainees, Ordnance officers estimated that about 1 out of 4 could bypass the first month of training, which was the elementary phase, without loss of efficiency. The question was how to *identify* the trainees who could bypass the elementary phase of training. Measurement of individual differences among trainees was the answer. A series of tests was developed for identifying those trainees who had, at the start, the equivalent of the elementary phase of training. This phase consisted mainly of exercises in tool usage and nomenclature. Its duration was 30 days. The tests found to be effective were measurements of knowledge of tools and automotive equipment. By use of the final tests of individual differences, it was found that 1 out of 5 of the trainees had the knowledge required to enter the second phase of training. Furthermore, these men could be identified by the tests. This procedure saved almost 20,000 man-months per month!

It is evident that individual differences among trainees are of two kinds: differences in attained knowledge or skill possessed at the start of training and differences in basic aptitude (learning ability). The example given above involved previously attained knowledge or achievement. In planning training in terms of the attained proficiency of trainees, the first step is to find out how much alike (homogeneous) or how different (heterogeneous) the trainee group is. If it is found that the group is fairly heterogeneous, it can be sectioned or split into two or more subgroups, each of which is relatively homogeneous. This was what was done in the case of the Army Ordnance Automotive trainees. They were split into a bypass group that did not take the elementary course and a regular group that needed the elementary phase to make progress in the more advanced phase of training.

The leader role includes knowing the skills of his group. Training needs of groups may be detected [3] and measured more readily when

[2] Roger M. Bellows, *Psychology of Personnel in Business and Industry,* 2nd ed. (Englewood Cliffs, N. J.: Prentice-Hall, Inc., 1954), pp. 316–17, from an unpublished study in 1943–44 by The Personnel Research Section, The Adjutant General's Office, War Department, conducted by the writer in collaboration with Calvin Taylor.

[3] Roger M. Bellows, M. Frances Estep, and Charles E. Scholl, Jr., "A Tool for Analyzing Training Needs: The Training Evaluation Check List," *Personnel,* American Management Association, XXIX (1953), 412–18.

mechanical skills, as contrasted to human relations skills, are involved. This is because devices for measuring mechanical skills are simpler and more precise than those for measuring human relations skills. The above illustration serves to show that at least some types of trainee needs can be measured. Can trainee needs in leader skill be measured in the same way?

Leader trainee needs

There are two ways by which needs of leader trainees may be identified with a view to correction by training. One of these is by measurement, the other is by action research.

First, measurement of needs of a leader or supervisor has been done by use of the *"How Supervise?"* test. Results of its use [4] on 169 foremen are shown in Part II of Table 1.1 in Chapter 1. The common misconceptions of foremen were identified by this device. For example, more than a third of the foremen believed that "the average worker cares little about what others think of his job so long as the pay is good." This and other misconceptions revealed by the measurement constitute training needs. Areas for remedial treatment by training are identified so that training can be focused on actual needs rather than assumed needs.

In other words, if the foremen referred to above are to become leaders, one of the first steps in training would appropriately be to dispel the attitudes and misconceptions directly opposed to the social-psychological concepts that are basic to leadership.

The second procedure in training leaders in terms of their human relations needs has been called action research. Applied research is the development and evaluation of tools to improve a situation. Action research is an extreme form of applied research. In it, the user of the hoped-for tool participates in the applied research and finds out for himself what he needs. He, the leader, trains himself by participating in the development of the tool. An illustration will serve to clarify the role of action research in leadership.

Whereas virtually all of 62 studies [5] have shown no clear relation between global morale and productivity of working groups, some studies that have isolated specific aspects of morale have revealed a strong relation-

[4] From an unpublished study by the author and associates, 1948.

[5] The first of these was by Arthur Kornhauser and Agnes Sharp, "Employee Attitudes: Suggestions from a Study in a Factory," *Personnel Journal,* X (1932), 393–401; the 62 are reviewed in Arthur H. Brayfield and Walter H. Crockett, "Employee Attitudes and Employee Morale," *Psychological Bulletin,* LII (1955), 396–424.

ship. One of these was a study by Lawshe and Nagle [6] which was concerned with one specific facet of morale—attitude of rank-and-file toward supervisor. What did the employees think of their boss? Some 223 workers were asked in a systematic way, by Lawshe and Nagle, some questions that would make visible their feelings. These workers belonged to 14 working groups; the working groups were rated as to group productivity. Answers to certain of these questions gave each supervisor a total score. This score was found to be significantly related to productivity. Among the questions were:

1. Does the supervisor give you straight answers?
2. Does he avoid you when he knows you want to see him about a problem?
3. Does he criticize you for happenings over which he knows you have no control?
4. Does he delay in taking care of your complaints?
5. Does he keep you informed?
6. Does he give you recognition?
7. Does he show interest in your ideas?
8. Does he follow through on his promises?
9. Does he give you sufficient explanation of why a work change is necessary?

This is indeed an interesting finding. We have not yet, however, illustrated the role of action research as it has been defined. Neither the research study nor its results is action research. The supervisors might be told the results of the study or they might be given the final report and recommendations for change in their behavior. But this is the usual way: tell them how to behave, order them, direct them, command them. We know how they should act—the study has told us—now all we need to do is to tell them. This is the authoritarian, the autocratic way. In general, it is likely to have little if any influence on their behavior.[7]

But action research is different, and this is an additional activity which the Lawshe-Nagle study reviewed above did not encompass. In it, each foreman would have participated in all phases of the study. He would have found out himself the things that were discovered by others, by a kind of do-it-yourself process. The results would have been *his*. He would say "the results are good, I believe in them—I did part of the study myself." There is no apprehension that he would not receive and

[6] Charles H. Lawshe and Bryant A. Nagle, "Productivity and Attitude Toward Supervisor," *Journal of Applied Psychology*, XXXVII (1953), 159–62; see also Roger M. Bellows, "Personnel Problems that Yield to Research," *Personnel Administration*, IXX (1956), 14–18.

[7] Roger M. Bellows, "Action Research in the Human Factor," New York: Society for Advancement of Management, *Advanced Management*, 1953. A paper presented at a meeting of American Association for the Advancement of Science, 1952.

act on the results; rather the fear would be that he would be "oversold" on them. The problem would not be getting across the results to him. Rather, *he* would tend to be the leader in getting across the results to others. Action research, while it has limitations, involves the user, and hence it is a communications device itself. And human relations training is largely a matter of communications.

Leader training and communications

Skill in communicating is believed to be one of the important earmarks of the leader who helps groups achieve goals through the new style of leadership we have discussed. In fact, the leader as we have defined him is the center of the communications network of the group. It is necessary for the leader not only to guard against the hazards of uncontrolled grapevine communications but also to take positive steps toward developing an adequate communications network.

The grapevine can be an insidious device. It conveys harmful misinformation when it grows and flourishes in a hostile social climate. When it thrives in a warm social climate it can facilitate other media for information exchange.

The grapevine seems to be self-starting. It swiftly carries either false rumor or accurate information. Poisonous rumor flows most freely and rapidly in the absence of other adequate media and when the climate is hostile. An example of malicious rumor, increasingly distorted as it progresses branch-by-branch along the grapevine, is illustrated by an example from Karl Menninger: [8]

Mrs. Adams to Mrs. Beck: "Where is Mrs. King today? Is she ill?"
Mrs. Beck to Mrs. Clark: "Mrs. Adams wonders if Mrs. King may not be ill."
Mrs. Clark (*who does not like Mrs. King*) to Mrs. Davis (*who does*): "I hear Mrs. King is ill. Not seriously, I hope?"
Mrs. Davis to Mrs. Ellis: "Mrs. Clark is saying that Mrs. King is seriously sick. I must go right over and see her."
Mrs. Ellis to Mrs. French: "I guess Mrs. King is pretty sick. Mrs. Davis has just been called over."
Mrs. French to Mrs. Gregg: "They say Mrs. King isn't expected to live. The relatives have been called to her bedside."
Mrs. Gregg to Mrs. Hudson: "What's the latest news about Mrs. King? Is she dead?"
Mrs. Hudson to Mrs. Ingham: "What time did Mrs. King die?"

[8] Karl Menninger, *The Human Mind,* 2nd ed. (New York: Alfred A. Knopf, 1937), pp. 289–90.

Mrs. Ingham to Mrs. Jones: "Are you going to Mrs. King's funeral? I hear she died yesterday."
Mrs. Jones to Mrs. King: "I just learned of your death and funeral. Now who started that?"
Mrs. King: "There are several who would be glad if it were true."

But if the social climate is less hostile, less distortion would be expected. And the errors that do creep in as the story progresses would not be expected to be so destructive. The social climate developed by the leader is seen to be important in communications.

Mutual understanding depends upon adequate communications. The fact that we have different psychological backgrounds makes each person different: our attitudes and behavior patterns are different; the social pressures that exist in our environment and the way we are related to each other and to different groups control, to some extent, our understanding. A common basis for mutual understanding, even of a word, is often lacking. C. G. Browne [9] points out that

> Some common basis of understanding is necessary if a word is to carry communicating value. Let us then define communication as the process of transmitting ideas or thoughts from one person to another . . . for the purpose of creating understanding in the thinking of the person receiving the communication.

Browne directed a study [10] which measured the differences in meanings of certain words between three groups of people. The three groups, of forty men each, were industrial psychologists, personnel managers, and foremen. The words used were

attitude	personnel
communication	policy
efficiency	practice
emotion	productivity
employee relations	profit
feelings	quality
foreman	research
incentive	scrap
job	security
management	standard
morale	supervision
motivation	training
opinion	turnover

[9] C. G. Browne, "Communication Means Understanding," *Personnel Administration*, XXXI (1958), pp. 12–16.

[10] Richard Bloom, "A Study of Communication Based upon Group Differences in Language Abstraction," (Master's thesis, Wayne State University, 1954).

Bloom found that not a single one of this list of 26 words commonly used in human situations was uniformly defined by the 120 men in the three groups. Specialized word meanings were found to vary widely between groups even though the groups had similar backgrounds. For example, for the word *communications,* only two psychologists and none of the others used the idea of understanding in their definitions.

Browne [11] points out that we use words as maps of a territory. The listener has one map or set of references; the speaker has another and very likely a different map. "From this it is obvious that understanding in the communication process cannot be realized simply because words are in agreement, but only if territories are in agreement." Conflicts arise in many cases when a man contradicts another without understanding what the other man is talking about. The role of the leader in communication includes the responsibility of arranging the situation for mutual understanding. The leader, to accomplish this, must consider the five basic parts to a communication: [12]

1. *The things around us* sometimes referred to as the environment or the context. All of these things are part of language or communication and the reactions which result on the part of the receiver. Failure to take them into account will decrease the value of the communication.
2. *The language maker or the speaker.* Too often he considers himself to be the only part of communication. Probably he is pleased and smiling because he is doing the talking and he makes the error of assuming that, because what he is saying sounds good to him, he is communicating well.
3. *The language itself.* When language is regarded as the only part of a communication, communication amounts to no more than ink marks or noises, since language by itself has no meaning and therefore can carry no understanding. It is important, therefore, that language be selected on the basis of the other parts of the communication process.
4. *The language receiver or the listener.* Many times he is not so pleased in the communication process because he is not doing the talking and further he may be confused by what is being said and what he is expected to understand from it.
5. *The evaluation or the judgment of the language receiver.* Through the communication the language receiver's evaluations should lead to understanding and acceptance. This, however, will be accomplished only if the language maker takes into account all of the various parts of the communication process.

Indirect and direct communications media are among the many devices used by the leader for achieving mutual understanding. Adequate leader

[11] Browne, *op. cit.;* cf. Alfred Korzybski, *Science and Sanity* (Lancaster, Pa.: The Science Press, 1933), p. 798; College Edition, New York: Harper & Brothers, 1957.
[12] *Ibid.*

training would take these into account to make the potential leader aware of pitfalls and to develop his skill in their use.

Indirect media are used for both small, informal groups and in larger, more formal organizations. They help to develop mutual understanding. They include all personnel procedures—situation and job analysis, job and employee evaluation, charter of organization, suggestion systems (discussed in Chap. 4, pp. 61–63)—that are used primarily for melding men and management into a working system and secondarily for communications.

Employee participation in decisions, like a suggestion system, is generally utilized primarily for purposes other than to engender mutual understanding. An organization that uses such activity knowingly as a basic communications device may be said to possess enlightened leadership.

Direct media consist of formally planned communications tools. In large organizations they may be listed in a roughly estimated order of frequency of use as follows:

Bulletin boards	Financial reports
Letters or bulletins	Films
Meetings and conferences	Other special booklets
Payroll inserts	Employee newspapers
Employee handbooks	Safety manuals
Employee magazines	Public address systems

Counseling

In this list it is noted that counseling is at the bottom and that meetings and conferences are toward the top. It is known that somewhat more than half of the companies in business and industry make use of the conference. It is used to a greater extent for salaried employees than for wage earners.

What can the leader expect from the conference as a method? How can it be used to engender maximum understanding? The next section will explore some of the aspects of the preliminary conference sessions; the next chapter will discuss the conference.

Preliminary conference sessions

There are several objectives of the preliminary conference session. We want the trainees to: (1) become acquainted with one another; (2) exchange problems and to become aware that their problems are not peculiar to them but that other people have them; (3) express their feelings about their problems; (4) orient each other concerning the objectives, scope, and limitations of the program; (5) think objectively and constructively about their own programs and those of others; (6) clarify and identify problem areas; (7) feel that human relations training can be a new source of help, orient the trainees themselves with facts, method, and results of leadership; (8) establish good working relations among group members; (9) become effective discussion leaders.

The first thing we hope to accomplish in a preliminary session is to get the trainees acquainted with one another. To do this each member introduces himself to the others, tells what his job title is and what his job consists of; he may be asked to mention a problem or two that he has had that pertains to human relations and leadership.

Trainees sometimes feel that they are "going back to school" in this group situation where there is no immediate urgency for accomplishing something and where the atmosphere is one of thinking and deliberation rather than action. This may contribute to what is sometimes called "loosening up." It is referred to technically by group dynamicists as the establishment of a group atmosphere in which group forces may play a part in the free-and-easy interchange and interaction among the members of the group. This feeling may help establish the conditions that are necessary for adequate communication on the part of the participants who are to learn from each other. The establishment of adequate communication bonds between the various members of a group of this kind is in itself a difficult task; theoretically, it could be said that the conditions for complete, free-and-easy communications are never entirely met. This is a matter of degree. It is hoped that the preliminary sessions will at least advance the group to some extent toward a condition which might be thought of as *rapport.*

At first some of the members are suspicious of the conference. They are apprehensive—afraid that they will "lose face" or lose prestige if they express themselves. Hence the silence that is often to be expected in a first meeting. With reference to willingness to participate, there appear to be two kinds of people in such meetings. The first kind will remain taciturn for a long period of time; the second kind will speak up early, apparently attempting to display leadership prowess and knowledge to the other members of the group. It should be realized that these people do not fall into definite "types" but overlap to a considerable extent, and that one person might display one kind of behavior at one time and another kind of behavior at another time, depending upon the other members who are present and the problems under consideration.

The second item: the exchange of problems. We mentioned briefly between our semicolons on p. 204 that we hoped each particular member of the group would find, in the preliminary session, that other members of the group had problems similar to his. And this is just what usually happens. In a preliminary session, when going around the group for the first time asking for statements of problems, we generally get from ten or twelve people only a few problem categories. Most of the problems that are mentioned fall in two, three, or four classes. The different members of the group rarely have unique problems. This finding on the part of the participants may itself result in a certain bond which may make for ease of communication. A member may find encouragement in the fact that others have problems similar to those he has been working on for two years, feeling rather sorry for himself and unique in his trouble.

The third item that we mentioned, a hope, really, was that the participants would begin to express their feelings about their problems. We hope that this "loosening up" will tend to reduce some frustration which usually adheres to an individual's problems. Again, taking an example from business and industry, a foreman found he had a clique among the people he supervised. He has had to deal with this clique for years. He has recently observed that the clique is an out-group as far as he is concerned. They do not behave in the same way that the other people in his unit do. He feels that they are always trying to impede the progress of the unit. They cut down the production in subtle ways, not by overt, clearly noticeable behavior, but more in the nature of a slowdown. He knows that they talk and communicate with one another more than they do with other members of the group. The other members of the group, he feels, are on the team, these people in the clique are not. And when he comes to that stage of maturity in human relations where he is willing to reveal and discuss this problem with his fellow trainees there is, we believe, a reduction in the amount of frustration that he has been experiencing for a long time. The mere fact that he is willing now to point to this problem and to discuss it openly with his colleagues may reduce frustration. The chances are that this supervisor had never been able to bring the problem out in the open and to discuss it either individually or collectively in a counseling, non-disciplinary style—in a permissive way. And he might get the enlightened idea, from displaying his difficulties to the trainee group, that he could reveal his feelings about this clique to all of the members of his own group. If he should arrive at this phase during the preliminary sessions, we believe he would be well on the way to becoming a better, more effective leader.

The fourth item has to do with orientation of the trainees concerning the objectives, the hoped for outcomes of the leadership training program. In some training programs that the author has helped conduct, particularly at the Western Electric Company Dellwood Conferences, the trainees are not informed as to objectives of the sessions. This is sometimes thought to enhance the value of the program. Trainees are not told the purposes of the program; but after some weeks, the trainees discover them for themselves. It is true that they do not have a uniform judgment as to the objectives of the program. Whether this approach is more efficacious than to lay out the aims of the program in the conventional manner during the first session is not known.

In the preliminary sessions the trainees realize that they actually are going to consider some of the real human aspects of their job duties. This prospect causes them to think a little bit differently and a little more deeply about the company and the objectives of the organization. They begin to revolve around in their heads the concept of morale of employees. They might ask the question about relation of productivity and morale. They almost always, in their work situation, talked in terms of productivity; and if morale was considered at all, it was a secondary objective, not a primary one. Motivation, to be sure, was considered as an exceptionally important requirement back in their manufacturing units: but it was not considered in an analytical way. Here in the preliminary sessions they begin to think about the program; what it is expected to accomplish; their human relations problems as the first order of business of the sessions; their misconceptions concerning human relations.

These misconceptions may be somewhat dispelled as the import of the program is grasped and as insights into the scope of the programs are gradually achieved by the trainees. They begin to realize that this is not an indoctrination program; that it is not a "cook-book" program where they are to memorize the recipes for conduct in human relations; that there are no panaceas or principles that are certain to generalize from one situation to another; that there is no mere bag of tricks for handling intrapersonal situations and the interaction of people in terms of the dynamics of the group.

Rather, the feeling grows that they are to formulate their own concepts of the values of the leadership styles that will be discussed as possible solutions to problems, and that these will require brand new attitudes which they themselves can develop as they see fit in terms of the human relations problems of their jobs. They are not directed to use the outcomes of the program in any way. This attitude maintains the nondirective, participative approach, carrying forward the nonauthoritarian style of leadership in the training program itself.

The fifth item: the beginning of constructive thinking on the part of the trainees. Some trainees, especially those who have been proponents of the extreme authoritarian style, are in the habit of becoming hostile as soon as a problem is revealed in the social setting. A person has not been producing—he should be punished. Reward, yes, if he does perform well, but certainly punish if he does not. He should be censored. He should be disciplined. The authoritative person thinks first in this manner. He does not think in terms of a constructive, remedial approach to human relations problems. Thus he finds himself first, in the orientation or preliminary session, in a state of confusion. He is likely to buck the idea of open discussion. But he sees open discussion progressing, and its vitality may result in constructive thinking on his part. He may begin to exchange ideas and experiences and later even help to initiate constructive thinking.

When problems of other people in the training session are brought up we see here a force at play which has been called by one applied psychologist the force of social facilitation—a concept to help explain motivation factors in particular social settings of this kind. When the "hard-boiled and practical man" comes to a point where he is willing to analyze the problems and review some of the methods that he has used in the past, he is apt to discover by this thinking that some of his methods have been ineffective. When he discovers that there are differences between effective and ineffective methods, he is well on his way to an analytical approach.

The sixth item that we wish to consider briefly here has to do with the identification, delimitation, and clarification of the problem area. We have mentioned that a large number of specific problems will tend to resolve themselves to a much smaller number. Problems fall into categories. Particular problems of general types may, for the purpose of the training program, be attacked as units. The members of the group begin to realize at the preliminary sessions that there are types of problems; that some types of problems are more frequent than others; that employees and, indeed, they, themselves, feel more strongly about some kinds of problems than about other kinds; that some kinds of problems are more amenable to solution than others; that there may be a theme of leadership style which pertains to most of the types of the problems.

It is hoped these insights are developed early in the training program, at least for some of the trainees. When problems become clarified and identified there is a tendency for consideration of them in a relatively nonemotional setting. After all, the culprit is not here; there is no point in getting mad. By the time the grouping of problems into various categories has been made, emotions and feelings will have been expressed and perhaps gotten out of the way. When we begin to classify things, we have the genesis of the analytical, objective viewpoint. This paves the way for a rational attack on the problem; it takes the place of the original, emotionally-loaded approach.

The seventh item: the trainee begins to see the human relations training program as a new source of help. It is part of human nature to resist change, or so it appears. We do not seem to have in our make-up "a set to be set for something that we are not set for." [13] On the contrary, we are set usually to resist anything that is new. It is commonplace for an industrialist, for example, to say, "We're getting along pretty well. We are making a profit right now. Our production was pretty good last month. Why should we change anything?" The military leader says, "Well, we won the last war. Why don't we keep on doing as we did then?" The fallibility of this way of thinking is immediately apparent. We see all around us change and growth. Everywhere we look we see change taking place. If we continue to persist in our old way we may not survive as an organization or as a civilization. But the human is apt, at first, to resist, to be hostile toward, to be suspicious of training.

Resistance may be quickly deduced during the preliminary sessions of the training program, especially if the setting of the program is developed in such a manner that there will be a warm atmosphere. The trainee sees that "bad" people are the product of misunderstandings, the social product of the organization rather than the product of "the devil within."

When the training program is problem-oriented—this being accomplished by taking up problems instead of personalities in the preliminary sessions—the trainee gets the notion that it is an applied program. Changes in his viewpoint may result. He begins to think how he can apply the content of the program to his problems.

Item eight is the establishment of good working relationships between group members. The goal is to make the trainee a participant in the program. The trainee becomes a trainer at the same time that he learns.

[13] C. G. Browne, "Leadership and Change," *Personnel Administration,* XX (1957), 43–46.

Thus the training program is conducted on a democratic basis. This is brought out in the early preliminary sessions when the trainee begins to realize that the nominal leader of the training program is not the only leader in the group. He, himself, is a leader. He begins to think of the mutual interest of the various trainees in the problems which are brought up. The main aspect of the preliminary sessions is perhaps the realization on the part of the trainees that they are not mere recipients of information, facts, methods, results, and techniques. It is participation, rather than reception, which we hope will very likely influence the trainee to apply what he has learned to the job situation.

The ninth item has to do with the training of discussion leaders. Often a discussion leader is drawn from the group itself by election or vote of the other members. He does not need, at the start, to be a highly skilled conference leader because if the situation is adequately arranged by the managers of the training program, he will learn. And so will the other participants. While he is leading discussion in some programs, the discussion leader changes places with others. The discussion leader does not necessarily need to be a so-called "expert" in human relations training. He can absorb the points of view and the results of research that are beginning to accrue and apply them to the problems of the group.

The discussion leader in permissive, nondirective training does not take a directing part in the program. He may guide the discussion as he sees fit, but he does not structure it or superimpose his own ideas on it to an extent greater than the other members of the group. The leader trainee's feeling of self-confidence increases from one session to another. This is a necessary, although not sufficient, condition for his ultimate success as a discussion leader.

We have seen that situation analysis is a desirable first step in leader training. From it the needs of the situation, for training, can be identified. The needs of potential leaders for different kinds of leader training can, we have found, be measured to some extent. At the very least, their misconceptions can be identified. And action research, in which the user himself helps develop the new and better ways of doing, may be recommended as a leader training device.

Mutual understanding depends upon adequacy of communications. The grapevine can be a destructive medium in a hostile social climate. The new leader, as a center of a communications net, needs training in this area: his success depends, perhaps in very large part, on his communications skill. The conference is discussed next as an important aspect of leadership activity.

Minds that have nothing to confer find little to perceive.

WILLIAM WORDSWORTH

14

Conference procedure

Training others in human relations and leadership—as in union leadership academies, management development programs, community activities—can be done in a variety of ways. We think that action research is one of the best approaches. We believe that any learning progresses more rapidly if activity in the actual situation takes place on the part of the learner. Learning, of course, can be accomplished through reading, discussion, and in experimental work with concepts, methods, and results. It can be accomplished through trial and application. And the conference provides one of the most fruitful methods.

The conference method

The conference method is one of the best starting points in a leadership training program. The conference approach can engender active participation. It can foster group interaction in analyzing problem situations and in formulating trial solutions. It can lead to active applications and to the formation of plans for approach, including action research. The conference seeks to impart valuable information *via* group participation in discussion. Human relations training, however, does not lend itself to the teaching of specific, stereotyped skills.

The training program in human relations differs from any other training with which leader trainees are likely to be familiar. As indicated in the previous chapter, the hoped for outcome of the conference is that new attitudes and orientation toward human relations problems will become part of the psychological repertory of each trainee who is a potential leader.

And we know by now through research that the conference method in human relations training does change attitudes of trainees. By the use of adequate psychological measurement procedures administered to a group of trainees before and after conclusion of the training, it has been found that significant gains—that is, changes of attitudes—occur.

At the present time, research is progressing. But how much of these gains are actually applied in the day-to-day situation in which the leader, supervisor, manager, or executive finds himself after the training course? This is an area in which research is now needed, because the final outcome—the payoff—the good that can be accomplished through leadership training lies in the future interactions of the trainee, not the mere attitude and knowledge changes that have been measured and are known to result from the training course. If we are to maintain the tough, as contrasted to the tender, approach we can only say that we do not have sufficient empirical evidence; that we should not conjecture and extend ourselves beyond our empirical knowledge. We would only be fooling ourselves, and perhaps precluding the adequate collection of the needed empirical evidence at a later time, if we were to claim more.

How should the conference leader prepare himself? The following several chapters are designed to give the conference leader knowledge of participative methods effective in leading an informal conference among his family at home or in a group in the community, a conference in the leadership training academy, a conference for business executives and management, a human relations conference, a conference in government, military, or school establishment. It is assumed that he will not possess "the authoritarian personality." The conference leader trainee will have an objective outlook upon interactions between people and between a person and a group. This is the outlook upon life situations that he hopes will be engendered in the members of the group. It is to be done in part through his efforts in arranging the situation so that they may develop new insights, attitudes, concepts, and approaches to leadership.

The conference leader may not direct the conference. He may not tell the members of the group what to do. He does, however, arrange a nondirective, democratic control over the conference. He does this in a nondisciplinary, permissive way. He does not structure rigidly the content of the conference. He guides through questioning, and especially through the timing of questions and suggestions. He asks for comments when (a) enough time has been spent upon a particular approach so that it has reached the point of diminishing returns, (b) when the participants are becoming more emotional than rational, and (c) when they lack interest in a too routine, monotonous discussion.

After some experience, the conference leader is able to achieve a desired degree of informality and at the same time arrange the situation through appropriate questioning and timing so that essential points will be talked out.

The degree of informality that may be appropriate depends, first, of course, upon the characteristics of the leader, and second, upon the characteristics of the group. Many a conference leader trainee has found that he must at first be formal and authoritarian simply because he finds it difficult to assume the more democratic, permissive role. Thus some leader trainees have much to unlearn from their previously learned habits of response. Others tend by their psychological equipment—again it has been learned—to fall naturally into the role of the nondirective conference leader.

The other set of factors involved here has to do with the backgrounds, the psychological equipment, of the conferees. If they have habitually been in meetings where the conference moderator pounded the table and, snorting with indignation, demanded action (or silence, or listening, or conformity, or productivity), then they would be somewhat surprised, even awed, at the change that has taken place, and they would be likely to utter some such remark as, "What goes?" Then, too, the group which has been in the habit of sitting at the feet of the director who is aloof, calculating, and logical would at first be somewhat confused if the leader appears before them with a more than usual friendly demeanor. They might say, again, "Aha, he is trying to sell us a bill of goods, let's find out what he is up to."

Above all, the group is quick to detect any semblance of lack of sincerity. Its members are apt to feel that the leader and the management he represents are manipulating them or drawing them into a trap that will confine them at some later time. So it is best for the conference leader to arrange in the preliminary meetings of the group to dispel these apprehensions. He can do this by stating clearly the objectives of the sessions and to follow through, reconfirming the impressions at appropriate times in succeeding meetings.

The care with which this aspect of the situation was handled was one of the main factors in the success of the Calco Chemical Division of American Cyanamid Corporation Round Table Training Conference. These conferences were set up and conducted with the collaboration of Francis Foster Bradshaw as consultant. "Round table" denotes the relationships for interaction among the members of the group that fit into the plan. It implies no differences in status and prestige among the members of the group. This is, in fact, difficult to achieve when there are evident status differences back at the work place or in the office. It is not easy to cut away these associations and stereotypes that the members possess. In the conference itself the interactions in terms of ideas, concepts, proposed solutions, and other interaction phenomena are valuable in their own right and are separate from the prestige of the individual.

The size of the group conference

There is little doubt that the size of the group makes a difference in how much interaction takes place among its members. We have defined a group as two or more people who communicate directly and interact with one another and who profit—that is, have their needs satisfied in some degree—by this interaction. How large can a group be for interaction which will involve direct communication and needs satisfaction on the part of the members? Ideally, perhaps somewhere between ten and fifteen people would be a maximum size. However, the maximum size would depend upon the composition of the group, the characteristics of the group leader, and the problems or materials being discussed. If the group is smaller than three or four, the conference leader might find that he does not have enough people involved to conduct the conference and to discuss all of the aspects in the situation. A sufficient range of views might not be available if the group is very small.

But if the group is too large, other disadvantages are imposed. If it is large, the social climate might be unfriendly and cold. It may lack the warmth of atmosphere that is necessary for intercommunication. Some of the members may not participate: often one person will be isolated; sometimes cliques will form and two, three, four, or more individuals will part from the "inner circle" group, forming splinter or satellite groups. This is a disadvantage. It results in a feeling of lack of mutual participation. The satellite group not infrequently goes off on its own and tends to combat the original group.

The size should be such that the group can be formed into a coherent, integrated whole.

Cohesiveness is one of the earmarks of a group that interacts adequately. When members of a group begin to value their membership, they are getting satisfaction from being a member. Cohesiveness is taking root. Cohesiveness grows with the "in" feeling and enhances the values of acceptance by the membership; approval by the group is the satisfaction of one of the predominating social needs of its members. When cohesiveness exists, it is easier for the discussion leader to utilize the group pressures that influence attitudes and behaviors of the participants. Because of this cohesiveness, a group should be easier than an individual to train. Then too, group interaction, engendered by social facilitation, promotes lively discussion in interchange of concepts. Members help one another learn. The group should be of such size that the members will have the feeling of satisfaction of their social needs through group membership.

What are some of the values of *buzz sessions,* sometimes called "Phillips 66," in which larger groups are broken down into small groups of two, three, four, five, or six people? [1] The main value, of course, is that interaction will take place among all the members. Sometimes buzz sessions are formed by the discussion head in an informal way: the individual members of the group are asked to turn to a neighbor and to engage in discussion for a few minutes. The discussion may be about the definition of the problem; an attempt to formulate the problem more precisely; an attempt to list possible or alternate solutions; or an attempt to summarize briefly what has been generally considered as the consensus of a group. There is no preparation and little formality in the buzz ses-

[1] J. D. Phillips, "Report on Discussion 66," *Adult Education Journal,* VII (1948), 181–82.

sion. It is not a highly systematized organization of groups. Small group buzz sessions can be used by breaking down large assemblies of a hundred or more people.

We might ask whether significant changes in behavior or attitudes are brought about by such informal, brief, but active, discussion activities. We might also inquire as to the kind of changes such buzz sessions might be expected to bring about. Will it bring about an exchange of knowledge? Might it induce changes in attitudes? These are the questions raised by Vinacke.[2] And in a carefully designed experimental approach he obtained some answers.

Here is what he found:

1. Buzz sessions really may bring about significant changes in either problem solving or attitude, or both.
2. Discussion may produce changes in either problem solving or attitude without changes in the other beyond those which might occur without discussion.
3. The kind and degree of change is, at least partly, a function of the task set for discussion.

Buzz groups tend to get activity and participation. They are especially useful when a group is large: it can be broken down into smaller groups for interaction. Other methods of group training can be combined with it. For example, it was combined with a film in one human relations training program.[3] The General Electric Company film, "The Inner Man Steps Out," was found by Speroff and Heydrick to lend itself to this use. Each small buzz group discussed interpretation of how changes in attitude, motivation, and frustration affect teamwork as depicted in the film.

Developmental discussion

Developmental discussion has sometimes been called "direct discussion" because its purpose is to direct the group interactions into action channels. When this method is used, questions or problems are presented to the group so that all members will consider the issues. In this kind of discussion, the discussion leader is perceived somewhat more as an expert and a person having somewhat more authority; the individuals in the group do not tend to look upon him as a nondisciplinarian.

[2] W. Edgar Vinacke, "Some Variables in Buzz Sessions," *The Journal of Social Psychology*, VL (1957), 25–33.

[3] B. J. Speroff and Allen K. Heydrick, "Buzz Groups Used with Films," *Personnel Journal*, XXXIV (1955), 19–21.

There is a slightly colder social climate and greater distance in communications between him and the members of the group than is the case in free discussion. The leader acts, in developmental or direct discussion, as a focal point for ideas. His function is to help clear up differences and assist the group in building mutually acceptable decisions. Contributions and interchanges are passed through him. He cannot bring about the degree of spontaneity that he may in nondirective, natural, free discussion.

It is clear that in the direct discussion method it would be more difficult to obtain free interchanges of attitudes and feelings; it is perhaps a better method for interchange of more rational or intellectual opinions not loaded with feeling. In any case, it is not expected of the discussion leader that he would be the person who knows the answers beforehand. His function is to set up the situation so that the best possible solution can be reached by group interaction and concurrence.

Developmental discussion is perhaps best used with groups whose members are mature and knowledgeable rather than with those who are just beginning to learn the work of enlarging their horizons of knowledge, of exchanging emotionally-toned opinions for the benefit of the group, of working together for the good of the group. Members who are knowledgeable, experienced, and mature are ready to participate, through directed discussion, in development and expression of ideas for solving problems for which there is adequate experience but lack of agreement.

Often in developmental or direct discussion, and sometimes in nondirect or free discussion, the discussion leader will use questions. He uses questions for the following purposes: to open the discussion; arouse interest; provoke thinking; accumulate data; distribute the discussion; direct observation; discover a point of weakness; arrive at conclusions; and limit or end the discussion. The discussion leader plans his questions so that they will be at least mildly challenging to the individual group members. In doing this he considers the differences between group members and attempts to adapt the questions to the level of verbal skill and knowledge of the members. When he directs a question at a particular member he has the level of verbal skill and knowledge of this individual in mind. He empathizes with him.

He attempts to center each question on one idea only. He hopes the answer that will be forthcoming will emphasize one point, and one point at a time. His questions may be phrased so as to state what he wants. He may want his respondent to classify, compare, criticize, define, discuss, explain, illustrate, justify, outline, review, summarize, or interpret. In directed discussion, his wishes should be clear to the respondent. The leader's questioning techniques should provide for: distributing questions fairly equally among the several members in the group; plenty of time for answering the question; consideration of each question by every individual in the group, both from the standpoint of response and from the standpoint of evaluation of the answer.

The conference leader who seeks improvement of himself and the group will check himself by systematic self-analysis. The following is an example of a self-analysis check list for use in assessment of developmental or direct conference procedure:[4]

1. Was my introductory statement clear, concise, and interest-catching, or was it wordy, confused, and formal?
2. Did I define unusual concepts and terms or was time wasted because of my failure to do so?
3. Did I guide the discussion by the intelligent use of questions or did I talk too much and dominate the meeting?
4. Did I keep control of the group or was the meeting characterized by frequent side discussions and irrelevant comments?
5. Did I express myself clearly and without hesitation or did I have difficulty in making myself understood?
6. Was there a spirited participation on the part of the group or was it necessary to prod or urge them to take part in the discussion?
7. Did most of the conferees participate or was the meeting monopolized by a few members?
8. Was the meeting characterized by an attitude of goodwill and cooperation or were the members indifferent or antagonistic?
9. Was I friendly and helpful or did I use sarcasm or reflect a patronizing attitude?
10. Did I refer questions from the floor to the conferees or did I answer them myself?
11. Did I make as much use as I should of charts, diagrams, and the blackboard?
12. Did I give credit to the participants and make them feel that it was their meeting or did I appear to "strut my stuff" like a prima donna?
13. Did I budget my time wisely or was it necessary to skip over essential points on the agenda?
14. Was my summary clear, complete, and forcefully presented or was it unorganized, incomplete, and ineffectual?
15. Did I present the summary as the findings of the group or as my own contributions?

If the problems at hand do not involve attitudes and feelings which must be adjusted through free discussion or the incident process, role-

[4] Waldo E. Fisher, *Conference Leader's Guide* (Pasadena, California: California Institute of Technology Bulletin No. 15, 1948), p. 28.

playing, or role-playing analysis, the discussion leader may choose to present human relations material by lecture or the method of directed discussion. Each method of presentation has its particular advantages and disadvantages. The lecture method has the main virtue of being a concise way of presenting materials. When a lecture is clearly laid out, it can be a time-saving method. For many kinds of subject matter, the trainees can learn a considerable amount from well-presented lectures. By itself, however, the lecture method has many distinct disadvantages as a way for imparting information.

The method of directed discussion affords the discussion leader a continuing examination, telling whether the subject matter is being understood and absorbed. The trainees, in their discussions of the subject matter, are engaged in active learning, compared with more passive learning in the lecture method. There is no need at this point to go into advantages of active learning as opposed to passive methods of learning—experimental evidence is quite clear-cut; it is in favor of active methods.

Developmental discussion is structured and at the same time somewhat democratic. Free discussion, to be considered below, is more *laissez-faire*. Maier and Maier[5] have studied the relative effectiveness of developmental and free discussion when an issue involving little emotion was decided upon.

They used 76 small groups: about half of the groups followed the developmental method; the other half used free discussion. Then the two groups were compared on quality of their decisions. In the free discussion groups, only 19 per cent of the persons reached high quality decisions, while 40 per cent of those in developmental groups reached high quality decisions. These investigators conclude: "It is the opinion of the writers that the above findings apply only to problems in which emotional involvement is not an aspect of the problem . . . with other types of problems the 'free' type of discussion may be more effective than the 'developmental.'"

Free discussion

In the method of free discussion, communication is not channeled through the discussion leader. He starts the discussion. But after that there is free communication among all the members of the group. The leader is permissive and acceptant. His main task is to be sensi-

[5] Norman R. F. Maier and R. A. Maier, "An Experimental Test of the Effects of 'Development' *vs.* 'Free' Discussions on the Quality of Group Decisions," *Journal of Applied Psychology*, XLI (1957), 320–23.

tive to the feelings of members and to reflect these feelings back to them so that they know they are understood. He stimulates interaction among the members. He limits them only to the extent of keeping the discussion from becoming a "free-for-all" with everyone talking at once. It is also his responsibility to keep minorities from being abused; to see that discussion doesn't wander too far from the problem at hand; and to summarize impartially the state of affairs at appropriate times.

Whereas the method of directed discussion is particularly advantageous in getting across material which is largely intellectual in the nature of ideas and analysis, the method of free discussion is primarily suited to areas in which strong feelings and resistances are likely to be involved. One must alter the attitudes of the trainees in human relations training. Since attitudes, particularly the stronger ones, are heavily loaded with feeling, a technique which is suitable for dealing with feelings is an essential human relations method. Various techniques for bringing about attitude change must be used. Among them the method of free discussion occupies an important place.

To those familiar with the techniques of nondirective counseling developed and described by Carl Rogers, the method of free discussion is quite easily recognized as being like a therapeutic technique, in the sense that attitude change tends to take place. Nondirective therapy and methods of free discussion have several aspects in common.

The techniques are basically alike in that the therapist and discussion leader both attempt to create a permissive atmosphere in which the participants are caused to feel free to express their feelings without any value judgments being made or without fear that the discussion leader is exercising censorship. Permissiveness in this situation is important. Unless the group members are led to feel that they are free to express themselves, their real feelings will not come out in the discussion.

Behavior which is based on feelings and attitudes tends often to be quite unreasoning and illogical; it may be hostile. When an individual reacts in a hostile manner to our own behavior, we tend, as a rule, to react in kind. In a serious quarrel, the participants create barriers to communication which prevent the feelings of either one from being dissipated. One person tends to egg on the other one until the situation reaches an *impasse,* or one of the two yields. However, when permissive methods are used, the one person is given an opportunity to express his feelings and thereafter is able to react in a constructive and logical way with regard to a problem. When the permissive atmosphere is created by free discussion methods, the situation not only permits but encourages expression of feelings. The group may come to see their problem solution as attitude change.

Psychotherapists in some situations have found it easier to change attitudes in groups than to change the attitude of an individual by himself. It is quite likely that social facilitation takes place when free discussion prevails among members of a group. One person may resist change when by himself; but in a group others are changing with him. Each person may make gradual changes without losing his security in the group. If a person attempts to change alone he may feel that he will be an outcast; but if he sees his friends, colleagues, or fellow members of the group interchange attitudes, opinions, and thoughts concerning new ways of acting or solving a problem, he, the individual, no longer has this fear of losing membership. Free interaction and expression in small groups may diminish resistance to change. A person may feel that certain attitudes would be unacceptable to others; but when he sees other persons change, he changes along with them; he is not retarded by fear. It appears that each member helps another to change his attitude, and security is felt by all because each is a group member.

The method of free discussion is perhaps most efficient when problems of acceptance are involved and when the group is in violent or strong disagreement. The permissive, nondirective style is important; direction, control, arbitrary or authoritative style would be a barrier to the very result that is to be accomplished.

Listening is sometimes an important activity for the discussion leader. He might find that he has done a good deal of the talking himself, perhaps even a larger proportion than the group has. It would seem a worthwhile goal if he were, let us say, to plan to set aside 80 per cent of the time for his group members to talk and 20 per cent for himself. Such a goal set at the outset will almost never be attained until the leader acquires considerable skill. After he has presented a topic a few times, has it clearly and comfortably in mind, and is accustomed to using the nondirective method, he will find that his skill in asking questions has developed. Having acquired this skill, he will be able to ask questions so that answers will not only be provocative of further thinking and development of ideas by the group, but that they will in effect be a step in the development of a concept of human relations. The discussion leader should hold himself to a minimum of talking, remembering that the problems of the group members, not his problems, are the ones to be discussed.

No one individual dominates the discussion. Rather, permissiveness is used as a way to exert control over the progress of the conference. Thus, ideas can be explored, feelings expressed. If we combine empathy and permissiveness and use them together as coordinate skills in conducting a training conference, we can tell when we have given a person some measure of satisfaction in expressing himself. At the same time, we have not exercised undue censorship of ideas. In addition, from the exercise of permissiveness, the leader and the group are both able to learn not only about the types of problems which exist, but also the kinds of feelings which potential leaders have about those problems. For the discussion leader that is probably the most important aspect of letting a leader trainee have his say without dominating or leading the discussion off its path.

Incident process

The incident process method was developed by Paul Pigors.[6] It is a modification of the case method to provide more action on the part of the trainee. Instead of presenting a case—such as those in chapters 5 and 6—for reading and later discussion by the trainee, the case is developed in the group. The case unfolds by question and answer, and each member perceives the details of the case from the same discussion. Each member has the same facts at the end of the case discussion. Thence facts emerge from the interactions of the group members.

The incident process starts by a brief statement of a problem by the discussion leader, and the episode unfolds. The first few minutes of an actual training session, conducted by F. Kenneth Berrien at an American Management Association seminar may help clarify the process. An executive personnel committee is discussing an episode:

Discussion Leader to Group: "Here is a problem that we want to solve. We want the group to help decide on what action to take on Mr. Watts." (*Long pause.*)

Group Member: "What did he do?"

D.L.: "He has been taking his secretary along to out-of-town meetings."

G.M.1: "Is that bad?" (*A few G. M.s laugh.*)

G.L.2: "That's what we want to decide about." (*Pause.*)

G.M.1: "When did it happen?"

G.L.: "The last time was last week, on last Tuesday and Wednesday at the sales meeting in Utica."

G.M.3: "What's the organization policy on this—on having a stenographer go along to meetings?"

[6] Paul Pigors and Charles A. Myers, *Personnel Administration: A Point of View and a Method*, 2nd ed. (New York: McGraw-Hill Book Company, Inc., 1951), 272–337, 369–71.

G.L.: "There is none."
G.M.5: "Is it done as a usual practice? Is there an approved precedent for it?"
G.L.: "Yes."
G.M.5: "Then why is it a problem in this case?"
G.L.: "Because people both in our Utica division and here at the home office are beginning to talk."
G.M.2: "Then public relations may be involved?"
G.L.: "Yes."
G.M.1: "What are Mr. Watts' duties as assistant sales manager?"
G.L.: (*Reads off a one-page summary of duties from Mr. Watts' position description; his duties include detailed written reports of out-of-town sales meetings.*)
G.M.3: "How about providing a local stenographer?"
G.M.5: "How about providing portable dictating equipment?"

Discussion proceeds, with question and answer, for another 20 minutes, and a solution is reached together with a recommendation that the policy committee write a general statement for the policy manual under the heading of public relations.

This particular case would probably not be written up and presented to the members of the executive personnel committee for briefing before the meeting.

The incident process method is a device for providing to all the members of the deciding group the pertinent facts that they want at the time they want them. These are built up from incidents and facts surrounding an episode. It is a democratic method that can engender a warm social climate.

The success of a leader is believed to depend in some measure on his conference skill. Conferences may be conducted by lecture, developmental or free discussion, or incident process. Each has advantages and disadvantages.

Developmental discussion is a structured, democratic procedure, useful in dealing with factual issues. Free discussion, like nondirective counseling, although more of a laissez-faire style, helps group members get insights into their problems and is especially useful when issues are emotionally toned. The conference leader usually talks too much himself. Skill in procedure is an important part of the leader's equipment. Buzz sessions can change attitudes in some situations. The incident process method is a modification of case conference procedures in which the small group develops the case. It has several advantages in obtaining group interaction. These may be valuable tools to the leader.

Another leader training tool, leadership simulation, is discussed in the next chapter.

*

All the world's a stage,
And all the men and women
merely players. WILLIAM SHAKESPEARE

15

Training by simulation

Synthetic team training is new. It has been used not much longer than a decade. The most systematic use of the synthetic crew trainer has been achieved by the U.S. Air Force. The Air Force use of the flight simulator will be discussed briefly to illustrate concretely the general purpose of the method and how it works; then we will be ready to turn to synthetic situations for training leaders. These situations include both role-playing and playing at war games as training in decision making.

The training simulator

The training simulator is used by the Air Force for transitional, refresher, and emergency procedure training. A forerunner of the modern crew flight simulator trainer was the Link trainer, familiar to many World War II trainees. It was a mock-up airplane cockpit which reproduced, on the ground, some of the situations a pilot experiences in the air. When pilots and crew must be transferred from obsolete to new aircraft, the simulator is used. Crews that had thousands of hours' experience in the B-29 had to be changed over to B-50D bomber aircraft. How could this be done most economically and efficiently? How could they be best trained in dangerous emergency procedure? The simulator supplied some of the answers.

The flight training simulator is called "synthetic" because it is not a real aircraft. It is simply an arrangement of a situation which simulates the real one. Thus, in a sense, the trainee pilot and crew play at flying; they do not actually fly.

There are several advantages to synthetic training. It is less expensive and less dangerous. Emergency maneuvers that would not be possible in actual training flight may be experienced and practiced. For example, a fire in an engine or in the cabin can be simulated. A combat "flight" can be taken over simulated enemy territory. Actually thousands of simulated combat flights are practiced by bomber crews now. And the crews become so involved in these training "flights" that they report on "return" that their experiences seemed real.

Briefing before such "flights," and especially critique upon "return," provide discussion of better ways to handle problem situations.

And not the least value of these simulated situations is their provision of a setting for the research evaluation and improvement of training methods. For example, the duration and kind of briefing and critique procedure can be objectively studied with a view of improvement.

The flight simulator aids training in not only technical information and manual skills, but also in teamwork. Intercommunications between various flight crew members and use of the intercom system are parts of the training.

Human relations and leadership training in labor unions, in business and industry, government, in the community, at home and in military organizations is not only feasible but is being accomplished in many situations. Role-playing is one of the synthetic training procedures that is coming into wide use.

Role-playing

A father is scolding his twelve-year-old. He "lays down the law," shouts, orders the boy never to do it again. But he does! And then the father thinks of another approach. He is about to say, "Now if you were in my place, what would you do?" But instead of saying that, he has the son play out the father's role, just for fun. The father takes the son's role—simulated role reversal. They sit facing each other and play out their roles. At the end of their little skit they discuss what happened, how each felt in the other's role.

Role-playing is alleged by some to be a human relations panacea. Do you want to settle an argument, combat resistance, get people on the team in jig time? Then use role-playing. But it is in no sense a cure-all for problems in interpersonal relations. It is merely another leadership training method that is useful in some situations. It is a training simulator—it imitates actual situations, so that participants can gain experiences and insights and agree on solutions to complex problems of human interrelationships.

People who resist change tend to resist training. When a man resists training, he seems to like being the way he is. A foreman, for example, may be proud to be known as "efficient and hard as nails." He likes to impress people by being the rugged individualist, the tough guy. Some resist training because they are unable to look at the problems from other persons' points of view: they lack empathy. Others resist because they see no reason for the training. People resist changing, too, if there is lack of visible reward for changing. A man might say, "Why should I change? The boss wouldn't appreciate it anyhow." Sometimes people resist if they have no idea of the final effect of the change. If the supervisor, for example, knows no other way of supervising than the one he is now using—which is probably an autocratic, authoritarian way—then that way will look good to him. One must, therefore, try to give a picture of what is to be expected after the change takes place. This prognosis may help this supervisor realize he might be more successful through training. People resist training when they are being "pushed into it." They want to feel that they are choosing this method themselves. Here it is obvious that the nondirective approach is indicated. Leading the horse to water will not necessarily create thirst. Simulated training such as role-playing is nondirective.

The role of any individual is the part he plays in the specific group to which he belongs. Thus, we have, each of us, many different roles.

When we are on the job our role may be that of a supervisor; at home we play the role of mother or father, wife or husband; in a grocery store, the role of customer. The behaviors are different in each of the situations, and yet there is consistency. If we were to get our roles switched and act like a foreman at home or like a father on the job, our behavior would be inappropriate. All of us belong to many different groups. We have learned certain ways of behaving which are more or less acceptable to each of these groups. The way of behaving is the role that we play.

In a training situation, role-playing may be deliberately undertaken with certain educational goals in view. Let us say that a training group has decided to act out a human relations problem situation. The training group consists of foremen and supervisors, or executives and managers of a company, or member trainees of a labor union training academy that hopes to train its members for leadership positions of greater responsibility.

The program training coordinator assigns the roles to be played by different persons in the training group. The problem to be played out is briefly discussed, and the skit gets under way with the actors spontaneously expressing themselves as the story unfolds. The job is then to analyze what has been going on among the actors. Who said what? How was it said? What feelings and attitudes were revealed? How did the actor feel? Role-playing attempts to get at these factors in behavior to enable the trainees to see more clearly the causes and to suggest possible remedies for ineffective behavior.

Role-playing is an educating process designed to bring about a change in attitude, set, and behavior of trainees. It may be thought of as a teaching method; it is especially appropriate for human relations training in many situations. Trainees grow in their degree of objectivity in viewing, analyzing, and interpreting the problems and motives of other people. They gain insights in terms of how to deal with these. They also learn how to use the role-playing method. Here are some ways in which it is being used: [1]

1. The most popular is in supervisory training in human relations and leadership. Role-playing especially provides plenty of opportunity for practicing the principles of leadership and human relations that are usually given in training. Many executive counselors have found it an exceptionally good way to get the

[1] Chris Argyris, *Role-Playing in Action,* New York State School of Industrial and Labor Relations, Bulletin No. 16 (Ithaca, N. Y.: Cornell University, 1951), pp. 2–3.

top officials of their organizations to see their own mistakes and to correct them.

2. Role-playing is also used to train personnel people, line supervisors, and shop stewards in such potentially difficult situations as layoff or discharge interviews, exit interviews, merit-rating interviews, and transfer interviews.

3. Role-playing is being used in training shop stewards and supervisory personnel to handle such problems as grievances. It is especially useful in teaching people how to listen more and talk less when an employee comes with a grievance.

4. Role-playing is an excellent method through which to study the problems involved in supervisor-worker or shop steward-worker communication. Supervisors, for example, by taking the role of the workers are able to see how it feels when they are ignored or not spoken to pleasantly. Skill in seeing the other person's point of view is important, and role-playing is especially suited for teaching it.

5. Role-playing may be used to give to training people practice in teaching. It has been used in practice teaching for such courses as lathe and drill press operation, drafting, mathematics, and other technical subjects. It helps (a) cut costs by pointing up the weaknesses of the instruction, thereby, (b) making instruction much more efficient, and (c) reducing learning time.

6. Role-playing is used effectively in orientation programs. It helps new persons to become more interested and involved in the program. Furthermore, it helps to bring into the open questions that may otherwise remain unanswered in new employees' minds. Finally, it is an excellent and interesting method by which to introduce people to such subjects as the organization's policies, attitudes, and goals.

7. A relative newcomer on the list of possible users of role-playing is the field of collective bargaining. Management and union officials have both found it extremely useful to role-play their points before presenting them in formal bargaining sessions. Weak points are usually discovered, ambiguities clarified, and, finally, new ideas may emerge from "taking the other side's position" during the skit.

The research-minded user of role-playing will see that it lends itself to research evaluation of human relations leadership training. One research problem that is obvious to the leader who would take an empirical research approach is this: for a given situation, is role-playing a more economical and efficient way of training than the direct, indirect, or lecture procedure? Some situations will lend themselves to finding an answer to this question. Such research presupposes a criterion of the outcomes in terms of changed attitudes and changed behavior of the participants in human relations leadership training.[2] It is hoped also that the reader will think of a research program of this kind in light of what was said in Chapter 13 concerning action research. When action

[2] Irving R. Welchsler, Robert Tannenbaum, and John H. Zenger, "Yardsticks for Human Relations Training," *Adult Education,* VII (1957), 152–69.

research is used for the purpose of evaluating role-playing, it is quite possible that a double-barrelled result can be achieved.

What can be said about role-playing as an educational device? This is the point-of-view of many who use role-playing regularly in human relations training: Education is a process of changing attitudes, prejudices, ideas, behavior patterns, concepts, and approaches to effective human relations. We all have erroneous predispositions toward the facts, methods, and results of human relations. Education requires unlearning, that is, doing away with common misconceptions and inappropriate habits, especially relating to our propensity for blaming a person for his behavior without analyzing it. It is here that role-playing can be effective. Re-education can bring about the elimination of inappropriate sets, attitudes, stereotypes, and habit patterns. Through it important changes in people, in the way one looks at others, the organization, the job, the school, the community, the country can be brought about. Value systems can be changed.

People do not learn, do not change, unless they want to change, unless their needs can be satisfied through change. As we have seen in the previous discussions, people resist change because they are set to continue rather than set to change. Role-playing is designed to provide concrete, down-to-earth, true-to-life experiences in which both the trainee and trainor are interested. Alternate solutions to problems arising from such experiences can be revealed through this technique. Both the trainer and the members of the group interact with a common set toward the material being role-played.

Re-education sometimes may be brought about more quickly when the participating members of a group have a chance to see and discuss ideas in a friendly atmosphere. Criticism is likely to be more constructive than vitriolic. The trainee begins to feel secure and confident as a member of this friendly group. It is thought that changes in attitudes, sets, and behavior patterns that occur in discussing true-to-life situations may be more permanent than they would be if the person merely thought through the ideas by himself and did not nail them down through group interaction.

Perhaps a true philosophy of education is that the teacher is a leader. He arranges the situation so that the work of learning can go forward toward a common goal. The common goal in this case is enlightment concerning human relations. The elimination of common misconceptions and the establishment of a readiness to change attitudes are primary requisites.

Role-playing puts the trainee in the other fellow's shoes. As a skit develops, the trainee sees characters acting in the play in the same ways that he, himself, acts in real life situations. This enables the trainee to empathize with the other person. He is able to get the feel of the problem of the other fellow.

Another value claimed for role-playing has to do with therapy. The trainee can get a lot of things off his chest. He can talk out his troubles through the role that he is playing in the skit. This can act as an emotional release to resolve tensions and satisfy needs. He has a feeling that somebody is listening. We believe that he may be able to look more clearly at his own human relations problems and to cope with them, having resolved undesirable tensions.

It will be interesting at this point to review the mechanics of role-playing. Just how is it done? It is assumed that the leader has in his preliminary sessions: (1) collected a list of problems, and that these are real problems for the trainees; (2) achieved interaction among the trainees and *rapport* between members and leader so that they consider him a permissive, nondisciplinarian coordinator. Role-playing is best adapted for spontaneous performance. In one session, for example, role-playing was begun when a supervisor remarked to another, "O.K., pal if you think you can do better, why don't you get up and show us?" In another session, group members did not understand a particular method of disciplining employees which a supervisor was trying to explain. One of the group members suggested that the supervisor act out the method, taking the role of the supervisor, with another member of the group taking the role of the employee being disciplined. The leader or coordinator was ready: he picked up the ball and arranged a role-playing skit on the spot.

In order to arrange the role-playing skit, the coordinator first sets up a problem and sees that it is common knowledge to the different participants in the human relations leadership training session. He does this by discussion and questions and answers. There are several basic items that the coordinator keeps in mind. The first of these is that the skit should contain material that is of interest to the majority of the trainees. It should bear upon a problem that the group is attempting to solve, preferably one of the categories into which several problems have fallen. The layout of the skit is set up in terms of the interest and backgrounds of the group. It is a simple skit; it does not have the complexity of a Broadway plot. Simplicity enables the different members of the group to role-play problems without rehearsals; the role-playing is spontaneous and free from formalities. The next step is to define the roles of the actors. This is done as a participative procedure with the coordinator acting as a summarizer of suggestions.

After the group has decided on the roles to be played and the actors for them, he then starts the role-playing by having each volunteer take a place at the table. Any distasteful role is best assigned, as suggested by Argyris,[3] to a member of the trainee group having a secure position in the group.

Multiple role-playing differs somewhat from the usual type of role-playing in which only two or three play the roles.[4] In multiple role-playing, all members of the group get into the act. There is no audience. Multiple role-playing is preferred when: (1) members of a small group might be embarrassed for one reason or another when putting on a demonstration before an audience, (2) it is desired to have all members participate, or (3) it is desired to obtain and later discuss a variety of ways of handling a human situation. The group is split into smaller groups of the size needed for the role-playing. Then each sub-group plays the same skit simultaneously. For instance, if there are twenty-one persons in the group and the skit involves three persons, then seven groups role-play the skit. If there is a member left over, he may act as observer or recorder and summarize the events that occur among the different groups. The role-playing is allowed to continue until all the groups have finished or until it is obvious that one or more groups are not going to finish within a reasonable time. The analysis of the role-playing results can be tabulated on a prepared form.

The frequency of types of outcomes may be compared, differences in solutions may be discussed and reconciled by the various members of the groups, and a consensus may be taken to determine the most feasible solution to the human problem.

Measures of attitude change and subsequent behavior change may be obtained as an appraisal, or criterion, of the outcomes of the role-playing. A research project, perhaps incorporating the action research principle, could be set up to gather data on outcomes. It is revealing, in some situations, to set up a control group which does not participate in role-playing, perhaps with background and characteristics similar to those of participating members, and to compare "before and after" attitudes of both groups.

[3] Argyris, *op. cit.*, p. 15.

[4] Norman R. F. Maier and Lester F. Zerfoss, "MRP: A Technique for Training Large Groups of Supervisors and Its Potential Use in Social Research," *Human Relations*, V (1952), 177–86.

An experimental design for action research could provide a before and after inventory of attitudes, such as the *"How Supervise?"* test, which is set up in comparable forms for use as before and after measurements of attitude change. Such a set-up in research design is provocative of definitive results.

Simulated war games

Decision-making games are a method of training which consists of a mock-up of an actual decision-making situation. The trainee engages in practice that would be impossible in the real situation. The method is similar to the flight simulator for training pilots and crew in emergency maneuvers. Practice in real maneuvers is too hazardous, but the play situation affords practice without danger. It is a way of learning by doing without risk.[5] The American Management Association developed the first large-scale, systematic, top management team decision-making exercise. It is called a new concept in management training.[6] The old-style manager relied on hunch or intuition; the new-style leader needs to learn to use facts and empirical evidence. A lifetime of practice on the job is insufficient, simply because the lifespan is not long enough to see the outcomes of the more crucial decisions.

The executive-training business war game is so arranged that the trainee team can, within a few hours of concentrated decision making, simulate years of experience. It is called "war game" because the military establishments originally conceived and conducted such games to train command officers. The procedure was adapted and developed for American Management Association by Franc M. Ricciardi in collaboration with Clifford J. Craft, Richard Bellman, Donald G. Malcom, and Charles E. Clark.

The game as arranged was not specifically designed to train leaders in human relations. Role-playing is the essence of the game. Decisions are made "four times per year"—20 minutes of teamwork is allocated for each decision. Player teams' decisions pertain to organizing companies, hiring consultants, financing all aspects of the business. Then teams are compared in the final outcome that the group decisions brought about. According to Ricciardi, since each trainee of the team takes the role of an executive in the simulated company, "inevitable inter-

[5] Franc M. Ricciardi, American Management Association, letter.

[6] Franc M. Ricciardi, "Business War Games for Executives: A New Concept in Management Training," *Management Review* (New York: American Management Association, 1957), pp. 46–56.

actions among the members" are part of the situation in which decisions are made.

In playing the game, the trainees or players are divided into five teams. Each team runs a company, starting with the same conditions, for example, its financial position.

Almost all the executives who have taken part in the various test plays agree that the decision game is a unique and valuable contribution to management training, because in a real sense it offers a dynamic case-study approach to the decision-making process.

The players face problems exactly like those top management meets in daily business. They are forced to do real strategic planning. They have to decide questions like these: Is our company going to get out on a limb on marketing? Should we plunge on research and development? Should we try for high volume at low margin, or turn out a high-quality product at a high price? Are we going to go in for price-cutting? Should we make a bid for price leadership?

Every few minutes they must repeat the decision process of selection, analysis, and action. For the questions, once answered, don't stay answered. Every period's results change the picture again. The players must be alert to trends, flexible enough to seize an opportunity when it is offered, and adaptable enough to switch to a new strategy if the original one doesn't work out.

Those who have played the game feel it has great possibilities for improving judgment and reasoning capacity. The game vividly demonstrates the complexity of running a modern business. It teaches the players—emotionally as well as rationally—that management by rule of thumb is no longer possible. As one participant put it, "The game's great merit lies in reminding players of the complex and interlocking nature of the factors that affect most decisions."

Another key value is the broader insight into company problems that the game provides. The marketing man begins to see that the money he is spending doesn't just appear out of nowhere; the financial man realizes that some of it comes back again.

And there are still broader implications. An obvious area for exploration is the use of some such gaming device for executive testing.[7]

The synthetic war games training situation, like the flight training simulator, lends itself to research for training improvement. What kinds of decision-making practice transfer most to the actual leadership situation? Are human relations practices improved by such training? What duration of training and what intervals between training periods yield most beneficial results? These are only a few of the questions that are to be answered in the future by research evaluation for improvement of training methods.

The war games leadership training procedure is in its infancy. A

[7] *Ibid.*, pp. 52–53.

beginning has been made in simulating situations. In the future, our organizations will be even more complex than these are today. Greater leadership skills will be required. Research is needed for evaluating and improving the training methods we have discussed.

Synthetic training devices—the air crew flight simulator, role-playing, war games decision making—have advantages in some leader training situations. Disastrous consequences of wrong decision and action are eliminated by simulating situations; they foreshorten the time needed for obtaining experience; they provide a setting for interaction of team members; insights based on facts can be achieved by group members who are unhampered by fear or emotional blocks to rational behavior.

This training setting provides an opportunity to improve various aspects of training through research. And finally, mutual understanding and mutual goals can be developed in groups under some situations by use of synthetic training procedure.

*

Knowledge which is acquired under compulsion obtains no hold on the mind. PLATO

16

Counseling and leader technique

Counseling is as much a part of the leader as it is of the leadership situation. It is at once a device used by leaders, a tool for training them, and a point of view which will help them develop further a philosophy of leadership.

Opportunity for a counseling relationship is present in many leader situations, particularly in small groups. The small group exists by virtue of direct face-to-face contact among its members. In school systems, principals have such direct contact with teachers; in business and industry, executives have it with other executives at the same and at higher and lower levels in the hierarchy of the organization; the foreman, especially, has such contact with the rank-and-file workers; the labor union leader has it with union members; the parent enjoys this relationship with the children in the family; the research director interacts in this way with research assistants in the department; everywhere in human relations we find this kind of interaction. Counseling can be part-and-parcel of the technique for motivating an individual or group to behave in a particular way. Thus in studying leadership we are concerned with counseling relationships between people.

Directive and nondirective counseling

The counseling method, as the conference method, may be either directive or nondirective. In the directive approach—somewhat more authoritative and autocratic—the counselor tends to tell or advise the counselee about his behavior; for example, "You had better do it this way." The directive approach is typified in the counseling interview session by: advice, argumentation, interrupting with questions, lecturing, telling the counselee he is wrong, cross-examination, breaking silences, kidding the counselee, or minimizing his troubles and taking responsibility for final action, adjustment, or behavior of the counselee. Nondirective counseling is quite the opposite of this. The counselor establishes *rapport,* listens, lets the counselee talk, uses few words himself, feels a conversational equal to the counselee, accepts the counselee's feelings and attitudes and reflects this acceptance, tries to achieve mutual understanding. He accepts intervals of silence. He helps the counselee establish insights into his problems which may lead him to better adjustment and self-solutions.

One of the proponents of directive counseling [1] believes non-directive counseling is appropriate when the counselee has ability to adjust for himself: "The general rule may be stated that the need for direction is inversely correlated with the person's potentialities for self-regulation, *i.e.,* the healthier the personality, the less the need for direction; the sicker the personality the more the need for direction." How far can we go with nondirective counseling? What situations lend themselves to its use? The quotation from Thorne suggests that some situations lend themselves to the nondirective approach and others do not. The inappropriate situations are those in which the group cannot maintain its own affairs, work consistently toward goals, or understand the meaning of teamwork. These situations lend themselves to directive counsel-

[1] F. C. Thorne, "Directive Counseling and Psychotherapy," *American Psychologist,* III (1948), 160–65.

ing. It is up to management or the leader to decide the degree of directivity that should take place.

The nondirective approach tends to minimize the importance of diagnosis or the consideration of past events for a study of the conflict. This less active procedure emphasizes present and future. The nondirective counselor is not concerned with the causes *per se* nor with specific treatments; his interest is in establishing new attitudes on the part of the counselee. He provides the setting for changing attitudes and behavior patterns. Thus, nondirective counseling may help to set up the situation so that the team can go forward in a shared direction. Although it does not endeavor to get at the underlying basis of behavior, it has been shown to help in attaining individual adjustment in some situations.

Counseling may mean individual face-to-face discussion of a personal problem with a fellow-employee, a fellow-student, or a fellow-member of any group. Each discussion has an element of counseling in it. Each interview can be a counseling interview, just as each training session can utilize the principles of nondirective counseling as discussed in the previous chapter.

In business and industry, much of the counseling is done by the supervisor. In some industrial enterprises, as in government bureaus and military establishments, there have been efforts to establish formal counseling programs. Some are based on paternalism. One example of this is a counseling program that was set up by Henry Ford a long time ago. This earlier one happened to be paternalistic. It contained some of the earmarks of the authoritarian style, as would be assumed from this quotation from Henry Ford's book, *My Life and Work.*[2] Henry Ford said, "I pity the poor fellow who is so soft and flabby that he must always have an atmosphere of good feeling around him before he can work." And again, "We do not believe in the 'glad hand' or the professionalized 'personal touch' or 'human element.'" Henry Ford said this in 1922. Many changes, both philosophical and organizational, have taken place since that time. If they had not, it is doubtful whether the company could have survived the requirements of the labor union which now can insist upon maintaining the dignity of the worker.

The Western Electric Company is a principal example of the development, based upon research, of a nondirective employee counseling program. This program has been described in detail by Dickson.[3]

[2] Henry Ford in collaboration with Samuel Crowther, *My Life and Work* (New York: Doubleday Page and Company, 1922), pp. 92, 263.

[3] William J. Dickson, *Understanding and Training Employees,* Personnel Series #35 (New York: The American Management Association), pp. 4–18.

It is typified by a nondirective approach in which the counselor and counselee share a sincere empathetic relationship. The counselor is interested in attitude and behavior change. But he does not direct the interview. His hope is that the counselee will initiate insights and change attitudes and actions of his own accord. The counselor maintains confidences. Sufficient time is allowed so that the counselee can talk it out. The counselor does not interrupt; he does not argue. The Western Electric Company looks upon its counseling program as a "humanizing agent."

The need for counseling

A case from the area of business administration illustrates problems that yield to counseling.[4] It involves the public accounting firm Glowacki, White, and Stern which was discussed in detail in Chapter 6. The concepts and methods discussed in this case problem would be, it is believed, as applicable to the administration of a labor union, for example, as it is for a public accounting firm. A counseling and communications program was indicated. The firm clearly needed to make supervisors aware of their responsibility for accomplishing communications and employee good-will.

A most frequent theme noted in the comments of the members of the staff: a felt need for adequate and frequent work reviews. They wanted to know how they were doing. Three-quarters of the group reported they never or rarely were told with promptness and regularity whether their work was satisfactory. On another item, about 20 per cent said their work reviews seldom or never revealed whether they were adequate or satisfactory. The effect of this condition is apparent on the attitudes of the employees. The group was interested in approval and recognition of their efforts as well as job security.

Post-appraisal counseling

Every day, we evaluate our peers, superiors, and those whom we believe to be below us. We usually do not do this in a formal or systematic manner: it just happens. We do it merely for fun, or by habit, for conversation or gossip. Sometimes we do it for a more serious purpose, as when an assignment is to be made and we want to judge which one of several people would be best for the task to be assigned.

[4] Roger M. Bellows, *Case Problems in Personnel Management* (Dubuque, Iowa: Wm. C. Brown Co., 1955), Case #3. Discussed in Chapter 6, pp. 16–17.

But even this last purpose of appraisal is not a main one. By far the most important use of appraisal of others is to help them to know and correct their weaknesses. This use unfortunately is as rare as it is important. It is new in business. It is the leader's use of appraisal. The authoritarian uses appraisal to "beat him down," or for firing purposes; the leader attempts to "build him up."

The primary purposes of ratings, evaluations, judgments, assessments or appraisals of others are twofold: informing the person of his weaknesses and strengths and coaching him for improvement. He needs to know how he is doing, a need revealed in Chapter 6. Telling him may, if properly done, supply satisfaction of social needs. It may allay apprehension and destructive fear.

Coaching can accompany telling him how he is doing. Coaching implies that improvement can be made. It requires tact. How can it best be accomplished?

The nondirective counseling approach has been applied to the post-appraisal interview by enlightened leaders. The leader-counselor emphasizes consideration. He uses several guidelines.

In the first place he realizes that all human appraisal of another's performance is fallible in some degree. He therefore strives to make his appraisal as objective and accurate as possible. He guards against his own tendency to bias and insincerity.

Secondly, he arranges the situation so that there will be a warm, not hostile, social atmosphere to promote rapport and mutual understanding. He puts the counselee at ease.

Third, he fosters self-analysis and self-appraisal on the part of the counselee by the permissive, nondirective approach. The counselee will, he hopes, bring out his own weaknesses. This is to be contrasted to the disciplinary interview of the authoritarian manager.

Fourth, the nondirective job counselor will let the counselee develop his own plans for corrective or remedial action, and at the close of the interview he will agree on a specific plan.

These principles of use of nondirective counseling in job coaching are well illustrated in classic interview material of Hill and Hann,[5] illustrative excerpts of which are shown below:

[5] L. Clayton Hill and Arthur S. Hann, "Counseling Interviews: A Procedure with Demonstration Interviews," Report No 5, Bureau of Industrial Relations, University of Michigan (Ann Arbor: University of Michigan, Publications Distribution Service, 1952), reprinted from John W. Riegel, *Executive Development* (Ann Arbor: University of Michigan Press), 1952, pp. 333–61, by special permission.

The First Interview (on a Thursday)

H (Hill): Hello, Art. You are right on time. I appreciate your staying after hours to visit with me. Please sit down, Art. Have a cigarette?

A (Art): Thank you.

H: How did the job go today?

A: Well, it went about as usual. We're pretty busy, you know, and we got mixed up on an order today—nothing unusual, but it did kind of make me a little mad. We sent out a wrong shipment of refrigerator door seals—sent out some Model 31's instead of 36's the other day, and we found out about it today. So I had to get into it and get it straightened out—and I just got finished.

H: You got into it yourself to straighten it out?

A: Yes. You know how it is—somebody makes a mistake and you try to get somebody to fix it up, and you usually end up by doing it yourself.

H: You feel you usually end up by doing it yourself?

. . .

(The interview progresses.)

. . .

H: Yes. That's it. I believe you developed that pretty much yourself, didn't you?

A: Oh, yes; I thought that out. I worked on it several nights, thinking that thing out—and we got it set up, and I think it's doing a good job. I'm glad you noticed it, too.

H: Well, Art, among your fine characteristics I am impressed by your knowledge of the job, ingenuity, and initiative. I would rate you very high on those factors. I think you do a very fine job in those areas. There are many examples I could mention where I have seen evidences of your doing an outstanding job in tooling, production methods, and plant layout.

. . .

(And then some home and family problems of Art are discussed; then the question of delegation comes up, introduced into the discussion by Art himself, who appeared to obtain new insights by discussing it. And then the first interview closed as follows.)

H: I see, Art. I think I'm beginning to understand how you feel. You want to be kept informed; you like to be in touch with these things, and you like to have these fellows consult with you before they take action—and if you see they get in difficulty, you feel the best and easiest and most effective way for you to get jobs done is to do them yourself.

A: I think—yeah; I think that about summarizes it. Let them do what they can and what they can't do, do yourself.

H: Well, Art, I think I now have a much better understanding of your feelings, and I don't want to keep you any later tonight. I appreciate your taking time to consider this problem of easing your work load by delegating more responsibility to your foremen. Would you say that is a possibility worth thinking about?

A: Yes, I'd kind of like to get my load lightened. I enjoyed hearing that you think I'm doing a good job on some things. I wish some of these foremen of mine would do a good job, too, along that line. I try to work hard and get my job done, spend a lot of time at it, and I kind of wish they would take theirs more seriously, too.

H: You wish the foremen would give you more help than they do?

A: Yes; I kind of wish they would. I sure can use some help.

H: You feel that is something for us to consider pretty thoughtfully?

A: Yeah—and I'll be glad to think about that.

H: Well, Art, I appreciate your coming in. Doubtless, we'll get in touch with one another sometime soon and have another visit on this problem of lightening your work load.

A: Okay.

H: Thanks for coming in for this visit. Goodnight Art.

. . .

(During the second and third interviews delegation—Art's problem of proper assignment of work to others—was discussed further; the third interview closed as follows.)

. . .

H: You believe in this way that you may be able to get more assistance from the foremen already here?

A: Well, yes, if I don't have to watch Bedford very closely. I don't think I will. It'll be tough, you know, letting him carry the complete responsibility for some of this stuff; but—

H: You feel it will really be tough?

A: Well yes; I do think it will be tough. For me, that is. I've been right in on most of his operations all the time, following everything day by day. It will be kind of tough for me to stand back and watch some of these fellows make a mistake once in a while; but I think I can hold back —that will be no cinch for me.

H: In your opinion, you'll want to get back in it? You'll be tempted to take over?

A: Yeah, you know, you've probably had the same experience yourself. You've probably seen Art doing some things once in a while you kind of wish you could get into. I must say I admire your holding back when you feel as though the jobs would move faster if you pitched in yourself. But you seem to give us the ball and expect us to carry it. I think I know how to do it—at least I will try.

H: Good. I'm confident you will do it, Art. And I am anxious to see you divide your work load with your subordinates. Well, I'll tell you, Art—it's getting late and time for you to get home to the family—but on the basis of your decision to share your responsibility shouldn't we celebrate? If Mrs. Hann has no objection, let's go over to Mike's and—

A: You aren't suggesting buying a drink to celebrate, are you?

H: Yes, and I'll buy you a dinner too. How about Mrs. Hann and the family though?

A: She will understand—Well, if it's on the company, all right.

H: All right, it's on the company, Art. I'll call Mrs. Hann and explain I'm taking you to dinner and tell her we're working on a deal to get you some help. I'll meet you down at the gate.

A: See you in ten minutes.

It is evident that a sound relation exists between two persons who come together to seek a solution to a delegation problem which is troubling them.

Adjustment counseling

The counselee may be emotionally unstable or feel so; he may feel immature; he may be afraid of imaginary dangers; he may be worried. The basis of the trouble may be in the uncertainties of the situation in which he finds himself. The unknown may be responsible for his insecurity.

In accordance with the principles of social need which have been discussed in previous chapters, an employee needs the feeling of acceptance, and so do people in other situations. The fact of cohesiveness of a small group depends upon this principle of acceptance in the group.

The nondirective method of counseling does not take on the responsibility for directing the life of an individual or a group. It is called "nondirective" to distinguish it from the general approach of advising, admonishing, exhorting, or attempting to force an individual or a group into certain pathways of patterned behavior.

Among psychotherapists of various persuasions, agreement seems to exist that some release from emotional tension may be gained by expressing feelings to someone else. Commonly we refer to this feeling of release as "getting things off the chest." One school of psychologists calls it catharsis. The Catholic Church would point to the confessional as serving this function. The emotional state which we have reference to is similar to the stress condition that we discussed in our fundamental approach to motivation. A person who is in the state of motivation has unresolved tensions to some degree. A person who has tensions or needs that have not been resolved may be in a disruptive emotional state if his behavior is not appropriate to the satisfaction of the need.

In some settings the employee's perception of the situational factors in his maladjustment will differ widely from that of the leader. Likewise, an employee's behavior might seem quite natural to him but not to his supervisor and fellow workers. This is the sort of case in which the counseling approach may be called for. In case of the junior accountants in the public accounting firm, Glowacki, White, and Stern, the attitude survey (Chapter 6) revealed that some of the juniors felt that they were not being recognized, their work was not being observed, and that they were better than their supervisors realized. Indeed, some did not even know, as the attitude survey revealed, who their supervisors might be! They wished to be counseled, in terms of their performance, by the resident partner.

It is abundantly clear from the results of this attitude survey, and from other employee attitude surveys of which this one is typical, that one of the central approaches to counseling can come from the need of the employee for a feeling of approval, approbation, security, or at least notice of his job performance. The employee is reluctant to initiate the situation. He is hesitant to ask his boss, "How am I doing?"

The rationale of nondirective counseling depends upon the self-reparative capacity of living things. This kind of counseling assumes that all persons have within their psychological make-up, itself mysterious, a capacity to improve, remediate, adjust, survive—with "a little luck" or help. This "luck" may be a situation so arranged that it will be favorable to such adjustment. The leader who uses the nondirective method attempts to provide only the setting for this remediation: the "little luck" or help. In the nondirective style of counseling, not a great deal of time is spent in delving into the past of the counselee. The immediate present and future of the person are the central matters that are dealt with. The dynamic pattern of needs satisfactions, which includes motivations, frustrations, and insights into adjustment by the counselee are all important in the nondirective counseling situation.

The warmth of the relationship between the counselor and the counselee is utilized by the counselor to assist in gradual growth of the counselee's psychological insights and adjustment of his behavior patterns to his social groups. The nondirective aspect of this counseling relationship does not remove the individual's initiative and independence, but instead it tends to cultivate these characteristics. The counselor does not solve the problem, but rather provides an environmental situation in which the counselee may solve his own problems.

Frustration disrupts the usual course of behavior, as discussed in Chapter 10. It does this in a number of different, sometimes subtle, ways. The usual efficiency in problem solving and adaptation to situations, which we call "mental alertness," sometimes cannot be resumed until frustration is sufficiently relieved. The counselee is likely to be one who is frustrated, one who has adjustment problems. The central purpose of nondirective counseling is to remove frustration so that usual, normal problem-solving behavior can take the place of frustrated behavior.

The first phase of a counseling program establishes initial contacts between the counselor and the counselee. Contact is generally best made first by the counselee. *The second phase* of the counseling program develops an understanding concerning the *modus operandi* of the counselor. The counselor makes it clear that he is not going to solve the counselee's problems for him. He emphasizes that the counselee will solve his own problems and that the role of the counselor is to provide the setting or help arrange the situation so that this can take place. The counselee *in the third and continuing phase* of the program talks about his problems and especially about the feeling tones that surround these problems, that is, aspects of frustration. In nondirective counseling, no progress is made until a sufficient degree of rapport has been established. This is a necessary but insufficient condition. Then the counselee starts to express his feelings. This is referred to as the "depth" part of nondirective counseling.

As the counselee begins to express his feelings they tend, at first, to be negative. His statements are characterized by complaint, hostility, aggressiveness, fear, worry, remorse; they are often, at this stage, characterized by unpleasantness, blame, and subjectivity directed toward a member or members of the several groups with whom the counselee interacts.

The nondirective counselor accepts these expressions. He shows that he understands them. He gives no indication of either approval or disapproval. This is, of course, a new situation for the counselee! He has probably not encountered this kind of understanding impartiality either at home or with groups in the community or work places. His ordinary life situation has been quite different. In these usual life situations he has been in the habit of criticizing and even fighting; here he does not need to criticize or fight; he begins to feel at ease. He finds that when he discusses other people unfavorably, he does not "get a rise" out of the counselor. In fact, the counselor does not show any of the emotional or retaliatory behavior that he is used to. No need is satisfied by negative behavior, since no special emphasis or notice is given it by the counselor. The counselee finds that he can express himself in a free and easy way and that he will have a good listener who will not criticize, discipline, or find fault with him. In expressing himself, he may recognize feelings and motivations that he has never before perceived in himself.

Sometimes the counselor may clarify, by a brief sentence or comment, some of the thoughts expressed by the counselee. He does this in a way that makes it apparent that he is attempting to clear up his own confusion rather than that of the counselee. He does not, however, make interpretations or diagnosis. His comments are limited to clarification. He merely expresses back to the counselee the feelings which the counselee had expressed; he does this to show that he understands them and not to imply that he is going to do something about them. This interest and striving for clarity on the part of the counselor tends to cause the counselee to examine his feelings still farther. And the permissive and acceptant atmosphere makes it easy for him to do so. The counselor is not very active—he listens and creates a warm, accepting climate.

Gradually the counseling periods become more and more positive as the counselee looks upon the more positive side of the feelings that he is expressing. Frustration tends to be dissipated and insight and intellectual evaluation begin to take its place. The counselee tends to become more socially functional, that is, he develops a less negative outlook toward people. He becomes able to choose substitute goals that are within his reach. This is the characteristic form of behavior that indicates a road to mental health. The stresses and tensions of the counselee become lessened; aspirations are adjusted to a realistic probability of achievement. Remediation is reflected by functional adjustment to groups. At this stage in the counselee's self-development, the counselor can begin to pay more attention to the rational aspects of the counselee's expressions. He can help him by being patient; he hopes the counselee will further clarify his thinking about the choices of goals and goal behavior that are available to him.

In this aspect of the counseling program the counselor may, with mutual profit to all, take a somewhat more active part. His interest here is exploring. Direction is a matter of degree. He still does not tell the counselee what to do. The counselee explores various possibilities of action; he still does most of the talking. And this exploration includes the possible consequences of alternate courses of action. The counselee gradually becomes more independent of the counselor.

It is at this point that the counselor is more directive than at any other time. He is the one who first suggests that the counselee does not need to come regularly to discuss his problems. Intermittent meetings, spaced two weeks to a month, or perhaps even at six months' intervals, may be appropriate, so that the counselor has an opportunity to follow up and observe the functional adjustment of the counselee.

We have been looking in the last few pages at the development of an interactive relationship that a psychotherapist develops with the counselee. In what ways are a leader and psychotherapist alike? In the first place, if the leader follows the democratic, participative, permissive, nondirective style, he is using the same approaches as the psychotherapist uses.

In the second place, the nondirective leader, while working with both individuals and groups, actually uses a modified form of nondirective counseling.

The method is congruous with the principles of needs satisfaction: alleviation of frustration, motivation, and the establishment of an atmosphere conducive to mutual understanding and mutual goals. Nondirective counseling is itself a specific application of these principles. The nondirective approach can, of course, be used with groups. It is the passive, indirect discussion-leading procedure. Role-playing contains ingredients of the nondirective approach. On-the-job-training and formal training and teaching may be done with the nondirective emphasis. The so-called incident process method depends upon the development of questions and insights on the part of the trainee. If he wants to grow in experience, he must ask questions. Before he will get further description of the incidents or episodes that make up the incident process procedure he must ask questions.

The nondirective counseling procedure is to the trained psychotherapist as the participative, permissive leadership style is to the leader. The leader using this style does not use coercion, admonition, discipline, orders, authority, vested power or fiat. Rather, he depends upon understanding of reasonable expectations and the establishment of mutual goals. A parent, teacher, or supervisor may use the nondirective approach when he is combining parenthood, teaching, or supervision with leadership. One can be a supervisor without being a leader. If he is using the extreme autocratic, authoritarian, directive style he is not, by definition, being a leader. To the extent that he does use this style, he is a leader—in terms of our operational definition of leadership.

Here is an example. Suppose a company (we may recall this example from business and industry) makes a formal employee evaluation every six months. The time has come for doing this. The supervisors rate the employees on a systematic, prepared rating form. A particular employee is found, through the rating process, to be excellent or good on some of his job aspects and unfavorable on one or two other aspects. The employee wants to know how he is doing on the job. How will the information be played back to the employee? Would it be done in terms of improvement? Can the situation be set up so that there will be mutual understanding? Will efforts be made towards remedial solutions, that is, helping the employee to unlearn his inappropriate reaction patterns and to develop new behaviors that will be more appropriate? How can this best be done? Can it be done by calling him on a carpet and disciplining him concerning his deficiencies? Or would it not be appropriate to do it through a nondirective counseling, post-appraisal interview?

If the nondirective interviewer calls the employee in and asks him how he thinks he got along during the past six months and then sits back and listens, he is likely to have the experience of hearing a self-appraisal substantially in agreement with the rating made out for the employee. The employee is likely to come up with constructive suggestions for improving himself. They might not be precisely the same as the suggestions which management might make, yet they might be appropriate. They may be even more appropriate because they are part-and-parcel of the thinking of the employee: they are his very own suggestions. And they are more realistic in terms of the psychological make-up of the employee himself. The employee certainly believes in and accepts his own suggestions. He is more likely to accept his own suggestions than management's. And this is especially true if there is a communications or group barrier between the two. His supervisor does not need to sell, manipulate, propagandize, coerce, force, threaten, or discipline. All the supervisor as a nondirective interviewer needs to do is to take, in a considerate, warm, friendly way, what the counselee has said about his own solutions to his own situation. But you as reader might say that this is an example of the ideal situation where all aspects of the scene have been set. True. And this is the job of the leader—to arrange the situation so that there will be mutual understanding and mutual effort toward a common goal.

A nondirective philosophy of leadership

Procedures known as nondirective counseling have emerged. These are based on the hypothesis that in all human nature there are remedial forces within. Thus it is the therapist's task to set the stage so that the patient himself can find adequate adjustments through developing goals and understandings concerned with his problems of maladjustment. In nondirective thearpy the clinical psychologist makes use of consideration rather than direction, of self understanding rather than coercion. That is, he lets the patient talk through his problems, and the patient, himself, finds his answers to them. These are not in the end the answers that the therapist sees, but they are the answers that are suitable, mutually satisfactory to both, and satisfying to the counselee. It is through the establishment of mutual goals, through sincere understanding and development of warm climate that the patient is helped. Scientific evidence based on quantitative research with use of adequate research designs and adequate samples, is available to support this approach.

Perhaps nowhere is the poverty of authority more evident than it is in the relationship of management and workers. History of the relationship of management to labor suggests that management, at first, thought of the employee as a serf or slave; later it looked upon the laborer as a commodity to be bought and sold, in terms of supply and demand. During the era of scientific management at the turn of the century, there was some consideration given to the feelings of the worker; but the trend mainly emphasized incentive devices that would enable him to live better off the job, and little thought was given to his happiness on the job.

Later still, especially during the 1930's as a result of strikes by labor and other overt evidences of labor unrest, management of business and industry was, like the mother and like the slave owner, forced to cast about for more effective devices for dealing with labor. Authority was no longer effective. The poverty of authority was evident: workers began in the middle 1930's to have more power, through their sanctions, than management. That is the situation, of course, today.

Coupled fortunately with these happenings were such studies as the Fritz Roethlisberger, William Dickson, and Elton Mayo Harvard University studies conducted first in the Western Electric Company's Hawthorne Plant. These studies highlighted the needs of the worker for social approbation and approval by management. These were found to be potent motivational influences.

Thus was born the technique for developing the area which we now call "human relations." Managements began to think in terms of methods which would enable them to communicate better in order to establish mutual goals and mutual understanding.

Now labor has begun to think it is not wholly good to spend too much time, energy, and resources in fighting over how the pie should be cut. Organized labor begins now to believe that it would be well to help management make a bigger pie, so that all could share in it. At the present time, labor unions maintain the controls of sanctions, thus preventing management from using its power. The power of one balances the power of the other. Since both are powerful, authority can be said to have little effect. And it is the manager of labor as well as the manager of industry who can become a creative leader through consideration, not authority. The stage is set for creative, nondirective leadership. Counseling in the nondirective way at once illustrates, and is a technique of, this philosophy.

We have examined nondirective counseling, developed by behavioral scientists as a human relations tool. We believe it is needed in all leadership situations, and we have illustrated this need from the case of Glowacki, White, and Stern. The attitude survey, discussed in Chapter 6, revealed it as a human relations need.

The post-appraisal interview, if properly conducted, can do two things: help allay apprehensions leading to feelings of insecurity and reveal weaknesses of team members in a way that the member will not only want to correct them but will himself find ways for remedy.

While the nondirective style of counseling has been used mostly as a form of psychotherapy, its uses in leadership are clear. It forms the basis of a new philosophy of leadership.

Measuring and Improving Teamwork

SIX

*

If we are measuring the wrong thing, it will not help us to measure it better. . . . ROBERT JAMES WHERRY

17

Measuring teamwork improvement

Our only hope for improved leadership is to submit our present ways to the acid test of measurement. The acid of the test is the *criterion.* Here we will have a look at different kinds of criteria and examine some illustrations; we then define *syntality* and *synergy;* then we look at five earmarks of "good" criteria and discuss, briefly, the reason we cannot provide you with a cookbook of recipes for leadership.

If we wish to improve ourselves in any way as individuals, or as teams, or groups, or collectivities, a first requirement for improvement is to know how we are doing now. We need a measuring rod or yardstick. We might be interested in "follow-up"—we'll make a change to see what effect the change has on future activity. Or we might choose to follow-back—we want to see how we are doing now compared to how we were doing a while ago under different and definable conditions. In either case, follow-up or follow-back, we need, of course, some kind of a *criterion.*

Some criteria are quite simple: money earned this year as compared to last; amount of growth of a child in terms of height or weight, or the average amount of growth of a group of children; the number of people that comprise the population of a group, community, village, city, or a nation from one year to the next or one decade to the next; the number of people who vote for a particular political party at one election period as compared to another. These are examples of what appear to be simple criteria, designed to reflect change, improvement or growth, decline or decrease. Such criteria aid us in describing the phenomenon that is being observed. We use them in our daily lives almost continuously. We like to observe and discuss change. It is abundantly clear that we need adequate criteria of leadership.

The various criteria that we use in our daily living, and that behavioral scientists use to test one way of doing as compared to another, fall into two classes. We now discuss these two kinds of criteria briefly. In the next sections, examples of criteria of leadership and team dynamics will be given; then we are ready to point to some ways of evaluating criteria and look into uses of criteria for improvement of teamwork, which is our goal.

Kinds of criteria

The two kinds of criteria have been called "subjective" and "objective."

Subjective criteria are not measurements but can, if we wish, be converted into numerical codes. We sometimes say, "the team did well" as contrasted to "the team did poorly." We could convert the word "well" or "good" into code "1" and the word "poorly" into "zero." However, in our ordinary day-to-day life situations we do not convert such adjective (adjectival) designations as "good, fair, and poor" or "outstanding, superior, or excellent," "good, above average, average, below average, inferior, poor, and useless" into codes. These are judicial criteria. They are called "subjective" because they depend upon judgment of a person as observer. In spite of the fact that we are able to superimpose a figure or code upon them, they are basically derived from judgment. And we see at once that such criteria are amenable to all of the foibles of human judgment, such as contagious bias, lenient tendency, halo, stereotype, incorrect observation, lack of basis for comparison, and other forms of human error.[1]

Objective criteria are of a different kind. They consist of counting the pieces or parts. Examples of this are population statistics, production of factory workers, number of children or average height and weight of groups of children, and the like. Such criteria are quantitative; that is, they are available at once in numerical form. And these criteria, unlike the subjective kind, are usually not amenable to human error except in counting, as might occur as arithmetic errors, or in reading a yardstick. Objective criteria at least appear to be much more scientific than subjective criteria.

In the field of behavioral science, however—and that is the field in which leadership and teamwork fall—it is not always possible to get adequate objective criteria. Usually we have to depend upon judgment, criteria of the subjective kind. Indeed we quite often have combinations of subjective and objective criteria and put these units or items together into a composite, as will, we hope, be clear in the examples of criteria that will be discussed below.

We should mention a word of caution with regard to objective criteria. Even when available, they are not perfect. In the final interpretation of a set of figures that reflect change or improvement, a subjective judgment is made. Of course, in observing and reading the scale or in adding items, a human judgment is made, too. When we deal with quantitative aggregates and use statistical formulas, we find that statisticians do not always agree among themselves as to which formula to use or which experimental design would be best to reveal the changes that we are studying or the improvement in which we are interested. Nevertheless, in using an objective yardstick we agree, I am sure, that there is less of the human element involved than there is in such adjective designations as "good" or "poor."

In studying the various phenomena of leadership it would be well to look at the several approaches that have been used in the past. In the first place, we might study changes that take place in the individuals comprising the group; second, we might look at interactions among these individuals; and third, we might look at their product or the outcome of group activities.[2]

[1] These are discussed in some detail in R. Bellows and M. F. Estep, *Employment Psychology: The Interview* (New York: Rinehart and Co., 1954).

[2] Raymond B. Cattell, "New Concepts for Measuring Leadership, in Terms of Group Syntality," *Human Relations*, IV (1950), 161–84.

The first one of these methods, which has been called the population approach, simply is concerned with each individual that comprised the group. Then an average of the individuals is taken. For example, a leadership test is given to each person before and after training, or before and after having an action research experience. Such a test would tend to reflect change in the average of the individuals; it would not measure change of the total group. If it is true that the behavior of the group is suprasummative—that there is more to group activity than there is in the sum of its parts—then we should not expect the study of individuals and adding or taking the average of the individuals comprising the group to reflect group changes, nor should we expect it to tell the whole story about the group. This is the old concern—the whole may be more than the sum of its parts.

The second way of studying groups and group change is to study interactions of members of groups. For example, we might use a sociometric approach and take choices of the people in the group, in terms of their preferences for co-workers: "With whom would you like to work?" Or we might study communications; how people communicate in groups. This would lead us into a study of organizational structure.

The third, and by far the most practical, way which has been used to study change is in terms of productivity or outcomes of group activity. Cattell calls this "syntality." [3] This is what we usually refer to as criteria of group performance. Behavioral scientists have been studying individual performance in job situations and in family, school, community, labor, business and in national affairs for a long time, perhaps fifty years. Everyone would tend to agree at once that the outcome, or productivity, or that which the group accomplishes, is the most important aspect of a group. So, as applied behavioral scientists and action research workers, we are concerned with practical outcomes. Our problems are in the applied areas—as contrasted to pure research which, it will be recalled, is conducted for the sake of extending the areas of knowledge rather than for applying or improving a situation. The theoretical constructs, new concepts and new findings relating to leadership are, we hope, to be applied to the actual situation. This is of considerable importance to us.

[3] The term *syntality* was first used thus by Raymond B. Cattell in "Concepts and Methods in the Measurement of Group Syntality," *Psychological Review,* LV (1948), 48–63. See also R. B. Cattell and L. G. Wispe, "The Dimensions of Syntality in Small Groups," *Journal of Social Psychology,* XXVIII (1948), 57–78; R. B. Cattell, "The Dimensions of Culture Patterns by Factorization of National Characters," *Journal of Abnormal and Social Psychology,* XLIV (1949), 443–69; and R. B. Cattell, "An Introductory Note on the Theory of Group Learning," *Journal of Social Psychology,* XXXVII (1953) 27–52.

Examples of syntality

We need criteria or measures of syntality in any applied science, so that we may reflect back upon different ways of doing, in order to improve these ways of doing. For example, assume we are studying a group of children and the purpose of the group is to learn, as in school, to use tools to produce useful objects such as book ends, bookshelves, picture frames, and the like. The criterion could be the number of objects of a standard quality that is produced by a group per unit of time. Now we could vary the ways of training the leaders of child groups; and using productivity as a criterion, we might note how it is affected by varying these features of the situation. Thus we might be able to tease out more efficient, economical, or effective ways of training child leaders, so that they could arrange the situation for the activity to progress toward the goal, productivity, in a shared way. This is our definition of leadership: it is seen that not one person, "the leader," is solely responsible; rather, the group as a whole is responsible for productivity.

One person might stand out as being the arranger, or the chief arranger, of the situation, the others participating in these arrangements. They may help in planning the arrangements. The teacher is considered as a formal leader, a chief arranger, but not the producer. The teacher arranges the situation so that learning can take place by the group in a most optimal and economical manner. The measure of syntality would be amount learned, since this is the goal of the group.

Now we might invoke an experimental design in which we varied certain features or aspects of the leadership situation to see under what conditions learning could take place most economically. Would it take place most economically in small or in large groups? Would it take place with an authoritarian and autocratic approach on the part of the teacher or would it take place most readily in terms of democratic style where the pupils would participate in the planning of the sessions? Is the lecture method, which is somewhat nonparticipative, more effective in producing results than is the discussion method which is somewhat participative and nondirective? Formal experimental designs have been set up by educational psychologists to study the influence of variables such as structure, organization, and interaction upon the criterion of syntality. In some cases the criterion is the amount learned per unit of time by the individuals in the group, or average learning of the group in terms of gains on, before, and after tests of the achievement type.

We may now consider criteria of effective leadership in the case of the family group—the most common of our life situations. What kind of criteria, to reflect the success of leadership within this group, would be appropriate?

It would seem, in the first place, that a number of different aspects of family life should be taken into account. This would suggest that, unlike the learning situation that was used above as an example of criteria of leadership, not one but many subcriteria would be used. These could possibly be put together into a composite or total over-all index of effectiveness of the family unit. It should be borne in mind that we are concerned not with family status at a particular time but with the on-going, continuous, dynamic, changing family relationships with other family units, with the community, school, the work situation of the father, and perhaps also of the mother, and other aspects of the activties of the family. It is possible that it would not be feasible to use quantitative criteria. The number of children in the family is one basis, but a family of ten children without adequate economic earnings would not be as good from the standpoint of community welfare as a smaller family. Thus any one criterion might be modified in terms of other situational aspects of the family. Some negative measures, such as the amount of delinquency or the number of contacts with the police and the courts would be a criterion aspect. Gains over a period of years in social and economic status would be a good sign, as would health. Illness can be traced to diet, living conditions, and emotional stresses that are more or less controlled by the leadership forces and dynamic conditions which accompany family life. These attributes of families are, in part, attributable to leadership.

Another example of leadership criteria has to do with the community, village, town, or municipal activities. A community that is "good" might be thought of as one that has an above average number of churches and good schools with effective physical facilities. The number of libraries, number of books in libraries, and the number of parks would be useful as criteria.

On the negative side, the absence of slum housing, relatively low juvenile delinquency rate, low crime rate, low number of divorce, manslaughter, and murder cases—these would all be indicative of a successful community. Certainly the absence of graft and corruption in the political government of a community would be taken into account in a total overall index of the goodness of a community. The number of saloons and gin mills in the community, the amount of alcohol consumed would be another negative aspect, whereas productivity in terms of gross dollars, and purchase and use of consumer goods would be a positive factor.

It is seen at once that as we get into larger groups and clusters of group phenomena, criteria become more complex, but it is not impossible to obtain such indices. We use less formal and less precise guesses as to community goodness in our daily conversation. We hear people say, "I do not like Chicago. It is too big. Both Detroit and Pittsburgh are smoky towns, and the traffic hasn't yet been taken care of. In Detroit there are a million automobiles, and there is a great deal of congestion in the downtown area. Los Angeles has too much smog, and that is unhealthy. I would neither live nor work in New York City. The crowds, and especially the subways, are very frustrating." Such expressions on the part of most everyone are commonplace statements.

Social scientists have attempted to do somewhat better than this. They tend to use more quantitative indices of goodness and, by studying the reliability of these indices, to interpret them in the light of carefully collected judgments of selected experts.

Such criteria reflect leadership conditions over a period of time; and it is only through study and improvement of the criteria that leadership in the myriad aspects of municipal life and government can be improved. Social scientists, in this as in other areas of leadership, are in the beginning stages of discovery. The surface is now only being scratched in terms of the quest for better ways of arranging situations to produce more desired results.

But we must have a start in these improvements, and starts come from definitions and concepts, the development of a body of knowledge, and from method which depends upon the criteria we have been discussing. Then from design of investigations, to reveal on an empirical or scientific basis the best leadership, we may expect to see improvement and advances in the decades to come.

Criteria pertaining to industrial, business, and military leadership have been worked on to a considerably greater extent than perhaps any other area. This is because industrial and military psychologists have, for a greater number of years, been concerned with individual criteria; more recently, during the last two decades they have studied group criteria, or criteria of syntality of teams. In some instances in industry it is possible to get objective criteria of success or achievement of groups in terms of production, or average hourly production, or production adjusted for scrap, or cost figures concerned with unit costs of product or product assemblies.

In one instance it was found desirable to obtain a criterion of achievement or productivity of a group of card punch operators. The criteria were collected on an individual basis. It was feasible to obtain the average hourly production of the card punch operator workers. It was also practical to count the number of errors that they made, since each punched card was reviewed and checked for errors. Then it was easy to charge back to the card punch operator the number of errors that the operator made, since a cost analysis procedure was in operation. The number of errors could be charged in terms of the number of equivalent units of work using the punched cards as a base. A criterion of syntality —production adjusted for errors—was derived and set up for each worker and each shift.

The group on the day shift produced, on the average, more errorless cards per hour than the night shift; the variability of performance on the day shift was lower than that of the night shift. Taking the two shifts together, it was found that the best card punch operator punched ten times more cards than the poorest card punch operator. The day shift's significant superiority to the night shift prompted inquiry into the reasons. This particular study was oriented toward selection of card punch operators, not leadership. However, leadership problems were involved in this situation, and it would have been well had the study explored leadership in addition to selection.[4]

There are many situations in which individual and group criteria can be collected in terms of syntality. There has been a great deal of work done on the development of such criteria of performance for sales personnel. Such variables as number of units sold, the gross dollar value of sales, per cent of quota achieved, number of returns, and sales cost by individuals and by groups are used as criteria. Other criteria in the sales field that have been used are of a different nature. These are subjective criteria. They involve ratings or judgments of sales people by supervisors or others who have observed their performance.

Industrial and business enterprises are, of course, interested primarily in productivity because they have to make a profit in order to stay in business. However, it is the goal of top management and other managers that profit be made over a long period of time. This emphasizes the need for productivity coupled with morale or happiness or satisfaction of the workers involved in the production.

Indeed, in some organizations morale is of primary importance. This

[4] William H. Stead, Carroll Leonard Shartle, and Associates, *Occupational Counseling Techniques: Their Development and Application* (New York: American Book Co., 1940), pp. 73–94.

is another aspect of syntality. Thus a labor union desires to develop and maintain a high degree of cohesiveness among the group members. It is interested in morale as an outcome of its activity.

Some industrial concerns, notably the General Electric Company, have recently been developing a measure of employee relations. This measure tends to reflect what we may call "the goodness of personnel handling." It may also reflect productivity, but not necessarily so. Union organizations could use similar measurements of dimensions of their organizations as criteria. With these, they could learn better methods of handling or managing their memberships. Similarly, it would not be out of place to mention that community groups could learn new and better ways of leadership. Some of these are now exploring the research done in the development and evaluation of criteria as indices of goodness of group relations and group performance, so that they can in turn develop and evaluate better methods of handling their problems.

Among the attempts to get an index of employee relations, to be used as a criterion to reflect different ways of leadership, there has been developed an employee relations index, labeled ERI. This has been found to be an interesting and promising tool. The ingredients of this index are: the amount of absenteeism, in terms of the number of absences in the group; the amount of turnover or the number of people who quit to work elsewhere; the amount of lateness or tardiness; the number of suggestions that have been submitted by members of the group for improvement of the working conditions and for the production; the number of initial visits to the company medical doctor or dispensary; the amount of participation in voluntary employee benefit programs.[5]

An index of employee relations or "the goodness of personnel handling" is a tap into one of the significant aspects of leadership. Studies have been made to determine what the relationship of a total over-all index such as ERI is to: (1) productivity and (2) morale as measured by a conventional employee morale index. In some plants of the company in which the ERI had been developed it was found that there was a relationship between ERI and both productivity and morale. The ERI is a promising device for the future; it ties down a large number of subcriteria and yields a composite criterion that is meaningful, reliable, and related to significant variables external from it, such as morale, determined by a separate procedure for measuring job satisfaction.

In the military establishments, the ultimate criterion of leadership

[5] Willard Merrihue and Raymond A. Katzell, "ERI—Yardstick of Employee Relations," *Harvard Business Review* (1955), pp. 91–99.

is winning a military engagement, battle, or war. However, there are many phases of winning such engagements. For example, the training of air crews, the noncommissioned officer leadership academies, the command and general staff schools for top management, and such establishments as the academies for training of Air Force, Army, Navy, Marine, and Coast Guard officers. A substantial share of the research in human relations that has been conducted thus far has been done by military establishments to improve leadership.

Syntality and synergy

Cattell defines and uses the concepts of syntality and synergy for analyzing group dynamics.[6] He looks upon a group as an arrangement that permits and controls energy expenditure of its members; it is a goal-achieving or need-satisfying device. The total energy commanded by the group is called "synergy."

Cattell conceives two kinds of synergy: maintenance synergy, which is that used in keeping the members together and effective synergy, the residue which the group uses to achieve its goals. These can be illustrated by reference to the family life group: maintenance synergy is energy used to keep the family group intact; and the remainder, the effective synergy, is used to achieve goals, for example, earning money, having and educating children, entertaining friends, and recreation.

The reader will think of examples of groups which exist merely for existing, not to accomplish anything. Most groups have "a cause" other than just to maintain themselves. Some do not. A social club may exist and "do nothing" but have fun. Amount of fun, then, is the only index or criterion of syntality.

The leader exists because he has an influence on group syntality. Several leaders, as defined, may be present in a group; one may stand out as having a greater influence on use of synergy in the group goal-seeking activity. And leadership often "passes from hand-to-hand" when new problems arise in the group. "Since every man affects the syntality measures, every man is more or less a leader." [7]

Measures of syntality reflect leadership: that leadership is best which yields greatest syntality. This is the reason for our interest in criteria of syntality. We turn now to ways of evaluating such criteria.

[6] Raymond B. Cattell, "New Concepts for Measuring Leadership," *Human Relations*, IV (1951), 161–84.

[7] *Ibid.*, p. 184.

Methods of evaluating criteria

Scientists working in the field of behavioral problems of leadership have been concerned with the evaluation of criteria of syntality. The development and evaluation of criteria itself is not a simple matter. We have said that two kinds of measurements can reflect leadership change: objective and subjective. Objective criteria are figures on, for example, productivity, lateness, and turnover. We have used these as illustrations of group performance criteria. How can they be evaluated? There are five ways:

1. *Such measurements as statistical reliability of criteria have been used.* A criterion, in order to be useful, must have some degree of internal consistency; that is, it must have reliability. A criterion with no reliability whatever cannot be useful as a base for guiding the way toward improvement in leadership.

Reliability is quite often assayed by a split-half method; the data are split up into two halves, and these are compared. An example of this is the comparison of productivity records of several groups of workers who are engaged in comparable production tasks. Let us say that we have a year's production figures by work weeks for a number of groups of bricklayer teams. Now suppose that we give each team a total score for their odd weeks of the year: weeks 1, 3, 5, 7, etc., and then suppose further that we give these same teams a total score for the even weeks 2, 4, 6, 8, and so on. We could then compare the relative standing of these teams on the total of the odd weeks and the total of the even weeks. We would expect them to maintain their same relative rank, and they would if there was high correspondence between the odd and even weeks. Or if there is some correspondence, we would expect them to tend to maintain their same relative rank. If they did not maintain their same relative rank in scores on the odd and even weeks—if there were no correspondence at all—we would then say that the criteria of syntality are not reliable. We would not expect such unreliable criteria to be predictable or to be related to any other kind of variable, such as the way the groups have been handled, led, or supervised. Other factors that might be related to productivity would not be revealed. Thus an index of reliability or internal consistency of the data is an evaluating procedure.

2. *A criterion should be related to other realistic measures of the success of the group.* Thus we would expect that turnover, absenteeism,

and productivity would be interrelated. If we find that there is no relationship between turnover and productivity, we would be somewhat suspect of the criteria of production. If the results of analysis do not indicate what is reasonably expected, we would say that the criteria are not very good criteria.

3. *Another earmark of the good criterion of leadership and change is the judgment as to whether the criteria are realistic to the situation.* We would not use the number of bills typed by billing clerks per unit of time if this was an unimportant aspect of their job or if they were kept busy on something else besides typing bills during a large share of their working period. Number of bills typed would not be realistic.

4. *A criterion of change must not be contaminated by external influences.* This is another fundamental rule in the development and evaluation of criteria. Artificial influences sometimes impose limits on a team or group of workers. The team does not have control over these artificial conditions. If there is poor lighting in some of the workrooms, we would not expect the groups operating under poor lighting conditions to perform as well as those working under good lighting conditions; those with poor equipment or machines perform less well than those with better machines. If quotas have not been realistically set, this would be an artificial limitation. A group of salesmen working in a territory that does not lend itself to sales of the particular product would be handicapped. Yet such a group might be working under the same quota as a group that is working in a "lush" territory where sales are easy. By the same token, we would not compare juvenile delinquency figures in two parts of the city—the downtown slum area and the more remote suburban area —without adjusting the quotas systematically.

In exploring the evaluation of criteria for appraisal of social change—for example, the influence of different modes of leadership on outcomes of group activity—it is readily seen that we are dealing with complex situations. We have suggested how reliability or internal consistency of criterion information is one earmark of the goodness of the criterion of group activity and performance. Interrelationships of one criterion with another reasonable or realistic criterion is another earmark of a suitable measure of social change. Both of these first two earmarks seem to be objective, inasmuch as they do not appear to depend on judgment or fallible human estimate, which is always subject to the errors of stereotyping and personal favoritism, halo, and prejudice. However, the third and fourth earmarks are influenced by judgment.

5. *A criterion must be free from contaminating bias.* No matter how

much the scientist tries to detach himself from his cultural habits, which lend themselves to errors of judgment, he has a difficult time in doing so. For this reason even in considering criteria that are really objective in nature, there is always a person making a judgment about it, evaluating it, and relating it to other criteria with which it might be combined into a composite index. The work of Merrihue and Katzell referred to above in connection with ERI is relatively free from such human bias, since these research workers used statistical methods to combine the different ingredients of the employee relations index. This is an unusual approach; it is one to be commended. In the future, more-and-more behavioral research scientists will utilize such methods.

We spoke in a previous chapter of some of the foibles of human judgment. We referred to contagious bias. The scientist himself is not free from contagious bias. He may fall into the insidious error of contaminating his data by allowing his own background prejudices to influence his view of what he finds. He may even project his own stereotypes or biases into what he observes, so that he sees certain things in terms of his own set, posture, or the predispositions of his psychological make-up. In the areas of evaluation of criteria, we call this error contamination. We have referred to it, in the case of criteria of individual performance, as illicit use of predictor information.[8] How does this work in the case of criteria of group performance and improvement?

We may draw an illustration from the area of industrial social psychology. Suppose that we are studying two styles of foremanship. Suppose that we have isolated what we might call the "worker-oriented" foremen and another group of managers which might be called the "work-oriented" foremen. When the worker-oriented foreman is asked what his job is, he is likely to reply that if he takes care of his men, his men will take care of him. He might say, "I have ten men on the production line, and my main job is to help them get out the work." He says that he pays close attention to management above him in the organization hierarchy, in order to be "in on the know-how and know-who," but he is likely to say that he does this so that he will be able to get things for his men, so that he can plan and initiate appropriate changes. When asked about the closeness of supervision—how continuously and rigidly he looks over the work of the men—he is likely to say "I don't breathe down the necks of the men." He is there when they need him. He has a feeling of consideration and cooperation, he tends to create a warm,

[8] R. M. Bellows, "Procedures for Evaluating Vocational Criteria," *Journal of Applied Psychology*, XXV (1941), 499–513.

not cold, atmosphere. Such a foreman would tend to provide a democratic rather than an autocratic, authoritarian environment.

We have also singled out a sample of foremen who may be considered the opposite of worker oriented; we have called these "work oriented." When we ask one of these foremen what his job is, he is likely to reply that his *raison d'etre* is to get production, get the finished product out the back door with a minimum of cost. When asked his relationships with management above him in the organizational structure, he is likely to say that he follows their edicts to the letter and he passes these down to the men in no uncertain terms. He supervises closely—"breathes down the necks of the men." We see in such a foreman a person who is the epitome of authority. He expects his men to behave in terms of his orders and not think about it. He lacks consideration, but he is a director of action. He, of course, would be classed as an autocratic authoritarian.

What we want to do is to prove or disprove the efficacy, or relative effectiveness, of the two different styles of leadership for a particular situation. So we go back to the groups that are supervised by the worker-oriented and the work-oriented foremen. We seek criteria of syntality, production, or other evidence of the efficiency of their activity. We are interested in outcomes, and we find that we can use production as the criterion. So we take all of the foremen who tend to have the worker-oriented style of leadership and get the average production of these groups. Likewise, we take the other groups, those supervised by the work-oriented foremen, and we compute the average productivity. Now, if we find a significant difference between these two averages of productivity, we might then feel that we could safely attribute the difference between the two kinds of groups to the style of leadership.

Is it safe to draw such a conclusion?

The answer to this question depends upon the care which has been taken in assembling and interpreting the criterion information. We are on somewhat firmer ground in dealing with the predictor side of the picture, that is the style of leadership, than we are when we are dealing with the criterion side. While both sides of the picture lend themselves to errors in human judgment, experience shows that there is more chance for contamination to enter into the picture on the criterion side. Even objectively, empirically, and quantitatively trained scientists who adhere rigorously to scientific method sometimes fall into the error of selecting their criterion information and their criterion groups in terms of predictor information. Since it is so difficult to evaluate, select, and combine subcriteria such as productivity, scrap, and errors, it sometimes happens that social scientists choose those criterion subassemblies which are most highly predictable. This is an insidious rule—predictability as an earmark of the good criterion—because it leads us to select from the various criteria those which show the results that we think are reasonable and that we expect to show.

It becomes easier and easier to see how contamination through contagious bias may influence what appears to be a highly empirical scientific result. This is not to say in any sense that scientific investigations are to be deplored. They are not. The design that we have discussed constitutes one of the only available general approaches to improving leadership. Yet we must emphasize the limitations of our present studies; this has been done through the illustrations of studies that are concerned with foremanship style. If there is some danger in the use of criteria such as production that is countable—that exists in terms of measurable quantities per unit of time—then such precautions would be doubly important when subjective ratings of group syntality or performance are utilized as the main basis for estimating change or improvement through different leadership styles.

What can we expect, in the next decade or two, by way of improvement of criteria? Robert J. Wherry [9] sets forth this prophesy:

> 1. Continued study of the ultimate criterion with emphasis upon clarification of purpose, refinement and definition, and improvement in measurement methods.
> 2. Increased emphasis in the field of criterion equivalence, *i.e.,* attempts to prove that more easily and cheaply obtainable criteria will actually accomplish the same results as would the ultimate criterion.
> 3. Improvement in methods of job and situational analysis techniques including a still better definition of the needed elements and of methods of estimating their presence. . . .
> 4. Studies to validate these rational approaches empirically so that they will represent true psychological scaling rather than mere clinical hunches.
> 5. Further attention as to how to select proper criteria to accomplish the tasks in hand. . . .

The incautious inference

Suppose, upon detailed and careful investigation in a company structure which has twenty different working groups, that certain aspects or segments of morale of the employees are found to be significantly

[9] Robert J. Wherry, "The Past and Future of Criterion Evaluation," *Personnel Psychology,* X (1957), 1–6.

related to syntality. Suppose that we have obtained a score on the leader, or foreman, concerned with what the workers think of him. Suppose we ask the workers whether they can say "yes" to the following questions:

Is he cooperative? Does he follow through on his promises? Is he available when you need to confer with him? Does he keep you informed? Does he avoid too close supervision?

Let us give each of the foremen a score in terms of the number of "yes" answers he gets from his men. Now suppose that we really do have adequate syntality criteria in terms of reliable ratings of production. Let us then compare the "yes" scores of the foremen with the syntality of their groups. Suppose we find a high degree of relationship or association between these two separate variables. We conclude that it is good in that situation to have as many "yeses" as possible. What can we say about another company or companies in general throughout the United States or companies in general throughout the world? Can we generalize? Can we infer that the device will work in other organizations? The answer is "No." We cannot generalize from specific situations to others.

We are, therefore, concerned with the stability of findings, the regularity, the number of times that experiments can be replicated to get equivalent results. Science has not gone forward sufficiently in terms of repeated experiments so that we will be able to generalize; we must await additional cross-validity studies. It is seen, then, how important is stability of findings and how cautious we must be in generalizing. It is for this reason that we cannot provide definite formulas for leadership.

In this chapter we have emphasized the need for improving criteria of syntality; our hope for improving leadership depends upon "good" criteria. There is no easier way to improve. We have looked over some illustrative measures of syntality and have defined synergy. We listed and discussed five earmarks of good criteria and warned against making incautious inferences or providing cookbooks.

With criteria of syntality as our base, we next discuss selection and prediction of leaders in Chapter 18, and then look at leader and situational characteristics in the final chapter.

*

Some great men owe most of their greatness to the ability of detecting in those they desire for their tools the exact quality that matters for their work. JOSEPH CONRAD

18

Why executives fail

Man has for many centuries endeavored to assess his fellow man. Some of these attempts have been crude, some dishonest, some brilliant, some validated and effective. Even Plato (427?–347 B.C.) was concerned with selection. He said, "In the first place, no two persons are born exactly alike, but each differs from each in natural endowments, one being suited for one occupation and another for another." [1]

Descartes spoke of animals as machines and the minds of men as

[1] Plato, *The Republic of Plato,* Book II, trans. by J. L. Davis and D. J. Vaughan (New York: Burt, 1866), p. 60.

amenable to analytical study—and was punished for his brashness. Wilhelm Wündt thought of psychology as a science and is said to have founded the first laboratory, in 1879, in which to study it.

Today, personnel psychology, pushed forward by programs of human relations research during two world wars, has grown apace. In leader selection, what does it have to offer? A little progress has been made. What is ready to apply?

It will be interesting in this chapter to see what top managements check as reasons why leaders fail, look into some technical problems that block immediate improvement of leader selection, then look at results of typical research. Then the question, "What are leader attitudes?" is asked and, to some extent, answered. Following that, leader behavior patterns as earmarks of leaders and leader characteristics will be studied.

Why executives fail

We have emphasized that the side of the picture which we call criteria —successful performance in the administrative position—is a difficult one to bring into focus. Most managers of various kinds of enterprises cannot agree very well on who is successful and who is not. One comprehensive survey of why executives fail yields a variety of answers. It will be interesting to review the results of this study [2] to see what characteristics tend to be avoided by those who select executives.

The items in the questionnaire survey were answered by 177 top executives in companies of various size and geographical location. Eight of the respondents were presidents and 86 were vice-presidents. They were asked to rank items concerning knowledge and personal factors as reasons why executives fail. Among the former, the two items that were checked most frequently were: lack of breadth of knowledge, checked 85 times, and lack of personnel and administrative knowledge, mentioned 69 times. On the personal factor side, inability to delegate responsibility was the most frequently checked item. Other personal characteristics considered important by executives were: ability to analyze and evaluate, to judge people, and to cooperate with others. Tables 18.1 and 18.2 summarize the results of the study.

Insofar as knowledge factors enable the leader to create (i.e. to initiate structure), they are important in leadership. Furthermore, knowledge influences social climate to some extent, and to the degree that it enables the leader to contribute more to the situation, it is significant.

[2] Frederick J. Gaudet and A. Ralph Carli, "Why Executives Fail," *Personnel Psychology,* X (1957), 7–21.

TABLE 18.1 · Frequency of Knowledge Items Causing Failure of Executives as Checked by 177 Top Management Executives *

Knowledge factor items	*Number of times checked*
1. Lack of breadth of knowledge	85
2. Lack of personnel and administrative knowledge	69
3. Lack of knowledge of marketing and distribution	28
4. Lack of knowledge of technical processes	25
5. Lack of liability knowledge	23
6. Lack of corporate organization knowledge	23
7. Lack of labor law and labor relations knowledge	10
8. Lack of finance knowledge	9
9. Lack of knowledge of materials	8

* Modified from Frederick J. Gaudet and A. Ralph Carli, "Why Executives Fail," *Personnel Psychology,* X (1957), 16. With special permission.

TABLE 18.2 · Frequency of Personal Items Causing Failure of Executives as Checked by 177 Top Management Executives *

Personal factor items	*Number of times checked*
1. Inability to delegate responsibility	91
2. Inability to analyze and evaluate	84
3. Inability to judge people	81
4. Inability to cooperate with others	79
5. Decision inability	71
6. Lack of drive	60
7. Lack of responsibility	47
8. Lack of perseverance	23

* *Ibid.*

We, for our purposes in studying creative leadership, are not so much interested in Figure 18.1 as in 18.2. To be sure, specific knowledge as required in an executive position is of importance. This is a specific, not general cause of failure. Personal factors, in Figure 18.2, are of utmost importance, and will be discussed in detail later in this chapter.

Specific and technical knowledge as well as general knowledge is not so important as sometimes believed. This is borne out by a study by Roach.[3]

He studied supervisors to determine the factors involved in supervision. He obtained 70 essays; 35 were descriptions of "good" supervisors and

[3] Darrell E. Roach, "Factor Analysis of Rated Supervisory Behavior," *Personnel Psychology,* X (1957), 487–98.

35 of "poor" ones. He analyzed 1091 statements and developed from them a questionnaire which was answered by 245 supervisors. Fifteen factors characterizing supervisory behavior emerged, which were called:

open-mindedness
a general bias factor
personal compliance
job knowledge
direction of employee performance
rewarding performance
company loyalty
cheerfulness
acceptance of responsibility
group spirit
approachability
personal drive
impartiality
poise
consideration

It would appear that only one of these 15 factors is concerned with specific job knowledge of the nonhuman relations kind. The other 14 involve personal or human relations factors.

Research orientation

Before reporting some facts, methods, and results on selecting leaders, it is necessary to agree on a way of evaluation. There are two ways, just as for William James there are two kinds of people: the tough-minded and the tender-minded. The tough way of evaluating our present status is quantitative, statistical, a posteriori, empirical, technical: it requires evidence. The tender way is clinical, intuitive, a priori, armchair, argumentative, sometimes nontechnical: it requires no evidence but depends on persuasion.

The tough method was perhaps first set forth clearly and in detail for the selection area by Clark Hull; [4] it is now exemplified in the work of such specialists as Robert Wherry, Harold Edgerton, Marian Richardson, T. W. Harrell, Edwin R. Henry, E. E. Cureton, and Raymond Katzell. Validity evaluations that appear in the Validity Exchange Department of the magazine *Personnel Psychology* result from the tough-minded approach.

The soft approach to description of usefulness of tests in selection is exemplified, on the one hand, by lay approaches such as that of William H. Whyte, Jr. in *The Organization Man.* He has a pessimistic, cynical view of selection techniques. He feels that our present tests are tests of conformity rather than predictors of potential for management: "Whyte seems to have the ancient tendency to look at a normal distribution and suggest that it is too bad that so many persons are in

[4] C. L. Hull, *Aptitude Testing* (Yonkers, N. Y.: World Book Co., 1928).

the middle."[5] It is, indeed, too bad that half of the people are, in a normal distribution, below average.

Most leadership selection items, designed to predict the success of leaders, are, as Whyte insists, contaminated by what is technically called "facade" or social set. What is meant here, in less technical language, is that an applicant can fake answers to personality and interest inventories—"Have you ever thought of beating your wife?" "No (of course not)." "Are you irritable?" "No (of course not)." But the applicant may not deliberately intend to fake. He merely may have a set or tendency to please the examiner—to give him what he expects or hopes to get. In either case the applicant's bias or set can influence his score on a so-called leadership personality or interest inventory.

The forced choice technique has fortunately been somewhat successful in minimizing these influences in the case of items relating to preference and interest; the so-called lie scales have aided interpretation of the Minnesota Multiphasic Personality Inventory scores; but no such objective devices are known to have been devised for the projective techniques such as the Rorschach ink blot tests. Here corrections, if any, are made in an intuitive way by the clinician.

Interdependent developments during the past two decades, and more especially since 1950,[6] have somewhat advanced the heritage of knowledge. Perhaps the most promising development in the leader selection field has been the evolution of the forced-choice method. This has been used as a tool for self-description as well as for description of performance by observer raters. It tends to eliminate, to some extent at least, some of the usual evils of rating, such as favoritism and lenient tendency. There are now some fifty published items on forced-choice methods; one of the more outstanding of these is by Richardson.[7]

The word *assessment*, referred to as an aid to personnel and leader selection, came into popular use in psychological circles as a result of publication of a book titled *Assessment of Men*. It reviewed methods devised by the OSS during World War II. It seems ironical that subsequent events have revealed that virtually all of the techniques reported

[5] Edgar F. Borgatta, "The Social Ethic and Rational Choosing," *Contemporary Psychology*, III (1958), 88.

[6] Cf. L. J. Cronbach, "Assessment of Individual Differences," 1956; J. M. Butler and D. Fiske, "Theory and Technique of Assessment," 1955; P. E. Meehl, "Psychotherapy," 1955; E. L. Kelly, "Theory and Technique of Assessment," 1954, *Annual Review of Psychology*. These sources contain some 562 references that relate to the problems discussed here.

[7] M. W. Richardson, "Merit Rating," *Handbook of Industrial Engineering* (New York: McGraw-Hill Book Company, Inc., 1957).

in that book are useless—as Cronbach says, "Assessment in the OSS style has now been proved a failure." [8] Assessment for predicting leadership involves incautious inferences: clinical intuition is simply not good enough for the problems at hand.

There are now several levels of the use of selection items and their combinations in leader selection. The layman uses them sometimes in an incautious way. His lack of caution results in misuse: his tendency to stereotype, contagious bias, common misconceptions and invalid halo all tend to result in poor decisions. The clinician may depend only on his experience and intuitive judgment, without validation. On the other hand, he may use verification information in a more or less formal way.

There are, in turn, several levels of verification of selection item combinations for use.[9] Among these are predictive validity, status validity, content validity, and congruent validity. Scores that have predictive validity are found to be correlated to some useful degree with specific criterion data (see Chapter 17) when these are collected in the future. Those that have status validity correlate with criterion data presently available. Content scores correlate with the criterion, since they sample the criterion, as in achievement items or samples of leader behavior in which the content of the item is a selected miniature of the leadership criterion situation itself. Scores that have congruent validity are found to be correlated with some other score that is known to have validity with an external criterion of leader performance.

Assuming that the criterion used is satisfactory, items verified by any of these designs have sometimes been found to yield useful data resulting in better leader selection. Congruent validity would be expected to be least useful, however, because of the loss in predictive power resulting from the remoteness of the criterion—the intermediate step results in a greater inference hazard.

Unfortunately, leader performance criteria as used for validation are always fallible to some degree (see above, Chapter 17).

In most situations in which decisions are made, none of these usual means of demonstrating validity is entirely satisfactory. As was pointed out some time ago,[10] this is because the criterion one wishes to predict

[8] Cronbach, *op. cit.*

[9] Some of these are set forth by the American Psychological Association Committee on Test Standards, "Technical Recommendations for Psychological Tests and Diagnostic Techniques," *American Psychologist,* VII (1952), 461–75. Few tests now used would meet the standards designated as essential by this committee.

[10] R. M. Bellows, "Procedures for Evaluating Vocational Criteria," *Journal of Applied Psychology,* XXV (1941), 499–513.

is always in the future, never in the present. Criterion conditions change from the experimental situation, in which the items were validated, to the applied situation in which the items are used. Any index of validity must always, for this reason, be phrased in the past tense; for example, "Validity was found to be .50," *not* "Validity is . . ." or ". . . will be .50."

Criterion situations are dynamic; they change. Thus, in reality, there is no such thing as validation for future use. Another way of saying this is, following Meehl,[11] that a new actuarial formula must be prepared for each new decision, and of course no statistical experience table can be prepared in advance. For this reason, emphasis must be placed on cross-validity and repeated validity studies. In a nutshell: *an employment decision aid in selecting leaders is likely to be best if it has been found to hold up frequently in the past—to have validity.*

It seems that neither the clinical nor the empirical method, by itself, is the complete answer in decision making in selecting leaders. Interpretative judgments are always necessary. Our only hope is to try to sharpen these judgments. How can this be done?

Two guiding principles for the selection of leader assessment tools to use in making employment decisions have been implied in what we have said.

The first is *the principle of minimum inference.* When observed behavior is used to predict a known or guessed criterion, without evidence that it really does so, we may say that an inference is being made. Sometimes this inference is rash, incautious. We may get agreement among those making the inferences when actual validity will subsequently be found to be lacking, as was the case, for example, in the study of Holtzman and Sells.[12]

The principle of minimum inference is violated in greatest degree perhaps by lay procedures; next by assessment and decision aids employing theoretical constructs without validation; somewhat less by procedures verified by means of congruent validity; somewhat less when empirical keys have been developed and where many recurrent cross and sustained validity checks have been made; and least when content validity is recurrently verified.

[11] P. E. Meehl, *Clinical vs. Statistical Prediction* (Minneapolis: University of Minnesota Press, 1954).

[12] W. H. Holtzman and S. B. Sells, "Prediction of Flying Success by Clinical Analysis of Test Protocols," *Journal of Abnormal and Social Psychology,* XLIX (1954), 485–90. Lack of validity of inferred predictors was also found in many studies reviewed by Symons, *Journal of Projective Techniques,* 1954 and by Kelly, *Personnel Psychology,* 1954.

The above paragraph is one way of saying something that perhaps can be said in a clearer, less-technical way: that inference is almost the same as guesswork and that proof by tryout takes the inference, or guesswork, out. We naturally strive for greater certainty. That is the essence of applied science; it is the essence also of prediction and control. Certainty, it should be emphasized, is a matter of degree. For example, if we have tried out a test and found it to be significantly valid on 100 samples of leaders, then we can be fairly certain that it will have some significant degree of validity on the 101st sample. There is little inference involved here. But if we have not tried the thing out at all and are depending merely on our "clinical intuition," then the inference is maximum. Now let us go to the second principle.

The second is the *principle of parsimony*. Simplicity in applied research is a desired goal, and it is often simpler and easier to change the situation. Greater emphasis can be placed on analysis of *the situation* in which it is hoped improvements will occur. This emphasis on situational factors might pay off more than exclusive emphasis on the psychological characteristics of the candidates for leadership. This will be illustrated in Chapter 19. A brief example will suffice here. In a certain company, employee-oriented, participative foremen tended to achieve high production from their work groups, and management-oriented, authoritarian foremen tended to get lower production from their work groups. Top management required management orientation on the part of the foremen. This was an autocratic, authoritarian company. It would seek and select hard-boiled, whip-cracking foremen. But it sought the wrong kind. What this management needed was to change the situation; that is, to change itself! A changed social climate would change the specifications of its first line leaders; then leaders of the employee-oriented variety could be selected. Since the goal of management is production, the situational change would be the simplest, most parsimonious way of achieving its goal.

Thus far in this discussion we have considered some of the problems of leader evaluation. How valid or "good" are the selection tools available for this evaluation?

Validity must be considered from an actuarial viewpoint; from the point of view of probability. In other words, the question should be: "Will they raise our batting average?" We cannot expect, even with the best methods available, to make a hit every time. Here, in Table 18.3, is what you can expect from good, fair, and poor tests.

TABLE 18.3

		GOOD TESTS			FAIR TESTS			POOR TESTS		
					Job performance					
		Low 1/3	*Mid* 1/3	*High* 1/3	*Low* 1/3	*Mid* 1/3	*High* 1/3	*Low* 1/3	*Mid* 1/3	*High* 1/3
Test Scores	High 1/3	1	3	5	2	3	4	3	3	3
	Mid 1/3	3	3	3	3	3	3	3	3	3
	Low 1/3	5	3	1	4	3	2	3	3	3

According to Table 18.3 you selected nine men, those above the double line running across the page. This double line we might call the "critical" or "knockout" score, a level below which you would not hire. With the "good" tests, you would select five men (instead of three, as by chance or by "poor," invalid tests) who would be like those in the highest third in leader performance.

We may picture these same results in a different way in order to bring out a different concept. I will do this as a way of approaching the subject of motivation as it is related to selection.

We can agree that we would like to identify *all* of those characteristics that make a leader successful. This objective is, of course, an impossible one. However, we can think in terms of the proportion of *all* those characteristics that make for success that we can identify or tie down by the selection tests. Here, shown in Figure 18.1, is how "good," "fair," and "poor" tests show up:

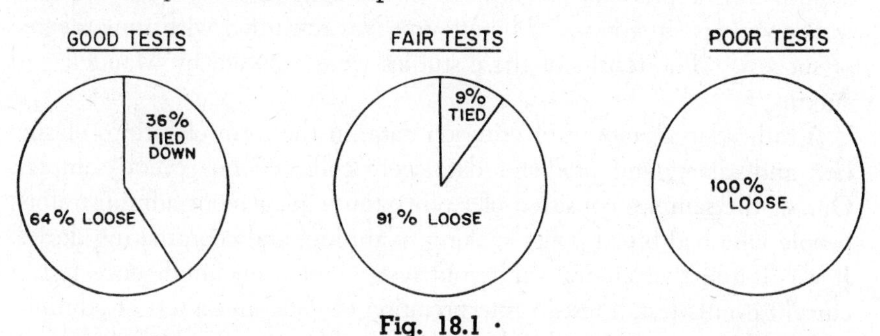

Fig. 18.1 ·

Now, of course, personnel psychologists—test and measurement specialists—are trying to improve selection tests. They have been trying for several decades. Some progress has been made, slowly. A plateau in this progress appears, to some observers, to have been reached. We cannot hope that the "good" tests will become very much better during the next decade or so. However, in some situations, the use of tests is very profitable indeed. This should, however, be emphasized: it depends on the peculiarities of the situation at hand.

Now, please glance back at the lefthand circle in Figure 18.1. At best, 64 per cent of all that makes for excellence of performance is "loose." Here is where the great contribution in leadership is to be made. Much of this 64 per cent can be ascribed to motivation as defined and discussed in previous chapters.

Selection research results

The U.S. Civil Service Commission has attempted to develop and evaluate tests to predict administrative competence. It has been realized that more accurate selection of better administrators and administrative trainees would yield large returns in economy and efficiency. But the difficulties in defining executive, administrative, and supervisory positions and in developing criteria of success against which predictors can be compared have delayed progress. Then, too, success in these jobs depends to an unknown degree on personal or personality characteristics of incumbents. And personal factors are more difficult to measure than most other psychological characteristics as more inferences are required in such measurement.

In one comprehensive program, the Civil Service Commission attempted to validate paper-and-pencil tests for predicting success in all administrative positions, regardless of the specific knowledge required in the various situations. The attempt was rewarded with some degree of success. The results of these studies were reported by Mandell and Adkins.[13]

A rather large amount of criterion data, in the form of ratings of success and salary, and predictor data were collected on several samples. One of the samples consisted of twenty top management administrators, people who had broad policy-making, planning, and coordinating duties. It was found that among the tryout tests chosen, an intelligence test, a current events test, a test in interpretation of data, and a test of administrative judgment appeared to have some usefulness. Each of these tests was found to "tie-down" about 40 per cent of all of that which makes up

[13] Milton M. Mandell and Dorothy C. Adkins, "The Validity of Written Tests for the Selection of Administrative Personnel," *Educational and Psychological Measurement*, VI (1946), 293–312.

administrative success as defined. They overlapped, however, so that a combination of them would not "tie-down" much more. These tests, while significantly valid under the conditions of the investigation, left much to be desired. This investigation may be said to be typical of a larger number of similar empirical studies.

Valid methods for selecting supervisors, administrators, or leaders are not necessarily valid in predicting success of leaders. Leaders are different from executives. The executive maintains the *status quo;* he is not necessarily creative, whereas the leader is creative. Most, in fact virtually all, of the hundreds of selection research studies pertain to selecting executives, administrators, or foremen; they do not pertain to selecting creative leaders as defined here.

Mandell, for example, developed an administrative judgment test [14] that had a considerable amount of validity. He defined an executive or administrative job as one in which it is estimated, from job analysis, that more than 50 per cent of the time is spent in planning and coordinating. He used a sample of 171 executives from several government bureaus.

He developed a multiple-choice test of administrative judgment to measure broad understanding of administrative problems and processes. Questions on the following topics were included:

1. Understanding of relationships between headquarters and field offices and between research and operating personnel.
2. Problems of timing programs.
3. Organization of the office of an administrator.

Two criteria of success were used: job performance in terms of the average of more than four ratings by peers and supervisors; the position, grade, or salary of the subject.

In addition to the administrative judgment test, a test of mental ability was tried out as a predictor of success. Both tests were found to be somewhat valid; the administrative judgment test was found consistently to be more valid than the test of mental alertness, for both crtieria and all samples. The former was found to "tie-down" about 25 per cent of success, whereas the test of mental ability only "tied down" about 15 per cent of it. Again, "success" is not necessarily creative leadership; this will be discussed later on.

[14] Milton M. Mandell, "The Administrative Judgment Test," *Journal of Applied Psychology,* XXXIV (1950), 145–52.

Other studies include one by Guilford and Comrey,[15] who state that attempts to predict success of administrators have not been very successful. They believe administration calls for a great number of characteristics and that these are difficult to isolate. These research specialists tried out biographical items to see which, if any, would be related to a criterion of administrative performance. The criterion used was only fairly reliable. They collected data from some 300 school principals and vice-principals. Each of them answered a 150-item questionnaire. The sample of 300 was split into three subgroups. Only 8 of the 150 items held up, that is, were related to efficiency for at least 2 of the 3 different groups. Among the items that held up in the study were those that pertained to such things as:

The administrator's father: the successful administrator's father tended to have employed more than five people.

Childhood confidences: the successful administrator tended to confide in brothers and sisters rather than the mother.

Care when ill during childhood: the successful administrator tended not to be cared for formally by a physician.

Membership in organized groups: the successful administrator tended to belong (during childhood) to an organized group of children between ages of 12 and 18.

Number of children desired: those who would like four or more tended not to be good administrators.

Guilford and Comrey conclude that for the conditions of their study, ". . . the biographical-data method has only limited promise of usefulness for the selection of school administrators."

Tryouts of nontest predictor inventories of interests, such as the Strong Vocational Interest Blank, have been made. Typical of these studies is that of Knauft.[16] He used 38 managers of bake shops to see how much the occupational interest scores on SVIB would be associated with managerial success as he defined it. None of the scores derived from the SVIB keys were of any use. These are 39 occupational keys which show how similar a respondent's interests as he expressed them on the blank are to those of successful members of the occupation. Knauft, however, developed an empirical key, by item analysis. This key yielded scores that were significantly associated with success as

[15] J. P. Guilford and A. J. Comrey, "Prediction of Proficiency of Administrative Personnel from Personal-History Data," *Journal of Educational and Psychological Measurement,* VIII, (1948), 281–95.

[16] E. B. Knauft, "Vocational Interests and Managerial Success," *Journal of Applied Psychology,* XXXV (1951), 160–63.

defined. Such empirical keys are usually unstable; that is, they do not tend to hold up on successive samples when cross validated. Knauft cross validated his key on a separate sample, and it "tied-down" some 25 per cent of that which makes for managerial success under the conditions of his study.

An interesting and useful analysis of supervisory and executive ability, using nontest predictors, was made by Jones and Smith.[17] They divided the executive's job into two parts: (1) those factors that are specific to the work, such as knowledge of the jobs supervised and technical, job-connected knowledge and (2) leadership in dealing with people.

They used a sample of 72 supervisors in the Milwaukee Electric Company on whom they developed 2 kinds of criteria: 5 superiors rated each of the 72 supervisors on over-all supervisory capacity; then ratings were made by those supervised by the 72 men—these were called "leadership ratings." The nontest leadership predictors tried out by Jones and Smith consisted of 3 types of multiple-choice inventory items: personality, personal history, and problematic items. Here is an example of a problematic item:

If a few workers in your department were needed to work overtime, you would:
1. Select the men with the most seniority.
2. Select the most efficient workers.
3. Give the work to the men with the least overtime.
4. Let the workers decide who should stay.

One provocative finding of the Jones and Smith study was that the items that were related to supervisor's performance ratings did not tend to be related to the performance ratings made by the employees supervised. It appears that the underdogs look for different leader performance behavior than does the boss of the boss. The question: who is most right, the boss of the boss or the underdogs? In our opinion, for many situations the underdogs are more likely to be right in their leadership appraisal.

Jones and Smith developed a leadership scale from the items: it was more closely associated with ratings of those supervised than with ratings of supervisors. To say this in another way, the leadership scale correlated higher with leadership appraisal than with the executive ability criteria. Jones and Smith believe that supervisory performance may well "include measures other than those based on the opinion of man-

[17] Omer R. Jones and Karl U. Smith, "Measurement of Supervisory Ability," *Journal of Applied Psychology,* XXXV (1951), 146–50.

agement officers." This study is related to many other recent studies the results of which emphasize the importance to leadership of attitude of employees toward supervisor.

The *history of military officer selection* shows continuous and urgent need of standard officer performance evaluation and prediction. The Personnel Research Section, Classification and Replacement Branch, AGO, developed and recommended officer selection procedures at the close of World War II. This project was known as PR 4061.[18]

The leaderless group discussion (interview board), merit rating, and other methods developed will be discussed briefly, since they have implications for any personnel program involving selection of executive, administrative, and supervisory personnel in the federal government and in industry.

Some 31,000 officers participated in the preliminary and final field trials in about 50 Army installations. The preliminary field trials were designed to improve workability of the trial procedures and get face validity. During the final trials 15,000 experimental officers were used. The composition of this sample will be described later when the criterion is considered. Several experimental or trial procedures were tested. These included an officer evaluation report, a new "board interview," and a biographical information blank.

The Officer Evaluation Report was the first of the trial procedures used. It was designed by the Personnel Research Section Staff primarily as an improvement over the procedure of averaging previous efficiency ratings. In preparing this new evaluation procedure, studies were first made of the War Department and Air Force forms. Two thousand of the War Department forms and 3000 of the Air Force forms, representing a 10 per cent sample of the first 30,000 Air Force forms processed, were used for analysis. Factor analysis of these data indicated that these latter two forms measure three groups of named qualities: (1) *leadership,* measured by such scales as leadership, force, initiative, perseverance, or industry; (2) *sense of duty,* measured by scales such as attention to duty, cooperation, loyalty, and judgment, and (3) *stability,* measured by such sales as stability under pressure, reactions in emergencies, force, endurance, and moral courage. In field trials at 13 different military installations the 10 War Department scales, 13 Air Force scales, and 68 additional experimental ones were given further

[18] Roger M. Bellows, "Evaluating Officer Performance," Joint Conference: Army, Navy and Office of Scientific Research and Development, August 16, 1945. An unpublished paper.

study. Statistical analysis of this material resulted in the final selection of 5 items composing a section of the officer evaluation report. These 5 items appear to measure all of the 3 major named rating factors: leadership, sense of duty, and stability.

The New Interview Board was a second instrument evolved. It consisted of a new kind of interview. Before discussing it, we might examine the typical selection board set up under Army regulations, particularly as it functioned at the close of World War I. The traditional Army board was a multipurpose instrument. Its purposes included the following:

1. To determine the intellectual qualities of the candidate through oral testing and examination of educational record.
2. To determine personal qualities through study of records, recommendations, and previous experience records, and an evaluation of interview behavior.
3. To determine the physical stamina and fitness of the officer.
4. To determine the technical fitness of the officer by reviewing previous civilian and military experience record.
5. To summarize all of the above, in order to arrive at a final over-all recommendation.

When the development of the new interview procedure was undertaken, two diverse approaches were debated. One group felt that some over-all integration approach similar to the traditional Army board above was indicated. Another group within the Personnel Research Section staff felt that such an interview situation was highly unrealistic and entirely too pretentious for a thirty to forty-five minute interview, and that only material capable of observation during the interview should be considered. The latter viewpoint prevailed; physical stamina was left for a medical examination, intellectual qualities were transferred to objective tests, the evaluation of background and certain of the personality characteristics have been transferred to an objective information blank, and the summarization function was performed by statistical analysis of the data.

The remaining function was an evaluation of the officer's ability to get along with people in line and staff functions. The interview form provided two work sheets upon which to record observations, reactions, and ratings on three areas called "bearing or manner," "voice and language," and "personality traits." The manual and prepared work sheets emphasized the social nature of the interview and minimized influence of prejudice by forbidding prior acquaintance of any one of the five-member board with the applicant, or any prior knowledge of general experience or background, or any attempt to explore or evaluate any phases of these not brought out indirectly in discussing personnel situations during the interview.

The Biographical Information Blank took over some other specific functions of the traditional Army board. Background information of a personal, educational, or occupational nature is combined with self-description of traits, attitudes, and habits. The blank is based upon previous experience of the National Research Council Committee on Selection and Training of Aircraft Pilots, National Defense Research Committee of Office of Scientific Research and Development, the Worker Analysis Section of Occupational Research Program of United States Employment Service, and the U.S. Navy. Preliminary field trials were carried on at 9 Officer Candidate Schools and involved somewhat more than 3000 student officers.

To test the efficacy of the various methods, criterion data were obtained by the staff at 45 installations. Approximately 15,000 officers were brought together in small groups of 15 to 30 officers who were well enough acquainted with each other's work to evaluate it. Each officer was requested to prepare two lists of the officers in his group, those High and those Low in general all-around value to the Army, listing them from highest to lowest, next highest, next lowest, etc. Each officer was requested to designate the five officers of the group most closely medium or middle with respect to over-all value. Further study was made only of officers who fell clearly into one of the three groups—High, Middle, or Low—in the sense of virtually perfect agreement of their fellow officers, never more than one dissenting vote for High or Low officers, and never more than two dissenting votes in the case of Middle officers. In addition, any officer placed over one group by his commanding officer was eliminated. For example, if an officer met the rigid requirements for membership in the Low group, and if the commanding officer nominated him for the High group, he was eliminated from the criterion groups. Using this very strict estimate of competence, about 4100 officers were selected on the above basis, but unusually high transfer rate, sickness, unavailability, and incomplete or unevenly completed forms reduced the final population to 3000 officers, 1359 of whom had been interviewed by the new interview board.

The efficiency of the various instruments will be described in terms of how well they succeeded in picking High and eliminating Low officers for retention. The Officer Evaluation Report (OER) was the most successful of the three new devices and did a better job of selection than did the average previous efficiency rating (PER). If each of these rating devices is considered separately as a predictor for selecting the top third of all applicants, the OER correctly selected 64.2 per cent High officers against 62.3 per cent of High officers picked by the PER, and erroneously picked only 5.6 per cent Low officers, whereas 12.7 per cent slipped by on the PER. If the two methods were used to eliminate the lowest 30 per cent of applicants, the OER correctly disqualified 68.2 per cent Lows against only 55.9 per cent for the PER, and erroneously rejected only 7.3 per cent High as compared with 15.9 per cent for the PER.

The Biographical Information Blank and the Interview did less well than either of the rating methods, but much better than the traditional Army Board; and when added to the Officer Evaluation Report to secure a Combined Point Index, it further improved the discrimination between High, Middle, and Low officers, assuring a still better selection program. Table 18.4 shows the percentages of officers falling into these three groups which would have been selected by a Combined Point Index that selected the top 30.9 per cent in terms of this predictor.

TABLE 18.4 · Selected by the Several Predictors, the Percentage of Officers Falling in Each of the Three Criterion Groups

Selection Procedure	Criterion Group		
	High	*Middle*	*Low*
Officer Evaluation Report OER	64	30	6
New Interview INT	58	25	17
Bio. Inf. Blank BIB	52	30	18
Combined Point Index	74	24	2
Previous Efficiency Report PER	62	25	13
Traditional Army Board TAB	45	26	29
Chance	37	32	31

From Table 18.4 it can be seen that: (1) the Officer Evaluation Report was superior to the average Previous Efficiency Rating; (2) each of the three proposed instruments was superior to the traditional Army Board; (3) the Combined Point Index, based on all three instruments was superior to the previous efficiency report (PER) and greatly superior to the traditional Army Board; and (4) the traditional Army board method was only slightly superior to chance. The Combined Point Index, on the other hand, doubled the number of High officers who were selected and decreased the Low officers from 31 to only 2 per 100.

Of course the proposed program would tend to work better if less than 30 per cent of the officer applicants are selected and more poorly if more than 30 per cent are selected for retention. With the upper score set at successive 20-point score intervals, the per cents falling in each criterion group are shown in Table 18.5.

TABLE 18.5 · Percentages of Officers that Would Be Selected by Each of Several Combined Point Index Cutting Scores, and the Percentage Falling in Each Criterion Group

Cutting Score Combined Point Index	Percentage Selected			
	From total group	*From High group*	*From Middle group*	*From Low group*
280	2.1	97	3	0
260	13.6	82	17	1
240	30.9	74	24	2
220	52.1	60	33	7
200	69.5	51	35	14
180	81.8	44	35	21
160	90.7	41	34	25

From Table 18.5 it is seen that no Low officers or only three Middle officers per hundred selected were picked if only 21 of each 1000 officers were accepted. The method worked as well accepting a quota of 907 of each 1000 officers as did the traditional Army Board when selecting a quota of only 320 per 1000 officers.

Since an important aspect of the job of an Army officer is said to be learning, two instruments were developed to check general learning aptitude and educational achievements: (1) Officer Classification Test, a measure of general ability or intelligence and (2) A General Survey Test, a measure of educational achievement. Neither of these was related to High, Middle, or Low criterion classification of the men, a finding which should have been expected since college graduation had been a prerequisite for most men directly commissioned and a standard score of 110 on the Army General Classification Test had been required for admission to OCS or cadet training.

It was concluded that the Combined Point Index has a satisfactory tendency to select officers on the basis of past and present performance. The adoption of this program, since it selected only 2 instead of 31 Low officers, could mean a saving of $2,900,000 for every 100 officers selected. These figures are based on the assumption that it costs at least $100,000 to induct, pay, train, maintain, and retire an officer selected for commissioning in the Regular Army at this time, and the further assumption that the value of any Low Officer, judged among the poorest by *all* his fellow officers, is zero (this may be too high an estimate of his worth if he decreases the morale of a division, makes decisions leading to disaster in combat, or alienates the affections of enough congressional committee members).

Leader attitudes as predictors

We could not expect a predictor which measures democratic leadership style to predict a criterion based on autocratic style. If the rater himself is autocratic, he rates others as to whether they are autocratic. Those who are, he tends to rate high; those who are democratic, he tends to rate low. We would expect a measure of democratic style to be negatively correlated with such criterion ratings. Thus if such a predictor correlates with this criterion, the correlation would be an indication of the kind of criterion we have rather than the validity of the predictor.

What the above paragraph means to us is this: the characteristics necessary for high rated performance depend upon the situation. If the situation calls for supervision without creative leadership, then measured creative leadership characteristics may not be found to be related to rated performance, or may even be negatively related. If, however, the situation calls for creative leadership characteristics, measures of them will be related positively to criteria. Then these measures will be found to be "valid." The problem is as simple, and complex, as that. We cannot state it more concisely.

There are several measuring devices that are believed to be, at least roughly, measures of creative leadership. Typical of these, the one most used and the one on which most scientific data are available, is the "How Supervise?" test or inventory. Illustrative items are shown in Part 2 of Table 1.1. It yields a measure which may be said, according to our viewpoint, to reflect creative, considerate leadership attitude. It is also said to measure human relations practices. Several studies have shown that scores on it are significantly related to supervisory performance as rated;[19] others have not. Typical of those studies that revealed no clear-cut significant relation is a study by Herbert Meyer.[20]

As a part of a larger study of supervisory selection in a plant of the General Electric Company, Meyer studied relation of "How Supervise?" scores to rated performance. The 95 subjects comprising the sample of supervisors used in the investigation were ranked on over-all job performance by 2 raters who rated them independently. Of those supervisors who had scored in the upper fourth on "How Supervise?" 32 per cent were rated low in present supervisory performance; of those in the middle half, only 13 per cent were rated low; of those in the lower fourth on "How Supervise?" 29 per cent were rated low in supervisory performance (see Table 18.6). Although these results suggest that the test is not useful as a selection device, it may throw light on the criterion.

TABLE 18.6 · Relation of "How Supervise?" Scores to Rated Supervisory Performance

Score on "How Supervise?"	*Per cent rated low in supervisory performance*
Those in upper quarter	32
Those in middle half	13
Those in lower quarter	29

Assuming this test as used does measure "desirable" supervisory attitudes and practices, we may appropriately ask this question: "Desirable to whom?" Those in the upper fourth on the test have these desirable attributes. But 32 per cent of them were rated low. These tended to be rated, according to our hypothesis, by raters who believe these practices are undesirable. What about the 29 per cent of those who made poor scores on "How Supervise?" and who were rated low by raters? These, according to our view, were appraised by raters who tended to be democratic, that is, who believed in desirable supervisory practices as measured by "How Supervise?"

We could not, therefore, expect to obtain significant validity of a trial predictor unless we know what the rater is looking for—what the situation requires. This remains the blind spot in prediction studies. Needed: more adequate situation study.

[19] Some evidence is reviewed in Roger M. Bellows, *Psychology of Personnel in Business and Industry*, 2nd ed. (Englewood Cliffs, N. J.: Prentice-Hall, Inc., 1954), pp. 323–24.

[20] Herbert H. Meyer, "An Evaluation of a Supervisory Selection Program," *Personnel Psychology*, X (1957), 499–513.

The big question is: "What does the job call for?" In predicting whether a man will be good or poor on a job it is absolutely necessary to know the requirements of the job situation. I have emphasized that the qualities that make a good leader do not necessarily make a good manager and vice versa. A manager will likely fail in a leader job if he does not have required leader qualities; a leader will likewise fail in a manager's job if he does not have the manager qualities that the job situation requires.

Chapter 17 outlined our present status of developing adequate criteria; this chapter focused on studies designed to predict success in supervisory, administrative, and executive positions; the next continues to examine leader and group leadership characteristics.

It is very often the opportunities which bring out the leadership qualities in a man.

ELEANOR ROOSEVELT, when asked to mention the leadership qualities of her late husband.

19

Leader qualities and opportunities

"Luck" plays a role in creating visible leaders. Luck may be considered as "opportunity," which is a name for the myriad social forces that influence the leadership situation.

We shall examine some of these forces in terms of what has been revealed by study of *leaderless group discussion,* sociometry, and interpersonal perception. Then we shall need a look at democratic versus autocratic style as related to leader situations, at leadership and "centrality" in communications networks, at cohesiveness as a group dimension. Finally, we shall be ready for a humble "last word."

Leaderless group measures

A new selection technique, the leaderless group discussion, LGD, offers an interesting and promising way to identify potential leaders. It consists, in general, of obtaining ratings of potential leadership by observing behavior in unsupervised small group discussion where no leader has been designated. We suggest this method is new: actually there are more than 50 research reports on it.[1] It has been evaluated and used in other countries, having perhaps first been tried by J. B. Rieffert who directed personnel research in the German military establishment during the 1920's.[2]

The U.S. Civil Service has developed the LGD as a selection screen. Some 190 civil service agencies use it, and its appearance in business and industry is increasing. A manual[3] of its application is available. Use in Britain, both in business[4] and in civil service[5] has been described.

Various modifications of LGD have been used as a situational behavior measurement to study leader potential. One study may be described as illustrative. In a study to examine its usefulness in identifying leaders, Walter Gleason[6] set up a procedure involving groups of seven and nine subjects in each. These men were leader trainees in a military training course. When each group was assembled, they were told the purpose: that duties of leaders involve working together.

They were given a topic, a problem of training men as leaders. They discussed the problem and its solution for fifty minutes. Each group was asked to rate the other members on the basis of leadership ability. These "peer ratings" were the trial predictors of later leadership performance.[7]

1 These are summarized and interpreted by Bass, who has initiated and directed a considerable share of them: Bernard Bass, "The Leaderless Group Discussion," *Psychological Bulletin,* LI (1954), 466–92.

2 The early history of the leaderless group discussion is reviewed by H. L. Ansbacher, "The History of the Leaderless Group Discussion Technique," *Psychological Bulletin,* IIL (1951), 383–90.

3 Milton M. Mandell, *The Group Oral Performance Test* (Washington, D. C.: U. S. Civil Service Commission, 1952).

4 J. M. Fraser, "An Experiment with Group Methods in the Selection of Trainees for Senior Management Positions," *Occupational Psychology,* XX (1946), 63–67.

5 P. E. Vernon, "The Validation of Civil Service Selection Board Procedures," *Occupational Psychology,* XXIV (1950), 75–95.

6 Walter James Gleason, "Predicting Army Leadership Ability by Modified Leaderless Group Discussion," *Journal of Applied Psychology,* XLI (1957), 231–35.

7 In some arrangements of LGD these ratings are made by observers rather than participants: this was the case in the Army selection study discussed in the previous chapter, and in several of the studies reported on industrial selection.

Four weeks later, at the end of the training course, the final leadership criterion measure was obtained on the 469 leadership trainees who comprised the experimental sample. This criterion consisted of several ingredients, including a faculty rating, buddy rating, and a situational test.

Results of the study were typical of those of a number of similar studies. It was found that the predictor ratings obtained from peer-participants in the LGD were significantly related to the final criterion scores of the candidates. The predictor, in fact, was found to contain or "tie-down" some 20 per cent of the criterion (see Figure 18.1). Thus the predictor, for use in selection, could be said to have "fair" validity, compared to tests and predictors in other studies. They do, of course, leave much to be desired. One might ask where the remaining 80 per cent of the loose variance is to be found!

A brief reference to two difficulties in method may be made at this point. The first difficulty involves ever-present problems concerning the criterion. The LGD validation methods, of course, require the best possible criterion. But the criterion used, as for example in the study by Gleason, is contaminated to an unknown degree (see Chapter 17). Gleason points this out himself,[8] but feels that the biases introduced in this way are not very serious. If this criterion contamination were removed, the obtained validity would be reduced an unknown amount.

Another problem has to do with the validity of a predictor in use in the operating situation as compared to obtained validity in the experimental situation. Because of differences in these two situations, we always can expect some reduction in validity of the predictors in use. And the amount of this decrease is almost always unknown.

In addition to its use as a promising aid in selection of leaders, LGD research has yielded insights that bear importantly on development of theoretical viewpoints regarding leadership. LGD performance as rated tends to correlate significantly with tendency to hold leadership office, "to initiate structure and interaction among associates and subordinates." [9] But it does not correlate at all, or as Bass says, negatively, with tendency to be considerate of their welfare.

Leadership is seen to be something more than establishing a friendly, comfortable social climate. The importance of initiating structure as a leader behavior pattern is emphasized.[10] Neither of these two leader

[8] Gleason, *op. cit.*, p. 234.

[9] Bass, *op. cit.*, p. 485.

[10] See Carroll Leonard Shartle, *Executive Performance and Leadership* (Englewood Cliffs, N. J.: Prentice-Hall, Inc., 1956), pp. 120–23.

activities is sufficient for leadership, but both are considered necessary. *Initiating structure* is planning for group goals, and consideration is the participative, democratic leader style.

Characteristics of successful leaders

An examination survey of some 124 studies on leadership was made by Stogdill.[11] He concludes that a classification of personal factors associated with leadership could be:

Capacity (intelligence, alertness, verbal facility, originality, judgment).
Achievement (scholarship, knowledge, athletic accomplishments).
Responsibility (activity, sociability, cooperation, adaptability, humor).
Status (socio-economic position, popularity).

But another significant factor is added by Stogdill:

Situation (mental level, status, skills, needs and interests of followers, objectives to be achieved, etc.).

If the *situation* is very important, and Stogdill and other research people believe it is, this is "devastating evidence against measurable traits." Traits that work in one situation do not work in another if leadership depends on the situation. Stogdill quotes Ackerson:[12]

the correlation for "leader" and "follower" are not of opposite sign and similar magnitude as would be expected of traits supposed to be antithetical. It may be that the true antithesis of "leader" is not "follower," but "indifference," i.e., the incapacity or unwillingness either to lead or to follow. Thus it may be that some individuals who under one situation are leaders may under other conditions take the role of follower, while the true "opposite" is represented by the child who neither leads nor follows.

Stogdill concludes:

The findings suggest that leadership is not a matter of passive status, or of the mere possession of some combination of traits. It appears rather to be a working relationship among members of a group. . . .

By selection of leaders we can only hope at very best to tie-down some

[11] Ralph M. Stogdill, "Personal Factors Associated with Leadership: A Survey of the Literature," *The Journal of Psychology*, XXV (1948), 35–71.

[12] L. Ackerson, *Children's Bureau Problems: Relative Importance and Intercorrelation among Traits* (Chicago: University of Chicago Press, 1942).

50 per cent of all that makes up success. Half is left over, loose. How do we identify this important half? We may call the factors that make it up "motivation." Motivation is the essential problem of leadership. Selection is only part of the story. And motivation, broadly defined and considered, is what we have been talking about in this book.

We have examined characteristics of leaders, leader behavior, and the leadership situation. Leader behavior is characterized by both consideration for others and tendency to initiate structure or bring order into a situation by planning and arranging the situation so the work can go forward in a shared direction. This is leadership.

Sociometry and leadership

Those interested in leadership phenomena will ask, "How may we find leaders?" or "What should I do to become a leader?" Both of these questions relate to what might be termed leader *visibility*. Simple, pat answers to these questions are not yet available from psychosocial studies, although social scientists have not been dragging their feet in attempts to come up with tangible suggestions for identifying and furthering emergent leadership potential.

Sociometry gives us, as does leaderless group discussion method, glimpses of persons functioning in a leaderlike manner within a circumscribed and defined group. These glimpses help us see how they interact effectively with group members and bring about on-going, constructive group activity.

The sociometric definition of a leader is "that person within a group who is chosen to a greater extent than other persons in the group." The leader is more visible than the nonleader. That this visibility is not necessarily related to dominance or the kind of "pushy" aggressiveness that is likely to be irritating to group members has been suggested by several studies.[13] We might view a favorable sociometric position as a condition for leadership; it is necessary, but insufficient.

Identification of the sociometric leader is relatively simple. Group members are asked to indicate which persons in the group they wish to "be near," "work with," or any other realistic basis of choice. This is what has been called a "sociometric test." Sociometrists prefer to regard it as a kind of action test. Sociometric choice is the opportunity for the group members to effect alteration of the group structure in line with their expressed preferences. For example, a group of women assemblers

[13] H. H. Anderson, "Domination and Integration in the Social Behavior of Young Children in an Experimental Play Situation," *Genetic Psychology Monographs,* XIV (1937), 343–408.

of small radio parts might be asked to choose which ones of the work-room group they would like to work near. Assurance that their choices "count" is made effective by appropriate rearrangement of their work locations after the choices are plotted.

In a study involving 133 delinquent girls in a state institution, Helen Jennings found high choice status to be related to broader community leadership. An election to a community council was held a short time before the sociometric test. An examination of the results of the election and the test showed that, of the 20 council members elected, 90 per cent were among the over-chosen in the sociometric test.[14]

Jennings reported some observations on the personal behavior characteristics of the over-chosen girls. Each over-chosen girl, to a greater or less extent:

Demonstrates ability to establish effective rapport with a variety of other personalities, adults as well as peers.

Shows initiative and ingenuity not only in starting new projects but in altering "problem" conduct of others.

Tends to be solicitous and helpful toward others.

Is cooperative and active in group projects even when assigned a menial role.

Whether these personality characteristics among the over-choosen delinquent girls generalize to other leader situations in the open community or world of work is problematical. However, they do conform to our notion of the leader as a nonauthoritarian, truly a group member who assists the group in accomplishing mutual goals.

An extension and amplification of leader selection on the basis of sociometric choice was a study by Borgotta, Couch, and Bales[15] to test the hypothesis that "The most effective group is the one which has the most adequate all-around leader . . ." The "all-around leader" or "great man" may be defined in terms of three factors: (1) *task ability*, composed of leadership rating by co-participants in a common task and an I.Q. score; (2) *individual assertiveness*, rated in terms of number of acts initiated per unit of time; (3) *social acceptability*, as revealed by sociometric choices on the basis of "enjoyed participation with."

Groups with and without leaders selected as above were studied in terms of their over-all effectiveness. It was found that:

[14] Helen H. Jennings, *Leadership and Isolation*, 2nd ed. (New York: Longmans, Green & Co., 1947), p. 119. "Over-chosen," for the purposes of this study, included all individuals receiving a number of choices a defined amount above the mean.

[15] E. F. Borgatta, A. S. Couch, and R. F. Bales, "Some Findings Relevant to the Great Man Theory of Leadership," *American Sociological Review*, LXX (1954), 755–59.

Groups containing "a great man" (or leader individual) have higher product rates of giving suggestions and agreements. Insofar as one has any reason to believe that this is related to the quality of solutions, the "productivity" of these groups is likely to be increased relative to the groups without "great men."

To the extent that a lack of showing tension is an indication of smooth functioning, groups with "great men" appear to show less inhibited response to the task situation with less anxiety and withdrawal from active participation. This may indicate greater satisfaction with the group. Further evidence of this is seen by the greater amount of positive social emotional behavior, reflecting friendly interpersonal relationships among the members of the group.

Effective leadership, then, would seem to result from a combination of factors, not the least of which is acceptable by the group as measured by the sociometric choice method. An individual has a greater chance, perhaps, under the conditions of this study, of becoming visible as a leader if he also possesses other qualities in addition to acceptance by the group. Examples of often listed qualities are individual assertiveness (willingness to take action) and intelligence. These were suggested as factors in the Borgatta, Couch, and Bales study.

But these qualities are examples only; they depend upon the particular situation. And no specific personal earmarks can be given for all situations. A genius could not be expected to become a visible creative leader of morons anymore than a moron could be expected to lead a group of geniuses. A social dilettante would not likely be chosen to lead a group of coal miners; a coal miner would not likely lead a group of socialites; a churchman would not be expected to be chosen for a leader by a group of murderous hoodlums, nor would a known hoodlum likely become a leader of churchmen. Such events are for romantic novels.

Interpersonal perception

We have seen in Chapters 8 and 9 that social perception, *la connaissance d'autrui,* is a significant aspect of the leadership situation. We discussed, in the section above, the relation of sociometric choice to leader visibility. We now turn to a particular aspect of leader visibility: measures of interpersonal perception.

Fred E. Fiedler studied 14 high school basketball teams to develop measures of interpersonal perception.[16] Each team consisted of from 9 to 18 players. Fiedler used a forced-choice questionnaire to obtain

[16] Fred E. Fiedler, W. Hartmann, and S. A. Rudin, *The Relationship of Interpersonal Perception to Effectiveness in Basketball Teams* (Urbana, Ill.: University of Illinois Bureau of Research and Service, 1952). This was a part of a study made under contract with Office of Naval Research.

so-called assumed similarity scores. He obtained these on individuals in the following way. Each person filled out a descriptive questionnaire 3 times: (1) he described himself on one form; (2) he filled out another form for "the person with whom you can cooperate best," predicting how this person would respond to the items on the form; (3) he filled out a third form for "the person with whom you can cooperate least," predicting how this person would respond to the items. Then Fiedler was able to obtain three scores:

ASp: a measure of assumed similarity obtained by comparing the person's self-description of his positive choice, the best co-worker. High ASp appears to be related to personal liking and perhaps warmth for the chosen person.
ASn: a measure obtained by comparing the person's self-description with his prediction of his negative choice. A high ASn may . . . indicate a feeling of personal closeness and warmth for the negative choice.
ASo: a measure obtained by comparing the person's prediction for his positive choice with his prediction for his negative choice. This measure is interpreted as "set" to differentiate between people . . .[17]

The criterion of teamwork used by Fiedler was a fairly reliable and realistic one. For basketball teams it consisted of proportions of games a team had won. For surveyor teams, used in another study by Fiedler, it was instructor rating of accuracy. Surveyor teams consisted of three or four men who were being trained as surveyors.

It was found that ASo scores—difference between predictions for a person's positive choice and his negative choice—of a team's most preferred work companion was negatively related to the criterion in three samples.

This may mean that a person who is more concerned with effective task performance—winning the game in basketball teams and accuracy in surveying teams—as a preferred co-worker is more likely to plan and initiate structure and less likely to be emotionally involved in group interrelationships.

Democratic vs. autocratic style

The style of control that is "best" for productivity also depends upon the group, as we suggested in Chapter 3. Such features of the situation as group needs, traditions, and expectations determine in part the style

[17] Fred E. Fiedler, "Assumed Similarity Measures as Predictors of Team Effectiveness," *Small Groups: Studies in Social Interaction,* eds. Paul Hare, Edgar F. Borgatta, and Robert F. Bales (New York, Alfred A. Knopf, 1955), p. 254; appears also in *Journal of Abnormal and Social Psychology,* XLIX (1954), 381–88.

of leadership that is most effective in terms of goal achievement.[18] For illustration, members of a group of executives undergoing seminar training in leadership said they understood and would like to apply democratic principles, but the president of the company was authoritarian—they could not see how they could apply it in the prevailing atmosphere of their company. Of course they were right.

Leonard Berkowitz [19] conducted a definitive experiment on relation of expectations of the group and the effectiveness of democratic style. He studied 72 small decision-making conference groups in business, industry, and government. He found that: (1) groups expected that the chairman would be the sole leader and that the leader and members would perform different functions; (2) sharing leader functions with group members tends to decrease group cohesiveness and satisfaction of members; (3) leadership sharing (an earmark of the democratic style) "is not generally reacted to negatively in groups with urgent problems. It may be that the group's motivation to reach an adequate problem solution as quickly as possible lessens the hypothesized group tradition."

This suggests that part of the task of the creative leader is to prepare the situation for participative leadership. This preparation, which involves, in many situations, changes in social climate, takes time. If the situation is urgent, if an emergency problem is at hand, time is not available. This illustrates a general set of conditions in which democratic style is inappropriate.

Leadership and centrality

Group structure determines, in part, the factor of *communications distance.* It is an important consideration for leadership. Does the strong man, the born leader, the person who is alleged to have leadership qualities always emerge as a leader? Or does "luck," opportunity contained in the situation, make the nominal leader? A study by Bavelas,[20] which has been called classic, is of considerable significance here.

[18] Situation characteristics that lend themselves to democratic leader style were discussed by R. L. French in a paper, "Leadership and the Authoritarian-Democratic Dimension," read at the Annual Meeting of The American Psychological Association, State College, Pennsylvania (Sept. 1950).

[19] Leonard Berkowitz "Sharing Leadership in Small, Decision-Making Groups," *Journal of Abnormal and Social Psychology,* IIL (1953), 231–38.

[20] Alex Bavelas, "Communication Patterns in Task-Oriented Groups," *The Policy Sciences,* eds. D. Lerner and H. D. Lasswell (Stanford, Calif.: Stanford University Press, 1951), pp. 193–202.

Each subject was given a card on which had been printed five symbols from a master set of six. Only one symbol appeared on all five cards. The subjects had to pass information along so that they could discover which symbol appeared on each of their cards. The task was finished when . . . each subject had identified the common symbol.

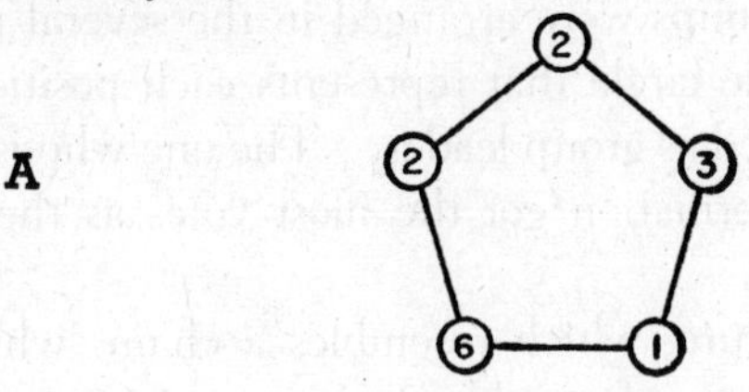

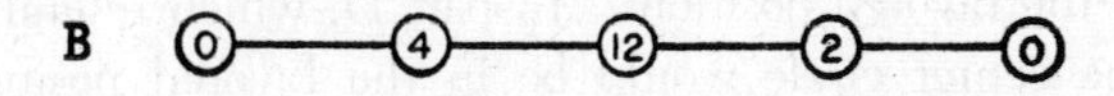

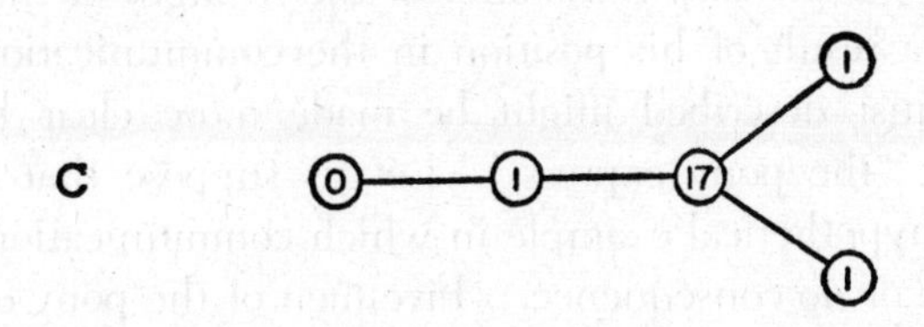

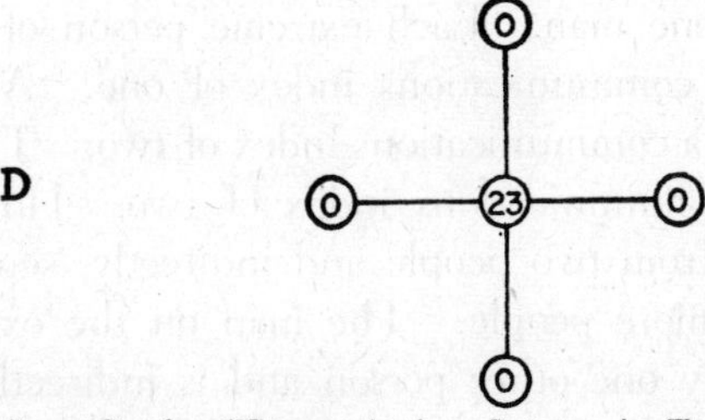

From Bavelas, "Communications Patterns in Task-oriented Groups," OP. CIT.

Fig. 19.1 · Centrality in communications structures and emergence of leaders; numbers within small circles are number of votes each man received as leader

At the end of fifteen trials the experimenter asked each subject: "Did your group have a recognized leader?" The selection of the leader did not depend upon his personal qualities. Instead it depended upon his position—"luck," opportunity—to receive information from the members of the group. The groups were arranged in the several patterns shown in Figure 19.1. In the circle that represents each position we find the number of votes received as group leader. The one who is in the favored position to receive information got the most votes as the recognized or visible leader.

In part *B* of the figure, which resembles a chain, which one of the five persons is in the most favorable position as far as structure of the group is concerned? Would you not expect the middle one to have more communications with the others than an end one? In part *C* of the figure, it is fairly obvious that the third one from the left, who connects directly with three other members of the five member group would be in the favored position. In part *D*, which resembles a wheel, obviously the center circle would be in the favored position in terms of communications distance brought about by the structure of the group, since he is at the crossroads of communication. Indeed, he was chosen as leader twenty-three times. The question is therefore asked, do you now believe that leadership is a matter of the strength of the personality of a leader or a result of his position in the communications network?

The study just described might be made more clear by reference to an example, "the pony express." Let us suppose that we are concerned with a hypothetical example in which communications outside of a network were of no consequence. Five men of the pony express interchanged information and communicated as freely as possible with one another. As in part *B* of Figure 19.1, the one on the left could not communicate with the one on his right, thus his direct communication could be with only one man. Each extreme person of part *B* of the figure would have a communications index of one. All of the other members would have a communications index of two. The middle man would also have a communications index of two. However, he gets information directly from two people and indirectly, separated by only one man, from two more people. The man on the extreme left gets information from only one other person and is indirectly separated by one other in the organization structure. The other two people are separated from him by more than one unit of communications distance. Thus we would expect the middle man in this lateral network of communication to have more information about the whole situation than the other people. We would expect that he would have the largest number of votes of these five men for leadership of the small group.

In part *C* of the figure we see only one man in direct communication with 3 others. He is the one also to receive the greatest number of votes; but part *D* illustrates this even more dramatically. The middle man at the crossroads of communication has direct contact with four people. None of the four has direct communication with more than the center man. He was the only one of the five to receive any votes in the Bavelas study. Thus we see a rough correlation between the communications distance which a man has with other members of the small group and his number of votes or choices for leadership of that group. We invoke the concept of centrality here. The more central a location in the network of communications, the more likely the man is to become a leader of the small group, if the results of this study are borne out in other situations.

Parts *A*, *C*, and *D* of Figure 19.1 do not lend themselves to the hypothetical example of the pony express. Rather, they seem to lend themselves more readily to the thought of ranchers who have located themselves appropriately in terms of a rugged terrain. They are pioneers. The five ranchers of part *A* of the figure have located their ranches an equal distance from one another in a more or less circular bowl, or plateau, surrounded by mountains. Each member communicates with only two other members. They have equal advantages in communications. There is no outstanding centrality for communications in the structure of this group. In part *B* of the figure, the ranchers have located themselves equally distant from each other along a valley surrounded by ranges of mountains. The communications structure is somewhat different from part *A*; the middle man has a greater degree of centrality. The two men next to him have greater centrality than the men terminating the network but less than the center man. In part *C* of the figure, one man obviously has greater communications centrality. These five ranchers are also located in a valley, but the brow of a hogshead-shaped mountain tapers down and extends between the two ranchers at the right. Clearly, the third rancher from the extreme left has greater communications facility, merely because of the happenstance, the opportunity of his location, than do any of the other four: he communicates directly with three others, whereas two of these three communicate only with him.

Next let us consider the rancher in the center of the cross. These ranchers are also located in a bowl. The bowl is surrounded by mountains and divided by escarpments, but the center of the bowl lent itself to a central location for a ranch. Obviously, this one man communicates with all four others, but none of the four others can communicate with anyone but him. Certainly his score of centrality is higher. He is likely the one who is better known, the one with whom the others are more familiar; he has more information, he can talk more "intelligently" to others about the total situation in the bowl. Would he not be the one, other things equal, who would be chosen as leader if there were reason for the group to have a high degree of solidarity and cohesiveness in fighting off enemies or in merely forming a ranchers' improvement association for the valley which they occupy?

Regarding communication networks we might ask a number of questions: Is there any one pattern that gives better performance than others when the group is involved in a specific task? Does one pattern tend to yield more syntality? The results of the highly artificial studies which have been reported in the literature pertain only to the conditions under which the studies were conducted. They are not generalizable to other conditions and situations involved in various kinds of home, school, community, labor union, and industrial situations or national and international organizations. We can nevertheless obtain from these investigations insights into the mysteries of communication networks. And, later on, as such studies are repeated and other variables brought into the picture, generalizable rules will emerge.

Communication networks have several dimensions. Such dimensions are the number of connections, the shape or symmetry of these connections, and the amount of information that the connections will carry to the recipients of the information. But suppose that we knew the optimal dimensions of communication patterns for a given group. A main point to be emphasized is that generalization to other groups is not feasible in terms of present research.[21] Leavitt conducted a study of some effects of certain communication patterns of group performance. He used four different communication patterns somewhat similar to those described in Figure 19.1. Here is what Leavitt concluded from his study:

> 1. The communication patterns within which our groups worked affected their behavior. The major behavior differences attributable to communication patterns were differences in accuracy, total activity, satisfaction of group members, emergence of a leader, and organization of group. There may also be differences

[21] Harold J. Leavitt, "Some Effects of Certain Communication Patterns of Group Performance," *The Journal of Abnormal and Social Psychology*, XLVI, (1951), 38–50.

among patterns in speed of problem solving, self-correcting tendencies, and durability of the group as a group.

2. The positions which individuals occupied in the communication pattern affected their behavior while occupying those positions. One's position in the group affected the chances of becoming a leader of a group, one's satisfaction with one's job and with the group, the quantity of one's activity, and the extent to which one contributed to the group's functional organization. The characteristic of communication patterns that was associated most with behavioral differences was centrality. . . .

3. It is tentatively suggested that centrality affects behavior via the limits that centrality imposes upon independent action. Independence of action relative to other members of the group is, in turn, held to be the primary determinant of the definition of who shall take the leadership role, total activity, satisfaction with one's lot, and other specific behaviors.

4. More precisely, it is felt that where centrality and, hence, independence are evenly distributed, there will be no leader, many errors, high activity, slow organization, and high satisfaction. Whatever frustration occurs will occur as a result of the inadequacy of the group, not the inadequacy of the environment. When one position is low in centrality relative to other members of the group that position will be follower position, dependent on the leader, accepting his dictates, falling into a role that allows little opportunity for prestige, activity, or self-expression.

We need a clue to lack of relationship between productivity and morale as shown by a review of studies of Brayfield and Crockett.[22] It will be recalled that these authors reviewed many studies pertaining to productivity and morale and found that virtually all of them revealed lack of relationship between productivity as measured and morale as measured with the exception of a study, for example, by Lawshe and Nagle.[23] It was noted in a previous chapter that favorable attitudes towards supervisor and ratings of productivity correlated highly. In this study, narrow or segmental aspects or facets of morale were being measured rather than global over-all satisfaction of the employees with the total job situation. The clue we need may be supplied by further studies of communication nets and centrality.

We have spoken of creative leadership as leadership by which the situation is arranged so that high productivity and high job satisfaction results. Another study, by Trow,[24] attacked this problem. Trow states

[22] Arthur H. Brayfield and Walter H. Crockett, "Employee Attitudes and Employee Performance," *Psychological Bulletin,* LII (1955), 396–424.

[23] C. H. Lawshe and Bryant F. Nagle, "Productivity and Attitude Towards Supervisor," *Journal of Applied Psychology,* XXXVII (1953), 157–62.

[24] Donald B. Trow, "Autonomy and Job Satisfaction in Task-Oriented Groups," *Journal of Abnormal and Social Psychology,* LIV (1957), 204–9.

in the beginning of his article that most findings of studies where communication nets have been varied systematically have shown that job satisfaction of a person varies directly with the centrality of his position in the net. Perhaps the person in the center of the net has more status attributed to him and, hence, more job satisfaction. How about the people out on the edge of the net? They have high peripherality; they do not participate very much in making decisions. They are the peon workers who do not get very much credit for what they do. No one recognizes them or approves of them or says they did a good job. The laurels go to the person in the center of the net. So then we would expect to have dissatisfaction when we have lack of diffusion, of participation. Trow's findings corroborate and support those of Leavitt. Here is the way Trow summarizes his study:

> The purpose of this experiment was to test the general propositions that the autonomy of positions and the level of need for autonomy of the persons occupying the positions are significant to the determinants of the job satisfaction and status perception of members of task oriented groups. The autonomy of a position was defined as a measure of its occupant's access to task-relevant information; it differs conceptually from centrality, which is a measure of access to communications channels, though the two may be found empirically to be positively correlated. . . .
>
> It was concluded, first, that positional autonomy is a major determinant of job satisfaction in task oriented groups, underlying the positive relationship between centrality and satisfaction reported in other studies. Second, the relationship between autonomy and job satisfaction is apparently mediated by satisfaction of a need for autonomy. Finally, doubt is cast on the contention that job satisfaction results from a prior perception of a favorable status relationship.

Trow's study includes an important variable not encompassed by Leavitt's. This variable is the need, on the part of members of the small group, for autonomy. Autonomy may be quickly defined as self-regulation. Some people appear to have need for self-regulation; others perhaps would prefer to be led—or regulated—by someone else. An example of this is the person who, when offered the job of supervisor, says he would prefer to remain a rank-and-file member. The person who claims to have need for autonomy needs a more central position, whereas the person who claims no need for autonomy would perhaps do well, as far as satisfaction is concerned, in the peripheral position.

It would not be appropriate, however, for us to say that the person without need for autonomy is better off being led and that the person who needs autonomy should be the leader. It would not be appropriate because we have defined leadership in a special manner. We see a large difference between leadership and supervision. Leadership is planning and arranging the situation so that the group goes forward in a shared direction to the satisfaction and benefit of all concerned. Supervision is something less than this: it is merely the act of relaying directions from above and seeing that the slaves do the work. It is a difference between the participative style, which is creative leadership, and the autocratic style, which is mere execution, administration, management, or supervision.[25]

Cohesiveness

Cohesiveness is another group dimension of importance for several reasons: more research work has been done on it than perhaps any other definable aspect of groups; it has been found to be related to other group dimensions as well as to leader behavior; it appears to be related to, or a part of, group satisfaction; it is a most promising area for future leadership research.

Definitions of cohesiveness are, in leadership writings, fairly precise. It is commonly thought of as synonymous with morale or effectiveness. Technically, it is the force acting on group members, pulling them toward the group. John Hemphill[26] calls it "viscidity" and defines it as "the degree to which members of a group function as a unit. It is reflected by the absence of personal dissension and personal conflict among members, by absence of activities serving to advance only the interests of individual members, by the ability to resist disrupting forces, and by the belief on the part of the members that the group does function as a unit."

In a questionnaire for measuring group dimensions[27] Hemphill uses twelve items which are scored for cohesiveness (viscidity). The respondent answers *A, B, C, D,* or *E,* designating definitely true, mostly true, both true and false, mostly false, or definitely false, respectively. The items are:

[25] Rensis Likert, Chris Argyris, James March, and Herbert Shepard, "Management Implications of Recent Social Science Research," *Personnel Administration,* XXI (1958), 5–14.

[26] John K. Hemphill, *Group Dimensions—a Manual for their Measurement,* Research Monograph No. 87 (Columbus: The Ohio State University Bureau of Business Research, 1956), especially p. 4 and p. 66.

[27] *Ibid.* This provides items for measuring thirteen dimensions of groups—autonomy, control, flexibility, hedonic tone, homogeneity, intimacy, participation, permeability, polarization, potency, stability, stratification, and viscidity. We believe viscidity or cohesiveness to be one of the most interesting and fruitful of those concepts.

There are two or three members of the group who generally take the same side on any group issue.

Certain members are hostile to other members.

There is constant bickering among members of the group.

Members know that each one looks out for the other one as well as for himself.

Certain members of the group have no respect for other members.

Certain members of the group are considered uncooperative.

There is a constant tendency toward conniving against one another among parts of the group.

Members of the group work together as a team.

Certain members of the group are responsible for petty quarrels and some animosity among other members.

There are tensions between sub-groups which tend to interfere with the group's activities.

Certain members appear to be incapable of working as part of the group.

There is an undercurrent of feeling among members which tends to pull the group apart.[28]

In one study, by Stanley Schacter and colleagues,[29] it was found that the relation of cohesiveness to production (team efficiency as defined in the study) depends largely on direction of "group induction."

Now we need another definition, one for *group induction.* Here is the way Schacter *et al.* define it: direction of influence of the group toward high or low production.[30] They theorize that if a group influences its members toward high production (positive induction), then groups of high cohesiveness would produce more than groups of low cohesiveness. Two previous studies, by R. L. French [31] and by Darley,

[28] *Ibid.*, p. 54–55.

[29] Stanley Schacter, Morris Ellerston, Dorothy McBride, and Doris Gregory; "An Experimental Study of Cohesiveness and Productivity," *Human Relations*, IV (1951) 225–38; also Dorwin Cartwright and Alvin Zander, eds. *Group Dynamics: Research and Theory* (White Plains, N. Y.: Row, Peterson & Company, 1956), pp. 401–11.

[30] In a factory, positive induction would result from membership in the management group, negative induction from membership in a "rate restrictor" group. Thus the reference group is all-important: see, e.g., Theodore M. Newcomb, "Attitude as a Function of Development Reference Groups," *Readings in Social Psychology*, 3rd ed., eds. E. E. Maccoby, T. M. Newcomb, and E. L. Hartley (New York: Henry Holt and Company, 1958), pp. 265–75.

[31] R. L. French, "Sociometric Status and Individual Adjustment among Naval Recruits," *Journal of Abnormal and Social Psychology*, IVL (1951), 64–71. In this study sociometric choice was used as a measure of cohesiveness.

Gross, and Martin [32] had found no relation between cohesiveness and productivity and Schacter *et al.* sought the reason. The added variable, direction of group induction as defined, yields useful insights into this problem. A common example of its operation is in a "slow down" group of employees in a factory: it is highly cohesive and negatively inducted; it is "set" to decrease production.

Schacter and his co-workers found that under the conditions of their study, cohesiveness and positive induction together contribute to, or are associated with, high production. A group with high cohesiveness "Hi Co" and positive induction "+Ind" produced 11.23 units, whereas one with "Lo Co" and "−Ind" produced only 6 units. A group with "Hi Co" and "−Ind" produced 4 units. They conclude that, in their study, cohesiveness was a determining influence "in the negative but not in the positive induction condition."

It is thus shown that cohesiveness by itself is not necessarily a factor in production and that other influences must be taken into account. We have additional evidence here that urges us to be cautious in our inferences. Leadership is a complex, multiple factor phenomenon that depends on the interaction of many forces in the total situation.

Schacter *et al.* conclude:

> We have considered some research findings which suggest four classes of variables to be consistently related to the productivity of an organizational group and to the psychological returns which the group offers its members. These classes of variables—the supervisor's ability to play a differential role, the degree of delegation of authority or closeness of supervision, the quality of supportiveness or employee orientation, and the amount of group cohesiveness—have been developed from a program of studies conducted in complex, ongoing organizations, the majority of them in business organizations.
>
> In reviewing these research findings, one finds confirmation . . . in that . . . the full motivation . . . in a complex organizational system can be tapped only when some system of functional representation assures them of an element of control in the larger organization as well as in the primary group.

A last word

The executive, administrator, manager, supervisor, or leader is primarily interested in the activities of people in an organization. He is especially interested in the results of their behavior—production. Insofar

[32] Jack Darley, N. Gross, and W. Martin, "Studies in Group Behavior: Factors Associated with the Productivity of Groups," *Journal of Applied Psychology,* XXXVI (1952), 396–403.

as he is a creative leader he will attempt to arrange the situation so that high productivity will be accompanied by understanding, satisfaction, and a feeling of mutual goals on the part of the people and groups involved. If the executive, administrator, or supervisor is an extreme authoritarian or autocrat he will not be concerned with these latter features. All he wants is production, and he issues orders without accompanying them with communications and a climate conducive to mutual understanding and a feeling of joint effort toward the goal.

The creative leader is one who considers the dynamics of the situation. He will be analytical. And in order to analyze, he will be interested in that broad and complex set of factors which we encompass in the one inadequate symbol, *P*. He will want to know as much about his people as he can.

Success is good management in action. Good management means: efficiency in achieving goals; satisfaction of the needs of the group; contribution to the general welfare of the group, organizations and society at large; maintenance and security; permanance. Success requires, by definition, harmonious working relationships and interactions. Good management in action—success—is not peculiar to business and industrial enterprises alone. It is an attribute of all kinds of organizations and working groups: labor unions; family activities; community groups; schools and school systems; government and military agencies and establishments; religious bodies; informal groups, and collectivities of people of all kinds, whether designed for actual productivity or for fun or just for "togetherness," itself.

We have noted a shift away from use of authority for accomplishing the ends of good management. The rapid growth of unions has changed attitudes of workers. People are no longer pawns to be moved about by management; rather, they have come to be able to control their own economic life. Man, through his organizations, has taken over control of his own destiny.

Authority as such is no longer a tool that is efficient for the achievement of good management. For this reason it has been necessary to arrange situations for training supervisors and managers as leaders. And, fortunately, there has been another development, concurrent with the shift from authoritarian to democratic leader style: the increased knowledge of methods for dealing with the problems that arise from organizational complexity itself, which brings about difficulties in communications and conflicts in human interactions.

Although research workers and students of leadership are approaching these increased problems with humility, realizing the scantiness of the knowledge and technique that is as yet available, there has been a rapid acceleration in the field of behavioral science. Products of this acceleration bear directly upon human relations. These products would go a long way, even at the present time, toward solution of problems if leaders were knowledgeable concerning them. It is this behavioral science approach which is, without doubt, our only hope for successful management of the future.

Bibliography

Achilles, P. S. and E. D. Achilles, "Estimates of the Military Value of Certain Character Qualities," *Journal of Applied Psychology,* I (1917), 305–316.

Allen, F. L., *The Big Change.* New York: Harper, 1952.

Allport, Gordon W. and Leo Postman, *The Psychology of Rumor.* New York: Holt, 1947.

Alpert, B. and Patricia C. Smith, "How Participation Works," *Journal of Social Issues,* V (1949), 3–13.

American business leaders, *Human Relations in Modern Business.* Englewood Cliffs, N. J.: Prentice-Hall, 1949.

Anastasi, A. and J. P. Foley, Jr., *Differential Psychology: Individual and Group Differences,* rev. ed. New York: Macmillan, 1949.

Ansbacher, H. L., "The History of Leaderless Group Discussion Technique," *Psychological Bulletin,* XLII, (1951), 383–91.

Argyle, Michael, *The Scientific Study of Social Behavior.* London: Methuen, 1957.

Arps, George F., "Work with Knowledge of Results versus Work without Knowledge of Results," *Psychological Monographs,* XXVIII (1920).

Asch, S. E., *Social Psychology.* Englewood Cliffs, N. J.: Prentice-Hall, 1952.

Baher, B. O. and J. Block, "Accuracy of Interpersonal Prediction as a Function of Judge and Object Characteristics," *Journal of Abnormal and Social Psychology,* LIV (1957), 37–43.

Bakke, E. W., *Bonds of Organization: An Appraisal of Corporate Human Relations.* New York: Harper, 1950.

Bales, R. F., "A Set of Categories for the Analysis of Small Group Interaction," *American Sociological Review,* XV (1950), 257–63.

Barker, Roger, T. Dembo, and K. Lewin, *First Ratio and Aggression.* Iowa City, Iowa: University of Iowa Press, 1942.

Barnard, C. I., *The Functions of the Executive.* Cambridge, Mass.: Harvard University Press, 1938.

Barthol, R. P. and M. Zeigler, "Evaluation of a Supervisory Training Program with 'How Supervise?'" *Journal of Applied Psychology,* XL (1956), 403–5.

Bass, Bernhard M., "An Analysis of the Leaderless Group Discussion," *Journal of Applied Psychology,* XXXIII (1949), 527–33.

———, "The Leaderless Group Discussion Technique," *Personnel Psychology,* III (1950), 17–32.

———, "Feelings of Pleasantness and Work Group Efficiency," *Personnel Psychology*, VII (1954), 81–92.

———, "The Leaderless Group Discussion," *Psychological Bulletin*, LI (1954), 465–92.

———, "Leadership Opinions as Forecasts of Supervisory Success," *Journal of Applied Psychology*, XL (1956), 345–46.

———, S. Klubeck, and C. R. Wurster, "Factors Influencing Reliability and Validity of Leaderless Group Discussion Assessment," *Journal of Applied Psychology*, XXXVII (1953), pp. 26–30.

Bass, Bernhard M. and O. L. Whilte, "Situational Tests: III. Observers' Ratings of Leaderless Group Discussion Participants as Indicators of External Leadership Status," *Educational and Psychological Measurements*, XI (1951), 355–61.

Bass, Bernhard M. and C. R. Wurster, Effects of the Nature of the Problem on LGD Performance," *Journal of Applied Psychology*, XXXVII (1953), 96–99.

Baumgartel, H. and F. Mann, "Research on Productivity and Motivation of Civilian and Military Personnel at Air Materiel Command Installations," *Technical Research Report* (April 1954). Mimeo.

Bavelas, A., "*Morale and the Training of Leaders*," *Civilian Morale*, ed. G. Watson. New York: Reynal and Hitchcock, 1942, 143–65.

———, "Communication Patterns in Task-Oriented Groups," *Journal Acoustical Society of America*, XXII (1950), 725–30.

Bell, G. B. and R. L. French, "Consistency of Individual Leadership Position in Small Groups of Varying Membership," *Journal of Abnormal and Social Psychology*, XLV (1950), 764–67.

Bellows, Roger M., "*Learning as Perceptical Evolution*," *Psychological Review*, XL (1933), 138–59.

———, "Personnel Methods in Business Management," *The American Psychologist*, III (1948), 539–40.

———, "Industrial Psychology," *Annual Review of Psychology*, II (1951), 187–88.

———, "*Action Research in the Human Factor*," *Advanced Management*. New York: Society for Advancement of Management, Inc., 1953.

———, "Personnel Problems that Yield to Research," *Personnel Administration*, IX (1956), 14–18.

———, "Selection and Motivation," *Personnel Administrator*, III, 1 (1958), 18–22.

——— and M. Frances Estep, *Employment Psychology: The Interview*. New York: Reinhart, 1954.

Bellows, Roger M. and R. G. Whisler, "A Consideration of Interacting Pattern Theories of Feeling and Emotion," *Psychological Review*, XLI (1934), 236–45.

Bender, I. E. and A. H. Hastorf, "The Perception of Persons: Forecasting Another Person's Responses in Three Personality Scales," *Journal Abnormal and Social Psychology*, XLV (1950), 556–61.

Benne, K. D. and Grace Levit, "The Nature of Groups and Helping Groups Improve Their Operation," *Review of Educational Research*, XXIII (1953), 289–308.

Berkowitz, L., "Sharing Leadership in Small, Decision-making Groups," *Journal of Abnormal and Social Psychology*, XLVIII (1953), 231–38.

Bernberg, R. E., "Socio-Psychological Factors in Industrial Morale: 1. The Prediction of Specific Indicators," *Journal of Social Psychology*, XXXVI (1952), 73–82.

Berrien, F. Kenneth and Wendell H. Bash, *Human Relations: Comments and Cases*, 2nd ed. New York: Harper, 1957.

Bion, W. R., "Group Dynamics: A Review," *International Journal of Psychoanalysis*, XXXIII (1952), 235–47.

Blake, R. R., "The Interaction—Feeling Hypotheses Applied to Psychotherapy Groups," *Sociometry*, XVI (1953), 253–65.

Bogardus, E. S., "Leadership and Social Situations." *Sociological and Social Research*, XVI (1931), 164–70.

Boring, Edwin G., *History of Experimental Psychology*, 2nd ed. New York: Appleton-Century-Crofts, 1950.

———, H. S. Langfeld, and H. P. Weld, *Introduction to Psychology*. Wiley, 1939.

Bradford, L. and R. Lippitt, "Role-Playing and Supervisory Training," *Personnel*, XXII (1946), 358–69.

Brayfield, Arthur H. and Walter H. Crockett, "Employee Attitudes and Employee Performance," *Psychological Bulletin,* LII (1955), 396–424.

Brayfield, Arthur H. and Harold F. Roth, "An Index of Job Satisfaction," *Journal of Applied Psychology,* XXXV (1951), 307–11.

Bregman, E. O., "Studies in Industrial Psychology," *Archives of Psychology,* No. 59 (1922).

Browne, C. G., "Study of Executive Leadership in Business I, The R, A and D Scales," *Journal of Applied Psychology,* XXXIV (1950), 12–15.

———, "Study of Executive Leadership in Business II, Social Group Patterns," *Journal of Applied Psychology,* XXXIV (1950), 12–15.

———, "Study of Executive Leadership in Business III, Goal and Achievement Index," *Journal of Applied Psychology,* XXXIV (1950), 82–87.

———, "Study of Executive Leadership in Business IV, Sociometric Pattern," *Journal of Applied Psychology,* XXXV (1951), 34–37.

———, "Communication Means Understanding," *Personnel Administration,* XXI, 1 (1958) 12–16.

——— and R. Shore, "Leadership and Predictive Abstracting," *Journal of Applied Psychology,* XL (1956), 112–16.

——— and Thomas S. Cohn, ed., *The Study of Leadership.* Danville, Ill.: Interstate Printers & Publishers, 1958.

Burnett, C. W., "Validating Campus Leadership," *Educational Research Bulletin,* XXX (1951), 67–73.

Burwen, L. S. and D. T. Campbell, "The Generality of Attitudes Toward Authority and Nonauthority Figures," *Journal of Abnormal and Social Psychology,* LIV (1957), 24–31.

Campbell, A., *Working Together.* A paper read March 24, 1955 at Sixth Annual Valley-Wide Cooperative Conference of the TVA, Fontana Dam, N. C. Mimeo.

Canter, Ralph R., "A Human Relations Training Program," *Journal of Applied Psychology,* XXXV (1951), 38–45.

———, "Psychologists in Industry," *Personnel Psychology,* I (1948), 145–61.

Carter, G. C., "Measurement of Supervisory Ability," *Journal of Applied Psychology,* XXXVI (1952), 393–95.

Carter, L. F., "Leadership and Small Group Behavior," *Group Relations at the Crossroads,* eds. M. Sherif and M. O. Wilson. New York: Harper, 1953, 257–84.

Carter, Launor, William Haythorn, Beatrice Shriver, and John Lanzetta, "The Behavior of Leaders and Other Group Members," *Journal of Abnormal and Social Psychology,* XLVI (1950), 589–95.

Carter, L. R. and Mary Nixon, "An Investigation of the Relationship between Four Criteria of Leadership Ability for Three Different Tasks." *Journal of Psychology,* XXVII (1949), 245–61.

Carter, R. E., Jr. "An Experiment in Value Measurement," *American Sociological Review,* XXI (1951), 156–63.

Cartwright, D., "Achieving Change in People: Some Applications of Group Dynamics Theory," *Human Relations,* IV (1951), 381–92.

Cartwright, Dorwin and Alvin Zander, ed., *Group Dynamics: Research and Theory.* White Plains, N. Y.: Row, Peterson, 1956. "Approaches to the Study of Groups: Introduction," pp. 3–14; "Group Cohesiveness: Introduction," pp. 73–91; "Group Pressures and Group Standards: Introduction," pp. 137–50; "Group Goals and Group Locomotion: Introduction," pp. 305–18; "The Structural Properties of Groups: Introduction," pp. 415–28; and "Leadership: Introduction," pp. 535–51.

Cattell, Raymond B., "Determining Syntality Dimension as a Basis for Morale and Leadership Measurement," *Groups, Leadership and Men,* ed. H. Cruetzkow. Pittsburgh: Carnegie Press, 1951, 16–27.

———, "New Concepts for Measuring Leadership in Terms of Group Syntality," *Human Relations,* IV (1951), 161–84.

———, D. R. Saunders and G. F. Stice, "The Dimensions of Syntality in Small Groups," *Human Relations,* VI (1953), 331–56.

Cattell, Raymond B. and G. F. Stice, "Four Formulae for Selecting Leaders on the Basis of Personality," *Human Relations,* VII (1954), 493–507.

Chamberlain, Neil, Frank C. Pierson, and Theresa Wolfson, eds., *A Decade of Industrial Relations Research.* New York: Harper, 1958.

Clapp, L. B., "Science and Human Want," *American Scientist,* XLVI, 2 (1958), 176–90.

Cleeton, G. U. and C. W. Mason, *Executive Ability: Its Discovery and Development*. Yellow Springs, Ohio: Antioch Press, 1934.

Cleven, W. A. and F. E. Fiedler, "Interpersonal Perceptions of Open-Hearth Foremen and Steel Production," *Journal of Applied Psychology*, XXXVII (1953), 312–14.

Chowdry, Kamila and T. M. Newcomb, "The Relative Abilities of Leaders and Non-Leaders to Estimate Opinions of Their Own Groups," *Journal of Abnormal and Social Psychology*, XLVII (1952), 51–57.

Church, A. H., *The Making of an Executive*. New York: D. Appleton, 1923.

Coch, L. and J. R. P. French, "Overcoming Resistance to Change," *Human Relations*, I (1948) 512–32.

Comrey, Andrew L., J. M. Pfiffner, and H. P. Beem, "Factors Influencing Organizational Effectiveness, I. The U.S. Forest Survey," *Personnel Psychology*, V (1952), 307–28.

———, "Factors Influencing Organizational Effectiveness II. The Department of Employment Survey," *Personnel Psychology*, VI (1953), 65–80.

Comrey, Andrew L., J. M. Pfiffner, and W. High, "Factors Influencing Organizational Effectiveness V. A Survey of District Rangers," *Personnel Psychology*, VII (1954), 533–47.

Comrey, Andrew L., W. High, and R. C. Wilson, "Factors Influencing Organizational Effectiveness VI. A Survey of Aircraft Workers," *Personnel Psychology*, VIII (1955), 79–100.

———, "Factors Influencing Organizational Effectiveness VII. A Survey of Aircraft Supervisors," *Personnel Psychology*, VIII (1955), 245–58.

Cousins, Norman, *Modern Man Is Obsolete*. New York: Viking, 1946.

Cowley, W. H., "The Traits of Face-to-Face Leaders," *Journal of Abnormal and Social Psychology*, XXVI (1931–32), 304–13.

Crissy, W. J. E. and James J. Regan, "Halo in the Employment Interview," *Journal of Applied Psychology*, XXXV (1951), 338–41.

Criswell, Joan H., "Sociometric Methods of Measuring Group Preferences," *Sociometry*, VI (1943), 398–408.

Crutchfield, R. S., "Psychological Distance as a Function of Psychological Need," *Journal of Comparative Psychology*, XXVIII (1939), 447–69.

Dailey, J. T., "Non-introspective Research on Human Motivation." Bureau of Naval Personnel, June 7, 1957. Mimeo.

Daniels, Harry W. and Jay L. Otis, "A Method for Analyzing Employment Interviews," *Personnel Psychology*, III (1915), 425–44.

Danielson, L. E. and N. R. F. Maier, "Supervisory Problems in Decision Making," *Personnel Psychology*, X (1952), 169–80.

Darley, J. G., N. Gross, and W. E. Martin, "Studies in Group Behavior: Factors Associated with the Productivity of Groups," *Journal of Applied Psychology*, XXXVI (1952), 396–403.

Davis, Keith, *Human Relations in Business*. New York: McGraw-Hill, 1957.

Department of the Army, *Leadership*, Department of the Army Field Manual: 22–10, 1951.

Deutsch, M., "A Theory of Cooperation and Competition," *Human Relations*, II (1949), 129–52.

Dickson, W. J., "The Hawthorne Plan of Personnel Counseling," *American Journal Orthopsychiatry*, XV (1945), 343–47.

Di Vesta, F. J., J. H. L. Roach, and W. Beasley, "Rating Conference Participation in a Human Relations Training Program," *Journal of Applied Psychology*, XXXV (1951), 386–91.

Dollard, J., N. E. Miller, L. W. Doob, O. H. Mowrer, and Robert Sears, *Frustration and Aggression*. New Haven, Conn.: Yale University Press, 1939.

Dubin, Robert, *Human Relations in Administration: The Sociology of Organization with Readings and Cases*. Englewood Cliffs, N. J.: Prentice-Hall, 1951.

Dunlap, Jack W., "The Management of Morale," *Personnel Psychology*, III (1950), 353–59.

Dunnette, M. D. and W. K. Kirchner, "Validation of Psychological Tests in Industry," *Personnel Administration*, XXI, 3 (1958), 20–27.

Dymond, Rosalind F., "A Scale for the Measurement of Empathic Ability," *Journal of Consulting Psychology*, XIII (1949), 127–33.

Employee Relations Department, Standard Oil Company (New Jersey), *"Made to Measure": Notes from a Conference on Personnel Management; Baton Rouge, Louisiana,* 1951.

———, *Employee Relations Research in Standard Oil Company (New Jersey) and Affiliates.* Number One, Vols. I, II, 1955.

England, G. W. and D. G. Paterson, "Relationship Between Measured Interest Patterns and Satisfactory Vocational Adjustment for Air Force Officers in the Comptroller and Personnel Fields," *Journal of Applied Psychology,* XLII, 2 (1958), 85–89.

Farnsworth, Paul R. and Quinn McNemar, eds., *Annual Review of Psychology,* Vol. 9. Palo Alto, Calif.: Annual Reviews, Inc., 1958.

Festinger, Leon, "Informal Social Communication," *Psychological Review,* LVII (1950), 271–92.

———, "Architecture and Group Membership," *Journal of Social Issues,* VII (1951), 152–63.

———, "Theory of Social Comparison Processes," *Human Relations,* VII (1954), 117–40.

———, A. Pepitone, and T. Newcomb, "Some Consequences of De-individuation in a Group," XLVII (1952), 382–89.

Fiedler, F. E., "Assumed Similarity Measures as Predictors of Team Effectiveness," *Journal of Abnormal and Social Psychology,* XLIX (1954), 381–88.

File, Quentin W. and H. H. Remmers, *How Supervise? Test.* New York: The Psychological Corporation.

Fine, H. J., S. C. Fulherson, and L. Phillips, "Maladjustment and Social Attainment," *Journal of Abnormal and Social Psychology,* L (1955), 33–35.

Finlay, W. W., O. Q. Sartain, and W. M. Tate, *Human Behavior in Industry.* New York: McGraw-Hill, 1954.

Fleishman, Edwin A., *"Leadership Climate" and Supervisory Behavior.* Columbus, Ohio: Personnel Research Board, The Ohio State University, 1951.

———, "The Leadership Role of Foremen in Industry," *Engineering Experimental Station News.* Columbus: The Ohio State University, XXIV (1952), 27–35.

———, "The Description of Supervisory Behavior," *Journal of Applied Psychology,* XXXVII (1953), 1–6.

———, "The Measurement of Leadership Attitudes in Industry," *Journal of Applied Psychology,* XXXVII (1953), 153–58.

Foa, Uriel G., "A Test of the Foreman-Worker Relationship," *Personnel Psychology,* IX (1956), 469–86.

Frazer, James G., *The Golden Bough: A Study in Magic and Religion.* London: Macmillan, 1922.

French, J. R. P., Jr., "The Disruption of Cohesion of Groups," *Journal of Abnormal and Social Psychology,* XXXVI (1941), 361–77.

———, "Role-Playing as a Method of Training Foremen," *Human Factors in Management,* ed. S. P. Hoslett. New York: Harper, 1947, pp. 99–116.

———, "Field Experiments: Changing Group Productivity," *Experiments in Social Process: A Symposium on Social Psychology,* ed. J. G. Miller. New York: McGraw-Hill, 1950, pp. 79–96.

French, R. L., "Sociometric Adjustment among Naval Recruits," *Journal of Abnormal and Social Psychology,* XLVI (1951), 64–72.

Frenkel-Brunswik, E., "Intolerance of Ambiguity as an Emotional and Perceptual Personality Variable," *Journal of Personality,* XVIII (1949), 108–43.

Fromm, Erick, *Man for Himself.* New York: Rinehart, 1947.

Fryer, Douglas H. and Edwin R. Henry, eds., *Handbook of Applied Psychology,* vols. 1 and 2. New York: Rinehart, 1950.

Gage, Nate L. and R. L. Exline, "Social Perception and Effectiveness in Discussion Groups," *Human Relations,* VI (1953), 381–96.

Gardner, B. B. and D. G. Moore, *Human Relations in Industry.* Chicago: Irwin, 1950.

Gardner, Martin, *Fads and Fallacies in the Name of Science.* New York: Dover Publications, 1957.

Gaudet, Frederick J. and A. Ralph Carli, "Why Executives Fail," *Personnel Psychology,* X (1957), 7–22.

Ghiselli, Edwin E., "New Ideas in Industrial Psychology," *Journal of Applied Psychology,* XXXV (1951), 229–35.

——— and R. Barthol, "Role Perceptions of Successful and Unsuccessful Supervisors," *Journal of Applied Psychology,* XL (1956), 241–44.

Gibb, C. A., "The Principles and Traits of Leadership," *Journal of Abnormal and Social Psychology,* XLII (1947), 267–84.

———, "An Experimental Approach to the Study of Leadership," *Occupational Psychology,* XXV (1951), 233–48.

Gilson, Thomas Q. and Myron J. Lefcowitz, "A Plant-Wide Productivity Bonus in a Small Factory. Study of an Unsuccessful Case," *Industrial and Labor Relations Review,* X (1957), 284–96.

Ginzburg, Eli, *Perspectives on Work Motivation.* New York: American Management Association, 1954.

Glaser, R., P. A. Schwarz, and J. C. Flanagan, "The Contribution of Interview and Situational Performance Procedures to the Selection of Supervisory Personnel," *Journal of Applied Psychology,* XLII, 2 (1958), 69–73.

Gleason, R. J., "Predicting Army Leadership Ability by Modified Leaderless Group Discussion," *Journal of Applied Psychology,* XLI (1957), 231–35.

Goodacre, D. M., "Group Characteristics of Good and Poor Performing Combat Units," *Sociometry,* XVI (1953), 168–78.

Goode, Cecil E., *Personnel Research Frontiers.* Chicago: Public Personnel Association, 1957.

Gordon, Oakley J., "A Factor Analysis of Human Needs and Industrial Morale," *Personnel Psychology,* VIII (1955), 1–18.

Gottlieb, Bertram and William Kerr, "An Experiment in Industrial Harmony," *Personnel Psychology,* III (1950), 445–54.

Gouldner, A. W., *Studies in Leadership.* New York: Harper, 1950.

Gray, J. and P. Stanley, *Psychology in Human Affairs.* New York: McGraw-Hill, 1946.

Gross, E., "Primary Functions of Small Groups," *American Journal of Sociology,* LX (1954), 24–30.

Gross, N., W. E. Martin, and J. G. Darley, "Studies of Group Behavior: Leadership Structures in Small Organized Groups," *Journal of Abnormal and Social Psychology,* XLVIII (1953), 429–32.

Guetzkow, H., ed., *Groups, Leadership and Men: Research in Human Relations.* Pittsburgh: Carnegie Press.

Haire, M., "Industrial Social Psychology," *Handbook of Social Psychology,* ed. G. Lindzey. Cambridge, Mass.: Addison-Wesley, 1954, Chap. 29. 2 vols.

Haire, Mason, *Psychology in Management.* New York: McGraw-Hill, 1956.

Hall, Calvin S. and L. Gardner, *Theories of Personality.* New York: Wiley, 1957.

Hall, D. M., *Dynamics of Group Action.* Danville, Ill.: Interstate Printers and Publishers, 1957.

Halpin, A. W., "The Leadership Behavior and Combat Performance of Airplane Commanders," *Journal of Abnormal and Social Psychology,* XLIX (1954), 19–22.

Hanawalt, N. G., Carol E. Hamilton, and M. Louise Morris, "Level of Aspiration in College Leaders and Nonleaders," *Journal of Abnormal and Social Psychology,* XXXVIII (1943), 545–48.

Hare, A. Paul, "Small Group Discussion with Participatory and Supervisory Leadership," *Journal of Abnormal and Social Psychology,* XLVIII (1953), 273–75.

———, "Situational Differences in Leader Behavior," *Journal of Abnormal and Social Psychology,* LXV (1957), 132–34.

———, Edgar F. Borgatta, and Robert F. Bales, eds., *Small Groups:* Studies in *Social Interaction.* New York: Knopf, 1955.

Harrell, Thomas Willard, *Industrial Psychology,* 2nd ed. Rinehart, 1958.

——— and R. D. Churchill, "The Classification of Military Personnel," *Psychological Bulletin,* XXXVIII (1941), 331–53.

Harris, Ewin F. and Edwin A. Fleishman, "Human Relations Training and the Stability of Leadership Patterns," *The Journal of Applied Psychology,* XXXIX (1955), 20–25.

Hatton, A. R., C. A. Carran, R. S. Childs, *et al., The Qualifications and Selection of a City Manager.* Chicago: International City Managers' Association, 1930.

Hedrick, C. B., "Feedback: A Method of Evaluating and Improving Management Training," *Personnel,* XXXII (July 1955), 16–29.

Hemphill, John K., "The Leader and His Group," *Educational Research Bulletin* (OSU) XXVIII (1949), 225–29, 245–46.

———, *Situational Factors in Leadership,* Education Research Monographs, No.

32. Columbus, Ohio: The Ohio State University, 1949.

——, *Group Dimensions. A Manual for Their Measurement.* Columbus, Ohio: Ohio State University Bureau of Business Research, 1956.

——, Pauline N. Pepinsky, Reuben N. Shevitz, William E. Jaynes, and Charlotte A. Christner, *Leadership Acts.* Columbus, Ohio: The Ohio State University Research Foundation, 1954.

Hemphill, John K. and C. M. Westie, "The Measurement of Group Dimensions," *Journal of Psychology,* XXIX (1950), 323–42.

Henry, W. E., "The Business Executive: The Psychodynamics of a Social Role," *American Journal of Sociology,* LIV (1949), 286–91.

Hepner, H. W., "A Business Ability Test," *Industrial Psychology,* II (1927), 17–27.

Heron, Alexander R., *Why Men Work.* Stanford, Calif.: Stanford University Press, 1948.

Heyns, R. W., *The Psychology of Personal Adjustment,* New York: Dryden Press, 1948.

——— and Alvin Zander, "Observation of Group Behavior," *Research Methods in the Behavioral Sciences,* eds. Leon Festinger and Daniel Katz. New York: Dryden Press, 1953, pp. 381–417.

Hilgard, E. R., *Introduction to Psychology.* New York: Harcourt, Brace, 1953.

Ho, C. J., "Personnel Studies of Section Managers in a Department Store," *Personnel Journal,* VIII (1929), 225–31.

Hollander, E. P. and W. B. Webb, "Leadership, Followership, and Friendship: An Analysis of Peer Nominations." *Journal of Abnormal and Social Psychology,* L (1955), 163–67.

Homans, G. C., *The Human Group.* New York: Harcourt, Brace, 1950.

Horowitz, M., R. V. Exline, and F. J. Lee, *Motivational Effects of Alternative Decision-Making Processes in Groups.* Urbana, Ill.: University of Illinois, Bureau of Educational Research, 1953.

Hoveland, Carl, "Psychology of the Communications Process," *Communications in Modern Society,* ed. W. Schramm. Urbana, Ill.: University of Illinois Press, 1948, pp. 58–65.

Husband, R. W., "Cooperative versus Solitary Problem Solution," *Journal of Social Psychology,* XI (1940), 405–9.

Hurwitz, J. I., Alvin F. Zander, and B. Hymovitch, "Some Effects of Power on the Relations Among Group Members," *Group Dynamics: Research and Theory,* eds. D. Cartwright and A. F. Zander. Evanston, Ill.: Row, Peterson, 1953, pp. 483–92.

Industrial Relations Research Association, *Research in Industrial Human Relations.* New York: Harper, 1957.

Jacobson, E. and S. Seashore, "Communication Practices in Complex Organizations," *Journal of Social Issues,* VII, 7 (1951), 28–40.

Jenkins, John Gamewell, *Psychology in Business and Industry.* New York: Wiley, 1935.

——, "Validity for What?" *Journal of Consulting Psychology,* X (1946), 93.

Jennings, Eugene E., "The Dynamics of Forced Leadership Training," *Journal of Personnel Administration and Industrial Relations,* I (Fall 1954), 110–18.

Jennings, Helen H., *Leadership and Isolation,* 2nd ed. New York: Longmans, Green, 1950.

——, "Sociometric Structure in Personality and Group Formation," *Group Relations at the Crossroads,* eds. M. Sherif and M. O. Wilson. New York: Harper, 1953, pp. 332–65.

Johnson, R. J., "Relationship of Employee Morale to Ability to Predict Responses," *Journal of Applied Psychology,* XXXVIII (1954), 320–23.

Jones, Margaret Hubbard, "The Adequacy of Employee Selection Reports," *Journal of Applied Psychology,* XXXIV (1950), 222–23.

Jones, O. R. and K. U. Smith, "Measurement of Supervisory Ability," *Journal of Applied Psychology,* XXXV (1951), 146–50.

Jung, C. G., *Psychology of the Unconscious.* London: Kegan Paul, 1921.

Kahn, Robert L., *The Importance of Human Relations Research for Industrial Productivity,* 1951. Mimeo.

——, "The Human Factors Underlying Industrial Productivity," *Michigan Business Review* (Nov. 1952), pp. 27–32.

——, *Two Kinds of Learning and Their Implications,* Personnel Series #155, American Management Association, 1953, pp. 25–29.

——— and D. Katz, *Leadership Practices in Relation to Productivity and Morale,* 1952. Mimeo.

Kahn, Robert L. and N. C. Morse, "The Relationship of Productivity to Morale," *Journal of Social Issues,* VII (1951), 8–17.

Kahn, Robert L. and A. S. Tannenbaum, "Union Leadership and Member Participation," *Personnel Psychology,* X (1957), 227–92.

Katz, Daniel and Herbert Hyman, "Industrial Morale and Public Opinion Methods," *International Journal of Opinion and Attitude Research,* I (1947), 13–30.

Katzell, R. A., "Testing a Training Program in Human Relations," *Personnel Psychology,* I (1948), 319–30.

———, "Measuring the Effectiveness of the Training Program," *Proceedings,* Ninth Annual Industrial Relations Conference, University of Minnesota, 1951, pp. 54–61.

Kidd, J. S., "Social Influence Phenomena in a Task-Oriented Group Situation," *Journal of Abnormal and Social Psychology,* LVI, 1 (1958), 13–17.

Klein, D. B., *Mental Hygiene,* rev. ed. New York: Holt, 1956.

Knickerbocker, I., "Leadership: A Conception and Some Implications," *Journal of Social Issues,* IV (1948), 23–40.

Larson, Cedric, *WHO: Sixty Years of American Eminence.* New York: McDowell Obolensky, Inc., 1958.

Lawshe, C. H. and B. F. Nagle, "Productivity and Attitude Toward Supervisor," *Journal of Applied Psychology,* XXXVII (1953), 159–62.

Leavitt, H. J., "Some Effects of Certain Communication Patterns on Group Performance," *Journal of Abnormal and Social Psychology,* XLIV (1951), 38–50.

Lesser, Gerald S., "Extrapunitiveness and Ethnic Attitudes," *Journal of Abnormal and Social Psychology,* LVI, 2 (1958), 281–82.

Levine, J. and J. Butler, "Lecture vs. Group Decision in Changing Behavior." *Journal of Applied Psychology,* XXXVI (1952), 29–33.

Lewin, Kurt, "Field Theory and Experiment in Social Psychology: Concepts and Methods," *American Journal of Sociology,* XLIV (May 1939).

———, "Frontiers in Group Dynamics: Concept, Method and Reality in Social Science: Social Equilibria and Social Change," *Human Relations,* I (1947), 5–41.

——— and Ronald Lippitt, "An Experimental Approach to the Study of Autocracy and Democracy: A Preliminary Note," *Sociometry,* I (1938), 292–300.

Lewin, Kurt, R. Lippitt, and R. E. White, "Patterns of Aggressive Behavior in Experimentally Created 'Social Climates,'" *Journal of Social Psychology,* X (1939), 271–99.

Likert, R., "Motivational Dimensions of Administration," *America's Manpower Crisis.* Chicago: Public Administration Service, 1952.

———, "Findings of Research on Management and Leadership," *Proceedings,* Pacific Coast Gas Association, XLIII (1953).

———, *Motivation: The Core of Management,* Personnel Series A155, American Management Association, 1953, pp. 3–21.

——— and S. Seashore, "Employee Attitudes and Output," *Monthly Labor Review,* LXXVII (June 1954), 641–48. Also in *Manpower in the United States.* New York: Harper, 1954.

Likert, R., C. Argyris, J. March, and H. Shepard, "Management Implications of Recent Social Science Research—A Symposium," *Personnel Administration,* XXI, 3 (1958), 5–14.

Lindbom, T. R., "Evaluating Supervisory Training at the Job Performance Level," *Journal of Applied Psychology,* XXXVII (Oct. 1953), 428–29.

——— and W. H. Osterberg, "Evaluating the Results of Supervisory Training," *Personnel,* XXXI (Nov. 1954), 224–27.

Lindgren, Henry Clay, *Effective Leadership in Human Relations.* New York: Hermitage House, 1954, pp. 287.

Lindzey, G. and E. F. Borgatta, "Sociometric Measurements," *Handbook of Social Psychology,* ed. G. Lindzey. Cambridge, Mass.: Addison-Wesley, 1954.

Lippitt, R., "Techniques for Research in Group Living," *Journal of Social Issues* (1946), 55–61.

———, "The Strategy of Socio-Psychological Research in Group Life," *Experiments in Social Process,* ed. J. Miller. New York: McGraw-Hill, 1950.

———, "Action-Research and the Values of the Social Scientists," *Journal of Social Issues,* IV (1950), 50–55.

———, L. Bradford, and K. Benne, "Group Dynamics and Social Action," *Freedom Pamphlet Series,* 1950. New York: Anti-Defamation League.

Lippitt, R., N. Polansky, F. Redl, and S. Rosen, "The Dynamics of Power: A Field Study of Social Influence in Groups of Children," *Human Relations,* V (1952), 37–64.

Liveright, A. A., "Role-playing in Leadership Training," *Personnel Journal,* XXIX (1951), 412–16.

London, Jack, "Evaluation: Continuing Problem in Adult Education," *California Journal of Secondary Education,* XXVIII (Dec. 1953), 472–74.

Maas, H. S., "Personal and Group Factors in Leaders' Social Perception," *Journal of Abnormal and Social Psychology,* XLV (1950), 54–63.

Maccoby, E. E., T. M. Newcomb, and E. L. Hartley, eds., *Readings in Social Psychology,* 3rd ed. New York: Holt, 1958.

Maier, Norman R. F., *Psychology in Industry,* 2nd ed. New York: Houghton Mifflin, 1946.

———, "The Quality of Group Decisions as Influenced by the Discussion Leader," *Human Relations,* III (1950), 155–74.

———, "The Contribution of the Discussion Leader to the Quality of Group Thinking," *Human Relations,* V (1952), 278–88.

———, *Principles of Human Relations.* New York: Wiley, 1952.

———, "An Experimental Test of the Effect of Training on Discussion Leadership," *Human Relations,* VI (1953), 161–74.

——— and Leonard M. Lansky, "Effect of Attitude on Selection of Facts," *Personal Psychology,* X (1957), 293–304.

Maier, Norman R. F. and R. A. Maier, "An Experimental Test of the Effects of 'Developmental' *vs.* 'Free' Discussions on the Quality of Group Decisions," *Journal of Applied Psychology,* XLI (1957), 320–23.

Maier, Norman R. F., Allen R. Solem, and Ayesha A. Maier, *Supervisory and Executive Development: A Manual for Role Playing.* New York: Wiley, 1957.

Maier, Norman R. F. and L. F. Zerfoss, "MRP: A Technique for Training Large Groups of Supervisors and Its Potential Use in Social Research," *Human Relations,* V (1952), 177–86.

Maller, J. B., "Cooperation and Competition: An Experimental Study in Motivation," *Columbia University Contributions to Education,* N. 384. New York: Teachers College, 1929.

Mandel, M. M., "The Administrative Judgment Test," *Journal of Applied Psychology,* XXXIV (1950), 145–47.

———, "Validation of the Group Oral Performance Test," *Personnel Psychology,* III (1950), 179–85.

Mann, Floyd C., "Changing Supervisor-Subordinate Relationships," *Journal of Social Issues,* VII (1951), 56–63.

Marquis, D. G., H. Guetzkow, and R. W. Heyns, "A Social Psychological Study of the Decision-Making Conference, *Groups, Leadership and Men,*" ed. H. Guetzkow. Pittsburgh: Carnegie Press, 1951, pp. 55–67.

Mayo, E., *The Human Problems of an Industrial Civilization.* New York: Macmillan, 1933.

McCormick, Fowler, "American Business and Its Human Relations," *Industrial Relations and Social Change,* Personnel Series No. 106 (New York: American Management Association, 1947), pp. 1–8.

McCuen, Theron L., "Leadership and Intelligence," *Education,* L (Oct. 1929), 89–95.

McDougall, William, *The Group Mind.* New York: Putnam, 1920.

Menninger, Karl A., *The Human Mind,* 2nd ed. New York: Knopf, 1937, pp. 289–90.

Merei, F., "Group Leadership and Institutionalization," *Human Relations,* II (1949), 23–39.

Meyer, Herbert H., "Factors Related to Sucess in the Human Relations Aspects of Work-Group Leadership," *Psychological Monographs: General and Applied,* LXV (1951).

Miller, D. C., W. H. Form, *Industrial Sociology.* New York: Harper, 1951.

Miller, J. G., "Toward a General Theory for Behavioral Sciences," *American Psychologists* (1955), 513–31.

Mills, T. M., "The Coalition Pattern in Three-Person Group," *American Sociological Review,* XIX (1954), 657–67.

More, Douglass M., "The Foreman: A Personality Portrait," *Journal of Personnel Administration and Industrial Relations,* I (1954), 60–75.

Moreno, J. L., *Who Shall Survive?* rev. ed. New York: Beacon House, 1953.

Morris, C. and L. V. Jones, "Value Scales and Dimensions," *Journal of Abnormal and Social Psychology,* LI (1955), 523–35.

Morris, R. T. and M. Seeman, "The Problem of Leadership: An Interdisciplinary Approach," *American Journal of Sociology,* LVI (1950), 149–55.

Mosel, N. N. and H. J. Tsacharis, "Evaluating the Supervisor Training Program," *Journal of Personnel Administration and Industrial Relations,* I (Fall 1954), 99–104.

Munson, Edward L., "Leadership for American Army Leaders," *Infantry Journal,* 1941.

Münsterberg, Hugo, *Psychology of Industrial Efficiency.* Boston: Houghton Mifflin, 1913.

Murdock, George P., *Social Structure.* New York: Macmillan, 1949.

Nakamura, C. Y., "Conformity and Problem Solving," *Journal of Abnormal and Social Psychology,* LVI, 3 (1958), 315–20.

National Planning Association, *Causes of Industrial Peace under Collective Bargaining.* Washington, D. C., 1948–1953.

Newcomb, Theodore M., "An Approach to the Study of Communication Acts," *Psychological Review,* LX (1953), 393–404.

———, "Social Psychology and Group Processes," *Psychological Review,* LX (1953), 393–404.

———, Eugene L. Hartley, *et al.*, eds., *Readings in Social Psychology.* New York: Holt, 1947.

Odiorne, George S., "An Application of the Communication Audit," *Personnel Psychology,* VII (1954), 235–44.

Packs, Donald S., "Survey of the Training and Qualifications of Personnel Executives," *Personnel Journal,* VII (1948), 256–66.

Patton, W. M. Jr., "Studies in Industrial Empathy: III. A Study of Supervisory Empathy in the Textile Industry," *Journal of Applied Psychology,* XXXVIII (1954), 285–88.

Peddiwell, J. Abner, *Saber-Tooth Curriculum.* McGraw-Hill, 1939.

Pelz, Donald C., "Leadership within a Hierarchial Organization," *Journal of Social Issues,* VII (1951), 49–55.

———, "Influence: A Key to Effective Leadership in the First-Line Supervisor," *Personnel,* XXIX (1952), 209–17.

Pepitone, A., "Motivational Effects in Social Perception." *Human Relations,* III (1950), 57–76.

Pfiffner, J. M., *The Supervision of Personnel: Human Relations in the Management of Men,* 2nd ed. Englewood Cliffs, N. J.: Prentice-Hall, 1958.

Piffner, Raymond W., "Participation as a Tool of Management," *Personnel,* XXV (1948), 143–54.

Pigors, Paul J. W., *Leadership or Domination.* Boston: Houghton Mifflin, 1935.

——— and F. Pigors, "Case Method on the Spot," *Adult Leadership,* III (1954), 7.

Pigors, Paul J. W. and F. Pigors, "The Incident Process: Learning by Doing," *Adult Education,* III (1955), 5.

Polansky, N. A., Ronald Lippitt, and F. Redl, "An Investigation of Behavioral Contagion in Groups," *Human Relations,* III (1950), 319–48.

Porter, L. W., "Differential Self-perceptions of Management Personnel and Line Workers," *Journal of Applied Psychology,* XLII, 2 (1958), 105–9.

Postman, L., J. S. Bruner, and E. McGinnis, "Personal Values as Selective Factors in Perception," *Journal of Abnormal and Social Psychology,* XLIII (1948), 142–54.

Preston, N. G. and R. K. Hehtz, "Effects of Participatory *vs.* Supervisory Leadership on Group Judgment," *Journal of Abnormal and Social Psychology,* XLIV (1949), 44, 345–55.

Purcell, T. V., "Packinghouse Workers' Dual Allegiance to Company and Union," *Personnel Psychology,* VII (1954), 48–58.

Radom, Matthew, "Industry's Contributions to Research in Industrial Relations," *Proceedings of the Eighth Annual Meeting, Industrial Relations Research Association.*

Redl, F., "Group Emotion and Leadership," *Psychiatry,* V (1942), 573–96.

Rice, Stuart A., "Contagious Bias in the Interview: A Methodological Note," *American Journal of Sociology,* XXXV (1929), 420–23.

Roach, Darrell E., "Factor Analysis of Rated Supervisory Behavior," *Personnel Psychology,* IX (1956), 487–98.

Roberts, A. H. and R. Jessor, "Authoritarianism, Punitiveness, and Perceived Social Status," *Journal of Abnormal and Social Psychology,* LVI, 3 (1958), 311–14.

Roethlisberger, F. J., "The Administrator's Skill: Communication," *Harvard Business Review,* XXXI (1953), 55–62.

——— and W. Dickson, *Management and the Worker.* Cambridge, Mass.: Harvard University Press, 1939.

Roff, M., "A Study of Combat Leadership in the Air Force by Means of a Rating Scale: Group Differences," *Journal of Psychology,* XXX (1950), 229–39.

Rogers, C., *Counseling and Psychotherapy.* Boston: Houghton Mifflin, 1942. Pp. 450.

Rohrer, J. H. and M. Sherif, *Social Psychology at the Crossroads: The University of Oklahoma Lectures in Social Psychology.* New York: Harper, 1951.

Ross, Ian C. and A. Zander, "Need Satisfactions and Employee Turnover," *Personnel Psychology,* X (1957), 327–38.

Rush, Carl H., Jr., *Group Dimensions of Air Crews.* Columbus, Ohio: The Ohio State University Research Foundation, no date.

Sanford, Fillmore H., *Authoritarianism and Leadership,* Philadelphia: Institute for Research in Human Relations, 1950.

———, "Leadership Identification and Selection," *Group, Leadership and Men,* ed. H. Gustzkow. Pittsburgh: Carnegie Press, 1951, pp. 158–76.

Sarbin, T. R. and R. F. Berdie, "Relation of Measured Interests to the Allport-Vernon Study of Values," *Journal of Applied Psychology,* XXIV (1940), 287–96. Reprinted in D. C. McClelland, ed., *Studies in Motivation.* New York: Appleton-Century-Crofts, 1955, pp. 89–101.

Sargent, S. Stansfeld and Robert C. Williamson, *Social Psychology,* 2nd ed. New York: Ronald, 1958.

Schacter, S., "Deviation, Rejection and Communication," *Journal of Abnormal and Social Psychology,* XLIV (1951), 190–207.

———, N. Ellerston, Dorothy McBride, and Doris Gregory, "An Experimental Study of Cohesiveness and Productivity," *Human Relations,* IV (1951), 229–38.

Schoenfeld, M. H. and J. N. Thurber, "Case Studies in Union-Leadership Training, 1951–52," U. S. Bureau of Labor Bulletin 1114, 1952, pp. 1–23.

Scholl, Charles E., "Selecting Executive Trainees in a Multi-Branch Bank," *Personnel Administration,* XXI, 3 (1958), 45–49.

——— and Roger Bellows, "A Method for Reducing Employee Turnover," *Personnel,* XXIX (1952), pp. 234–36.

Scott, Ellis L., *Perceptions of Organization and Leadership Behavior.* Columbus, Ohio: The Ohio State University Research Foundation, 1952.

Seashore, S., "Group Cohesiveness as a Factor in Industrial Morale and Productivity." Ann Arbor: University of Michigan, 1954. Ph.D. thesis.

———, "Teamwork—Key to Production?" *Adult Leadership,* III (1955), 20–21.

——— and R. Likert, "Action Research for Better Community Programs in International Affairs," *Adult Leadership,* II (1953), 23–25.

Selznick, Philip, *Leadership in Administration.* Evanston, Ill.: Row, Peterson, 1957.

Shartle, Carroll Leonard, "A Clinical Approach to Foremanship," *Personnel Journal,* XIII (1934), 135–39.

———, "Leadership and Executive Performance," *Personnel,* XXV (1949), 370.

———, "Ohio State Leadership Studies," *Engineering Experimental Station News.* Ohio State University, XXIV (1952), 16–21.

———, *Executive Performance and Leadership.* Englewood Cliffs, N. J.: Prentice-Hall, 1956.

——— and Ralph M. Stogdill, *Studies in Naval Leadership: Methods, Results, and Application. Final Technical Report.* Columbus, Ohio: The Ohio State University Research Foundation, 1953.

Shaw, M. B., "A Comparison of Two Types of Leadership in Various Communication Nets," *Journal of Abnormal and Social Psychology,* L (1955), 127–34.

Sherif, Muzafer, *An Outline of Social Psychology.* New York: Harper, 1948.

——— and Carolyn Sherif, *Groups in Harmony and Tension.* New York: Harper, 1953.

Siegel, A. I., "An Experimental Evaluation of the Sensitivity of the Empathy Test," *Journal of Applied Psychology,* XXXVIII (1954), 222–23.

Snygg, D. and A. W. Combs, *Individual Behavior*. New York: Harper, 1949.

Solem, Allen R., *The Influence of the Discussion Leader's Attitude on the Outcome of Group Decision Conferences*. Ann Arbor: University of Michigan, 1953. Doctoral dissertation.

———, "An Evaluation of Two Attitudinal Approaches to Delegation," *Journal of Applied Psychology*, XLII, 1 (1958), 36–39.

Stagner, R., "Attitudinal Climate," *Labor-Management Relations in Illini City*, Vol. 2. Explorations in Comparative Analysis. Champaign, Illinois: University of Illinois, Institute of Labor and Industrial Relations, 1954.

Stead, W. H., Carroll Leonard Shartle, and associates, *Occupational Counseling Techniques: Their Development and Application*. New York: American Book, 1940, pp. 98–101.

Stettinius, E. R., Jr., "The Selection and Development of Executives in American Industry," *Harvard Business School Alumni Association Bulletin*, XIII (1936), 43–50.

Stogdill, Ralph Melvin, "Personal Factors Associated with Leadership," *Journal of Psychology*, XXV (1948), 35–71.

———, "Leadership, Membership and Organization," *Psychological Bulletin*, XLVII (1950), 1–14.

——— and Staff Associates, *Aspects of Leadership and Organization*. Columbus, Ohio: The Ohio State University Research Foundation, 1953.

Stogdill, Ralph Melvin and Kathleen Koehler, *Measures of Leadership Structure and Organization Change*. Columbus, Ohio: The Ohio State University Research Foundation, 1952.

Stogdill, Ralph Melvin, Ellis L. Scott, Alvin E. Coons, and William E. Jaynes, *The Prediction of Navy Officer Performance*. Columbus, Ohio: The Ohio State University Research Foundation, 1953.

Stogdill, Ralph Melvin, C. L. Shartle, and Associates. *Patterns of Administrative Performance*. Bureau of Business Research Monographs No. R-81. Columbus: Ohio State University, 1956.

Stogdill, Ralph Melvin, C. L. Shartle, E. L. Scott, A. E. Coons, and W. E. Jaynes, *A Predictive Study of Administrative Work Patterns*. Bureau of Business Research Monographs No. R-85. Columbus: Ohio State University, 1956.

Strodtbeck, F. L. and A. P. Hare, "Bibliography of Small Group Research: (From 1900 through 1953)," *Sociometry*, XVII (1954), 107–78.

Strong, E. K., "Vocational Guidance of Executives," *Journal of Applied Psychology*, XI (1927), 331–47.

Sumner, W. Graham, *What Social Classes Give to Each Other*. New York: Harper, 1883, pp. 91–92.

Swanson, G. E., T. M. Newcomb, and E. L. Hartley, eds., *Readings in Social Psychology*, rev. ed. New York: Holt, 1952.

Taft, R., "Use of the 'Group Situation Observation' Method in the Selection of Trainee Executives," *Journal of Applied Psychology*, XXXII (1948), 587–94.

Tagiuri, Renato and Luigi Petrullo, eds., *Person Perception and Interpersonal Behavior*. Stanford, Calif.: Stanford University Press, 1958.

Tannenbaum, A., The Relationship Between Personality Variables and Adjustment to Contrasting Types of Social Structure. September, 1954.

——— and F. Massarik, *Participation by Subordinates in the Managerial Decision-Making Process*, No. 14. Los Angeles: Institute of Industrial Relations, University of California, 1950, p. 11.

Tead, Ordway, *The Art of Leadership*. New York: Whittlesey House, 1935.

Thelen, H. A., *Dynamics of Groups at Work*. Chicago: University of Chicago Press, 1954.

Torrance, E. P., "Methods of Conducting Critiques of Group Problem-Solving Performance," *Journal of Applied Psychology*, XXXVII (1953), 394–98.

———, "The Behavior of Small Groups Under the Stress of Conditions of 'Survival,'" *American Sociological Review*, XIX (1954), 751–55.

Toynbee, Arnold J., *A Study of History*. New York and London: Oxford University Press, 1954.

Turner, Ralph H. and L. M. Killian, *Collective Behavior*. Englewood Cliffs, N. J.: Prentice-Hall, 1957.

Uhrbrock, Richard S., "Attitudes of 4,430 Employees," *Journal of Social Psychology*, V (1934), 365–77.

U. S. Civil Service Commission, *Leadership and Supervision,* Personnel Management Series No. 9, 1955.

Valentine, W. L., "Common Misconceptions of College Students," *Journal of Applied Psychology,* XX (1936), 633–58.

Van Dusen, A. C., "Measuring Leadership Ability," *Personnel Psychology,* I (1948), 67–80.

Van Zelst, R. R., "Empathy Test Scores of Union Leaders," *Journal of Applied Psychology,* XXXVI (1952), 293–95.

Villers, R., *The Dynamics of Industrial Management.* New York: Funk & Wagnalls, 1954.

Viteles, Morris Simon, *Industrial Psychology.* New York: Morton, 1932.

Weaver, C. H., "The Quantification of the Frame of Reference in Labor-Management Communication," *Journal of Applied Psychology,* XLII, 1 (1958), 1–9.

Wechsler, I. R., M. Kahane, and R. Tannenbaum, "Job Satisfaction, Productivity and Morale: A Case Study," *Occupational Psychology,* XXVI (1952), 1–14.

Wechsler, I. R., M. A. Klernes, C. Shepherd, "A New Focus in Executive Training," *Advanced Management,* XX (1955), 19–22.

Weitz, Joseph and R. C. Nuchols, "A Validation Study of 'How Supervise?'" *Journal of Applied Psychology,* XXXVII (1953), 7–8.

———, "Job Satisfaction and Job Survival," *Journal of Applied Psychology,* XXXIX (1955), 294–300.

Wherry, Robert J., "Criteria and Validity," *Handbook of Applied Psychology,* eds. Douglas H. Fryer and Edwin Ruthvan Henry. New York: Rinehart, 1950.

———, "The Past and Future of Criterion Evaluation," *Personnel Psychology,* X (1957), 1–6.

——— and D. H. Fryer, "Buddy Ratings: Popularity Contests or Leadership Criteria?" *Personnel Psychology,* II (1949), 147–59.

White, R. K., *Value-Analysis: The Nature and Use of the Method.* Society for the Psychological Studies of Social Issues, 1951.

Whyte, William Foote, *Pattern for Industrial Peace.* New York: Harper, 1951.

———, *Leadership and Group Participation,* Bulletin 24, New York State School of Industrial and Labor Relations, Cornell University, 1953.

———, *Money and Motivation.* New York: Harper, 1955.

Wickert, Frederic R., "Turnover and Employees' Feelings of Ego-Involvement in the Day-to-Day Operation of a Company," *Personnel Psychology,* IV (1951), 1–14.

———, "How Supervise? Scores Before and After Courses in Psychology," *Journal of Applied Psychology,* XXXVI (1952), 388–92.

Willerman, Ben, "The Relation of Motivation and Skill to Active and Passive Participation in the Group," *Journal of Applied Psychology,* XXXVII (1953), 387–90.

Williams, S. B. and H. J. Leavitt, "Group Opinion as a Predictor of Military Leadership," *Journal of Consulting Psychology,* XI (1947), 283–91.

Wilson, Robert C., W. S. High, H. P. Beem, and A. L. Comrey, "Factors Influencing Organizational Effectiveness, IV. A Survey of Supervisors and Workers," *Personnel Psychology,* VII (1954), 525–31.

Woodworth, Robert S., *Dynamics of Behavior.* New York: Holt, 1958.

Worthy, James C., "Factors Influencing Employee Morale," *Harvard Business Review,* XXVIII (1950), 61–73.

Wyland, R. R., "Measuring the Results of Supervisory Training," *Factory Management and Maintenance,* CX (Jan. 1952), 110–11. The following related work is being obtained: Betty B. Pond, "Performance on File—Remmer's 'How to Supervise' Test before and after Supervisory Training," unpublished Master's thesis, Pennsylvania State College, 1951.

Yoakum, C. S., "Can Executives Be Picked by Mental Tests?" *Forbes,* IX (1922), 259–60.

Yoder, D., *Personnel Management and Industrial Relations,* 4th ed. Englewood Cliffs, N. J.: Prentice-Hall, 1948.

Young, A. H., *Relations of the Supervisor to His Men.* American Management Association Production Executives' Series, No. 29, 1926.

Young, E., ed., "Proceedings of Tenth Annual Meeting," *Industrial Relations Research Association,* Publication 20.

Madison: University of Wisconsin, 1958.

Zander, A., "Problems of Sensitivity and Resistance in Changing Attitudes," 1949. Mimeo.

Zerfoss, L. F. and Norman R. F. Maier, "Improving Staff Procedures in Training," *Journal of Industrial Training,* VI (1952), pp. 5–16.

Index

C

E

F

G

C